Gift of the

Arminta &
Stanley Berry

fund

STRICKEN FIELD

The old Custer Battlefield archway, 1930s

STRICKEN FIELD
The Little Bighorn since 1876

JEROME A. GREENE

Foreword by Paul L. Hedren

UNIVERSITY OF OKLAHOMA PRESS : NORMAN

Also by Jerome A. Greene

Slim Buttes, 1876: An Episode of the Great Sioux War (Norman, 1982)

Yellowstone Command : Colonel Nelson A. Miles and the Great Sioux War, 1876–1877 (Lincoln, 1991; Norman, 2006)

(ed.) *Battles and Skirmishes of the Great Sioux War, 1876–1877: The Military Views* (Norman, 1993)

Lakota and Cheyenne: Indian Views of the Great Sioux War, 1876–1877 (Norman, 1994)

Frontier Soldier: An Enlisted Man's Journal of the Sioux and Nez Perce Campaigns, 1877 (Helena 1998)

Nez Perce Summer, 1877: The U.S. Army and the Nee-Me-Poo Crisis (Helena, 2000)

Morning Star Dawn: The Powder River Expedition and the Northern Cheyennes, 1876 (Norman, 2003)

(with Douglas D. Scott) *Finding Sand Creek: History, Archaeology, and the 1864 Massacre Site* (Norman, 2004)

Washita: The U.S. Army and the Southern Cheyennes, 1867–1869 (Norman, 2004)

Fort Randall on the Missouri, 1856–1892 (Pierre, 2005)

Indian War Veterans: Memories of Army Life and Campaigns in the West, 1864–1898 (New York, 2007)

Library of Congress Cataloging-in-Publication Data

Greene, Jerome A.
    Stricken field : a history of the Little Bighorn Battlefield / Jerome A. Greene ; foreword by Paul L. Hedren.
        p.   cm.
    Includes bibliographical references and index.
    ISBN 978-0-8061-3791-9 (hardcover : alk. paper) 1. Little Bighorn Battlefield National Monument (Mont.) 2. Little Bighorn, Battle of the, Mont., 1876. I. Title.
    E83.876G75   2008
    973.8'2—dc22

                                                            2007022664

1 2 3 4 5 6 7 8 9 10

To the memory of my friend Clifford L. Nelson, 1945–1996, who loved this place and whose murder by a cowardly miscreant was compounded by a miscarriage of justice

Contents

List of Illustrations   ix
Foreword, by Paul L. Hedren   xiii
Preface and Acknowledgments   xvii
Maps   xxi

  1. Signal Event   3
  2. Recognition   19
  3. War Department Years: The National Cemetery, 1880s–1920s   37
  4. War Department Years: Transitions, 1920s–1940   57
  5. National Park Service Administration, 1940–1969   75
  6. National Park Service Administration, 1970–2000   147
  7. National Park Service Interpretation   170
  8. Research and Collections   194
  9. Nonprofit Support Groups and Interest Groups   213
10. Indian Memorial   226

Afterword   239
Appendix 1. National Cemetery/National Monument Legislation   241
Appendix 2. Little Bighorn Battlefield National Monument
      Park Visitation Totals, 1940–2003   257
Appendix 3. War Department and National Park Service
      Superintendents and National Park Service Historians
      at Custer Battlefield National Monument/Little Bighorn
      Battlefield National Monument, 1893–2003   259

Notes   263
Bibliography   321
Index   337

Illustrations

Maps

Map showing the Little Bighorn battlefield   xxii–xxiii
Maps of early land status   xxiv–xxv
1942 National Park Service master plan   xxvi
1960 National Park Service boundary study   xxvii
Plat showing work completed under auspices of Mission 66   xxviii
General Management Plan of 1985   xxix

Photographs

The old Custer Battlefield archway, 1930s   *frontispiece*
Custer's Last Fight, by A. R. Waud, 1876   101
Principal Seventh Cavalry commanders at the Little Bighorn   102
Leaders of the Indian coalition at the Battle of the Little Bighorn   103
Lieutenant General Philip H. Sheridan   104
The Place Where Custer Fell, photograph by John H. Fouch   105
Views of the Little Bighorn battlefield   106–107
View to the west toward the Little Bighorn River, 1883   108
"Erection of the Monument on Gen. Custer's Battle-Field"   109
The Custer Monument   110
Two views of the battlefield in the 1890s   111
The Custer Monument and Last Stand group in the early 1890s   112
View south-to-north along Battle Ridge, 1910   113

Graves from Fort Phil Kearny, Wyoming Territory 113
Aerial views of the battlefield and national cemetery in the 1930s 114
The Reno–Benteen Memorial 115
Two-story stone lodge and stable 115
The rostrum in the national cemetery 116
A view to the northwest of the seventy-fifth anniversary
  proceedings, 1951 116
Cemetery view looking toward the newly completed visitor
  center and the monument, 1952 117
Graveside service for returned World War II dead at the
  national cemetery, July 1949 118
Cemetery view, June 1980 118
Stone House renovation, 1998 119
Battle survivors in front of the Seventh Cavalry Monument,
  June 25, 1886 120
A firing demonstration with troops from Fort Custer during
  the tenth anniversary observance in 1886 121
Cavalry soldiers, Memorial Day 1897 121
Attendees of the semicentennial observance of the Battle of
  the Little Bighorn, June 1926 122
Brigadier General Edward S. Godfrey and White Bull, 1926 123
Commemorative medal sold during the 1926 fiftieth
  anniversary proceedings 124
General Jonathan Wainwright, Edward S. Luce, and Art Bravo,
  June 25, 1952 124
General Jonathan Wainwright paying homage to the dead of
  Custer's command during the 1952 dedication ceremony 125
Interment of the remains of Major Marcus A. Reno,
  September 9, 1967 126
Harold G. Stearns speaking at the centennial observance
  of the Battle of the Little Bighorn, 1976 127
Indian activists, 1988 128
The Indian Memorial, *Spirit Warriors* sculpture 128
Dedication of a marker to Dog's Backbone, 2003 129
Elizabeth B. Custer 130
Sketch of proposed "memorial hall" 131
Custer Battlefield National Monument Museum and
  Visitor Center 132
Dedication ceremonies for the museum, June 25, 1952 133
Visitor Center observation deck 134

Four-unit apartment building for seasonal employees   134
View of the area, 1958   135
Mari Sandoz and Superintendent Luce, September 1949   136
Walter Brennan, Superintendent Thomas Garry, and
    two Crow youths, 1965   137
William H. White in front of the superintendent's house, 1920s   137
Exhibits in the museum, 1952   138–39
Early National Park Service interpretive markers   140
Examples of interpretation in the late 1960s and early 1970s   141
Living history exhibits, 1974 and 1995   142
Relocation of the marker for First Sergeant James Butler,
    July 21, 1949   143
Park Historian Don Rickey, Jr., ca. 1956   144
Archeological excavation, 1958   144
Blackened scape and markers after the grass fire of
    August 10, 1983   145
Archeology research at the park   146
A gallery of superintendents   260–61

All illustrations are courtesy of Little Bighorn Battlefield National Monument unless otherwise indicated.

Foreword

Jerome A. Greene's *Stricken Field* is a layered, complex, uniquely perceptive administrative history of Little Bighorn Battlefield National Monument in southeastern Montana. This special unit of the National Park System possesses political and social importance transcending the moments of utter chaos occurring on June 25 and 26, 1876, when George Armstrong Custer and elements of his Seventh Cavalry were overwhelmed by Lakota and Northern Cheyenne warriors in easily the most phenomenal battle of the Great Sioux War and perhaps all of America's Indian wars.

The battle story itself has been told and retold many times before and is not the focus of this work, although the event is deftly recounted in Greene's opening contextual chapter. The root of this study lies instead in the National Park Service's institutional need to appreciate and understand the evolutionary imprint of its management on an extraordinary place, included more than a half-century ago in the nation's revered national park system. Traditional administrative histories answer obvious questions. What political actions led to the establishment of the unit, and what did citizens, or Congress, or one or another U.S. president do, and why? And why does today's tour road follow such-and-such a route? What led, finally, to the construction of a park's visitor center, and what determined its symbolic or more commonly bland architectural style? What notables attended critical anniversaries and what did they have to say? Such details fill dozens of park administrative histories, all serving to aid managers, interpreters, and rangers who

successively staff the sites. These matters are usually of minor consequence to the public at large and such studies are rarely published by
major university presses.

The Little Bighorn Battlefield National Monument is different.
The Little Bighorn was never a typical unit of any system, and no con-
ventional administrative history serving the National Park Service alone
would ever suffice. From the start it has been a place of swirling intrigue,
mystery, aversion, and controversy that boils to the very present. Also
from the start Little Bighorn was a hallowed memorial to the slain
Custer, the boy general's death symbolic of a price paid by Anglo-
Americans in the settlement of the West. Such a notion was offensive
to Indians broadly, of course, and most particularly to the descendants
of those who defeated Custer. Deservedly, attempts at reconciling
cultural differences and attitudes is a persistent theme in *Stricken Field*.
But even as today's visitors enjoy a contemplative Indian memorial constructed on Last Stand Hill adjacent to an aged granite burial monument
erected by the army, interpretation, landscape preservation, and public
use issues churn anew and work to keep the park at the very center of a
meaningful national conversation over how and for whom the National
Park Service manages the units in its charge. Greene's story is riveting,
timely, and, frankly, unsettling.

For all, of course, the battlefield itself is the central focus. Many
Americans see Little Bighorn as the Gettysburg of the West, the location of a pivotal episode in the broad sweep of American history. For
most, Little Bighorn is a reverential landscape, a place of infamy, what
Brigadier General George Crook's aide, Lieutenant John G. Bourke,
called "sacred ground." For them, it's where the enigmatic contest of
late June 1876 played out across a wide valley floor and over undulating
eastern highlands, with heralded cavalry companies dying to a man
amid explanations as vaporous as a hot Montana summer breeze. The
field drew visitors and speculation almost from the start. Lieutenant
General Philip H. Sheridan, one of the army's senior commanders
during the western Indian wars, paused to reflect there in July 1877.
Custer was a friend, and Sheridan needed to understand how a friend
met death. More than anyone, he championed the initial preservation
of that stricken field, or at least that portion where most of the Seventh
Cavalry soldiers had fallen. By 1879, Sheridan's vision was realized
when Congress authorized Custer Battlefield National Cemetery,
bringing a mantle of federal protection to a square mile of sage-dotted
prairie centered on Last Stand Hill.

The War Department administered Little Bighorn for some sixty years, the tending of the eventual mass grave and budding national cemetery at first falling to the commanding officer of nearby Fort Custer, then to a succession of government custodians. The battlefield was transferred to the National Park Service in 1940, and a Park Service superintendent occupied the army's old stone lodge and oversaw modest but growing visitation, some tourists motoring up from the Custer Battlefield Highway, U.S. Route 87, connecting Sheridan, Wyoming, and Hardin and Billings, Montana, with points east and west. Park amenities in those days were unpretentious, limited to an entrance gate and dirt roads leading to the granite cavalry memorial on Last Stand Hill overlooking scattered marble markers on the battlefield, and a quiet cemetery with Stars and Stripes flown from a towering garrison flagstaff. Cemetery burials were largely limited to soldiers reinterred from abandoned military posts scattered throughout the region and to a few veterans from the Spanish American War and World War I.

The casual pace at Custer Battlefield National Monument, as it came to be known in 1946, as at other parks and monuments throughout the country, witnessed a remarkable transformation following World War II. In the wake of the Great Depression and wartime self-sacrifice, America blossomed, and in its new-found prosperity citizens discovered the nation's national park system anew. As the popularity of the parks skyrocketed in the 1950s and '60s, NPS managers undertook expansions and improvements to accommodate increased use. At Little Bighorn the dirt trace to the Reno-Benteen segment of the park was transformed into a paved, two-lane road (and the jutting Weir Point, critical to the battle story, skinned by road graders). In 1952 the Service dedicated a long-anticipated visitor center at the monument, built on a sector of the field made prominent by Cheyenne warriors and even Custer himself, but which provided an excellent view of Last Stand Hill to the east and Deep Ravine to the south. In 1960–61, and again in the interest of accommodating spiraling public use, the Service constructed four living quarters for its expanding staff, and a maintenance facility, all on battlefield ground not heretofore compromised by development. The National Cemetery saw expansion too, immense squares of prairie grasses and sage giving way on the cemetery's original western margins to accommodate veterans of World War II, Korea, and Vietnam. Visitation growth through the era justified it all, so it was said, jumping from 14,000 in 1943 to 130,000 in the mid-1950s to more than 400,000 annually by the mid-1990s.

By the 1980s some senior National Park Service officials expressed due concern over the footprint of development creeping across the same original square mile of battlefield set aside in 1879. The cemetery eventually closed to further expansion, and the Service evinced a desire to relocate certain visitor facilities to neutral ground and actually restore sacred ground where possible. But facility relocation has not come easily at Little Bighorn Battlefield. With an alarming persistence spurred by demands to better handle crowds driving ever larger vehicles and having ever greater amenity expectations, roads still get widened, parking areas expanded, new wayside exhibits, memorials, and monuments erected, new trails built, restroom facilities constructed on parking lot islands, and proposals floated to expand the existing visitor facility, because expansions are so much easier to effect than all-new construction on neutral turf.

Stricken Field is a brilliantly conceived story of the Little Bighorn Battlefield, the place, the decisions made about it, and the resulting imprint. The infamous battle certainly sets the stage, but this is every bit the chronicle of burials and reburials, the Stone House, an extraordinary national cemetery, and roads, markers, a visitor center, and adoring and contentious visitors. It is also the story of colorful and well-meaning staffs and affinity groups, and of the politics involved in managing a place that in the end is sacred to all people.

Foremost, however, this friend of the battlefield and the National Park Service sees Greene's story as a cautionary tale. Do we of the National Park Service, in our capacity as stewards of America's unique national park system, toiling in the embrace of our own institutional credo to conserve the scenery and the natural and historic objects thereon "by such means as will leave them unimpaired for the enjoyment of future generations," work finally to minimize development and preserve resources at Little Bighorn? Or shall we be remembered for our ability to endlessly impose and expand the stamp of development on a very small tract of land, a mere square mile, a place made sacred by the blood of Americans both white and red?

Enjoy Greene's *Stricken Field*, an enlightening history of Little Bighorn Battlefield National Monument. His disquieting narrative serves us well, and serves notice, too.

Paul L. Hedren
O'Neill, Nebraska

Preface and
Acknowledgments

My association with Little Bighorn Battlefield National Monument extends back to the late summer of 1960, when, as an ardent Custer buff just out of high school, I ventured alone from upstate New York to pay homage to the site that had already captivated me for several years. In those days, the gates remained open after park hours, and late in the afternoon I made my way from the bus station in Crow Agency to the Seventh Cavalry Monument and Last Stand grouping to stand silently in awe before proceeding to unroll my single-layer sleeping bag and—despite proscriptions against camping—spend an especially cold and fitful night somewhere in the vicinity of Deep Ravine. The next day I hiked toward the Reno–Benteen Entrenchment Site some four miles away, but an encounter with a rattlesnake dissuaded me and ended the trek. That night in nearby Hardin I sold the Polaroid land camera my parents had given me for graduation and the next morning paid fifty-seven dollars for a ticket home and took the bus east.

Despite the brevity of my sojourn, the site—then called Custer Battlefield National Monument—continued to fascinate me. So began an intermittent association that has beckoned me as college student visiting from South Dakota, as ranger-historian assigned there in the summers of 1968, 1970, and 1971, and irregularly thereafter through three decades as a research historian with the National Park Service. As I now finalize an administrative history of the park, it is apparent that the place I experienced as a youth has changed immensely in notable

ways. Visitation has mushroomed, creating manifold parking and circulation problems, and there exist multiple land issues affecting interpretation and administration to varying degrees, all ultimately affecting
protection, public use, and enjoyment. Continuing private development
or its imminence on all sides of the park threatens visitor experience as
well as significant battle-related resources, further confounding park
management and compounding matters affecting its stewardship. Not
all is necessarily negative, however. Conversely, and most immediately
noticeable, is the presence of the recently completed Indian Memorial
that honors the Indian dead in the Battle of the Little Bighorn. In so
doing, the structure distinguishes other peoples and registers values
and meanings hardly comprehended for the park in 1960. Dedicated
in 2003, the Indian Memorial effectively acknowledges variant perspectives for the purpose of achieving truth; its existence helps reconcile
elements of the human spirit and signifies what Little Bighorn Battlefield National Monument, as a fixture of our society, represents to all
Americans at the outset of the twenty-first century.

Anything associated with the Little Bighorn story is potentially
complex and rife with controversy and opinion. That has been the
nature of the beast since 1876. While the following history of the site
and park deals only peripherally with the battle story and only as it
has affected park operations, it is, nonetheless, omnipresent, and its
arguable aspects continue to produce debate. Despite this reality, the
research and production of this study has not been contentious thanks
to the help of numerous people who gave generously of their time or
provided relevant material for my study and use. Foremost, I thank the
staff of Little Bighorn Battlefield National Monument, particularly
Superintendent Darrell Cook, who has supported the project from the
time of his arrival there; Park Historian John Doerner, who provided
documents and other data throughout the duration of the research and
writing and who has assisted with his counsel and in numerous other
ways; and former museum curator Kitty Belle Deernose, for furnishing
materials from the collections in her charge. For contributions throughout the project, I must thank Chief of Interpretation and Visitor Services
Kenneth Woody; Administrative Officer Cathy Not Afraid; Chief Ranger
Michael Stops; Facility Manager Lonnie Hergenrider; and Clerk Typist
Prudence Pretty On Top. Former superintendents Neil C. Mangum
(also a former park historian, and who, as superintendent, promoted
this study), Alpine, Texas; Gerard Baker, Mount Rushmore National
Memorial, South Dakota; Barbara Sutteer (formerly Booher), Phoenix,

Arizona; Dennis Ditmanson (also a former ranger-historian), Pecos National Historical Park, New Mexico; and James V. Court, Billings, Montana, reviewed the study, answered questions, and furnished information on my request, as did former National Park Service chief historian and assistant director for cultural resources Robert M. Utley, Georgetown, Texas, who served at the park as a historical aide in the 1940s and early 1950s. Former park historians Douglas C. McChristian, Tucson, Arizona; Richard J. Rambur, Pilot Hill, California; L. Clifford Soubier, Charles Town, West Virginia; B. William Henry, Jr., Florence, Oregon; as well as the late Don G. Rickey, Evergreen, Colorado, likewise provided relevant data. (Rickey's classic *History of Custer Battlefield* was an invaluable asset to the present study.)

Others who made available pertinent documentary materials or who offered assistance in other ways include former superintendents Daniel E. Lee, Cave City, Kentucky; William A. Harris, Kitty Hawk, North Carolina; and Eldon G. Reyer, Santa Fe, New Mexico; and past and present park ranger–historians John D. McDermott, Rapid City, South Dakota; Margot Liberty, Sheridan, Wyoming; Ben F. Irvin, Boise, Idaho; Randy Kane, Williston, North Dakota; Daniel A. Martinez, Honolulu, Hawaii; the late Douglas Keller, Pea Ridge, Arkansas; Michael Donahue, Temple, Texas; and Gerald B. Jasmer, Billings, Montana. For favoring me with essential data throughout this work, I must thank my fellow National Park Service colleagues Douglas D. Scott, Midwest Archeological Center, Lincoln, Nebraska; Chris Jones, Denver Service Center, Lakewood, Colorado; Rudolph A. Lobato and Rick Frost, Intermountain Region Office, Lakewood, Colorado; Paul L. Hedren, Niobrara-Missouri national park group, O'Neill, Nebraska; Tom DuRant, librarian, and John Brucksch, media division, Harpers Ferry Center, Harpers Ferry, West Virginia. Special thanks for sharing records, manuscripts, and reports go to James S. Brust, San Pedro, California; Sandy Barnard, Terre Haute, Indiana; the late Brian Pohanka, Alexandria, Virginia; Nan V. Rickey, Evergreen, Colorado; Paul Andrew Hutton, Albuquerque, New Mexico; John C. Paige, Lakewood, Colorado; Michael J. Koury, Johnstown, Colorado; Bob Reece, Longmont, Colorado; Tonia Horton, State College, Pennsylvania; Anita Donofrio, Buffalo, New York; Art and Chris Sowin, West Hills, California; William P. Wells, Malibu, California; Thomas R. Buecker, Crawford, Nebraska; and to six special librarians: James Curry, Montana Room, Parmly Billings Library, Billings, Montana; Eric Halverson, Big Horn County Library, Hardin, Montana;

Karen Woinosky, Wyoming Room, Sheridan County Fulmer Public Library, Sheridan, Wyoming; David Hays, Western History Collections, University of Colorado Libraries, Boulder; and Jim Kroll and Philip Panum, Western History/Genealogy Department, Denver Public Library. In addition, I acknowledge the help and support of the Montana Historical Society, Helena; the Big Horn County Museum, Hardin, Montana; and the National Park Service Technical Information Center, Denver Service Center, Lakewood, Colorado.

To all of these individuals, offices, and institutions, I extend my sincere appreciation.

MAPS

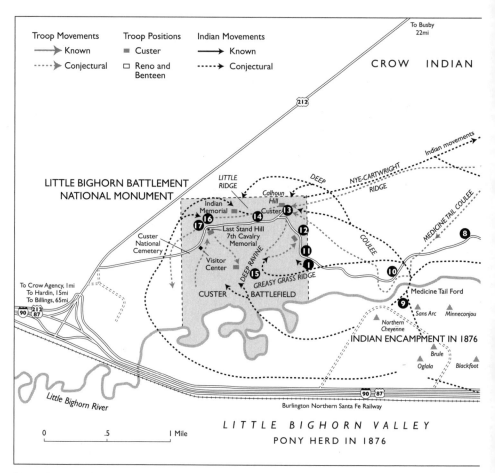

Map showing the Little Bighorn battlefield and various troop and Indian movements and battle positions, as well as modern highways and the boundaries of Little Bighorn Battlefield National Monument. Adapted from brochure map *Little Bighorn Battlefield* (National Park Service).

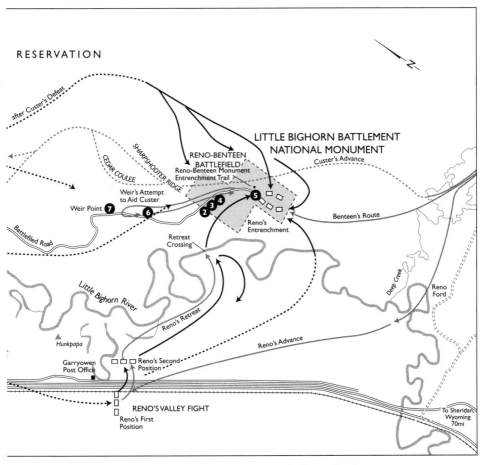

RESERVATION

after Custer's Defeat

LITTLE BIGHORN BATTLEMENT
NATIONAL MONUMENT

SHARPSHOOTER RIDGE

CEDAR COULEE

RENO-BENTEEN
BATTLEFIELD
Reno-Benteen Monument
Entrenchment Trail

Custer's Advance

Weir's Attempt
to Aid Custer

Weir Point ❼ ❻ ❷❸❹ ❺

Benteen's Route

Battlefield Road

Reno's
Entrenchment

Retreat
Crossing

Little Bighorn River

Deep Creek

Reno
Ford

Reno's Retreat

Hunkpapa

Reno's Advance

Garryowen
Post Office ☐☐☐ Reno's Second
Position

RENO'S VALLEY FIGHT

Reno's First
Position

To Sheridan,
Wyoming
70mi

1. Indian Encampment
2. Custer's Advance
3. Valley Fight
4. Retreat
5. Hilltop Defense
6. Sharpshooter Ridge
7. Weir Point
8. Medicine Tail Coulee
9. Medicine Tail Ford

10. Deep Coulee
11. Greasy Grass Ridge
12. Lame White Man Charge
13. Calhoun Hill
14. Keogh–Crazy Horse Fight
15. Deep Ravine
16. Last Stand Hill
17. Memorial Markers

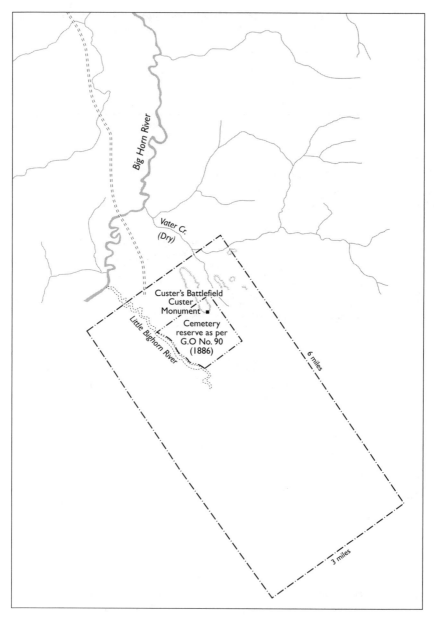

Maps of early land status. One of 1879/1881 (above) shows the six-by-three-mile tract originally sought by the War Department for a reservation embracing the National Cemetery. Adapted from "Map of Military Reservation of Fort Custer, M.T.," 1879. The second (opposite), of 1885, shows the acreage as ultimately scaled back to one square mile.

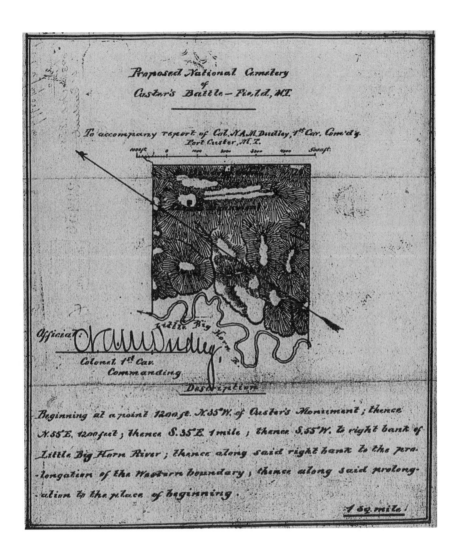

Proposed National Cemetery
of
Custer's Battle-Field, M.T.

To accompany report of Col. N.A.M. Dudley, 1st Cav. Com'd'g.
Fort Custer, M.T.

Little Big Horn R.

Official
Colonel 1st Cav.
Commanding

Description

Beginning at a point 1200 ft. N. 35° W. of Custer's Monument; thence
N. 55° E. 1200 feet; thence S. 35° E. 1 mile; thence S. 55° W. to right bank of
Little Big Horn River; thence along said right bank to the pro-
-longation of the Western boundary; thence along said prolong-
-ation to the place of beginning.

1 sq. mile

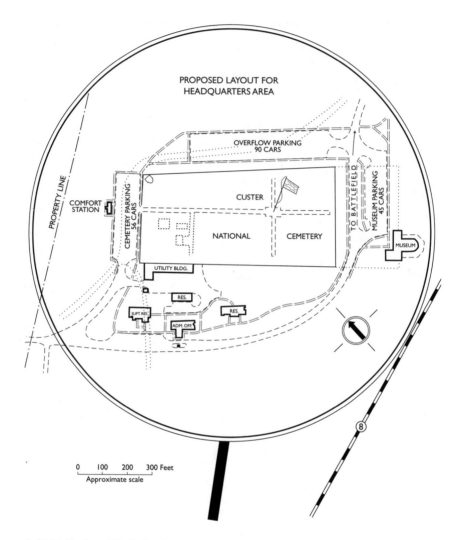

A 1942 National Park Service master plan called for the placement of museum, residences, administrative offices, and appurtenant maintenance facilities all within tight orbit of the national cemetery. Most provisions of the plan, including these, were never enacted because of the national emergency of World War II. Adapted from "General Development Plan Part of the Master Plan for Custer Battlefield National Cemetery," January, 1942.

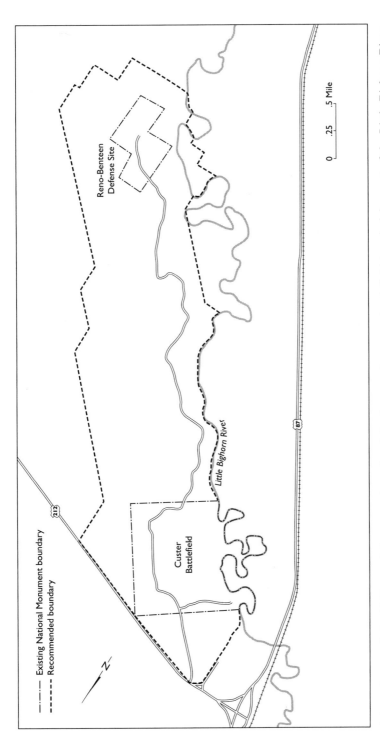

Existing National Monument boundary
Recommended boundary

Reno–Benteen
Defense Site

Custer
Battlefield

Little Bighorn River

212

87

0   .25   .5 Mile

A boundary study in 1960 urged the expansion of park lands to enclose most battlefield terrain lying east of the Little Bighorn River. Tribal and congressional politics have combined to repeatedly thwart efforts to incorporate into the National Park Service holdings the contiguous property on which the Battle of the Little Bighorn occurred. The land question continues to bedevil park administrators. Adapted from "Land Ownership and Recommended Boundary Adjustment," 1960.

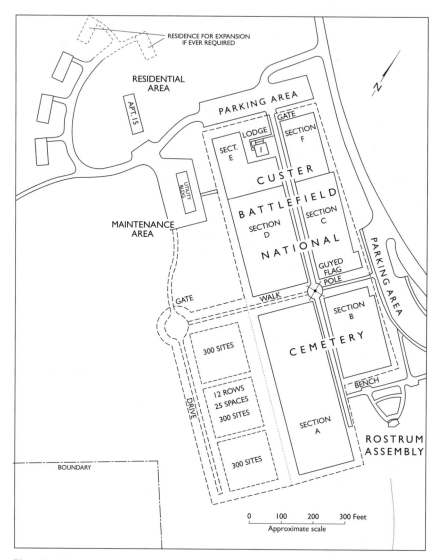

RESIDENCE FOR EXPANSION
IF EVER REQUIRED

RESIDENTIAL
AREA

APT. 15

PARKING AREA

GATE

LODGE

SECT.
E

SECTION
F

CUSTER

BATTLEFIELD

UTILITY
BLDG.

MAINTENANCE
AREA

SECTION
D

SECTION
C

NATIONAL

GUYED
FLAG
POLE

PARKING AREA

GATE

WALK

SECTION
B

CEMETERY

300 SITES

BENCH

12 ROWS
25 SPACES
300 SITES

DRIVE

SECTION
A

ROSTRUM
ASSEMBLY

BOUNDARY

300 SITES

0   100   200   300 Feet

Approximate scale

N

Plat showing work completed under auspices of Mission 66, including cemetery expansion and the construction of utility and residential units, which were built in 1961–62. Adapted from "Plat of Mission 66 Work," 1966.

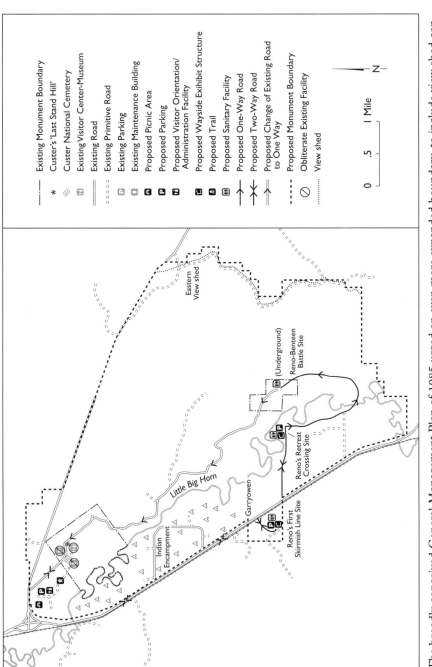

Existing Monument Boundary

* Custer's 'Last Stand Hill'

Custer National Cemetery

Existing Visitor Center-Museum

Existing Road

Existing Primitive Road

Existing Parking

Existing Maintenance Building

Proposed Picnic Area

Proposed Parking

Proposed Visitor Orientation/
Administration Facility

Proposed Wayside Exihibit Structure

Proposed Trail

Proposed Sanitary Facility

Proposed One-Way Road

Proposed Two-Way Road

Proposed Change of Existing Road
to One Way

Proposed Monument Boundary

Obliterate Existing Facility

View shed

N

0   .5   I Mile

The broadly conceived General Management Plan of 1985 urged an even more expanded boundary, to include view shed considerations as well as the site of the Indian village. The interpretation-driven design envisioned the tour to start near Garryowen and properly follow the flow of battle from south to north. Largely because of land considerations, it was never enacted. Adapted from "General Management Plan Alternative B," 1985.

xxix

STRICKEN FIELD

CHAPTER 1 Signal Event

For most of its existence since 1876, the land on which the Battle of the Little Bighorn occurred has been a stricken field. Beginning with the profound episode with which it has ever since been identified and continuing to the present, the overwhelming appeal of this place of conflict has not only validated its historical agelessness but has assured its gradual and continuing physical detriment. Through various administrations of the Little Bighorn battlefield as a government-managed entity, there have always been questions of appropriate balance, questions perhaps more starkly apparent at the beginning of the twenty-first century than ever before. Nowhere in the National Park System have the issues surrounding public use versus preservation been more dramatic, and nowhere have the consequences been more profound than for the historic ground. As the battlefield has changed over the past 131 years from a memorial shrine honoring army dead to an inclusive historic site welcoming all perspectives, it has reflected the evolving maturity of a nation of disparate values uniting for broader meaning and harmony of spirit. Just as important, the decades following the Battle of the Little Bighorn have witnessed a continuum of development, as appointed government agencies, with respect to their defined purposes, have sought first to steward and then accommodate the growing attention the place has commanded. Therein rests the conundrum of this most fascinating and enigmatic ground: where lies the balance of visitation, interpretation, and development of this historic site when weighed against its preservation for future generations? It is anticipated that the perspectives presented in this study will guide future managers of Little Bighorn Battlefield National Monument in shaping decisions to help answer these and other questions affecting the prospectus for the park.[1]

Little Bighorn Battlefield National Monument, which embraces major portions of the lands composing the Little Bighorn battlefield proper (while interpreting most of the rest of the outlying historic property), lies in southeastern Montana adjoining the Little Bighorn River. The National Park Service unit is approximately sixty-seven miles southeast of modern Billings, Montana, and approximately seventy-four miles north of modern Sheridan, Wyoming, along U.S. Interstate Highway 90, which runs between those cities, and near its junction with U.S. Highway 212. The monument lies in Big Horn County, whose seat is at Hardin, some fourteen miles to the north. The monument grounds constitute an enclave in the middle of the Crow Indian Reservation, whose administrative facilities occupy buildings in the town of Crow Agency, three miles north of the park.

For most of their existence before mid-1876, the lands composing the area of the Little Bighorn battlefield lay more or less dormant. In terms of regional geomorphology, they are part of the Missouri Plateau section of the Great Plains Physiographic Province, characterized by eroded uplifts and terraced lands segregated by myriad streams, and whose gravelly soils of sand, clay, and volcanic ash run from yellowish to ash gray in color. They are the products of all preceding geologic periods, including a time when much of present-day Montana comprised inland seas. (A rare short-necked plesiosaur gave evidence of Mesozoic marine life in eastern Montana when workers discovered its skeleton in Custer Battlefield National Cemetery in 1977.) With the distant northwest-coursing Big Horn Mountains forming a horizon on the south, and the Pryor range splayed similarly on the west (both likely uplifts of the Eocene epoch of the Tertiary period, Cenozoic era), the battlefield proper, some 2,750 feet above sea level and further defined by the presence of vast sandstone and shale formations topped by depositions of sand and gravel, comprises the lowlands portion of Big Horn County. Farther east are the low-lying Wolf, or Little Chetish, Mountains and the Davis range, upon which geomorphologists postulate influences of both the Oligocene and Pleistocene epochs of the Tertiary period.

Landforms in the immediate vicinity of the battlefield and adjoining the Little Bighorn River consist of dissected and alluvial bluffs, furrowed hillocks, erosion-resistant hogback ridges, broad drainages, twisted swales, and deep-running ravines, mostly adjoining the east bank of the stream, along with erosionally sculpted bench lands gradually rising away to the west from the Little Bighorn. That river heads in the Big Horn Mountains and flows north to meet the Bighorn River near Hardin; the Bighorn joins the Yellowstone about twenty-five miles farther north. Deeply fissured canyons, carved over eons, trace the country adjoining the Big Horn Mountains and include those through which pass the Bighorn River (a unit of the National Park System) and the headwaters of the Little Bighorn River. In the vicinity of the Little Bighorn battlefield vast deposits of bituminous coal and lignite exist, while petroleum and coal methane presently command rapt commercial interest.[2]

Southeastern Montana is an area of short grasslands sparsely punctuated in the higher elevations by scattered scrub pine and cedar trees. Cottonwood, poplar, ash, willow, alder, and other deciduous trees abound along tributary streams, such as the Little Bighorn. The climate is semiarid, with precipitation averaging around sixteen inches per year. High winds are common and typify much of the winter season, when driving blizzards accompanied by fast-freezing temperatures can occur. Snowfall is usually under fifty inches, while winter temperatures average 20 degrees Fahrenheit but can reach extremes of -50 with the chill factor. Conversely, at the height of summer, temperatures average in the 60s and 70s, with extreme highs occasionally climbing to 100 degrees or more. Precipitation and alternating temperatures foster the ground cover, which besides trees consists of diverse grasses, including wheat grass, bluestem, and grama, all punctuated by prickly pear cactus, yucca, sagebrush, and greasewood (salt sage). The grasses sustained the vast herds of buffalo that once grazed the region and today support cattle and other livestock. Other wildlife that traditionally roamed the country include deer, elk, pronghorns, bears, mountain lions, wolves, coyotes, bobcats, jackrabbits, porcupines, raccoons, and foxes. Native bird species included bald eagles, golden eagles, crows, magpies, various hawks, grouse, sage hens, and killdeers, while reptiles and amphibians included the ubiquitous prairie rattlesnakes, bull snakes, garter snakes, water snakes, horned lizards and various smaller lizards, and frogs and toads. While buffalo are largely gone from the region, their numbers decimated by hide hunters in the 1880s, many of these other creatures continue to dwell in the country around the Little Bighorn battlefield.[3]

The historical presence of buffalo and other game animals promoted initial occupation of the region by humans. While the earliest
hunters and fishermen appeared in parts of southeastern Montana
as many as nine thousand years ago, more recent arrivals to inhabit
that country and northern Wyoming, and who factored significantly
in the history of the Little Bighorn battlefield, were the Crows, a
Siouan-speaking people related historically and culturally to the village
Hidatsa in present North Dakota and with likely prehistoric ties to
the lower Mississippi area and southeastern North America. By the
early nineteenth century, the formerly sedentary folk, who obtained
horses in about 1730, had migrated west into the Yellowstone–Powder
River hinterland and beyond, separating into two groups. The Mountain Crows generally inhabited the country below the Yellowstone
River, including the Bighorn and Little Bighorn drainages south into
modern Wyoming and west to the Wind and Absaroka ranges; the River
Crows traversed the lands between the Yellowstone and Missouri rivers
and north to Milk River, not far from the present-day Canadian border.
(After 1850 a third division, the Kicked in the Bellies, occupied part of
central Wyoming above the North Platte and Sweetwater rivers.)

Transient in their region, the Crows became avid traders whose
contacts with distant tribes east and west gradually modified their culture. They participated in the emerging American fur trade during the
early decades of the nineteenth century, providing tanned buffalo hides
and receiving guns and ammunition, knives, axes, pans, and assorted
ornaments, as well as sugar, flour, coffee, and alcohol. Like other tribes,
they followed herds of buffalo for trade and subsistence, and their
economy reflected their dependency on the beasts. In their occupation
of favored game lands, besides their wealth in horses and trade goods,
the Crows drew the enmity of neighboring peoples but managed lasting
accommodation with some groups, such as the Assiniboins, that supported their endurance. After a major success against an enemy coalition
of Lakotas, Cheyennes, and Arapahos at mid-century, which established
the tone of regional intertribal relations over the next two decades,
the relatively small Crow Tribe (about five thousand in 1870) actively
aligned themselves with the federal government. They had earlier
signed the Fort Laramie Treaty of 1851, broadly recognizing tribal
boundaries, and later signed the Fort Laramie Treaty of 1868, which
more specifically defined (and reduced) their tribal lands. During
1876, 1877, and beyond, members of the Mountain Crows served as
scouts for the army against the Lakotas, Northern Cheyennes, Nez

Perces, and other tribes. In 1883 Bureau of Indian Affairs administrative offices were established at the present-day Crow Agency.[4]

Other tribes eventually made inroads into Crow lands, notably the aforementioned Lakotas, Cheyennes, and Arapahos, groups of eastern origin with similar agricultural antecedents. The Lakotas (also known as Teton Sioux) were Siouan speakers, while the Cheyennes and Arapahos spoke languages of Algonkian origin. In their migrations west, these tribes had reached the Black Hills in present-day South Dakota by the end of the eighteenth century, thereafter moving into competitive buffalo ranges with the smaller Crow tribe, with whom territorial conflict was inevitable. As indicated, by the 1850s and beyond, the Crows on the one hand, and the Lakotas, Cheyennes, and Arapahos on the other, were major constituents of the intertribal rivalries that dominated Indian occupation of the plains and that exacerbated long-standing open warfare among them. Whereas the latter tribes at one time often fought among themselves, by the mid-nineteenth century they had generally consolidated into loose alliances grounded in familial associations and cultural affinity. (The Cheyennes and Arapahos each eventually divided into northern and southern components, with the southern divisions migrating to the southern plains.) By the 1870s the Lakotas asserted their dominance over most of the lands east of the Bighorn River and threatened domination of the Crow territory beyond. Streams like the Little Bighorn became popular summer religious rendezvous sites for the various bands of the tribe.[5]

The hostility between the Crows and the Sioux–Northern Cheyenne–Northern Arapaho coalition grew in the 1860s, as whites began making concerted inroads through Indian lands. Previous interest by whites, following the Meriwether Lewis and William Clark army expedition of 1804 to 1806 to explore the lands of the Louisiana Purchase of 1803, was mainly confined to the fur trade, in which the tribes profitably participated through the 1850s. Early activities promoted by St. Louis entrepreneur Manuel Lisa occurred in the Yellowstone–Bighorn River country, beginning with the 1807 establishment of the trading post of Fort Manuel at the mouth of the Bighorn River. Among the first non-Indians operating directly in the proximity of the later battlefield were John Colter, who had been with Lewis and Clark and who accompanied the first fur trading expeditions to the Missouri-Yellowstone country in 1806–1807 (Colter viewed the spectacle of what became Yellowstone National Park in 1807 and visited Bighorn Canyon in the same year); Edward Rose, a trapper and guide of mixed Caucasian, black, and Indian heritage who lived with the Crows between 1810 and 1820; and James Beckworth, of Caucasian and black ancestry, who lived with the Crows variously from 1825 into the 1860s. Ultimately, raids on the Crows by enemy Blackfeet Indians brought the abandonment of Fort Manuel in 1811, and British authority was temporarily reasserted in the region with the outbreak of the War of 1812.

The fur trade factored seriously in the configuration of Indian alliances and produced long-term implications. Following the War of 1812, American dominance was reasserted. At the mouth of the Big-horn River along the Yellowstone, the Missouri Fur Company erected another post where Fort Manuel had stood, proliferating trading oppor-tunities among the Crows and other tribes. The Blackfeet continued their alliance with the British Hudson's Bay Company, occasionally clashing with the Americans and finally driving the Missouri Fur Company from the region. But other companies persevered, and more stations were erected along the Yellowstone. Changes in world markets and commerce gradually affected the trade, however, and by the 1860s it had declined forever in the region.[6]

By then, gold prospecting had begun, and in 1863 a party from Bannack City, Montana Territory, under James Stuart, journeyed down the Yellowstone to the mouth of the Bighorn, then ascended that stream to the Little Bighorn. Stuart's party found traces of gold but abandoned its quest following an attack by Indians near Bighorn Canyon. Eight years later, another party from western Montana intent on examining the Powder River country for gold was repulsed by Lakotas and driven away. And in 1874, a group of 147 men from Bozeman, comprising the Yellowstone Wagon Road and Prospecting Expedition and equipped with two cannon, penetrated the area of the Yellowstone and Rosebud Creek seeking gold. They too encountered the Sioux. On April 11, in a confrontation along the west side of the divide between the Rosebud and Little Bighorn, Indians laid siege to the entrenched prospectors for two days. (The site of the exchange was near the route of Custer's command little more than two years later.) The party subsequently passed west to Lodge Grass Creek in continuing back to Bozeman. For the most part, however, following the passing of the fur trade and despite these aborted mining ven-tures, whites generally avoided the area, leaving the Bighorn country to the Indians.[7]

By that time, as indicated, Sioux migration into Crow country was far along. Compounding all was the federal government's purchase of

Fort Laramie, in present-day southeastern Wyoming, from the American Fur Company in 1849. Thereafter, a tide of gold- and land-hungry emigrants bound for California and Oregon began passing through the disputed tribal lands, despite government acknowledgement of tribal ownership by way of several treaties with the people. Within the next decade the first regional army campaign against the Sioux took place following a confrontation in which warriors wiped out a detachment of soldiers from Fort Laramie. Meantime, to the north and east, increasing steamboat navigation of the Upper Missouri and the establishment of Fort Benton at the head of navigation with its roads and trails leading to remote settlements further anticipated a reality in which white interests and influences would thoroughly circumscribe Indian lands.

Consequently, on the northern plains, particularly in modern eastern Montana and Wyoming, western North and South Dakota, and western Nebraska, the years of conflict between Indians and U.S. forces beginning in the 1850s involved American Indians whose own expansionistic designs were by then being superseded by those of white Americans. Growing regional white hegemony preceding the Civil War only intensified the existing intertribal conflict. Elements of some peoples moved south or pushed west as Lakotas increasingly occupied parts of eastern Montana Territory. The cultural and social connections among the Lakotas, Cheyennes, and Arapahos presaged loose military alliances, and smaller tribes like the Crows found themselves squeezed territorially. For security, the Crows gravitated toward the U.S. government in their disputes with the Sioux and their allies.

Events leading to the Great Sioux War of 1876–77, in which occurred the Battle of the Little Bighorn, were grounded in the invasion of Indian lands by whites during the 1860s. On the northern plains, treaties concluded with the Lakotas, Northern Cheyennes, Northern Arapahos, Crows, and other groups attempted to segregate them from one another and to remove them from the principal routes of emigration, notably the Oregon Trail, as well as areas of potential government economic interest. A major flaw in the treaty process was the government's failure to comprehend that Indian signatories often lacked authority to represent kinsmen in other bands who rejected the instruments. Eventually, when federal efforts failed to enforce compliance from tribesmen who were not direct parties to the accords, the army was called in to force their acquiescence. Then two events, the Santee Sioux uprising in Minnesota in 1862 and the Sand Creek Massacre in Colorado Territory in 1864, all but guaranteed future disaster in government-Indian relations. In the former instance, army campaigns to prosecute the Santees carried the warfare westward from Minnesota, inflaming tribes in the Yellowstone country while fueling the fears of whites throughout the trans-Mississippi frontier. And the massacre of a purportedly peaceful village of Southern Cheyennes by volunteer troops in southeastern Colorado further alarmed Indians throughout the Great Plains. Sand Creek mobilized the plains tribes and sent avenging Sioux, Cheyenne, and Arapaho warriors on a rampage against settlements and trails in Colorado and neighboring territories, including present-day Wyoming.

In Wyoming (then part of Dakota Territory), white emigration increased in the 1860s with establishment of the Bozeman Trail, which spurred northwest from the Oregon Trail to the gold fields of south-western Montana Territory. Intent on punishing the tribes following their reaction to Sand Creek, Brigadier General Patrick E. Connor headed a multicolumned movement into northern Wyoming and southern Montana in 1865 that ultimately failed because of logistical problems and deteriorating weather conditions. When Lakotas, Cheyennes, and Arapahos persisted in their resistance to the influx of travelers through their hunting grounds, the army raised and occupied three posts along the Bozeman, thereby inciting major conflict. Following several well-publicized engagements—including the annihilation by Sioux and Cheyennes of Captain William J. Fetterman and his command near Fort Phil Kearny on December 21, 1866—the government abandoned the region altogether, ending the so-called Red Cloud War (after the Lakota chief of that name) and conceding, at least temporarily, Indian suzerainty there. The treaty of 1868, signed at Fort Laramie, designated hunting territory and established for the Lakotas and their allies the Great Sioux Reservation in western Dakota Territory. Many of the people settled at the reservation agencies, although Sioux known as "northern roamers" continued to hunt the Yellowstone–Powder River region on lands recognized as belonging to the Crows. In the refusal of the Northern Sioux to yield to reservation life lay the seeds for future confrontation with the army.

Relations with the tribes never improved. Ironically, the so-called "Peace Policy" fostered during the administration of President Ulysses S. Grant, wherein the government promoted involvement in Indian administration by religious organizations, clashed starkly with the army's forceful prosecution of the Indians, further jeopardizing peace. On the northern plains, a major contest loomed with the Lakotas and

Northern Cheyennes. In the summer of 1873, a Northern Pacific Railroad survey expedition penetrated Sioux hunting grounds in Montana, during which accompanying Seventh Cavalry troops commanded by Lieutenant Colonel George A. Custer twice skirmished with Indians—once near the mouth of the Bighorn River. And during the following year, Custer headed an expedition into the Black Hills portion of the Great Sioux Reservation that resulted in the discovery of gold in that country. In the summer of 1875, moreover, an army exploration of the Yellowstone River occurred, which ascended the Bighorn twelve miles preparatory to anticipated military operations in the area. Late that year, after the nontreaty Lakotas seemingly spurned federal directives to move to the agencies and reservation tribesmen refused to yield the gold-rich Black Hills portion to federal negotiators, warfare was assured.[8]

The Great Sioux War, of which the Battle of the Little Bighorn was the climactic engagement, occupied twenty months between February 1876 and September 1877, during which various U.S. Army troops took the field. Warfare occurred in a broad region encompassing approximately 120,000 square miles of present-day Montana, Wyoming, South Dakota, and Nebraska. Initial army strategy called for three columns of troops to close on the nontreaty Lakotas in the Yellowstone–Powder River country. Brigadier General George Crook was first afield, leading a column north from Fort Fetterman, Wyoming, amid frigid temperatures in February 1876. At dawn on March 17, part of Crook's command under Colonel Joseph J. Reynolds attacked a village on the Powder River in southeastern Montana Territory believed to contain Crazy Horse's Oglala Lakotas but that instead mainly held Northern Cheyennes under Chiefs Old Bear and Two Moon. Reynolds's men drove the people out and captured their ponies before destroying the camp, with casualties light on both sides. Warriors from the village, however, later recaptured most of the ponies, and Reynolds's destruction of Indian supplies on which Crook hoped to subsist his troops forced the general to abandon the field. Importantly, Reynolds's attack on the Northern Cheyennes further solidified the Lakota-Cheyenne alliance and served to bring more warriors directly into the fray with the army. News of the fight with Reynolds's soldiers created discord among the Indians on the Sioux reservation, compelling many of them to join their relatives in the Yellowstone country the following spring to help fight the soldiers.

The army reversal at Powder River portended similar actions by tribesmen desperate to maintain their freedom and confident enough to press the troops sent against them. In the spring, when Crook started north to cooperate with columns sent from Dakota Territory and western Montana, the Lakotas and Northern Cheyennes initiated combat with his soldiers. On June 9, 1876, as his men bivouacked along the Tongue River in northern Wyoming, a force of Northern Cheyennes boldly opened fire on them from bluffs above the camp.

Eight days later, more than a thousand Sioux and Cheyenne warriors attacked Crook's soldiers and Crow and Shoshoni auxiliaries as they wended north along the headwaters of Rosebud Creek. The Battle of Rosebud Creek lasted most of June 17 and ranged over some five square miles of difficult terrain. During the fighting, the Indians killed ten men and wounded twenty-one more, while the soldiers killed eleven warriors and wounded five. In the end, Crook held the field as the warriors melted away to the north. As he pondered the significance of such fierce opposition, he decided to withdraw his command back into Wyoming to await reinforcements and supplies. Strategically, with their defeat of Crook at the Rosebud, the coalition of warriors under such men as Crazy Horse, Sitting Bull, Gall, and Two Moon would effectively nullify army plans for the duration of the summer.[9]

Crook's decision to withdraw following the Rosebud was filled with implications for what happened subsequently. He did not directly notify the other army commands of his action and whereabouts. By then, forces under Brigadier General Alfred H. Terry and Colonel John Gibbon had converged along the Yellowstone River near the mouth of Rosebud Creek. Terry's column of nine hundred horse and foot troops, which had left Fort Abraham Lincoln, Dakota, in May, included the Seventh Cavalry, almost seven hundred men strong, commanded by Lieutenant Colonel George A. Custer. Gibbon's column, from Forts Shaw and Ellis, Montana, consisted of four hundred men of the Seventh Infantry and Second Cavalry. With Crook's location uncertain and reports of large bodies of Indians in the vicinity, Terry and Gibbon decided to seek them out and force a confrontation.

Custer's regiment was destined to find the Indians. The thirty-six-year-old commander, a widely regarded Civil War hero, had registered previous successes against Indians in November 1868, when his regiment attacked and destroyed a Southern Cheyenne village at the Washita River in the Indian Territory (present-day Oklahoma), and in August 1873, in the aforementioned skirmishes of the Seventh Cavalry with the Sioux along the Yellowstone. Now he was directed to lead his troops south to an Indian trail discovered days earlier. Departing the Yellowstone on June 22, Custer followed the Rosebud for two days before turning west in pursuit. On Sunday morning, June 25, from the divide overlooking Rosebud and Little Bighorn valleys, Custer's Crow and Arikara scouts spied an Indian village some fifteen miles to the west, beyond bluffs along the Little Bighorn. In fact, the scouts had located an immense summer encampment containing as many as five thousand Lakotas and Northern Cheyennes, including perhaps fifteen hundred warriors, some of whom had fought Crook but a week earlier.

Unaware of the true size of the targeted village, Custer determined to conceal his regiment behind the divide, wait until dark June 25, then advance and place his command at the ready to strike at dawn. But fate intervened. Fear that the Indians had learned of the presence of the cavalry in the hills near the divide forced a change of plan. Believing that word of the proximity of troops would cause the village to break up and its occupants scatter, Custer ordered the regiment to advance directly toward the Little Bighorn, reconnoitering en route. Soon after crossing the divide, he sent Captain Frederick W. Benteen with three companies (D, H, and K) to the left and southwest of his main column in an apparent precautionary probe of the country intended to prevent villagers from possibly escaping in that direction. As Custer's command drew nearer the Little Bighorn, word of fleeing Indians made him order Major Marcus A. Reno and three more companies (A, G, and M) to move ahead rapidly, ford the stream, and charge the Indians expected to be in the valley. Custer told Reno that he would "be supported with the whole outfit." As Reno set out, Custer and five companies (C, E, F, I, and L) continued moving toward the river. Far in the rear, Company B of the Seventh under Captain Thomas M. McDougall ushered the advancing pack mules and their cargo of extra ammunition.

Thus were the troop components of the Seventh Cavalry arranged at the onset of the Battle of the Little Bighorn. While Benteen proceeded on his scouting mission, Reno's battalion crossed the river and opened an attack on the south end of the Indian village, so large that it stretched north for possibly a mile and a half. As Reno's troops, revolvers drawn, galloped forward, they discovered a large body of warriors massing to meet the command. That spectacle caused Reno to order his men to halt the charge, dismount, and fight on foot, and the men quickly fell into skirmish formation to meet the Indians. With no sign of Custer, the soldiers stretched their ranks across the bottom and opened fire at the warriors before them. After twenty minutes, the Indians gradually turned the west flank of Reno's position, causing him to retire east into a thick grove of cottonwoods bordering the river. There the troops kept the gradually encircling warriors at bay. But with the Indian numbers increasing rapidly, Reno was desperate to keep them from completely infiltrating the timber. After fifteen minutes of this exchange, Reno—in a movement ever since clouded in controversy—led a mounted retreat from the woods to the bluffs beyond the river that saw heavy casualties inflicted among his men. Closely pursued by warriors, the desperate soldiers, often struggling hand to hand in the rush, forced their horses into and through the stream, up its slippery banks, and through twisted draws to surmount the heights.

As survivors of Reno's rout in the valley gained the high ground, Benteen's command appeared from the south. He produced a note from Custer directing Benteen to hurry forward with the pack train and its ammunition reserves. But no one knew precisely where to the north Custer had gone. Although a few of Reno's men fighting in the valley had briefly spotted him moving in that direction atop the bluffs, the support he had promised had seemingly not materialized. With Reno's battalion reduced from the traumatic events in the valley, Benteen aided in securing the hilltop position, and together the troops sought shelter from the Indians' fire behind hurriedly raised breastworks and saddles and the carcasses of dead horses. Fortunately, the warriors had not captured the pack mules, and the animals with their troop escort shortly arrived on the hill, contributing both men and ammunition to support Reno. Presently, most of the warriors withdrew downstream, where sounds of gunfire confirmed Custer's probable location. At that, a company under Captain Thomas W. Weir started north from Reno's position to find and reinforce him. Weir's men, shortly followed by the balance of the command, advanced a mile to a ridgetop viewpoint from which clouds of dust and smoke rising some three miles farther north marked the likely position of Custer and the Indians. Soon, as the distant warriors started toward Reno's soldiers, the major directed his men back to their hilltop defenses, and there the troops settled in to defend a mounting siege of their lines. The question of Custer's exact whereabouts and actions remained unresolved.

In fact, after Reno had advanced to ford the Little Bighorn in his approach to the village, Custer had followed on his trail for some time. Well before Custer reached the river, however, he diverted his five companies to the right, or northwest, gaining the general hilltop area where Reno later took refuge and where some troops in the valley had seen him waving his hat to inspire them in their objective. Informed conjecture suggests that Custer, perhaps motivated by Reno's dismounted condition, considered a flank attack on the village and was seeking a point where he might descend and initiate it. He shortly led his command past the site of the later Weir Point sortie, generally north through a draw that emptied into a broad drainage, later called Medicine Tail Coulee, then started for the river, beyond which lay the tepees of the Northern Cheyennes.

From that point on, Custer's exact movements and purposes become murky, clouded by speculation and controversy. Aided by the results of archeology conducted during the 1980s, however, together with Indian accounts collected later, the course of Custer's route to destruction can nonetheless be discerned with some confidence. Following its emergence in Medicine Tail Coulee, it appears that part of Custer's command, perhaps as many as three companies, passed down the drainage in anticipation of fording the Little Bighorn, while the remaining units occupied the high ground north of the coulee, possibly a reserve intended either to cover the troops at the ford or to establish contact with Benteen's anticipated battalion. By the time Custer's men reached the ford, however, Reno had largely been driven onto the bluffs east of the river, thereby freeing hundreds of warriors to stream north to meet the new threat on their homes and families. Evidently, few, if any, of Custer's soldiers crossed the Little Bighorn and breached the village. Instead, the Indians succeeded in repulsing the command, driving it back from the ford, out of Medicine Tail Coulee, and across a deep, dry rift today called Deep Coulee. As more Indians crossed the river to confront them, Custer's troops fell farther back, fighting to stem the onrush. Skirmish lines of dismounted soldiers helped stay the Indians' advance but subsequently crumbled with drastic consequence as the tribesmen drove off army horses bearing precious ammunition-laden saddlebags.

At some point, the troops occupying the high ground bordering Medicine Tail opened fire on the Indians, perhaps those approaching them from different parts of the coulee or those threatening the companies withdrawing from the ford. In any event, these soldiers began a movement down and across Deep Coulee and up to the presently designated Calhoun Hill, at the south end of a lengthy hogback ridge along which the troops arriving from the ford area were coalescing. Archeological evidence suggests that an ensuing crossfire fusillade directed there from Indian positions east and southwest of Calhoun Hill destroyed most of Company L. Company I and the survivors of

Company L clustered farther along on the east slope of the hogback, perhaps in supporting proximity to Companies C, F, and I, and were there dealt a similar fate by warriors positioned three hundred feet northeast of the northernmost point of the ridge.

It is possible that part of Custer's battalion passed down the northwestern slope of the hogback and beyond the area of the present-day National Cemetery toward the Little Bighorn River. Whatever the reason for this movement, the warriors ultimately forced the soldiers back to the ridge, where they apparently attempted to unite with the remaining units. Some troopers possibly established a skirmish line in the broad swath below and south of today's Custer Hill area to check the Indians' advance. And as the military situation further deteriorated, some troops tried to run down the slopes toward the river; some of them perished in a yawning culvert now known as Deep Ravine, whose recesses trailed down to meet cliffs overlooking the stream. Meantime, the remaining officers and men, including Custer and his staff, besides several civilian members of his family, pulled together on the northwest face of the hogback, near its top. Here they arranged dead horses as last-hope barriers against arrows and bullets that tore into the group, but in the end they succumbed, possibly in "last stand" fashion, with the remaining soldiers of Custer's battalion. This phase of the Battle of the Little Bighorn from the time the troops entered Medicine Tail Coulee until the last shots echoed away on Custer Hill and elsewhere probably lasted no more than two hours.

Following their annihilation of Custer's troops, the warriors redirected their attention to Reno's and Benteen's soldiers, who after their movement to Weir Point had withdrawn to their former positions behind breastworks on the hills overlooking the Little Bighorn. Flush with their victory over Custer four miles away, the Sioux and Cheyennes now besieged Reno's men from neighboring ridges and hillocks, opening a lively yet intermittent fire that wounded some and occasionally inflicted fatalities among them. The only surviving surgeon remained busy, establishing a field hospital in a low swale behind the defenses and protecting it from Indian marksmen with the bodies of dead mules and horses. Although firing slackened during the night of June 25, the men on the line remained alert. At dawn on the twenty-sixth, warriors resumed their shooting. When the doctor called for water for the wounded, volunteers bravely slipped down to the river and filled canteens. By midday, however, the Indians had largely withdrawn, the great encampment packing up and heading south, upstream toward the Big Horn Mountains. Relieved to see them go, the troops feared a ruse and remained alert on the hill through the night of June 26. But nothing occurred. The Battle of the Little Bighorn was over.

On the morning of June 27, Reno's men discerned a massive dust cloud to the north. It proved to be the soldiers of General Terry and Colonel Gibbon advancing up the river. A detachment from Terry's command found the dead of Custer's companies strewn over the hills and ridges east of the stream, most of the bodies stripped and muti- lated by Indian women in the aftermath of the fighting. Only after Terry gained the bluffs did Major Reno's worn and anxious command learn the fate of Custer's men. As the surviving members of the Seventh Cavalry buried their comrades on June 28, Terry, Gibbon, and Reno tallied the casualties. The engagement ultimately yielded losses of 268 officers and men (including 251 soldiers, 7 civilians, and 3 Indian scouts, plus 7 soldiers who died later from wounds). It is believed that fewer than 100 Indians were killed in the battle.[10]

Little Bighorn was the greatest victory for the Indians in the Great Sioux War, as well as the worst defeat suffered by U.S. troops to that time since the close of the Civil War. While the Indian triumph exerted immediate confidence among the Lakotas and Northern Cheyennes, it also mobilized the federal government in its military prosecution of the people. Little Bighorn did not mark the end of the Great Sioux War; it instead caused the government to bring to bear all resources necessary to punish the tribes and drive them permanently into the agencies. With concurrence of Congress, army authorities took over the Sioux agencies on the Great Sioux Reservation. General Sheridan imposed a policy of disarming and dismounting the reservation tribes- men while focusing troop reinforcements in the Yellowstone region. To that end, over the next year General Crook and Colonel Nelson A. Miles campaigned through the region, registering substantive successes over the tribes at places like Slim Buttes, Dakota; Cedar Creek, Mon- tana; Red Fork of Powder River, Wyoming; and Wolf Mountains, Montana. In each instance, the soldiers killed warriors (and some- times noncombatants), destroyed villages and food stores, and captured ponies, visiting on the tribes ceaseless havoc and ultimate starva- tion. Devoid of renewable resources, the destitute people surrendered at forts or at the agencies in Dakota Territory and Nebraska. Some followed Sitting Bull and other Sioux leaders into Canada, where they remained until 1881. But in reality, by autumn 1877 the Great Sioux War was over.[11]

Of all the actions between the army and the Lakotas and Northern Cheyennes in 1876–77, the Battle of the Little Bighorn captured public attention as most previous and subsequent army-Indian engagements did not. Partly because of the totality of the Indian victory, as well as of the mystery surrounding the demise of Custer's battalion, Little Bighorn came to loom large in public consciousness. Custer had been one of the most prominent officers of the army when he was killed, a status that combined with the nature of his death to assure his immortality in American history. The events of the Great Sioux War, and Little Bighorn in particular, further fueled growing patriotic sentiment by white Americans over ensuing weeks and months. In time, "Custer's Last Stand" assumed mythic proportions and came to symbolize a national perception of warfare between whites and Indians in the trans-Mississippi West while assuring its standing in the country's popular history and culture. Furthermore, by its dramatized heroic aspects and evolved (and ever-changing) symbolism in artistic, literary, and cinematic endeavors, the Battle of the Little Bighorn has contributed significantly to the nation's cultural history.

CHAPTER 2

Recognition

The decision, presumably by General Terry, to bury Custer's dead at the scattered places where their bodies were found (and likely where they fell) on the battlefield, rather than collect them in some form of mass grave, would strongly influence subsequent development and future interpretation of the Little Bighorn battle site. The judgment reflected the nearly three days' decomposition of the remains and thus the inability to transport them. "Warm weather and the flies had worked their will on the wounds of the soldier dead," recalled one veteran. "The conditions were revolting." Another witness reported that "hands, heads, feet and legs are cut off and scattered here and there." Furthermore, there was a sense of urgency to get medical help for the wounded of Reno's command, while the dearth of available picks and shovels was severely felt. (There were none with Custer's command, and but a half dozen or so, besides some axes, were found in the village area.) Nonetheless, because of the overwhelming nature of the army defeat and the large number of officers who perished, it was considered impractical to gather up any remains. As one officer noted, "It was simply impossible to bring in these bodies."

The surviving men of the Seventh Cavalry spread over the field armed with knives, hatchets, and tin cups, each company responsible for completing burials within a given sector. Except for Custer and his brother, Captain Thomas W. Custer, most of the dead, including officers, received but a modicum of attention, and some were apparently barely covered with a few scoops of the ashy soil or with branches of sage. Most of the officers' bodies were marked "with the means at hand." According to then-General Edward S. Godfrey speaking many years later, Captain Henry J. Nowlan "marked the grave of each officer with a stake driven below the surface of the ground. The name of the officer was written on a slip of paper, the paper put in an empty cartridge shell, and the shell driven into the top of the stake." Nowlan also made a sketch map of the locations of the officers' graves. By late in the afternoon of Wednesday, June 28, the burials of more than 260 men were complete (at both the Custer and Reno ends of the battlefield), and the troops began a labored trek north along the Little Bighorn River. At the mouth of that stream, their comrades helped the wounded aboard the steamer *Far West*, which began a grueling and storied descent of the Bighorn, Yellowstone, and Missouri rivers to reach the hospital at Fort Abraham Lincoln, Dakota.[1]

During the interments, several of the Seventh Cavalry officers with Custer—specifically second lieutenants James G. Sturgis and Henry M. Harrington, First Lieutenant James E. Porter, and Assistant Surgeon George E. Lord—were not identified and possibly were never found. A specific search for these officers was conducted and a tentative identification made of one body, thought to be Lord's, on Custer Hill. Captain Otho E. Michaelis, who was ordnance officer for the Department of Dakota, claimed that a shirt and socks, besides his moustache and "shapely hands," certified that the man was Dr. Lord. "The remains were lying near Col. [First Lieutenant and Regimental Adjutant William W.] Cooke's, somewhat higher (a few feet) on the hill, and where the final and most desperate fighting was done." Despite the probability that the man was Lord, he was initially carried as "missing in action." By September 1876, however, General Terry, now convinced of the evidence in Lord's favor, authorized his notation to be officially changed to read "killed in action."[2]

The issue regarding Dr. Lord's identification demonstrates the esteem in which the remains of all of these men were held within the army community. As in all aspects of army life, however, and in accordance with strictures of discipline, lines of authority, and etiquette of military rule, officers fared better than humble enlisted personnel in the discriminatory system of command. There were obvious differences also in responsibility, pay, quarters, and work assignments. In the nineteenth century, moreover, officers often came from cultured backgrounds. Most had received formal educations from assorted civilian colleges and universities, and many had been schooled at the prestigious Military Academy at West Point or at other military institutes. Although some officers had risen from the lower ranks under special circumstances of appointment (and were not always accepted as such by their supposedly more learned peers), they nonetheless helped compose the stratified class system existing between commissioned and enlisted status. Often, officers hailed from prominent political or business families, and relationships within and among those circles as they related to the military establishment were more or less omnipresent. Thus, in the army caste system the bodies of officers killed in the line of duty on the frontier were generally transported home or to cemeteries designated to receive them, while enlisted men so lost were usually interred in the field.[3]

Given the social realities of U.S. Army composition in 1876–77, it was only a matter of time before the families of Little Bighorn officer fatalities began to assert their desire to retrieve their dead. As early as March 26, 1877, General Terry wrote divisional commander Sheridan that he was "much pressed by the friends of the officers who fell with Custer on the 25th of last June in the Battle of the Little Bighorn, to bring in their bodies." Within days, Sheridan substantially modified Terry's letter to include wives as well as friends. He requested that the secretary of war provide funds to recover and bury all the bodies but Custer's at Fort Leavenworth. "Mrs. Custer wants Gen. Custer buried at West Point, and I recommend that she be gratified in this desire." Terry asked that a War Department "incidental fund" be used to purchase cases and coffins for the "bodies or bones," while Sheridan proposed detailing an officer to deliver the remains in boxes to Fort Lincoln, where they would be transferred to appropriate coffins. "The satisfaction it will give to the wives, families and friends of the officers will be very great." Commanding General Sherman endorsed the project, which was approved by the War Department.[4]

In early May, Sheridan notified the secretary that he had appointed his brother and aide-de-camp Lieutenant Colonel Michael V. Sheridan, himself a captain on detached duty from the Seventh Cavalry, to carry out the duty of recovering and properly interring the officer dead and requested $1,000 to begin the work. "I cannot tell what the expense will be," wrote the general. "It may be a little more than this amount, or may be less."[5] Two days later, Colonel Sheridan received formal published orders that were vague as to purpose. He was to proceed by way of St. Paul, Bismarck, and the Missouri and Yellowstone rivers "to the site selected for a new post near the mouth of the Little Big Horn river, on business connected with the public service."[6] That same day, he received more explicit instructions from his brother:

> In compliance with the authority of the Hon. Secretary of War, herewith enclosed, you will proceed to the battlefield of the Little Big Horn, and recover, as far as it is practicable, the bodies of Lieut. Colonel Geo. A. Custer and other officers who fell with him on June 25th 1876, and bring them down to Fort Abraham Lincoln, where they will be properly prepared for burial.
>
> The body of Lieut. Col. Custer will from thence be trans-shipped to the cemetery at West Point, New York, and those of the other officers to the National Cemetery at Fort Leaven-worth, unless the relatives and friends of the officers desire to take possession of the bodies for interment at such places as they may elect.
>
> In the performance of this duty the most rigid economy will be required, and the expense will be paid by the Hon. Secretary of War out of the Contingent Fund of the Army.
>
> All commanding officers will be required to give Lieut. Col. Sheridan such assistance in the way of details and transportation as he may find necessary to make a requisition for, and Brig. Gen. Terry is requested to detail Capt. Nowlan, 7th Cavalry, to accompany Col. Sheridan to the battle field and assist him in his duties.[7]

Colonel Sheridan's visit to the scene of Custer's defeat in July 1877 for the specific reason of removing the officers' remains represented the first purposeful effort by the federal government to recognize the unique qualities of the place—a place of horrific military defeat that would be long remembered. On July 1, 1877, Sheridan's small party left the site of the old trading post of Fort Pease, five miles below the mouth of the Bighorn. Near the junction of the Bighorn and Little Bighorn he joined Captain Nowlan, who had helped bury the dead in 1876, and members of a reconstituted Company I, Seventh Cavalry, who would accompany him to the battlefield. Guided by scouts who had been with Custer, including the Crows Half Yellow Face and Curley, as well as George Herendeen and Thomas H. LeForge, the caravan halted at Post No. 2 (to be designated Fort Custer in November of that year), then being raised at the confluence of the Bighorn and Little Bighorn rivers to watch over Sioux country and prevent such an assembly of the tribesmen as had occurred the previous year. From that post, Sheridan's group, followed by four ox-drawn wagons, journeyed the thirteen or so miles south to Custer's battlefield, camping en route and reaching the site on the morning of July 2. The area of the immense Indian village was littered with lodge poles and destroyed camp debris. Sheridan crossed east of the river at Medicine Tail Ford. It had been just over a year since the burials, and it became quickly apparent that they had not fared well in the interim. Heavy rains on the ashy soil had quickly bared the remains, and wolves, coyotes, and other creatures had dragged many from the shallow graves to feast.[8]

Over the following days, Sheridan's men performed their duties. They canvassed the ground southeast of Custer Hill without success for evidence that might help identify the remains of Lieutenants Sturgis, Porter, and Harrington and Dr. Lord (despite his tentative identification). Guided by the previously numbered stake markers, Nowlan's map, and a map prepared the previous summer by First Lieutenant Edward Maguire of Terry's staff, they exhumed portions of the other officer remains and placed them in pine boxes fashioned at Post No. 2. The remains of Custer and his brother Captain Thomas W. Custer were disinterred along with those of Captains Keogh and George W. Yates and Lieutenants Cooke, Algernon E. Smith, Calhoun, and Reilly. The remains of Custer's youngest brother, Boston Custer, were evidently also recovered. Four miles away, the soldiers retrieved the remains of Lieutenants Benjamin H. Hodgson and Donald McIntosh and of Dr. James M. DeWolf. "Few entire skeletons were found," wrote one observer. "The skulls, especially, were missing, or smashed in, evidently by wolves and Indians." The remains of scout Charley Reynolds, who had fallen in the valley with Reno, filled but a handkerchief.[9] Those of Custer (marked as stake no. 1) were debated. His remains were problematic; those first selected were dismissed, and Sergeant Michael C. Caddle of Company I explained, "I think we got the right body the second time." More easily identified were those of Lieutenant Cooke. Colonel Sheridan later wrote to Cooke's family that "the wolves had disturbed the grave a little but about all except the more perishable parts of his body was [sic] found." Sergeant Caddle was able to help identify most members of Company I by clothing lying in the vicinity of their tightly massed position.[10] In addition, the remains of Mark Kellogg, the news correspondent who had accompanied Custer, were found and reburied. Some headboards were erected, notably one marking the grave of

Second Lieutenant John J. Crittenden, whose remains were placed in a coffin and reburied where they lay at the southern tip of the battle ridge, per his family's request. What was left of the bodies of each individual exhumed was placed in a box filled with dry grass. "As the climate and soil had assisted in the destruction of the remains," noted a correspondent for the Bozeman Avant Courier, "most of them go to the East mingled with Mother Earth."[11]

Sheridan next dispatched parties in all directions to search for exposed remains to re-cover. "As I had no lumber with which to make coffins, it was thought best to simply re-cover the graves and mark them with cedar stakes, so that the remains could be collected hereafter and buried in a cemetery, if one be declared there, or else removed to the cemetery at Post No. 2." Second Lieutenant Hugh L. Scott, who supervised this work, remembered that it had been perfunctory at best: "We had neither the time or the force to bury the whole command in deep graves." Finally, the colonel ordered a thorough search for bodies of the encompassing ground south to Reno's crossing. "I believe that all have now been buried, though it is possible that in the breaks and ravines, some may have escaped us."[12] On July 4, Sheridan's party conveyed the remains of Custer and his officers to Post No. 2. Three days later they were hoisted aboard the steamboat *John G. Fletcher* for the trip down the Yellowstone and Missouri to Fort Abraham Lincoln, where they arrived on July 12, 1877. Hodgson's remains, which had been properly casketed at Post No. 2, were sent on their way to Philadelphia. Following the arrival at the post of caskets sent from Chicago, the rest of the bodies were variously dispersed: Cooke's to Hamilton, Ontario; Riley's to Washington, D.C.; DeWolf's to Norwalk, Ohio; Keogh's to Auburn, New York (all at the families' expense); Custer's to West Point; and Captains Custer and Yates and Lieutenants Calhoun, Smith, and McIntosh to the National Cemetery at Fort Leavenworth, Kansas, where final burial took place on August 4. Custer's funeral occurred on October 10, 1877.[13]

Within days of the departure of Colonel Sheridan's party, the first photographer to capture the scene visited the battlefield. He was John H. Fouch, who had his office at the Tongue River Cantonment. Fouch's image, titled "The Place Where Custer Fell," likely shows the precise spot where Custer perished. The view embraces the knoll atop Custer Hill with the grisly litter of horse bones and weathered cavalry gear, together with planted stakes that just days before had marked the graves of officer dead. (The image, discovered in 1990, constitutes an exceptionally significant contribution to the battlefield's interpretive history.)[14]

Less than three weeks after Colonel Sheridan's departure from the battlefield, his brother and commander of the Military Division of the Missouri went into camp opposite the field, west of the Little Bighorn on ground once occupied by the Indian village. Lieutenant General Philip H. Sheridan, joined by Brigadier General Crook and other officers, had journeyed by rail from his Chicago headquarters and overland from Wyoming en route to consult with Commanding General William T. Sherman and Brigadier General Terry over army occupation of the Yellowstone country in the closing stages of the Great Sioux War. (Sherman was ascending the Yellowstone on an inspection tour that over the course of three months would take him and his party into the new national park as well as to sites in the Pacific Northwest.) In the afternoon of July 21, Sheridan's entourage established Camp Seventh Cavalry on the west bank of the Little Bighorn. Inspecting the field at Sherman's request, Sheridan noticed corpses exposed from heavy rain, despite his brother's recent work there. Crook's adjutant, First Lieutenant John G. Bourke, saw "portions of the human anatomy and skeletons of horses" along with clothing, hats, and boots strewn over the ground. A Fifth Cavalryman recalled seeing "the skeletons of six men, and a seventh showing fragments of chevrons, on the ground a short distance from where we forded the creek." Sheridan detailed an aide, Major George A. Forsyth, to take seventy men and thoroughly examine the area and gather for burial any remains found on the surface (Forsyth reported burying seventeen "total skeletons and parts of skeletons"). "I then visited the main portion of the battle-field," recounted the general, "and found all the graves nicely raised as in cemeteries inside civilization, and most, if not all, marked with head-boards or stakes." Sheridan's party next day proceeded on to Post No. 2 and on the following day met with Sherman aboard the *Rosebud* on the Bighorn River. The meeting lasted two hours. Sheridan and Crook then steamed east down the Yellowstone and Missouri rivers. Sherman proceeded to the army station next day but on the twenty-fifth started downriver to the Yellowstone and continued west. For unknown reasons, despite his proximity to Custer's battlefield and his likely interest in inspecting it, Sherman passed on the opportunity and instead pursued his itinerary.[15]

Despite the attempts of General Sheridan's party to cover the remains of the dead, it did not succeed. A correspondent for the *New York Sun* lamented the condition of the dead on the field the day after

Sheridan departed, concluding after a lengthy and graphic description that "bad as it may seem in print, it is a thousand times worse in reality." Yet General Sheridan's visit, coming on the heels of that of his brother, proved of inestimable importance for what happened subsequently at Custer's battlefield. It appears to have influenced Sheridan's recommendation that the site, located but thirteen miles from Fort Custer (former Post No. 2), "be set off as a national cemetery, if possible." The proximity of the army station made its proper care a certainty. The general wrote Sherman of his wish in April 1878. If the national cemetery were not approved, he planned to "this summer have the remains removed to the cemetery at Fort Custer and there buried."[16]

It is likely that Sheridan's thoughts were influenced to a considerable degree by the fact that the particulars of Michael Sheridan's visit had been purposely kept from the press, at least initially, and that when word of the recovery of officers' remains got out, families of the enlisted dead protested. At least one letter of criticism was written to Congressman William W. Rice (Rep.-Mass.) by the father of Corporal Samuel F. Staples, who had died with Company I at the Little Bighorn. Samuel E. Staples, beyond grieving for the loss of his son, consoled himself with the conviction that "all who fell remained together," a belief shattered with news in the summer of 1877 of the expedition to retrieve the officers' remains. "This proceeding appears to have been purposely kept out of the daily papers and from the knowledge of the friends of the soldiers." Compounding the notion that he could otherwise perhaps have thus retrieved his son's remains, there appeared statements in the press alluding to the poor condition of the dead on the field of action.[17] Staples demanded to know the truth. "If true," he wrote to Rice,

> I think the government can do no less than to give these remains decent burial, by putting them in coffins, and remove them to some suitable place. . . . It is hard for me to understand how the remains of the officers could be in condition for removal, . . . while those of privates and non-commissioned officers had become food for wolves. . . . I want to secure the body of my son. If not, I want that he with those who fell with him should have decent and suitable burial at some permanent post or at the National Cemetery where their bodies can rest undisturbed, and some fitting monument erected to their memory.

Staples's sentiments were ultimately conveyed via Representative Rice through the War Department to General Sheridan, who, in light of his own experience on the field, likely took them to heart in his recommendation to Sherman in the spring of 1878.[18]

By that time, the accounts of wayfarers passing the battlefield essentially verified the statements regarding its neglected condition in so remote a land. In August 1877, less than a month after Generals Sheridan and Crook had been there, not much had improved. A gold seeker en route to Post No. 2 reported that he had viewed many of the remains "with only a little layer of earth thrown over. . . . [It was a] terrible sight." Another described graves scarcely covered with heads and feet protruding. And in October, Frank M. Fleming, a worker building Post No. 2, visited the scene and saw a field "strewed with feet, legs, hands, and arms, which had been wrenched from the shallow graves by the coyotes, the nationality of their owners being shown by an occasional shred of the army blue." Fleming said there were "feet still covered by the cavalry boot and with the flesh gnawed clean from the exposed parts. . . ."[19] Soon after, a correspondent for the *New York Herald* accompanied a detachment under Lieutenant Colonel Albert G. Brackett to view the site in late September 1877. He reported on the entire battle area in more tempered tones:

> On the hill where Reno made his stand the numerous rifle pits and breastworks show what his men did for their defence. Down the hill about a hundred yards lie the remains of forty-six horses, killed at the picket line. . . . [On Custer's field] bones were scattered in every direction, but not human bones. So many horses had been killed on these bluffs that their bones were met with on every side. . . . There was found above ground only twelve human skulls and some bones, evidently dug up by Indians and coyotes. In two or three cases skulls were found stuck upon the grave stakes. Colonel Brackett immediately set about collecting these bones and had them re-interred as well as it was possible to do with knives and horses' shoulder blades, the only implements at hand.[20]

A year later it was much the same, if not worse, when "many of their bones and several skulls have been washed out and are laying [*sic*] upon the ground." The writer of that statement, moreover, took as souvenirs "a few buttons, a hors [*sic*] shoe (off Custer's horse), and a few cartridge shells from the battle field." There were even reports of a nearby stage station operator taking a "trophy" skull from the battlefield to be sent to his company proprietor. And in June 1878, Colonel Nelson A. Miles led a party of officers and cavalrymen to the scene to interview Sioux and Cheyenne participants of the battle. Two months later he was back with a twenty-man infantry detachment and some thirty Cheyenne chiefs and warriors accompanying the mother and sisters of Lieutenant James G. Sturgis to the ground to view a fabricated grave covered with stones and perhaps effect some closure. On that visit an associate described the bleaching bones as "never properly buried." Another wrote that "the horrible sight of bleached bones of horses, and the skulls of human beings cannot fail to remind one of the Valley of Jehosophat."[21]

The comments, and especially the published remarks, reflected a reality that would not go away. It is likely that Mrs. Sturgis's visit, during which she as the mother of a Little Bighorn officer victim had to endure the dreadful condition of the field, climaxed the cumulative lament and brought action to improve the site. On October 29, 1878, General Terry—in a missive laden with implications for the long-term future of Little Bighorn Battlefield—notified Lieutenant Colonel George P. Buell, Eleventh Infantry, commanding Fort Custer, as follows:

> There have been lately several reports in the public print that the remains of Custer's men have never been properly buried. The Department Commander directs that you take the first favorable opportunity to make a careful examination of the field of battle on the Little Big Horn, and, if there are any human bones there exposed, that you cause them to be carefully collected at some one point, there securely buried and a high cone or pyramid of loose stone to be built up over the grave, so as to protect the remains from any future depredations by wild animals. Let this be done by an adequate force and in a thorough manner. The Department Commander thinks that the most suitable location for the grave is the highest point of the ridge, just in rear of where General Custer's body was found. He directs also that, if it has not heretofore been done, the high broken ground to the north and east of the battle-field be thoroughly examined for a distance of five or six miles to see if any trace can be found of the remains of about thirty men who are supposed to have escaped, for a time, from the

main battle field. If such remains should be found, they will be carefully collected and brought to the main grave. The graves of most of the commissioned officers were originally marked. If any of these remain so, and are secured against depredations, they should not be disturbed, but made more secure if necessary by having stone upon them.[22]

Terry's order reached Fort Custer on November 18. By then, the onset of cold weather precluded immediate enactment by Buell, and it was postponed until spring. The Terry directive significantly formalized in official manner the caring attention that the army would henceforth apply to Custer's field to ensure an appearance appropriate for its status as a place where American soldiers had died in combat. In April 1879, Buell's successor, Lieutenant Colonel Albert G. Brackett, sent Captain George K. Sanderson and a detail from Fort Custer to perform the directed work. Sanderson was unable to find stone, so he instead collected cordwood. He prepared a large grave at the point designated by Terry at the top of Custer Hill, then collected human bones (from "parts of four or five different bodies") and placed them within. He covered them with wood for a height of four feet above the ground, then continued building, stacking the wood on the sides. Sanderson filled in the center (presumably above the wood atop the grave) with horse bones scavenged from the field. When completed, the informal monument stood eleven feet high and ten feet square. "It is built on the highest point immediately in [the] rear of where Gen'l Custer's body was found." Then the work detail attended to the individual graves, which Sanderson reported were reshaped and a stake placed wherever one had previously existed. The captain blamed the incredible news reports on the presence of the horse bones, which his men had collected and placed in the cordwood mound. He concluded:

> The whole field now presents a perfectly clean appearance, each grave being remounded and all animal bones removed. I would respectfully suggest, that if it is the intention of the Government to do anything further to mark this spot, that a stone wall be built around where the mound now stands, . . . that either all the remains be gathered together and placed in one grave and a stone mound be built over it, or that stone head stones be placed at each grave, as they now are [in wood]. Either would be an enduring monument.

Photographs of the cordwood mound, along with other views of the battlefield, taken by Stanley J. Morrow of Yankton, Dakota Territory, accompanied Sanderson's report. Significantly, the document was forwarded through the secretary of war to Representative William W. Rice of Massachusetts, whose constituent Samuel E. Staples, father of a common soldier who died at Little Bighorn, had doubtless influenced these proceedings. Meantime, unquestionably inspired by recent events, on January 29, 1879, the secretary of war authorized the establishment of a national cemetery on Custer's battlefield. On August 1, 1879, by virtue of General Order No. 78, Headquarters of the Army, the ground was designated a national cemetery of the fourth class, meaning appropriate boundaries would yet be determined. (This date has since been recognized as the park's Establishment Day by the National Park Service.)[23]

Captain Sanderson's recommendation of a monument for the Little Bighorn dead, either in the form of a stone wall surrounding the cordwood depository or head stones at each grave, anticipated, in large effect, that very treatment of the site. The site, moreover, required steady maintenance, and his visit to the battlefield in 1879 began a tradition that became formalized, whereby troops from Fort Custer cared for the ground, policed it on an irregular basis, and monitored the graves, and re-covered them as required. Following Sanderson's 1879 effort, other parties ventured there to attend to the remains that were more or less constantly being re-exposed. "The last time I was at the battlefield," reported one captain, "no remains appeared exposed. The graves being mostly in the ravines and sides of the hills, are now well covered with a thick bed of grass; indeed, the rank patches of grass are about the only remaining marks of the graves." The officer urged that "as soon as the monument is put up, that the bones be collected and all deposited at its base . . . as the most reasonable and appropriate manner of finally burying the remains."[24]

The matter of raising an appropriate monument to honor the dead soldiers at Little Bighorn went back to the immediate aftermath of the battle. In the wake of the first reports of the army disaster and the universal public dismay ("Dead? Is it possible! He, the bold rider / Custer, our hero, the first in the fight / Charming the bullets of yore to fly wider / Shunning our battle king's ringlets of light!"), contributions from citizens, including army personnel, signified a widespread desire to properly commemorate the dead. Friends of the deceased officer tentatively set up the Custer Monumental Association. A widow's relief fund was started simultaneously, with the *Army and Navy Journal,* the professional military tabloid, urging solicitations to honor the living as well as the dead. In tribute, the Montana territorial legislature changed the name of the Little Bighorn River to Custer's River, and the *New York Herald* called for erection of a monument to the fallen. And although Elizabeth B. Custer, widow of the Seventh's commander, registered an interest in such a tribute, her immediate attention rested with the retrieval of her husband's body and its burial at West Point rather than with the monumentation of the battlefield on which he died. In May 1877, nearly a year after the event, the *New York Herald* called for a monument "to the memory of all [who fell there]."[25]

Preceding Sanderson's recommendation by several months, and doubtless unknown to the captain, the army's quartermaster general, Brigadier General Montgomery C. Meigs, had already promoted a design for such a memorial. Meigs called for "a granite monument, of sufficient size, to receive in legible characters the names of all the officers and men who fell in that fight." It would be "massive and heavy enough to remain for ages where placed—a landmark of the conflict between civilization and barbarism." Throughout his planning for the monument, Meigs apparently kept Mrs. Elizabeth Custer informed of its progress and later sent her copies of the plans and the names inscribed thereon. The general thought that the monument might be prepared during the winter of 1878–79, then shipped by way of steamer and wagon to the battlefield. He anticipated that all remains collected be interred "in a vault and the monument set up over them." Later, he urged that the national cemetery designation be granted as early as possible and that a survey of its metes and bounds not be delayed so that "there may be no difficulty about the payment for the monument ordered and now ready for shipment."[26]

Yet it was nearly three years before the monument was erected. A contract was let on February 21, 1879, to the Mount Auburn Marble and Granite Works, Cambridge, Massachusetts, for a pyramid-shaped stone edifice measuring six feet wide at its base, three feet six inches at its top, eleven feet six inches in height. The names of the 261 dead, including officers, enlisted men, Indian scouts, and civilians, would be carved into the facets so that the total cost stood at $1,000. As executed by Alexander McDonald, the monument consisted of three granite pieces—a base and two sectional components forming the shaft—together weighing 38,547 pounds. (Generally, the sections are described as weighing seven tons, six tons, and five tons, respectively.) By July 21, 1879, the pieces were ready for shipment and within a month had arrived at Governor's Island, New York Harbor. From there they journeyed by way of the St. Lawrence River and Great Lakes to Duluth, Minnesota, then on to Bismarck, Dakota, by rail, then by steamer up the Missouri and Yellowstone, and by sledge up the Bighorn River to Fort Custer, where they arrived in 1880. On February 12, 1881, the commanding officer notified department headquarters that the three stones for the monument had each been hauled by sledge (dragged by twenty-four mules) from the post to Custer Hill, crossing the ice-bound Little Bighorn three times, and waited only the thawing of the ground to be raised.[27]

In July, First Lieutenant Charles F. Roe headed a detail of Company C, Second Cavalry, under Second Lieutenant Alvarado M. Fuller, to raise the monument. Employing a derrick crane made of ash cut from along the Little Bighorn, together with posts and a capstan, the whole powered by mules, "the stones were moved into position with comparatively little trouble." Roe placed the obelisk where the cordwood structure had been raised, "on the point of the hill within six (6) feet of the place where the remains of General Custer were found after the fight." Roe offered the following particulars regarding the finishing of the monument:

> I [previously had] had a hole dug eight (8) feet square and six (6) feet deep and then filled it in with a concrete of stone and mortar making it perfectly solid, which brought the foundation to the surface of the ground. On that I built a foundation of large flat stones seven (7) feet square and two and a half feet above the surface; binding it (the upper foundation) together by four (4) iron rods running each way with iron plate washers on the outside, so that it will probably last for a great many years. . . . The stones were then placed in position and a trench dug ten (10) feet from base of monument on four (4) sides, for the remains. I took great pains in gathering together all the remains from the Custer Battle Field, Reno's Hill and the valley, giving it my personal attention and scouting very thoroughly over the whole ground and miles back, so that I feel confident all the remains are gathered together and placed at base of monument. Stone [was] put immediately on top of remains, and then earth, so that now they are well buried and will never be exposed again in all human probability. It was impracticable to place remains in crypt or tomb under

monument, as the stone was of such nature as only to make a good solid foundation.

Whenever I found the remains of a man [on the field], I planted a stake, well in the ground, so that future visitors can see where the men actually fell. The earth was mounded up against the monument so as to cover the built foundation and gives it the appearance of being on a mound. The work was completed on the 29th of July. . . . I take this opportunity of commending Mr. Irishman, Wheel[w]right, and Private Bannon, "F" Troop, 2d Cavalry, stonemason, for their intelligent assistance and zeal. The remains of Lieutenant Crittenden were well buried where he fell and the stone sent by his father put in position.[28]

Despite Roe's canvassing of the battlefield for remains and the final interment of approximately 220 at the base of the monument in 1881, human skeletal parts continued to appear intermittently during subsequent years. In August 1884, for example, a group of cowboys herding horses past the site came across the bones of a soldier in a ravine several hundred yards southeast of the monument. That discovery, and others like it either reported or unreported, signified both the attention that the place commanded publicly, as well as the need to attentively monitor the grounds of the new national cemetery. Because the cemetery (i.e., the entire battlefield) was administratively tied to Fort Custer, that post was responsible for caring for the graves and all related maintenance. As a national cemetery, moreover, the site warranted periodic inspection. One in the spring of 1882, scarcely nine months after the monument's erection, noted that frost had "split off quite a number of pieces from the shaft and if this continues it will soon be badly defaced." The inspecting officer, Major William W. Sanders, called for securing the remains of the dead, as well as protecting the base of the monument, with an iron fence that could not be destroyed by prairie fires. He further urged that "if it is the intention to permanently mark the different points where the officers and men fell in this battle, . . . iron posts be supplied to replace the present sticks that now mark the different points, [as] these sticks are destroyed by prairie fires and cattle." The Division of the Missouri inspector general, Colonel Nelson H. Davis, concurred in the proposal for a fence "or stone wall" but noted that "to mark the spot where individuals fell would be a change of the course followed by the Gov't heretofore in similar cases."[29]

As the effective ward of Fort Custer, the national cemetery became the object of social and commemorative outings too. In June 1886, the tenth anniversary of the Battle of the Little Bighorn saw attendance by several army and Indian veterans, including the Hunkpapa Lakota Gall, a principal leader of the Indian coalition, who ushered visitors over the ground and gave his personal remembrances of the action. Other Sioux and Cheyenne battle participants appeared, along with the Crow scout White Swan. Army participants included Major Frederick W. Benteen, Captains Edward S. Godfrey, Winfield S. Edgerly, and Thomas M. McDougall, Dr. Henry R. Porter, Corporal John Hall, and former trumpeter George Penwell, while a company of the Ninth Cavalry arrived from Fort McKinney, Wyoming. The event was organized by First Lieutenant Herbert J. Slocum, Seventh Cavalry, and facilitated by Colonel Nathan A. M. Dudley, commanding officer of Fort Custer. On June 25, commemorative tributes and volleys were fired near the monument. Troops of Company K, Fifth Infantry, from Fort Keogh (former Tongue River Cantonment) established a field station named Camp Crittenden and provided skirmish demonstrations for attendees, and photographer David F. Barry of Bismarck captured images of the events. On June 28, perhaps as many as one thousand persons from the fort and around the region toured the Custer and Reno fields.

Most visits to the battlefield, however, were more subdued. Each Memorial Day, a delegation from the John Buford G.A.R. Post at the fort journeyed the thirteen miles to pay respects at the battlefield, despite difficulties in fording the Little Bighorn, usually swollen with the melting snows of the Big Horn Mountains. On May 31, 1887, a party setting out from Fort Custer had to climb atop their saddles to keep dry in crossing the stream. At the battlefield, members held services at the monument and at the grave of Lieutenant Crittenden, leaving floral wreaths and garlands before departing to Reno Hill, then back to Fort Custer. Similar ceremonies took place in 1888 on the anniversary of the battle. The monument also became the focal point for Fourth of July observances. On Independence Day 1890, more than four hundred Crow families pitched their lodges at the base of Custer Hill while the Indians paraded, danced, and performed a sham battle. In 1891 the celebration was repeated, with a twelve-pounder cannon from Fort Custer being discharged at regular intervals. The twentieth battle anniversary in 1896 was observed by some veterans of Reno's engagement, but most of the attendees were Sioux who were there visiting the Crows.

Some of the Indian participants accompanied visitors over the ground and explained the battle. And the twenty-fifth in 1901, while promoted as a big affair, turned out to be rather subdued, with Indian children gracing the monument with tossed flowers.[30]

As eastern Montana and northern Wyoming became increasingly settled, more people beyond army personnel from Fort Custer passed through the country in carriages or on horseback and stopped by to see the national cemetery. Many picked up battle-related cartridges that were strewn over the ground or chipped souvenirs of their visits from the headstones and/or monument (see chapter 3). Throughout these early years, any regular interpretation of battle-related events rested with Fort Custer residents who had been in the country for years. Two prominent persons who could speak with authority were Thomas H. LeForge and James Campbell, both of whom had been on the scene during the initial burials. LeForge had been a scout with Gibbon, and he often led tours of the field from the post. Campbell, who succeeded LeForge as chief scout at Fort Custer, likewise had served as a scout with Gibbon and reportedly had helped mark the graves with the first wooden stakes. Both men functioned in the capacity of unofficial guides and likely presented the first substantive interpretation of the Little Bighorn battlefield.[31]

Fort Custer's role in the establishment and maintenance of the national cemetery at Custer's battlefield continued until the post's abandonment in 1897. As indicated, the fort had been established in July 1878, under authority of Congress approved on July 22, 1876, in the wake of the Little Bighorn disaster, to establish a permanent presence (with Post No. 1, subsequently named Fort Keogh) in the Yellowstone country. In addition to the fort proper, a military reservation was needed, along with a reservation at the newly designated national cemetery, as well as land for a limestone reserve located near the old post of Fort C. F. Smith. Through the Department of the Interior, the Crow Indians, who owned the land by virtue of the Fort Laramie Treaty of 1868, objected to the War Department's request for tracts of four hundred square miles for the post, eighteen square miles for the national cemetery, and nearly four square miles for the limestone reserve. The cemetery tract had been surveyed by Lieutenant Maguire in 1879, and the eighteen square miles represented a six-by-three-mile declaration respecting the entirety of the Little Bighorn battlefield, including the national cemetery. Colonel Dudley complained that the Indian Department intended "to reduce this declared Reservation or Cemetery ground to the vicinity of 'Custer's Hill.' Some forty (40) men were killed . . . on 'Reno's Hill,' and some in the bottom opposite this Hill on the left bank of the Little Big Horn, but all the bodies have been removed to the 'Custer Monument' grounds."

The matter was not resolved until the mid-1880s. By then, as Dudley reported, "many Indians are located on, and have been allotted farms within the grounds originally declared reserved for a National Cemetery." Thus, the army negotiated for less acreage—thirty-six square miles for the Fort Custer reservation and one square mile for the national cemetery, with minimal disruption of Indian holdings. In regard to the latter, "this covers most of the ground known as 'Custer's Battlefield,' Lieut. Crittenden's grave, a good river front, a plot of good grazing ground, and sufficient agricultural ground to be occupied by a superintendent, if ever required." Metes and bounds of the proposed tract were as follows:

"Commencing at a point 1,200 feet north 350 west of Custer's monument, and running thence north 550 east 1200 feet; thence south 350 east one (1) mile; thence south 550 west to the right bank of the Little Big Horn River; thence along said right bank to the prolongation of the Western boundary; thence along said prolongation to the place of beginning. Area: one square mile."

On December 7, 1886, President Grover Cleveland by executive order proclaimed the described tracts for military purposes. General Order No. 90, Headquarters of the Army, implementing the proclamation, were published on December 15, 1886. The State of Montana ceded the designated lands in accordance with a general act of cession approved in 1891. In theory, that cession justified the taking of the reservations as an "absolute military necessity," thereby granting to the federal government all right, title, and interest held by the Crow Indians, who were not compensated by Congress for their loss of land until 1930.[32] Custer Battlefield National Cemetery, at least in its initial configuration, was formally complete.

CHAPTER 3 | # War Department Years

The National Cemetery, 1880s–1920s

The erection of the monument to the army dead on the Little Bighorn battlefield represented the first permanent improvement at the more or less one-mile-square national cemetery. From that time until 1940, the site would remain under the control and authority of the War Department, reflecting in its military administration both a cemeterial component and a generally small but evolving interpretive component. The tentative beginnings of the cemetery-battlefield's commemoration, coupled with its progression into a more standard military cemetery facility, continued over the decades of the 1880s and 1890s, and by 1900 the site had assumed the characteristics that essentially marked it throughout much of the twentieth century.

As stated, Fort Custer, through its commander and his quarter-master officer, continued nominal stewardship of the site until the post was abandoned in 1897. Both the military and national cemetery reservations remained surrounded by Crow Indian land. In 1882 the Crows sold the western part of their land to be opened for settlement by whites. A year later, their agency was moved to the present Crow Agency, and many of the tribesmen settled along the Little Bighorn and Bighorn rivers in the vicinity of the Fort Custer and Custer Battlefield National Cemetery reserves. A reservation established in 1884 for the Northern Cheyenne Indians immediately abutted the east boundary of the Crow tract. Troops from Fort Custer carefully monitored the potentially volatile conditions between these traditional enemies, now placed side by side. Both tribes eventually accepted the concept of severalty, whereby their tribal lands were allotted for individual ownership and farming.

In the autumn of 1886, the allotment issue on the Crow Reservation became complicated by the arrival there of none other than Sitting Bull—to whites the purported mastermind of the destruction of Custer and the Seventh Cavalry—just three miles from the Crow Agency headquarters and scarcely ten years earlier. The Hunkpapa leader, along with one hundred Lakotas from the Standing Rock and Cheyenne River agencies, took part in a peaceful pilgrimage to the Crows. The visit lasted two weeks, during which the former enemy tribes comingled, feasted, and reminisced, and Sitting Bull held forth within miles of his 1876 victory. During the stay, the chief told the Crows that he wanted his own allotment delayed. That pronouncement henceforth affected the progress of the allotment program among the Crows and caused consternation for their agent, Henry E. Williamson. As a result of Sitting Bull's influence, declared Williamson, "several of the Crow chiefs, who had never uttered a word against allotment, took the same stand as Sitting Bull said he had taken at his agency." Long after the Lakotas had departed, allotment efforts among the Crows remained stalemated.[1]

Occasionally, disturbances arose requiring a military presence. In the fall of 1887, during a brief uprising of a faction of the Crows, troops from Fort Custer camped near the national cemetery to monitor events at the nearby agency. A skirmish between soldiers and Indians erupted there in which Wraps-Up-His-Tail (Sword Bearer), a collaborator of a perceived messianic disturbance, was killed. None of the action spilled over onto the cemetery reservation, and the so-called Crow Rebellion became the last military operation against Indians in its immediate vicinity (although troops from Forts Custer and Keogh operated in the area during the period of the Wounded Knee Massacre in December 1890).

Instead, army caretakers worked to improve the site. The recommendations for an iron fence and repairs to the monument, as called for by Major Sanders in 1882, were fulfilled two years later when expenditures of $900 ($800 for the fence and $100 for repairs) were authorized by the Department of Dakota. (The fence comprised four panels of iron rods, each approximately ten feet long, "well-pointed and cramped through holes bored through heavy flat horizontal plates, also of iron.") For the next several years, no disbursements affecting the battlefield occurred. On October 24, 1888, in keeping with its designation as a national cemetery, the site received the remains of 111 soldiers and civilians from the old post cemetery at Fort Phil

Kearny, Wyoming Territory, abandoned since 1868. Under supervision of Captain James M. J. Sanno, these remains, which included the fatalities from the so-called Fetterman Massacre of December 1866, were buried in three parallel rows on Custer Hill, the graves laid out in a north-south configuration a short distance south of the monument. The headstones for the Fort Phil Kearny dead were installed in October 1889, during which time soldiers from Fort Custer under Captain John H. French, Twenty-fifth Infantry, also reburied the remains of four of Custer's men that had become exposed.[2]

In August 1889 Lieutenant Colonel George D. Dandy, deputy quartermaster of the depot quartermaster's office in Washington, D.C., visited the field and complained about its overall condition. He found the monument defaced from visitors chipping on it, coupled with the "marks of pistol bullets." In looking over the area, Dandy concluded that it lacked formality. "With the exception of this monument, there is no semblance of a [real] cemetery at this place. The points where the bodies of the officers were found have been marked by stakes, and there is an appearance of graves at certain places. There are also human bones to be found scattered about the field, some of which have been carried away by visitors." Dandy urged appropriate setting off and maintenance of the grounds with the enclosure of a strip (300 feet by 3,172 feet) containing twenty-five acres along the battle ridge sufficient to encompass the monument, the Fort Phil Kearny dead, and the grave of Lieutenant Crittenden. He further suggested that a superintendent be assigned to look after the grounds. The enclosure, high enough to keep out vandals and animals, was also to be fireproof, and Dandy recommended construction of an iron railing six feet tall. To house the superintendent, he recommended a lodge be built near the Little Bighorn River so that water might be accessible. Dandy estimated total cost of the improvements at $29,000. "If this cemetery is to be maintained," he concluded, "it should be enclosed with the least possible delay. It has been and is now only an open burying ground, though classed as a National Cemetery." (On October 28 and 29, 1889, Sergeant Herman W. Vance, Troop B, First Cavalry, from Fort Custer, formally surveyed the entire mile-square cemetery reservation. Two days later, iron posts were placed at the corners of the tract.) Doubtless influenced by the presence of the Fort Phil Kearny interments, Colonel Dandy observed that the grounds, when properly upgraded, would afford a place "to which the remains from other posts can [likewise] be removed when necessary or desirable."[3]

Another visitor to the battlefield in the summer of 1889 was U.S. senator James Burnie Beck (Rep.-Ky.). James Campbell accompanied him over the ground and evidently influenced his decision to seek markers and fencing for the site. On his return to Washington, Senator Beck drafted legislation calling for the replacement of the deteriorating wooden stakes marking the supposed burial places of Custer's men. Two hundred forty-nine headstones were crafted in the pattern authorized for national cemeteries, but specifically inscribed for enlisted men with "U.S. soldier 7th U.S. Cavalry fell here June 25, 1876," and for officers with name, rank, and unit, together with the words "Fell here June 25, 1876."[4] All were subsequently sent to Fort Custer to be erected on the battlefield. Between May 1 and 12, 1890, Captain Owen J. Sweet commanded Company D, Twenty-fifth Infantry, in completing the work. Because only 217 graves had been marked (exclusive of those for Boston Custer, Harry Reed, and Lieutenant Porter, whose body had not been found), Sweet's men moved over the terrain carefully in skirmish formation to find the rest. He reported that his officers and men indeed accounted for, and reburied as appropriate, the twenty-nine others, including "four bleaching skeletons [that] had remained unburied and with God's canopy to cover them for 14 years."

Sweet's report described the difficulties in identifying grave sites after the lapse of so many years and long after the initial inadequate burials and field tallies. Nonetheless, he concluded that

> the remains of all the soldiers on the Custer field are buried where they fell. . . . This lapse of time had tended to nearly obliterate all traces of the graves where only slightly marked, and many were only found by digging into every spot that bore the slightest resemblance to a grave, or spots where the grass was much greener and more luxuriant than in other places. . . . To avoid digging up the bones, which were found in all the graves during the first hour or two of the work, it was found necessary to dig the holes for the headstones at from 10 to 20 in[ches] from the mounds.

Captain Sweet went on to offer what is apparently the first substantive interpretation of the troop movements based wholly on the disposition of the graves on the battlefield. In all, he reported, "246 . . . headstones were erected on the Custer field, two headstones, one for Lieut. McIntosh, and the other for Dr. DeWolf, being erected on the Reno field, and that of

Lieut. Porter [whose remains were never found] being returned to the post and turned over to the Post Quartermaster, accounts for 249 head-stones." Wooden headboards were used to mark the places where Boston Custer's, Reed's, and Mark Kellogg's bodies were found. Significantly, Sweet noted that "several headstones were set near the graves previously marked where indications led to the possibility that more than one body rested. This was resorted to only at the end of the work, when guided by many days' experience, and a judgment well matured thereby." The stone for Lieutenant McIntosh was placed below Reno Hill and west of the Little Bighorn, in the field where he died. Sweet stated that the positioning of the McIntosh and DeWolf markers "may be slightly in error, . . . but they are correct for memorial purposes." He further advised the placement of a fence around the McIntosh marker to keep livestock from damaging it, while acknowledging an oversight in not having a marker to place where Lieutenant Hodgson fell on the east bank of the river. Sweet suggested that the Reno end of the battlefield had been neglected, and advised that troops should later canvas the ground there, with any retrieved remains either buried there or removed to the monument for interment.

As for the Fort Phil Kearny dead, the captain politely tendered his opinion of their reinterment on Custer's field:

> As the Custer battle lines enclose an irregular square it is believed to have been but a duty and in honor of those who fell there that this should have been sacredly reserved to them alone, and it is thought the use of the ridge near the monu-ment, and within the limits of these lines, for the purpose of re-interring the remains of our comrades who fell at . . . [Fort Phil Kearny] was unfortunate, and is to be regretted as there are numberless excellent locations outside of these lines that could have been most fortunately & appropriately selected for the purpose. As the remains of the dead from Forts Ellis, McGinnis [sic] and Sisseton, and many other posts, will even-tually be sent there, it is urgently recommended that proper representations be made to the proper authorities, to prevent an irregular placing of other bodies as in the case above cited.

At the time Captain Sweet performed his work of installing the head-stones, a small crew from Fort Custer under Second Lieutenant Samuel Burkhardt, Jr., labored to survey the boundaries of the national cemetery reservation. Following the survey, a "substantial barbed-wire fence" with gates was installed around the perimeter of the battlefield-cemetery, finally enclosing the mile-square tract authorized in 1886.[5]

Sweet's efforts in May 1890 were substantial and went a long way in cleaning up the battlefield, establishing order, and arranging for the security of the site. Although his work resulted in the placement of 246 stones where but 210 men had fallen, his rendering of the groupings of markers was ever after significant in influencing interpretations of the battle action. (For example, 52 markers were placed on Custer Hill where only 42 bodies were found; others appear to have been placed to the southwest, giving rise to theories of a well-attended skirmish line in that vicinity. Furthermore, Sweet placed no markers in Deep Ravine, where a concentration of bodies was known to have been found.)

Also in 1890, the remains of forty dead from the abandoned Fort Sisseton, Dakota Territory, arrived for reburial. Possibly in deference to Sweet's expressed concerns, those dead were interred on a flat several hundred yards west of the Custer monument. Lieutenant Colonel J. Ford Kent, acting inspector general, visited the battlefield-cemetery in July 1891 and reported the fence "intact and serviceable," although "both gates" were open and one unhinged, "the enclosure thus being open to stock, and a party of emigrants, apparently, encamped in same." While the headstones generally remained in good order, that for Custer—as well as the monument—had been chipped "by curiosity hunters." Moreover, vandals had apparently used a sledgehammer on the fence panels, effectively turning two of them into gates, allowing entrance to the monument. "The base of the monument, where it rests upon its pedestal, has been chipped all around," while the face of the stone had been further marred by a bullet shot. With hopes for preventing recurrences of the delinquency, while at the same time anticipating that more dead from abandoned forts would soon be arriving at the Little Bighorn site, Kent urged the hiring of a permanent superintendent.[6]

Continually completing repairs from Fort Custer proved an ongoing chore. Much of the damage was blamed on the Crow Indians, who, it was said, repeatedly broke through the gates and turned stock loose to range inside the enclosure. "As a consequence, the graves are tramped over and headstones knocked down by the stock." The regimental quartermaster of the First Cavalry at the post called for hiring a "keeper," and for him the construction of a suitable lodge would be required. For the keeper, or superintendent, to perform his duties, he would need such tools as shovels, hoes, picks, and rakes, along with several spools of barbed wire and staples. In addition, for maintaining the road to the cemetery, he would need a team, a wagon, a plow, and a scraper. These recommendations were forwarded through channels to the quartermaster general in Washington, D.C., who in October 1891 requested an appropriation of $29,900 "to erect a permanent fence and Superintendent's lodge at that Cemetery."[7]

Over the course of the next year, the final configuration of what ultimately became the Custer Battlefield National Cemetery of today was defined. By then, numerous other reburials from cemeteries from abandoned posts across the northern plains had been made on the flat below the monument and adjoining those from Fort Sisseton. They comprised the army dead, dependents, and civilian workers from Forts Totten (27), Abraham Lincoln (160), Bennett (25), Rice (146), Abercrombie (undetermined), and Pembina (25), Dakota Territory, and from Forts Shaw (77), C. F. Smith (17), and Maginnis (22) and Camp Poplar River (13), Montana Territory. (The Fort C. F. Smith dead, which included men killed in the Hayfield Fight of 1867, were accompanied by a large obelisk monument originally erected in that post's cemetery in 1868. Photographic evidence indicates that the Fort C. F. Smith reburials were initially made in the area presently designated Section F, westernmost of the cemetery, and were later [at least by 1901] removed to the area designated Section B. The Fort C. F. Smith monument was reestablished with the post reburials at the national cemetery.) These burials influenced a plan to enclose appropriate acreage, initially including the Custer monument "and the present graves," in a tract dedicated solely to cemeterial purposes. Andrew N. Grover, who assessed the property for the Quartermaster Department, however, concluded that the grounds incorporating present and future fort interments could not include the monument and graves, "owing to the rough and uneven surface of the ground . . . [and because] the [fort] interments that have already been made are far outside of such limits." Grover indicated an area adjoining the recent fort reburials as most appropriate. There "the sod is firm and not liable to wash out as it is on almost every part of the Battlefield, especially near the monument." He additionally recommended several sites for construction of a lodge in the vicinity of that ground. The Tenth Cavalry regimental quartermaster concurred and on June 24 urged the quartermaster general to settle on an eight-acre tract including the fort burials surrounded by a stone wall.[8]

Despite earnest intentions for the cemetery-battlefield, its neglect continued with little funding appropriated for either needed repairs or to implement the development plans. Early in 1893, department quarter-master Major John V. Furey requested $500 for improvements while summing up the site's deficiencies: "The cemetery has received but little attention as to its care since its establishment—the gates have been broken down and cattle and horses allowed to roam at will therein, destroying what little there was of grass as well as breaking and knocking over the head stones. The monument has been defaced by relic hunters, as well as the stones marking the place[s] where General Custer and others fell."[9] Furey advocated the appointment of Fort Custer guide James A. Campbell as temporary overseer of the cemetery pending appointment of a permanent superintendent. Later that year, when the requested funds were approved, Campbell supervised repairs with brick and cement to the monument, notably an addition to the badly chipped bottom portion. Campbell put up signs warning visitors against defacing the property, then installed along the barbed-wire reserva-tion enclosure arched double gates for wagons and a turnstile for entering pedestrians. Around the perimeter of the reserve he directed the straightening and redriving of hundreds of fence posts, and his workers reset some 475 headstones with brick and cement. Total cost for the work was $478.71. It was noted that "visitors and relic hunters have almost entirely destroyed the headstone marking the place where Gen. Custer fell."[10]

In the summer of 1893, army veteran Andrew N. Grover was appointed the first superintendent of the national cemetery at Custer's battlefield, assuming his duties there on July 11. Grover had previously worked at Fort Custer and had been highly recommended for the posi-tion by the commanding officer of that post. He occupied a probationary appointment beginning in November 1892 and had since performed a six-month detail as assistant superintendent at the Fort Leavenworth National Cemetery. Grover was described as "a very nice kind of man—modest, unassuming, rather taciturn."[11] Within a week of his arrival, Grover received civil engineer W. H. Owen at the site. Appointed by the depot quartermaster in Washington, D.C., Owen was to survey and establish an enclosed cemetery area within the reservation, "even though it should require removal of the [fort] remains heretofore buried there and their re-interment in parallel rows and in consecutive order in accordance with the numbering of the graves in the burial register."[12] Owen carefully assessed the battlefield and recommended against Dandy's cemetery site (a ridgetop strip of twenty-five acres including the monument and Crittenden's grave) and settled on the ground below the monument, where the fort reburials had already occurred, as being the ideal tract for the cemetery:

Below the [battle] ridge towards the gate & distant 500 to 1200 feet from the monument, there is a plateau, nearly level, n.w. & s.e. & sloping gently towards the river (s.w.). This plateau has a much better soil, & aside from considerations connected with the monument & the battlefield, would make an excellent site for the cemetery. Five to ten acres of suitable ground can be had in a rectangle. On this site are interred the remains, about 17, brought from [Fort] C.F. Smith & at one end of the site but nearly on a spur outside of the proper boundaries of a rectangle such as I would select for a cemetery enclosure are the remains of about 500 from [Forts] Sisseton, Totten, Poplar River, Pembina, McGinnis, Ab. Lincoln, & Rice &c. This plateau is about 50 ft [in elevation] (roughly esti-mated) below the monument & 150 to 200 ft above the river. It is in part protected from the north by the monument ridge, & the soil is better & less stony.

Owen noted that most of the five hundred or so fort reburials existed on a spur of land (possibly present Section A). To bring them into the planned cemetery enclosure would require the manipulation of the proposed rectangular tract. (He initially urged instead that the fort reburials be relocated. These graves had seemingly been made hap-hazardly and with improper alignment. Though the work would be costly, Owen advised their relocation so that "the numbering could be made straight which is now very crooked & mixed up.")

Regarding the plan to include the monument within the bounds of the cemetery proper, Owen concluded:

No suitable connection could be made between this site & the monument to enclose both within one wall, even if money was available. . . . If the whole battlefield is to remain enclosed as at present with a substantial plank & wire fence & its historical features—the monument, the stones marking the spots where each man fell—preserved & kept in proper condition, I see no reason *necessary* for the enclosure for cemetery to embrace the monument, & if the other conditions—topography, character of soil, nearness to water, lower elevation, &c. make it very desirable to select the lower site, I think it should be done without regard to the monument.

As Owen indicated, the requirement of water to enable trees and shrubbery, and the ability to obtain it, preferably by way of a steam pump or windmill at the river, would be the final determinant, although he clearly favored the lower site. Owen further advised the practicality of raising the superintendent's lodge of brick, which might be obtained inexpensively at Crow Agency. Until such a lodge was raised, Superintendent Grover and his wife and teenage daughter would camp in tents on the site.[13]

On August 3, 1893, Owen filed his survey report, recommending that the cemetery enclosure be established on the ten-acre plateau below and west of the monument. "It would be better in my opinion, as a matter of sentiment and historical fitness, to leave the battlefield intact, and to establish the Cemetery elsewhere for the interment of others than those who fell in the Custer fight, and for the residence of a Superintendent who should have the care of the whole Reservation." His final recommended tract encompassed nearly seven (6.91) acres and accommodated the previous fort interments. At that place, he noted, "there is a fine site for the buildings. The remains already there need not be disturbed. It will only be necessary to remove the 111 from Fort Phil Kearney [sic], buried on the ridge near the monument."[14]

In the meantime, Grover and his family needed shelter other than tents for the upcoming winter, and funding was quickly approved to provide the superintendent with lumber sufficient to construct a temporary house near the river, with the notion that the completed building might later be converted to a pump house. By November, Grover had basically finished work on his temporary quarters, a simple two-room, roofed lean-to building of rough boards and batten measuring fourteen by twenty-eight feet and approximately ten feet in height. As of early 1894, he and his family were quartered therein, although funding had by then been appropriated for an eight-room lodge with cellar, expected to be raised near the entrance to the newly designated enclosed cemetery tract. By that date, total burials stood at 927.[15]

On the eighteenth anniversary of the Battle of the Little Bighorn, June 25, 1894, excavation proceeded for building the superintendent's lodge, contracts having been signed with the firm of Fisk J. Shaffer of Helena. The structure as completed and inspected late that year cost $4,663.63. Overall, the gabled, two-story native stone lodge measured thirty feet square, with a single-story front porch measuring twenty feet eight inches long by six feet eight inches wide. Nicely appointed with keystone-arched doorways and windows, the lodge boasted a full basement and attic, with each floor containing nine hundred square feet. Circular windows were in each gabled end, and chimneys for fireplaces were of brick. The roof was shingled. Complementing the stone exterior, the woodwork was painted a variety of earthen colors, with sills and porch frames a matching stone shade, dark brown for the porch surface, dark terra cotta for projecting gutters, sashes, cornices, and downspouts, and dark green for all window frames, exterior doors and frames, and shutters. Each floor contained four rooms; those on the first floor included an office, living room, kitchen, and entrance hall, while those on the second comprised bedrooms and a hall area adjoining a balustered staircase. Some distance behind the lodge, a roofed board-and-batten privy house was built. A six-thousand-gallon cistern of brick and concrete provided water.[16]

With anticipated closure of Fort Custer, administration of the Custer Battlefield National Cemetery Reservation was by late 1895 turned over to the depot quartermaster in Washington, D.C., to whom Grover reported (although throughout his tenure he apparently never received a copy of national cemetery regulations). During that year efforts looked to acquiring additional headstones for the fort reburials, as well as for contracting with Edward Flinn for erecting a stable, a stone outbuilding, and a covered walkway in the new cemetery. (These were all completed by late October 1895.) In June of that year, sixty-one boxes of army remains arrived for reinterment from Fort McKinney, Wyoming, along with twenty-six headstones. Later that summer, Grover received funds to remove sagebrush and cacti from the new tract. Early the following year, the superintendent called for relocating the Fort Phil Kearny dead from the battle ridge to the cemetery, echoing Surveyor Owen's earlier sentiments, but this was not immediately accomplished. Later in 1896, Grover ordered marble headstones to replace the headboards memorializing where Boston Custer, Harry Reed, and Mark Kellogg were found. (For unexplained reasons—possibly because neither youth was a permanent government employee—the stones for Custer and Reed did not arrive or were never placed; wooden headboards marked their spots until at least 1909, and by 1916 stone markers had been emplaced.) A stone for Kellogg was provided in July 1896 by the *New York Herald* publishing company.

By that time, what remained of Custer's marker had been carried off, and a wooden cross erected in its place was disappearing quickly as visitors removed pieces to take with them. In April and May 1896, 119 more remains arrived for reinterment from Forts Custer and Buford, Montana. Besides required repairs to the Custer monument caused by frost moving bricks in the foundation, efforts in the cemetery were complicated by introduction of a new numbering system, mix-ups in names and headstones for burials, and the irregular placement of stones and grave measurements in the southeast section. Other improvements to the cemetery in the form of a flagstaff, purchase of grass seed, repairs to the water cistern, and construction of wooden sidewalks around the lodge were completed in 1897. Although Grover urged construction of a rostrum as well as a pressurized water delivery system, neither project was immediately approved. On the anniversary of the battle in 1897, a contingent of bicycle riders arrived on the bench land west of the river and opposite the cemetery. They were members of the segregated Twenty-fifth Infantry, officered by whites, who had peddled from Fort Missoula, in western Montana, with the army's experimental bicycle corps en route to St. Louis, Missouri.[17]

The laying out of the national cemetery in the 1890s, together with the completion of the stone superintendent's lodge and its ancillary structures and the 1881 monument and the 1890-placed markers, created effective associative resources that eventually augmented the primary battlefield resource in the memorialization of the Little Bighorn dead. These, together with the later monument placed on the hill at the Reno–Benteen Defense Site, came to compose the onsite tangible resources that today constitute Little Bighorn Battlefield National Monument. Over time, differentiation between the battlefield proper, where the historic event occurred, and the superimposed developed resources, both commemorative and support-oriented, would often become blurred in terms of the site's interpretation and public perception.

Because the battlefield had been established as a national cemetery, the War Department's interpretation of the ground where the Battle of the Little Bighorn occurred was minimal at best. Superintendent Grover was on hand to answer the questions of visitors, but mostly he functioned as caretaker of the active cemetery, and the work was highly dedicated to developing and improving that tract, besides caring for the monument and the markers. Throughout Grover's tenure, it was clear that the cemetery reservation was but an enclave in the heart of the Crow Reservation. The Indians often mistook the land for their own, and occasionally they would cut timber for fuel on the cemetery reserve. Complicating the issue, two small land patents within the cemetery reservation had been granted by the Bureau of Indian Affairs (the matter was not resolved until 1930 through a settlement with the Crow claimants). During the early years, the Crows referred to the superintendents as "ghost herders," whose task was to prevent the spirits of the dead from roaming beyond the cemetery. As late as 1912, the view persisted among many tribesmen that when the flag rose over the cemetery each day, the soldiers' spirits returned to their graves.[18]

In October 1902 Major Alfred Reynolds, inspector general of the Department of Dakota, toured the site, commenting on the need for an improved water supply from the Little Bighorn for irrigation "if it is deemed advisable to plant trees and otherwise improve the cemetery proper." Respecting the battlefield component, he added the caveat that "it occurs to me that the scene of this memorable fight would be better left in its natural state."[19] Through the first years of the new century, more remains arrived for reinterment, including four dead removed from the site of Reno's engagement. By the spring of 1903 there were 1,221 burials in the cemetery. Two soldiers killed at Canyon Creek, Montana, during the 1877 Nez Perce War and buried at the site of that encounter west of Billings were scheduled for burial at the cemetery in the summer of 1905. But before they could be removed and transported to the cemetery, a sudden deluge swept the remains away. They were not found again until 1915, when they were buried in the Custer Battlefield National Cemetery. Meantime, through the years occasional discoveries were made of Little Bighorn soldiers' bones and skeletons on the battlefield proper. These "unknowns" were collected and buried as such in the cemetery tract. In 1905 a veteran soldier who had helped bury the dead in 1876 led a party to Deep Coulee, a considerable distance south of the principal Custer battalion casualties. There the buried remains of First Sergeant James Butler of Company L, Seventh Cavalry, were disinterred for reburial in the cemetery, apparently as an "unknown."[20]

In April 1906, after nearly thirteen years, Andrew Grover transferred to the national cemetery at Springfield, Missouri. His replacement was W. H. H. Garrett, formerly assistant superintendent of the cemetery at Jefferson Barracks, Missouri, who arrived at the battlefield in the same month. Like his predecessor, Garrett directed his attention to developing and maintaining the cemetery. Meantime, the markers on the battlefield proper continued to deteriorate because of vandalism by visitors. In 1902 the visiting inspector general noted that "the spot where Custer fell is marked by a wooden cross, as tourists have demolished the original stone." Although as early as 1900 it was anticipated that an iron post would replace the cross erected in 1894, this was never accomplished. A graphic portrait of the neglected condition of the battlefield emerged following a visit early in 1908 by a reporter for the *New York Times*, whose piece also gave insight into egregious interpretive data being put forward by Superintendent Garrett. (E.g., the Fetterman graves, said Garrett, represented dead from "the Fort Phil Kearney [*sic*] massacre. That was after [*sic*] the fight of the Little Big Horn and their bodies were brought here. Through a mistake at the time they were all buried up there where the Seventh's men lie.")[21]

As regards the battlefield, the correspondent observed that many of the stones in the grouping below the monument were in derelict and damaged condition. He reported that Garrett had told him that two stones previously marking Custer's spot had been totally chipped away and a third had been entirely carried off. "A wooden cross for Custer!" he intoned. "Only a wooden cross, nothing more! A cross, if you please, made of an upright piece of wood, rough, 5 feet high, an inch thick, and a couple of inches wide, with a cross piece of the same width 2 feet in length roughly nailed on. No marking or lettering of any kind. That's all for Custer!" The headstones for other officers and men had been ruined by the near-constant vandalism. One was "so chipped and hacked that not more than a jagged piece a foot in height stood above the ground." Thomas Custer's marker likewise had been marred by souvenir seekers, "seemingly as if with a hammer or an axe." Captain Yates's, said the reporter, "is chipped and mutilated by miscreants who have no reverence for the memory of those who gave up their lives that these very vandals might . . . be enabled to visit the valley of the Little Big Horn." These same people had also chipped away on the monument "without mercy." The unidentified newsman concluded that "the proper authorities seemingly care not enough for the memory of those who died . . . to keep the spots where they fell from being defiled by relic hunters."[22]

The continuing deterioration of the battlefield resources in fact signified the neglect of that facet of the national cemetery reservation during the early years of the twentieth century. Routine activity of the superintendent and his staff (which by 1908 included a number of Crow Indians hired from the agency) focused on the cemetery proper, where most activity occurred. During the year 1908, 173 remains arrived from

Fort Keogh, on the Yellowstone River near Miles City. These included Indian war dead from the various Sioux campaigns of Colonel Nelson A. Miles. (A monument from the Fort Keogh post cemetery was also forwarded to the national cemetery.) Two casualties from the Battle of White Bird Canyon of June 1877, during Nez Perce War, also arrived from Grangeville, Idaho, for reburial. Improvements to the cemetery in 1908 included the erection of a seventy-five-foot, iron, two-section flagstaff with guy wires to replace the one installed in 1891, which had been destroyed by lightning in 1907. A new iron gate was also installed. The flagstaff was inspected by an officer from Fort Mackenzie at Sheridan, Wyoming. On July 31 a prairie fire of unknown origin ravaged the cemetery but was apparently quickly extinguished. In early 1909 Superintendent Garrett reported that the Crow Indian Curley, a prominent local resident who had served as a scout for Custer at the time of the 1876 engagement, had erected a fence on a portion of the cemetery reservation. Admonished to remove it, Curley evidently complied.[23]

Garrett's tenure ended in March 1909, when the War Department transferred him to the national cemetery in Florence, South Carolina. His replacement was Oscar Wright, who received $60 per month, and under whose administration the first telephone line connecting the lodge with the trunk facility at Crow Agency was installed at a cost of $145. That year contracts were let for replacing the shingle roof on the lodge and its porch with one of tin, along with new spouting and conductors, the work completed by B. H. Daly of Sheridan. The Fort Keogh marker previously received was set and erected in October by the Hazleton Tombstone Company of Butte, Montana, and an iron tablet bearing President Abraham Lincoln's Gettysburg Address arrived for placement in the cemetery. Changes on the battlefield included the June burial at the base of the monument of an arm bone purportedly from a Custer trooper received from Fort Logan, Colorado. Elsewhere on the field, Wright further complicated the interpretive picture by placing markers for the missing Harrington, Sturgis, Lord, and Porter. (He also placed one for Hodgson, killed with Reno's command, on the hilltop near the Reno defense site). Although Wright stated that he had placed the markers "at their proper places," it is unknown how that determination was made. After little more than a year on duty, Superintendent Wright transferred to Fort Gibson, Oklahoma, replaced by G. W. Thomas, who arrived at the national cemetery in late July 1910.[24]

Emphasis on cemetery maintenance continued much as before under Superintendent Thomas. In October permission came to level off all of the mounded graves. Meantime, remains arrived from the long-abandoned post of Fort Reno, Wyoming, and probably from the cemetery at Fort McKinney, near the town of Buffalo, Wyoming. In 1912, 173 others were received from Fort Assinniboine, Montana, including the remains of 20 army fatalities from the Battle of the Bear's Paw Mountains in 1877. (These burials appear to have been the last until 1917, when the dead from the post cemetery of Fort Yellowstone, in Yellowstone National Park, arrived for reinterment.) Footstones placed long ago were removed from some graves in 1910, while two iron tablets relating to congressional establishment of national cemeteries and army designation of such were received for installation at the tract. This was followed in January 1911 by the arrival of a set of iron tablets bearing the stanzas of Theodore O'Hara's famous poem "Bivouac of the Dead" for placement in the Custer Battlefield National Cemetery as it was in national cemeteries throughout the nation.[25]

Thomas's service ended in June 1912. He was succeeded by an acting superintendent, James McGowan, for one month. Then Daniel Dommitt, a veteran of Gibbon's column during the Great Sioux War of 1876–77, assumed the permanent position. Another frontier army soldier succeeded Dommitt in December 1913, when former cavalry and infantry soldier Eugene Wessinger became superintendent. Under Wessinger, a gasoline-powered pump installed in a frame shack by the river was able to deliver small amounts of water to the cemetery but was insufficient for irrigating the graves until 1915, when only two trees stood in the plot. Wessinger had served at Fort Custer as early as 1877, and his mode of operation at the national cemetery reflected his performance as a hard-bitten noncommissioned officer. To facilitate burials in winter, he dynamited frozen terrain. He reportedly salted the battlefield terrain with cartridge casings from the abandoned shooting range at Fort Custer so that tourists might "find" a relic to take home with them. In 1914 Wessinger completed substantial improvements on the base of the monument, replacing the badly cracked brick with an eight-inch concrete girdle. Because of continuing vandalism in the adjacent group of markers, he urged the War Department to install a high iron fence, although this was not immediately accomplished. In 1915, in response to War Department interest in improving the roads, Wessinger oversaw grading of a road through the cemetery as well as the old wagon trail leading to the monument. Two years later, concrete sidewalks encircled the superintendent's lodge and led into the cemetery.

Wessinger's tenure at the national cemetery was a relatively long one; he remained until 1929.[26]

Despite continued focus of the War Department administration on the cemetery, visitors continued to be drawn to the battlefield. By the late nineteenth and early twentieth centuries, interest in western history and American heroes had accelerated, due largely to then-current illustrators like Frederic Remington and writers like Theodore Roosevelt and Owen Wister. William F. ("Buffalo Bill") Cody's Wild West show also excited curiosity about the West as it toured through the land. (Cody had visited the battlefield in 1894.) Hotels and resorts now proliferated in areas around Yellowstone National Park and the Big Horn Mountains. As early as 1902, promoters in Sheridan staged a reenactment of Custer's fight at that community in which Crows playing Sioux attacked Wyoming national guardsmen from Sheridan, Buffalo, and Newcastle and the whole degenerated into a melee. In 1903 a trainload of news correspondents arrived by way of Sheridan. Crow Indian police conducted them over the field in wagons and by horseback. Five years later, the Dixon-Wanamaker expedition documented with film an early battle reenactment staged near Crow Agency. Yet another reenactment using Crows and Montana national guardsmen took place in the hills near the battlefield in 1909, and a film of it by a Chicago firm titled *On the Little Big Horn; or Custer's Last Stand*, was distributed around the country ("the finest battle film ever made," said one contemporary). Beyond the boundaries of the Crow Reservation, white settlement had increased, and towns like Sheridan and Billings, burgeoning rail centers, rose in population along with smaller communities like Hardin. More interest was thus generated in the cemetery and battlefield, where in 1910 a rutted and worn single-lane wagon road traversed the north-to-south length of the ridge crest between the monument and the Crittenden grave. By the summer of 1915, the road had been graded and widened to twelve feet, including a loop at Calhoun Hill, so that automobiles could be accommodated. A line of the Chicago, Burlington and Quincy Railroad, opened through the valley in 1894, frequently dropped passengers at Crow Agency to visit the site.[27]

With the growing appeal of the place, there was much public interest in and curiosity about the battle. Yet the War Department offered little information on the site, save for a few artifacts exhibited in the superintendent's lodge as early as 1896. When, in 1909 Superintendent Wright requested from the War Department "a definite and accurate account of the Custer massacre . . . [to] enable the Superintendent of this National Cemetery to more fully explain to visitors the facts connected with this historic event," he received a sheaf of documents about the battle. And in 1913 Superintendent Dommitt noted an upsurge in battle-interested visitors following construction of a bridge across the Little Bighorn River at Crow Agency. For all practical purposes, however, interpretation remained a low priority in relation to the superintendent's cemeterial duties.[28]

Until Fort Custer closed, picnickers transported by army ambulances had frequented the site at opportune times of the year, and Memorial Day events organized by the post's Grand Army of the Republic members transpired there annually. Thereafter, G.A.R. posts in Billings and Sheridan made annual Memorial Day visits to the cemetery, and in the early 1900s the flag-decorated graves often received flowers from Crow Agency schoolchildren. Extensive annual Memorial Day ceremonies at the cemetery began in 1919 under the auspices of Hardin's American Legion Post No. 8, though the event was initiated and coordinated by Superintendent Wessinger. Early in the century, two ethnological expeditions factored the Little Bighorn into their agendas. In 1907 the expedition of Edward S. Curtis, underwritten by financier J. P. Morgan, visited the battlefield while gathering photographs and cultural data about the Crows. Curtis's images of some of Custer's former Crow scouts are well known today. And in 1909 the philanthropist Rodman Wanamaker funded Joseph K. Dixon's great Indian council, headquartered at Crow Agency, which sought to obtain photographs and historical and ethnological information about the western tribes. Throughout this period, no formal interpretation about the battlefield was available, and often inexact information came from Crows and others who accompanied visitors to the area. In 1908 retired Brigadier General Edward S. Godfrey toured the battlefield and complained about the misinformation being dispensed there.[29]

In 1916 the fortieth anniversary of the 1876 engagement brought wide attention, with perhaps six thousand attendees arriving by special trains from Billings and Sheridan, as well as by horseback and in an estimated three hundred automobiles. Although many battle participants had by then passed away, many others attended the observance on June 25. In a pervasive spirit of reconciliation, General Godfrey—he who as a young Seventh Cavalry officer had accompanied Custer to the Washita in 1868 as well as to the Little Bighorn eight years later—rode across the field with aged ethnologist George Bird Grinnell and photographer Laton A. Huffman from Miles City. Approaching Custer Hill and the monument, the trio met a small body of feather-bedecked Indians—Northern Cheyennes—gathered around a spring wagon containing an elderly blind man. He was Two Moon, a leader of the Cheyennes in the battle, and in peaceful gesture he extended his hand to Godfrey. Following a prayer by one of the Indians, the old general dismounted and climbed into the wagon, then stood and read an address prepared by Elizabeth B. Custer, who had declined an invitation to attend the ceremony. This was followed by Godfrey's own remarks comparing "the whole region" to a former "wilderness without civilized habitation." White Man Runs Him, one of the Crow scouts in 1876, then spoke. Finally, Two Moon rose and spoke in his own tongue, his translated words in part saying, "Forty years ago we had a fight here with Custer. I came to fight Custer. We wiped him from the face of the earth. But now we are brothers under the same flag." Then came a rendition of "Garry Owen," the Seventh Cavalry marching song, performed by a band composed of schoolchildren from Crow Agency. Tributes by speakers followed, then a salute of rifle volleys, and finally the playing of "Taps" by members of the Billings chapter of the United Spanish War Veterans. Photographer Huffman captured images of the events. The crowd adjourned to the Crow Agency fairgrounds to watch races and rodeo events and to hear closing addresses.[30]

While War Department attention to the operation of the national cemetery following the fortieth anniversary commemoration continued much as before, the event indeed became something of a watershed in the history of Little Bighorn Battlefield. Whereas before that observance the site was considered remote and isolated, within three years of the anniversary travel there was encouraged by regional civic groups interested in promoting tourism in Montana and adjoining states during an age of the Model T and of flourishing automobile clubs. A touring road designated along existing arteries in 1919–20 passed through the valley fronting the national cemetery reservation and was named Custer Battlefield Highway. The thoroughfare, complete with nearly one hundred campgrounds, originated in Des Moines, Iowa, and terminated in Glacier National Park in northwestern Montana, yet its name posted in red and white markers through its entire length reflected widespread promotion of the battlefield site. (A booster brochure promised "no sand or heavy mountain grades [and . . .] mosquitoes as scarce as hen's teeth.") When former commander-in-chief of the Allied

Armies Marshall Ferdinand Foch toured the battlefield in 1921, he manifested much interest in it, passing along the battle ridge and back in an automobile. His visit in many ways signified the dawn of a new age for the site.[31] By the post–World War I era, the Indians wars had become an anachronism in an age of mechanized combat and internationalism; the Battle of the Little Bighorn, in effect, had passed from current event into history, and as history the resulting attention would forever change the focus at Custer Battlefield National Cemetery.

CHAPTER 4 | # War Department Years

Transitions, 1920s–1940

By 1920 burgeoning interest in the Battle of the Little Bighorn, together with increasing ceremonial commemoration at the national cemetery reservation, forecasted a subtle administrative shift away from the cemetery and toward interpretation of the battlefield portion of the reserve. Despite the thrust in attention by the public, however, few concessions by the War Department occurred immediately. Insofar as Superintendent Wessinger was concerned—and despite his awareness of the evolving attention—efforts at Custer Battlefield National Cemetery proceeded much as they had earlier. The monument continued to serve as a memorial to the government victims of the battle; the markers represented the places where individual soldiers had fallen in combat (or at least, presumably, where their bodies had been found); and the cemetery—the primary functional element of the reservation—continued receiving veteran and dependent dead for burial. Whatever interpretation existed—doubtless muddled by the ridgetop presence of the Fort Phil Kearny burials—largely remained the province of individual visitors and whatever resources or knowledge they might bring with them.

Because of concern over continued vandalism of the markers adjacent to the monument in the so-called Last Stand grouping, a wrought-iron fence was erected around the fifty-two headstones in 1930. For the most part, however, the War Department effort at Custer Battlefield National Cemetery (the entire military reservation) remained focused as before on the cemetery. This work included, besides maintenance of the grounds, roads, walks, and buildings and their appurtenances, the facilitating of burial services for veterans (and their dependents), not only of the Civil War and Indian wars, but now including the Spanish-American War and World War I.

A major improvement to the superintendent's lodge during the late 1920s involved the installation of pipes for inside plumbing, although fixtures were not mounted immediately, apparently at Wessinger's discretion. After Wessinger departed in 1929, two successive acting custodians—Joseph Morrow (December 1929–January 1930) and Alex Naylor (January–August 1930)—took over pending the appointment of Victor A. Bolsius, who took charge as superintendent in August 1930. In 1931 electrical wiring was installed in the lodge, with power temporarily provided by a gasoline-fueled generator until a line was hooked up in 1932. In 1934 a stone garage/storage facility was built behind and south of the frame maintenance building in the rear of the lodge. (Later, in the 1940s, a concrete safe deposit vault was constructed where a coal bin existed.) This latter two-story building had been converted from a stable/outbuilding initially erected in 1895, and in 1932 it was refurbished as a government machine shop with living quarters placed in the former hayloft.

Notable work in the cemetery consisted of the planting of trees along the drive and the seeding for grass of part of the cemetery tract. In the winter of 1931 a number of cottonwood and white ash trees were planted, and in the spring of 1933, 25 red cedars and 150 blue spruce trees were transplanted in the cemetery. By then a water system installed in 1932 permitted more plantings. In the late 1930s a honeysuckle hedge was planted along the north and west sides of the cemetery.

A frame comfort station with four toilets was built along the south boundary in 1932, followed two years later by erection in the northwest corner of a rostrum as initially called for by Superintendent Grover in 1897. Built of native stone and concrete, with wooden ceiling and a stone podium, the rostrum measured 14½ x 23 feet and played a major role in subsequent Memorial Day observances. The rostrum was dedicated in grandiose style on Memorial Day 1935, with an estimated throng of eight to ten thousand on hand to hear Montana governor Frank H. Cooney's address.

Further improvements in the early 1930s included the installation of ornate double iron gates at the entrance to the cemetery along with gates for pedestrians accessing the grounds. Bronze tablets cast with the words "Custer Battlefield" and "National Cemetery" were mounted on the stone portals erected on either side of the gates. Sidewalks and curbs were upgraded and irrigating lines and drains installed. A graveled parking area now bordered the tract in front of the lodge, and a sewage disposal area was located on the slope 136 feet south of the south edge of the cemetery plot. Late in the decade, an invasion of Mormon crickets confounded the staff when the insects often became trapped several inches deep in open graves. A low metal barrier fence was temporarily raised around the cemetery to help keep the crickets out.

Meantime, interments continued. Late in 1931, seven from the post cemetery at Fort Logan, Colorado, represented the last of the fort interments. A major change to the cemetery ongoing in 1932–34 was the removal to Section B of the 111 Fort Phil Kearny remains, finally relocated from the ridge near the monument after forty-four years.

Earlier, against considerable local opposition, the remains of Lieutenant Crittenden, buried on the field at his parents' behest since 1876, were removed to the cemetery plot along with the privately purchased headstone furnished by his family. Crittenden's remains were reinterred with military honors on September 11, 1931. (A request to the War Department to replace the marker where Crittenden had been buried was at first denied; a headstone for him was not placed on the field until 1938.) The relocations were required to conform policy-wise with an intent to have no remains buried outside the cemetery. Practically, they were needed to accommodate anticipated construction of a graded oil-surfaced road along the ridge, besides a reservoir, a drain, and a graveled parking area east of the road.

In 1933 the cemetery proper was described as comprising 6.21 acres, enclosed by an iron fence. Only a single interment had taken place in 1932, and there remained 2,436 gravesites available. The quartermaster of the Ninth Corps Area noted that "in view of the isolated locations, it is improbable that any portion of the reservation other than the area now in the cemetery proper will ever be required for interments of the remains of military personnel."[1]

During the 1920s and 1930s questions arose respecting decades-old land issues affecting the Custer Battlefield National Cemetery Reservation and ownership claims by certain Crow Indians. One in 1927 involved the "arbitrary boundary" of the Little Bighorn River on the west side of the reservation. There, because of the meandering nature of the Little Bighorn, the fence had been established a short distance east of the riverbank. In 1905 and 1907, three twenty-five-year trust patent allotments to Crows had inadvertently overlapped into the reserve east

of the river. Recognizing the mistake, the Indians had not claimed ownership of the tracts until 1927, when one occupant tried to cut timber there.
The Indians claimed precedent rights by virtue of the 1868 treaty granting
the Crow lands. The army insisted that the 1905 and 1907 patents
were voided by the fact that they had been awarded long after the 1886
executive order creating the national cemetery reservation. In 1928, in
estimating compensation for the Crows, War Department and Department of the Interior officials determined that the three claims—Plain
Shield (7 acres), Plenty Wing (18 acres), and White Goose (8 acres)—
totaled $295 in value (based on estimated worth of $5–10 per acre).
Moreover, with recognition that the Crows had not been paid for the
original 1886 taking, officials factored an additional valuation of $2,750
(an estimated $5 per acre for 550 acres) for a total of $3,045. This
compensation was paid to the Indians with conveyance of title in accordance with an act of April 15, 1930. In addition, in 1932 the Department of the Interior further granted a fifty-year right-of-way over allotted
Indian lands for the electrical power line to the cemetery. In 1937 the
government leased for grazing purposes the ground between the Little
Bighorn River and its fence at a rate of $40 per year.[2]

Although the claims issues occupied War Department attention and
operational matters regarding the cemetery proper continued to take
precedence under that department's administration, public interest in
the site continued to rise. Locally, American Legion Post 8 in Hardin
continued to sponsor Memorial Day observances at the cemetery. In
1920 the Hardin High School band entertained some 750 attendees
with patriotic airs followed by a picnic at the park in Crow Agency. In
1921 introductory services took place at Hardin's Harriet Theatre and
were followed by a parade of various veteran groups, clubs, schools, and
fraternal bodies. Ceremonies followed in the Custer Battlefield National
Cemetery. Similar observances continued throughout the decades of the
1920s and 1930s, all under the auspices of Hardin American Legion
Post 8. In 1935 Post 8 organized the May 30 activities for all Memorial
Day ceremonies and activities at the cemetery.[3]

Beyond this local attention, two events were key to focusing national
interest on the Little Bighorn in the 1920s and were likely instrumental
in marshalling sentiment for increasing interpretation of the battlefield
component. By this time, the new scenic highway brought increasing
numbers of sightseers to contemplate the field where Custer and his
men fell. Tourism literature touted the "silence [that] still falls on the
visitor as he stands on the brown hills and listens to the requiem of the

winds played in sad cadences among the lonely graves." In 1921 the celebration of the forty-fifth anniversary of the Battle of the Little Bighorn, organized by the townspeople of Hardin, Billings, and Crow Agency, featured an Old West theme and attracted approximately four thousand automobiles, many towing trailers, and fifteen thousand attendees at the various ceremonies marking the occasion. General Godfrey, citing illness, did not attend, but seventeen other Indian war veterans appeared and received public acknowledgement. Besides observances at the national cemetery, a major offsite attraction was the dedication of a Custer monument in the city park in Hardin, participated in by Montana governor Joseph M. Dixon and J. Bronson Case of Kansas City, a cousin of the absent Mrs. Custer, who delivered an address on her behalf. (Mrs. Custer nonetheless prepared a pamphlet featuring articles by Godfrey and others that was widely sold at the event, and she loaned one of her husband's buckskin suits for exhibit at the Hardin Carnegie Library.) In addition, a reenactment presented by the Hardin American Legion featured Crow Indians performing a war dance and taking the parts of Sioux warriors. An aerial show, carnival, parades, and picnic captivated the throng, and an all-Indian rodeo at Crow Agency rounded out the proceedings.[4]

While the forty-fifth anniversary proceedings went a long way in promoting interest in Custer and the Little Bighorn, it paled in comparison with the offerings five years later. The fiftieth anniversary observance in 1926 coincided with a burst of regional boosterism and brought out hordes of people—perhaps as many as fifty thousand. By that time rail systems and gravel highways, both rampantly advancing tourism, afforded ready means of travel throughout the state and region to facilitate visits to the national cemetery and battlefield. Tourism by then was up at the national parks in Wyoming (Yellowstone) and Montana (Glacier), and even Custer Battlefield National Cemetery had boasted some ten thousand visitors during the summer of 1924. In the fall of 1925, with the semicentennial fast approaching, the Billings Commercial Club organized the National Custer Memorial Association to coordinate events and raise funds. Civic-minded folk from assorted towns in Wyoming and Montana joined in the effort, as did the states' politicians and congressional delegations. Billings resident James A. Shoemaker was appointed secretary. A commemorative badge was even to be struck for the occasion. Officials shortly named a blue-ribbon commission of forty-nine notables in western history to adorn the association's letterhead, among them George Bird Grinnell, Grace

Raymond Hebard, John G. Neihardt, Colonel William A. Graham, Earl A. Brininstool, and retired brigadier general Charles King—all stellar names in the field of Indian wars and Little Bighorn history. Photographer David F. Barry, who had chronicled the 1886 proceedings, was also on the list.

As before, the occasion highlighted the army role in events, largely omitting formal Indian participation in its planning and organization, albeit encouraging their participation seemingly for symbolism and visual effect. General Godfrey, as national chairman of the association, headed a distinguished (and mostly honorary) executive national committee composed of ex-Seventh Cavalrymen or their descendants and including the long-retired Winfield S. Edgerly, Luther Hare, and Charles A. Varnum, as well as Mrs. Custer. But the nuts-and-bolts work rested with lesser luminaries who provided publicity to promote attendance. Godfrey championed the event as a rendezvous for Indian war veterans, and it was advertised as such in the various veterans' tabloids. Certified Little Bighorn veterans—including Indians—received free railroad tickets, while other Indian war veterans received lower train fares. Of the surviving officers, however, only Godfrey attended; Edgerly, Varnum, and Hare declined because of physical infirmities.

Under the reunion theme "Burial of the Hatchet," organization of the events proceeded. A central feature was to be the interment of a Seventh Cavalry trooper's remains discovered by road workers in May 1926 near the site of Major Reno's retreat from the valley in 1876. Plans called for burial in the national cemetery, with consecration of a thirty-foot-tall monument to soldier veterans of all Indian wars interred there. Instead, however, and to the apparent consternation of Superintendent Wessinger, the remains were placed in a crypt near A. G. Carter's Garryowen store fronting Custer Battlefield Highway, evidently with the concurrence of General Godfrey. Committee hopes that Elizabeth Custer would attend the ceremonies, finally visiting the site where her husband died fifty years earlier, went fleeting when the widow politely demurred, unable to "suppress the emotions that the day, the ceremonies, the place, would surely call forth." Instead, Mrs. Custer was to deliver a radio presentation, but in the end she declined involvement entirely. In her place she sent a grandniece, May Custer Elmer, and her husband.

Hundreds of people gathered in the days leading into the activities, some coming by special trains routed from Billings and Sheridan to

Crow Agency, others by automobile. Sixty special policemen ranged through the tent city that went up near Crow Agency. In all, more than one hundred veterans of the Indian wars attended, including seven who had been with Reno and Benteen at the Little Bighorn: Charles Windolph, William C. Slaper, Theodore W. Goldin, William E. Morris, Fremont Kipp, Daniel Jewell, and Peter Thompson (three of them—Windolph, Goldin, and Thompson—were Medal of Honor recipients for their roles in the battle). Some eighty Sioux and Northern Cheyennes also appeared, courtesy of their agencies. Three of the Lakotas were identified as Shoots Walking, Young Hawk, and Little Moon. Another Lakota was Red Tomahawk, the man who had killed the Hunkpapa leader Sitting Bull in 1890. Cheyennes present included White Horse, Black Whetstone, Lone Wolf, Limpy, Hollow Wood, Kills Night, Sun Bear, Dog Friend, Beaver Heart, Fast Walker, and Pine.

On June 20, a contingent composed of three troops—about 250 officers and men—of the modern Seventh Cavalry arrived by train from Fort Bliss, Texas, to participate in the events. They went into camp at the Crow Agency fairgrounds, over ensuing days entertaining visitors with drills and maneuvers and joining in a mounted excursion of the battlefield with Godfrey, Colonel Fitzhugh Lee, commander of the Seventh Cavalry, and Crow historian Russell White Bear. Each evening at the Crow Agency fairgrounds, the Seventh Cavalry band performed for whites and Indians. The events gradually took the form of friendship between the two groups, and even tribes who had shared traditional enmity for the moment found solidarity with one another. One celebrity who came to Crow Agency to visit Lakota friends was screen idol William S. Hart, who had contributed much to Indian causes. Eschewing the attention normally accorded him, Hart permitted the Indians to honor him in a special private ceremony at Little Bighorn battlefield, where the Sioux respectfully designated him "Crazy Horse." Another prominent attendee was novelist Mary Roberts Rinehart.

The fiftieth anniversary celebration opened the morning of June 24 with demonstrations of aerial acrobatics over Crow Agency provided by army and navy pilots and their planes brought in from Texas and Virginia. Next, the Seventh Cavalry paraded on a street lined on either side by Indian and army veterans, and troops replicated a horse-charge of old through the Little Bighorn, an event filmed by a crew from Universal Pictures in California. A band concert took place in the park, followed by a Crow rodeo, and, in the evening the tribe hosted a traditional dance.

The sole activity centering on the cemetery-battlefield occurred earlier in the day when representatives of the press visited the sites of Major Reno's actions with veteran soldiers who had been there in 1876.[5]

Formal observances began the next day at the battlefield, where the hilltops and ridges brimmed with hundreds of Model Ts and thousands of spectators who watched a formation of planes wing by overhead to open the ceremony. The mounted Seventh Cavalrymen advanced from the southeast along the battle ridge headed by Colonel Lee and General Godfrey, sword in hand, and former Crow scout White Man Runs Him. A comparable column of Cheyennes and Sioux, war bonneted and donned in traditional garments, approached from the north. As they met near the monument, the two bodies halted and White Man Runs Him raised a pipe toward heaven, then passed it to the Lakota leader, White Bull, nephew of Sitting Bull and himself a Little Bighorn participant. Godfrey then sheathed his sword in symbolic testament to peace, firmly grasped White Bull's extended hand, and presented him with an American flag. The old Lakota in turn handed the general a prized wool blanket. The none-too-subtle message was that the tribesmen, once demonstratively hostile to the government, were now acceptably subordinate to it.

Following this presentation and speeches by Godfrey, Lee, and other dignitaries, White Bull, the general, and the Seventh Cavalry veterans laid wreaths at the mass grave surrounding the monument while a squad of modern soldiers fired a salute above the Last Stand markers and the notes of "Taps" wafted through the assembled crowd. Then the Seventh Cavalry horsemen paired off with the Indians and filed down the hill in a solemn column of unification, "following the American flag from the spot where, a half century earlier . . . they had met as deadly enemies." After the ceremony on Custer Hill, commercialism took hold. Two airplanes promoting a Custer movie opening in Sheridan, Wyoming, took passengers on flights over the cemetery and battlefield while hordes watched from below. With planes overhead and automobiles arrayed across the ground, the momentary dichotomy between the events of 1876 and the rise of twentieth century technology could not have been greater.

On June 26 the unknown soldier was formally entombed at Garryown with Seventh Cavalry chaplain George J. McMurry leading the service. A procession of cavalry accompanied the casketed remains while the elderly veterans watched. Following the volleys and a playing of "Taps," General Godfrey offered remarks about "burying the hatchet."

White Bull presented his tomahawk, and the general placed it in the crypt. The memorial committee members added photos, newspapers, and other paraphernalia before the tomb was closed. Later that day, the fiftieth anniversary ceremonies concluded with the placement of a painted wooden cross on Reno Hill. The Seventh Cavalry troops marked the occasion with a reenactment of Reno's "charge" to and through the river and up the ravines to the bluff top. Another Indian rodeo and more aerial exhibitions followed at Crow Agency. That evening the Seventh Cavalry squadron paraded one last time. The Hardin American Legion hosted a party for the veterans, the regimental band played a closing concert, and a fireworks display sponsored by the Custer Memorial Association ended the semicentennial observance. When all was said and done, the overriding significance of the commemoration, beyond the events themselves, lay in the prolonged national exposure that they and their record attendance generated. Evermore, Custer Battlefield National Cemetery became fixed in public consciousness as a foremost tourist attraction in Montana and the American West.[6]

None of the subsequent anniversary observances approached the 1926 activities in terms of attendance, symbolism, or immediacy via the presence of a strong cadre of battle participants. No events took place in 1931, and by the time of the sixtieth anniversary in 1936, Godfrey and the other veteran officers were dead and the number of surviving battle participants was rapidly dwindling. Elizabeth Custer had herself passed away in 1933. Nonetheless, perhaps inspired by recollections of the 1926 proceedings, more than fifteen thousand people, including twenty Indians war veterans, turned out in 1936 in soaring temperatures to witness aged Charles Windolph, formerly of the Seventh Cavalry, and Louis Dog—a thirteen-year-old Northern Cheyenne at the time of the battle—memorialize the event. Also in attendance was Grace Harrington, whose father, Second Lieutenant Henry M. Harrington, had died with Custer. The proceedings, sponsored by the Hardin Lions Club, included an address by Montana governor Elmer Holt followed by a firing salute and the playing of "Taps" at the monument. Speeches by various dignitaries then took place at the rostrum. No modern Seventh Cavalry troops attended, and sole army representation rested with a single troop of the Fourth Cavalry from Fort Meade, South Dakota, that staged a small reenactment with a few hundred Sioux, Crows, and Northern Cheyennes below the battle ridge.[7]

The anniversary activities of 1921, 1926, and 1936 testified to a mounting and pervasive national interest in the Battle of the Little

Bighorn. Although the cemeterial functions remained a constant there, it was clear that the battle and its personages—as evidenced by the intermittent anniversary commemorations—had struck a responsive chord with people and that visitation at the battlefield and cemetery would continue to grow. The natural result became interest in making the battlefield complete by adding to it the related sites in the valley and on the bluff tops where the forces of Major Reno and Captain Benteen had fought the Sioux and Cheyennes. As early as 1917 the Montana state senate had urged Congress to legislate

> the purchase or reservation of additional [land] so as to include the site of the [overlooked] opening fight in the valley, and all of the land east of the river as far as the top of the bluff, from a point three thousand feet south of the De Wolf marker to the present reservation on Custer Ridge, comprising a strip to include Reno Hill. [Congress should also,] for the authentic information of future generations, . . . provide that the lines of battle on the two fields specified be marked in an appropriate manner, and that a practical road or highway be built from and connecting the National Cemetery on Custer Ridge with Reno Hill and the site of Reno's fight in the valley, including a bridge over the Little Big Horn River between the two points last named.[8]

Congress did not act immediately, however. A visitor in 1924 lamented that "the government has never spent one dollar to cut away the sagebrush, build roads, or establish signboards to give the tourist a practical idea of the battle. . . . It seems only fitting that . . . [Reno's battlefield] should be properly marked. Today only the markers showing where Hodgson and Dr. De Wolf were found prove to the passerby that once a battle occurred here. [Moreover,] there is no wagon road leading from the Custer battlefield back to Reno's entrenchments." The complainant allowed that

> in order to reach this equally historic place it is necessary to go down into the valley from the Custer battlefield, thence straight south on the Custer battlefield highway about six miles to Reno Creek, and then up Reno Creek about a mile and a half to an old cow camp. If the cow punchers chance to be at home you may be able to hire a team and wagon to take

you across Reno Creek and onto the Reno battlefield. This is entirely unnecessary, for with but comparatively small expense a road can be graded from the east side of the Custer battlefield to the Reno entrenchments. . . . Thus this battle-field is neglected and the tourist is prohibited from making a careful study of Custer's last stand in its entirely.[9]

The Reno Hill site was indeed a significant component to understanding the battle action and was in pristine condition. "One may still, with knife or spoon," observed one writer, "dig a little way down into the rifle pits, even now visible, and unearth bullets which once whizzed their menace about the heads of Reno's men. All about are bleached skeletons of horses undoubtedly the bones of the mounts of the Seventh Cavalry, lying where they fell fifty years ago."[10] Legislation cosponsored by Second District representative Scott Leavitt (Rep.-Mont.) and U.S. senator Thomas J. Walsh (Dem.-Mont.) and approved on April 14, 1926, just weeks before the semicentennial, authorized the Interior Department to acquire "by condemnation or otherwise, such land as may be deemed appropriate, not exceeding one hundred and sixty acres, on the site of the battle with the Sioux Indians in which the commands of Major Marcus A. Reno and Major [*sic*] Frederick W. Benteen were engaged, and to erect thereon a suitable monument and historical tablet." Because of long-established land allotment and ownership rights, the act did not affect the valley area. Funding of $2,500 was authorized for implementation but was not immediately forthcoming.

Interest in the Reno–Benteen phases of the 1876 action remained high throughout the semicentennial activities, when several formal visitations to the sites transpired. The National Custer Memorial Committee planned a memorial at the site, but Godfrey and others—including Mrs. Custer—adamantly objected to the inclusion of any reference to Reno, whose actions in not immediately moving to Custer's relief during the engagement they considered cowardly. The events were tempered, and, as noted, a small marker was emplaced pending the erection of an appropriate monument. Funds, however, were not forthcoming until 1928, when a revised amount of $2,300 was made available. An added stricture called for maintenance by the Quartermaster Corps of the army "in conjunction with the Custer Battle Field Monument." Work on the memorial began immediately, with a contract let to the Livingston Marble and Granite Works in Livingston, Montana. Not surprisingly, the finished monument reflected the units involved in the defense of the hill but made no specific mention of Reno or Benteen.[11] (Efforts as late as 1939 to add Reno's name did not succeed, although the memorial by then had become informally dubbed "Reno's Monument" and later became known as the Reno–Benteen Memorial.) Erection occurred in July 1929, and official dedicatory ceremonies took place on August 14. The rough-cut, tapering dark granite shaft, standing 9½ feet high, rested on two receding slabs, the larger measuring approximately 3 x 5 feet, its polished face bearing the inscription. Because land acquisition for the site had not yet occurred, the monument remained under control of the Bureau of Indian Affairs until August 7, 1930, when jurisdiction to 160-acres of Sections 34 (Township 3 South) and 3 (Township 4 South) passed to the War Department.[12]

The establishment of the monument on the Reno–Benteen hilltop position produced increased interest in that aspect of the Battle of the Little Bighorn. Already, a headstone marker stood on the hill representing Lieutenant Hodgson. Another stood partway down the slope for Dr. DeWolf. Yet a third had been placed in the valley for Lieutenant McIntosh. (And in August 1938, through the efforts of Billings resident and Yellowstone County clerk and recorder George Osten and Robert S. Ellison of Manitou Springs, Colorado, a privately raised granite marker with bronze tablet would be dedicated in a well-attended ceremony at the site where scout Charles ["Lonesome Charley"] Reynolds fell during Reno's valley engagement.) Growing interest by students and visitors in the Reno–Benteen phase of the 1876 action, especially following the erection of the monument there, would permit a more holistic view of the Battle of the Little Bighorn. The expanding attention necessitated a means to access the remote site by visitors to the national cemetery and monument, located some four miles north.

In effect, the War Department once more acknowledged growing public sentiment to learn of the events that transpired on the battlefield. Plans for a road to be developed between the Custer monument and the "Reno battlefield" had evolved partly concurrently with those for a new entrance road leading from the valley highway. That route had been surveyed as early as 1924, but right-of-way approval from the Crow Reservation superintendent had been delayed until 1934. Big Horn County leased the right of way to the War Department, but the Crow landowners awaited payment of ten dollars per acre; the issue was not settled until the summer of 1936. In 1930, meantime, a rough road was run from the Custer site to the Reno site, and in 1931 the Big Horn County surveyor charted a more formal route that departed from the existing improved lanes along the battle ridge at the south boundary of the cemetery reservation. From there, the projected grade dipped south toward Medicine Tail Coulee Ford before heading southeast, back from the river, in its approach to and through the 160-acre Reno battlefield tract before turning due south for one and one-quarter miles to ford Reno Creek and make junction with a county road. By the spring of 1934, planning for construction of the passage through the cemetery reservation was underway, the War Department acknowledging that "the area is visited by thousands of people annually, and there is a growing demand for an improved highway." The Depression-era Public Works Administration funds would finance the work.

Yet, beyond planning, nothing was immediately accomplished. Because the proposed route passed through the Indian lands south of the cemetery reservation, Quartermaster Corps officials awaited approval of a sixty-foot right of way from Crow Reservation superintendent Robert Yellowtail, who in January 1938 notified the army of the landowners' consent. In June Yellowtail further gave his endorsement to blueprints for the work, which got started that year under contract with the D. M. Manning Construction Company of Hysham, Montana.

During the 1938–40 construction of the two-lane gravel-based roadway (twenty feet wide with five-foot shoulders on each side), at least five major developments occurred that—owing to the lack of period sensitivity regarding historic landscapes—materially affected the original condition of the battlefield and possibly altered interpretive conclusions about the site. For one thing, the grading that took place near the monument at the north end of the battle ridge likely disturbed and distorted the primary landscape in the area of the monument and Last Stand group. Similar construction seems to have demolished several hillocks that appeared on the 1891 topographic map of the field. Further along the route, near the area of Medicine Tail Coulee Ford, construction of a reinforced concrete culvert over Medicine Tail Creek necessitated significant realignment of the creek channel from its probable 1876 configuration. At the significant Weir Point site, a modest dip in the terrain where Reno and Benteen's forces gathered to watch action on Custer's distant field was drastically modified into a gap for the road to pass through. Finally, completion of the road terminus near the Reno–Benteen Memorial likely graded away and otherwise destroyed significant battle-related landforms. Construction included bituminous surfacing of the road all the way south past Medicine Tail Coulee to the approximate middle of Section 23. From there to the Reno monument the road was gravel. In all instances, the lack of proper advance archeological clearance was detrimental to the likelihood of finding significant artifactual evidence from which substantive battle-related conclusions might have been made.[13]

Efforts to include the lands of the Reno–Benteen phase of the Battle of the Little Bighorn roughly paralleled a campaign to establish on the cemetery reservation a full-blown museum where visitors might view artifacts of the engagement and learn something of how the fighting occurred. Although this clearly was beyond the scope of responsibility of the War Department, the army nonetheless grudgingly made concessions to mounting popular attention through the 1920s and 1930s.

One of the earliest proponents of a museum there was Elizabeth B. Custer. In the early 1920s, the widow called for development of "a memorial hall of some kind where pictures, books, arms, and objects" reflecting the service of "our soldiers and frontier men" might be preserved. In 1923 she envisioned a hall dedicated not only to the men who fell with Custer but to the soldiers as well as settlers who endured the Indian wars of the northern plains, and she engaged architect Carlton Van Walkenburg to design an adobe edifice complete with specifications and estimates. "What I have in view is a very simple concrete building that would hold all those things used by the settlers. Whatever pictures or prints or books or furniture that pertained to that day. Whoever has seen that wonderfully historical & faithful moving picture "The Covered Wagon" must realize that a collection of articles, pictures, books, [and] letters could be obtained now that would help to tell the history of the settlement of the Great West." Yet perhaps understandably, Mrs. Custer visualized a one-sided exhibit; nowhere in her ruminations did she see reason to include the story of the "warlike Sioux" and Cheyennes.

Late in 1923, Mrs. Custer learned from Senator Walsh of his plans to introduce a bill for construction at the cemetery of a building for the custodian with additional rooms appropriate for those attending interments as well as persons visiting the battlefield. She hoped that the building might be enlarged to accommodate "the arms, uniforms, [and] accoutrements of our soldiers." She enlisted the aid of retired Lieutenant General Nelson A. Miles, who wrote members of Congress urging that $40,000 be appropriated for construction of "a commodious Memorial Building that would store the trophies and shelter the thousands of friends who visit the grounds." She also wrote Montana Democrat David Hilger of Lewistown, Secretary of the Montana Historical Society, to gain state support for her plan, telling him, "I hope that once this proposed building is built there may be additions—a real museum of frontier objects—letters, pictures, and perhaps some of the clothing and farming utensils and possibly a covered wagon!" Walsh's bill and its $15,000 appropriation, introduced in the Senate on December 6, 1923, was referred to the Committee on Military Affairs, where it subsequently died.[14]

Walsh promised to resubmit the bill, and Mrs. Custer continued her efforts. She continued to lobby Walsh, even presenting him with the plans for her adobe museum. Likely at her urging, in 1924 her cousin J. Bronson Case of Kansas City, Missouri, petitioned Montana Governor Dixon to use his influence with Walsh and U.S. senator Burton K. Wheeler (Dem.-Mont.) to introduce a bill for a museum and memorial, something larger than Walsh had initially envisioned. Said repository, according to Case, "would house all of the relics of General Custer, . . . including a display of the heads of animals that have been mounted and were killed by him." He suggested dedicating the structure at the upcoming semicentennial, and he offered (presumably with Mrs. Custer's acquiescence) to produce her for that purpose. But the effort subsequently faltered, derailed by the rising Teapot Dome scandal and Senator Walsh's chairmanship of the Senate investigation of it that followed.[15]

By the mid 1930s, virtually all of the former champions of the museum movement had passed from the scene. Elizabeth Custer had died on April 4, 1933. Senator Walsh had died in office the same year. Soon after Elizabeth's death, the Billings Commercial Club, a local conclave of boosterism, passed a resolution calling for building a Custer museum to house relics left by the widow and forwarded it to the attention of the Montana delegation in Congress. Spurred on by word of a movement afoot to place the artifacts with the Custer State Park in the Black Hills of South Dakota, museum supporters hoped that such a facility might be built as part of the public works program then before Congress. By that time too even the War Department was responding to the steadily mounting public interest in the Little Bighorn site, and in 1938 Superintendent Harvey A. Olson issued an interpretive brochure about the site that included information about the battle. Moreover, during the thirties a guide brought on by Olson unofficially provided interpretation of the site for visitors. He was eighty-one-year-old William H. White, a soldier who had served in the Second Cavalry in 1876 and who had been on the scene with Gibbon's command two days after the battle. Beginning in 1932, White rented a room in the superintendent's lodge, supplementing his meager government pension selling booklets about aspects of the Custer fight written by Dr. Thomas B. Marquis of Hardin. According to one contemporary report, White was the only man permitted to serve "as a guide at the Custer battlefield . . . in recognition of his services following the famous battle." Marquis referenced White's work as follows: "He has made thousands upon thousands of personal acquaintances and many warm friends throughout the United States. As visitors to the historic place they have listened enthralled to his ungarnished and convincing stories of what he saw there just after the battle and of what he then learned as to the details of it." In time, White's advanced years hindered his abilities as a guide. Failing health forced his departure from Custer Battlefield National Cemetery; he died in 1938.[16]

In that year Senator Wheeler, in company with several serious students of the Battle of the Little Bighorn, reopened the matter of a museum at the cemetery. With support from former cavalryman Edward S. Luce, who was then publishing a manuscript titled "Keogh, Comanche, and Custer"; Earl A. Brininstool, a well-known author of books about Custer and the Indian wars; and Eugene D. Hart, author with North Dakota congressman Usher L. Burdick of a then-forthcoming biography of Jacob Horner, Wheeler pushed new legislation for a museum. In January 1939 he introduced Senate Bill 28 authorizing the secretary of war to choose a site within the cemetery to establish "as a memorial to Lieutenant Colonel George A. Custer and the officers and soldiers under his command at the Battle of the Little Big Horn River, June 25, 1876, a public museum suitable for housing a collection of historical relics . . . [and] to accept on behalf of the United States for exhibit in such museum the collection of relics now a part of the estate of Mrs. George A. Custer, deceased . . . [and] other historical relics as he may deem appropriate for exhibit therein." The bill permitted the secretary of war to complete the museum "under such conditions as he may prescribe . . . without regard to civil-service requirements and restrictions of law governing the employment and compensation of employees of the United States." The bill further authorized the appropriation of $75,000 to carry out the work.[17]

Wheeler's bill was referred to the Senate Committee on Military Affairs, which solicited the views of War Department officials. On May

16, 1939, Secretary of War Harry Woodring endorsed the legislation, acknowledging heightened interest in the site and noting that "the cemetery is visited annually by thousands." He viewed the projected museum as a place where other Indian battles might also be studied, thus reflecting representation in the cemetery of soldiers who had participated in other Indian campaigns. "The proposed memorial building could . . . be used as a repository for historical records and relics of . . . [other] battles with the Indians also, thus preserving them to posterity. In the opinion of the War Department it would be a well-deserved tribute to the hardy soldiers who participated in the winning of the West." Budgetary constraints, however, affected the measure, and the House of Representatives amended it to reduce funding to $25,000. The Wheeler bill, after passing both houses, was signed into law by President Franklin D. Roosevelt on August 10, 1939. Funding, however, was not immediately forthcoming, and with the onset of World War II the museum project went into abeyance.[18]

Meantime, the gradually changing perceptions among the public, as well as among politicians and War Department officials, to embrace Custer Battlefield National Cemetery as a viable place for visitation and contemplation based on its history corresponded to a trend that had been germinating through parts of the government since before World War I. In 1916 the National Park Service had been created to protect national parks and monuments, and its enabling act had promoted the notion of consolidating under its administration the fragmented array of parks and monuments administered by the War Department and the Department of Agriculture. While a powerful Forest Service lobby successfully resisted the transfer of its properties, Park Service officials focused on War Department administration of historic sites that they believed to be wrong both from economic and interpretation standpoints. Besides providing no literature for visitors at its parks, the army employed park guides who often lacked subject-matter proficiency. Thus began a crusade to unite administratively all federal parks and monuments under the aegis of the National Park Service.

The movement culminated on June 10, 1933, when President Roosevelt approved Executive Order 6166, which effectively turned over to the National Park Service "all functions of administration of public buildings, reservations, national parks, national monuments, and national cemeteries." The transfer affected work and properties "of the National Park Service of the Department of the Interior and the National Cemeteries and Parks of the War Department which are located within the continental limits of the United States." Under authority of Executive Order No. 6228, July 28, 1933, which further clarified the June order, forty-seven War Department properties— national military parks (e.g., Gettysburg, Petersburg), national parks (e.g., Fort McHenry), battlefield sites (e.g., Antietam, Fort Necessity), national monuments (e.g., Big Hole, Statue of Liberty), miscellaneous memorials, and national cemeteries—were immediately transferred to the National Park Service. Although eleven national cemeteries were conveyed under the authority, they "included only those within or adjoining the military parks transferred." Custer Battlefield National Cemetery was not among them, its status defined in section 2 of the order that generically postponed such transfer "until further orders." The reason was that Custer Battlefield National Cemetery, unlike the long-closed national cemeteries associated with Civil War parks in the East, was still open for burials. Both the National Park Service and the War Department desired that the latter office retain control and maintenance over its active cemeteries, and that is what was done.

The action proved but a deferral, however. Enhanced public attention to the historic battlefield component of the cemetery reservation dictated that the site eventually join other former War Department properties under custodianship of the National Park Service. On July 1, 1940, seven years after passage of the sweeping transfer legislation, Custer Battlefield National Cemetery joined the National Park System by virtue of Executive Order No. 8428.[19] Henceforth, the site would take an abrupt tilt farther away from emphasis on the cemeterial function, while continuing to effect that former War Department responsibility, to emphasis on accommodating public visitation of the battlefield component. Although hardly perceptible at its beginning, National Park Service administration promised a new direction that would one day facilitate a more comprehensive and inclusive interpretation of this largest and most diversely symbolic of all of America's Indian war battle sites.

CHAPTER 5

National Park Service
Administration, 1940–1969

The transfer of Custer Battlefield National Cemetery to the National Park Service on July 1, 1940, brought no immediate perceptible difference. The historical name was initially retained, and, for the moment, activities continued much as before the site's change from War Department to Department of the Interior administration. Under the National Park Service, the former national cemetery reservation was aligned as a coordinated unit organizationally tethered to Yellowstone National Park, a status that would continue until 1953. Following the transfer, War Department personnel continued maintaining the cemetery, and Superintendent Harold Montague, who had arrived in December 1939, remained on duty through November 1940. The first National Park Service personnel did not arrive until December 1940, and the first National Park Service superintendent did not come on duty until early the following year, although his assignment had been determined perhaps as early as the spring or summer of 1940 and he had spent several months training for it while serving with the War Department at Arlington National Cemetery in Virginia.[1]

In many ways, Superintendent Edward Smith Luce seemed the perfect choice for the job. A lengthy army background that included enlisted service in the Seventh Cavalry early in the twentieth century tendered him military bearing and administrative talents, besides a consuming and intellectual interest in the Battle of the Little Bighorn and the history of his old regiment, for which he had gathered much historical information. He knew many army and civilian students of the battle, including participants Godfrey, Edgerly, Varnum, and Hare, and was widely recognized for his own recently published work, *Keogh, Comanche, and Custer* (1939). Over the course of his superintendency, Luce, who went by the sobriquet "Captain" and later "Major" Luce (the latter a self promotion), became a legendary fixture who cast a long shadow that extended well beyond his fifteen-year tenure there. One who worked for Luce offered these insights of him:

> "Cap" Luce stamped his mark deeply in the memory of all who knew him. None who visited Montana's Little Bighorn Battle-field between 1940 and 1956 is likely to forget him. He wore the green uniform and distinctive "Montana Peak" Stetson of the National Park Service, but every fiber bespoke his "Old Army" antecedents. With ample frame, red face, hawk nose, and Pall Mall in a long cigarette holder, he became as familiar a feature of Custer Hill as the battle monument itself. His bull voice, developed on long-ago parade fields, commanded instant obedience from park rangers, laborers, and erring tourists. His fund of anecdotes and adventure stories, spun with great gusto, if not always scrupulous respect for accuracy, unfailingly delighted all who fell under his spell.[2]

Accompanying Luce to the cemetery was his wife, Evelyn, whose interest in, and exertions on behalf of, Custer Battlefield were second only to those of her husband for the duration of his term.

Under Luce's leadership, the Little Bighorn battlefield began a transformation that—over the course of several decades—turned the site into one of the most popular tourist destinations in the National Park System. Among the first tasks confronting Luce were the resetting of battlefield markers that needed stabilizing and a major repair to the Custer monument that had begun to list to the south. In June 1941 the southeast corner of the mass grave was opened and some three tons of concrete poured into the base to secure the monument. In addition, the last 2.8 miles of the road leading from Custer battlefield to the Reno–Benteen area was graveled, improving access to the distant site, although during wet weather the road remained closed. Cemetery work accomplished in 1941 included removal from the grounds of all sage-brush, the planting of new trees, and sodding of the tract. (In February, there were 2,342 burial sites available.) In September, looking to improve the cemetery landscape, Luce arranged for 140 evergreen trees to be planted therein. The water supply, heretofore ever a problem because of uncertainties of the pump house and the potentially flooding Little Bighorn, continued to vex the superintendent. (In 1941 the flooding stream disrupted electrical power for three days.) Late in 1945, he attempted to sink a well, but the water yield was so poor that it was never used. When the water extension line to the cemetery and museum rusted out in 1952, Luce had it replaced with a cement-asbestos composite called Transite pipe. Within three years, he replaced the line from the pump house by the river to the cemetery, also with Transite pipe.[3]

The 1940s saw the furtherance of an evolution that would one day supplant attention formerly devoted almost exclusively to management of the cemetery. Beginning with Luce's arrival, and increasingly ever after in line with its mission and policies, the National Park Service addressed such matters as planning and development, resource protection and management, interpretation, research, collections acquisition and preservation, and, later, legislative compliance. The development and direction of these programs, besides the many issues and controversies that they invariably generated through the years beginning under Luce in the 1940s and continuing through subsequent superintendents, became the hallmark of National Park Service stewardship of the site and its resources.

Yet, from the 1940s through succeeding decades, many changes were to take place that were not always good for the battlefield resource, changes that have gradually affected the approximately one-square-mile tract of Custer's field as well as the added acreage at Reno–Benteen and that have tended to cumulatively manipulate an ever-expanding footprint and threaten the sanctity of the historic scene. Preservation and development always share a tenuous coexistence, and such has been the situation at the battlefield since the assumption of park service stewardship there. Whereas during the early years the issue scarcely surfaced (despite repeated assaults on the terrain by construction activities), it became more serious after the 1960s, when sweeping federal historic preservation law sought to protect such properties in the face of increased public visitation and accommodating development. Too often regarding the Custer battlefield, the statute was ignored or winked at by senior management, with accruing egregious results. Too often irreparable damage to the landscape or threats of such would be caused either unconsciously by custodians at best oblivious or indifferent to the law or perhaps consciously by those at worst disdainful of it.

These concerns, of course, did not immediately register with park service officials in 1940 at the inception of their management of Custer Battlefield National Cemetery. In 1941, as Luce took stock of his new domain, he found that its ground area consisted of the roughly one-mile-square national cemetery reservation as set aside in 1879, which included the cemetery proper, the Custer monument, and a portion of Custer's battlefield, most of it within a fenced area. It also included the 160-acre Reno–Benteen Defense Site, as established in 1929, some four miles south of the monument, as well as a small part of the entrance road and the oiled road right of way connecting the two tracts. Two gravel roads on the sloping ground below the cemetery joined into one leading down to the Little Bighorn River, where a new concrete pump house (1938) and a gravel pit were located. A four-inch pipe ran from the pump house to the cemetery. Phone and power lines (one of the latter running between the superintendent's lodge and the pump house) connected to the site from Crow Agency. Near the Custer monument, east of the road, was a parking area adjoined on its north end by the concrete reservoir. Appurtenances built under War Department administration in the area of the cemetery and lodge included the sewer, septic tank, and disposal field southwest of the lodge and its collateral buildings.[4]

Luce's arrival and assumption of charge over this physical plant shortly coincided with an upsurge in interest in the Custer story brought on by the 1941 release of Warner Brothers' *They Died with Their Boots On*, starring Errol Flynn and Olivia DeHavilland. The movie played in theaters well into 1942 and likely inspired increased visitation at the national cemetery. Added interest came in 1943 with serial publication in *The Saturday Evening Post* of Ernest Haycox's "Bugles in the Afternoon," based on the Custer story and for which Luce had provided the author various historical military data. By then, however, with World War II well underway, gasoline and tire rationing contributed to reduced numbers of visitors to the site. (Visitation in a peak month like June fell from 10,348 in 1941 to 4,161 in 1942 and to 1,687 in 1943.) Nonetheless, increased attention to Custer and the battlefield component of the cemetery reservation during the early forties stemming from Hollywood portrayals and the national press contributed to the decision to change the name of the National Park Service unit from Custer Battlefield National Cemetery. On March

22, 1946, the Seventy-ninth Congress passed Senate-introduced legislation effecting the change to Custer Battlefield National Monument, which brought the site into conformance with other commemorative units of the park system. The act stipulated that the "national monument shall be entitled to receive and to use all moneys heretofore or hereafter appropriated for the Custer Battlefield National Cemetery."[5]

Soon after his arrival, Superintendent Luce, working with regional personnel, began devising a master plan for the site in accordance with National Park Service policy for new parks. Land ownership and property line studies were completed in 1942, though most of the year was occupied with formulating the related master plan, with final approval following submission to National Park Service authorities lasting until mid-1944. Each component property of the site would be affected—the cemetery, the Custer battlefield, and the Reno–Benteen Defense Site (then called Reno battlefield). (Luce foresaw an expansion of the battlefield based on his own field research findings that indicated new areas of Custer's movements between the Reno–Benteen site and the Custer field [see chapter 8].) The plan envisioned major park development, to include an expanded headquarters area concentrated off the southwest corner of the cemetery containing two duplex residences for employees, a utility building and service court, an expanded superintendent's residence, and enhanced parking. A new comfort station would be built west of the entrance to the cemetery. The anticipated museum, along with additional parking, was to stand where the easternmost sections of the cemetery were located, and the plan called for moving more than five hundred sets of remains from the affected part, Section A, for reburial in Section D to accommodate the new development. More parking capacity would be located along the north side of the cemetery. Accompanying drawings suggest that the existing stone lodge, employees quarters, and garage were to be razed and the cemetery tract expanded into that section. Planned new road work included realigning the oiled entrance road from near the southwest corner of the cemetery to run along the south side of the proposed headquarters area and access the museum and the existing road (termed the "Battlefield Highway") leading past the Custer monument toward the Reno–Benteen site. Meantime, the existing road bordering the north boundary of the cemetery leading to the monument would be removed. A network of sidewalks and trails would connect together all aspects of the new development.[6]

As grandiose as the master plan was, the wartime emergency assured that funds would not be immediately forthcoming to complete it, and, except for a few later-enacted components, the design went largely unfulfilled. In 1946 a measure provided authorization for appropriations for repairs to the entrance road and the road to the Reno–Benteen area and was apparently the authority the park service sought for completing the surfacing of the latter. More important from Luce's standpoint was the museum, the centerpiece of his master plan.[7] Support came from the Montana legislative assembly, which early in 1949 passed a joint memorial to the president and Congress requesting appropriate funding "for the building of the Custer Battlefield Museum at Custer Battlefield National Monument, Montana." Receipt of the memorial was acknowledged in the Congressional Record in February. Meantime, during the immediate postwar period, Luce's employees remained busy in the cemetery with interment in Section D of World War II dead received from Europe and the South Pacific. (The first World War II dead had arrived for burial in March 1942.) Each reburial was attended with full military honors. In March 1948 Luce wrote that "we are getting about ten bodes [*sic*] a month and this will last for another three years." Compounding this work, in August 1948 the cemetery received for reburial the remains of at least thirty-six soldiers from the post cemetery at Fort Harrison, Montana.[8]

With the conclusion of the war in 1945 and the relaxing of emergency gasoline and tire restrictions, visitation at the national cemetery-battlefield shot up quickly. Whereas in August 1945, a peak month of the year, only 2,858 people visited the site, in August 1946 more than 10,000 showed up, a figure that continued to increase dramatically in subsequent years. Whereas visitation in 1943 totaled but 14,046 people, in 1946 it stood at more than 51,000. These figures supported Luce's contention that the new museum for the site was long overdue. Planning for the museum, meantime, continued with Region 2 personnel in Omaha, Nebraska. Luce recounted that "particular attention was given to the view which would be obtainable from the orientation room. The group agreed that for the funds which we believe will be available, the proposed plans will be most practical." The visits of National Park Service director Newton B. Drury in July 1948 and September 1949 must have given Luce further opportunity to lobby for the project, for which $96,000—because of rising costs—had been identified in the National Park Service Physical Improvement Program.

Finally, in 1950—eleven years after the project had been approved—funding was forthcoming and final plans and specifications completed. Bids were opened on June 5 at Yellowstone National Park, and a Billings,

Montana, firm, the J. C. Boespflug Construction Company, received the contract on June 28. Exhibit plans, prepared by historian Merrill J. Mattes and curator Harry Robinson of the regional office, were reviewed and approved. Groundbreaking for the building, to be located just northeast of the cemetery, occurred on July 17, with Custer's grand-nephew, Colonel Brice C. W. Custer, symbolically turning the first spade. At the ceremony, Luce spoke, followed by Custer and Lawrence A. Frost, a podiatrist and Custer authority who curated the Custer Room of the Monroe County Museum, Monroe, Michigan. American Legion Post 8 of Hardin furnished colors for the occasion. The James Louk Post, Veterans of Foreign Wars, provided a military salute, and the ceremony concluded with historical aide Robert M. Utley playing "Taps" on a bugle.

During the interim between the groundbreaking and dedication of the new museum the seventy-fifth anniversary of the Battle of the Little Bighorn was observed. American Legion Post 8 in Hardin organized the event because the National Park Service had no funding available for the purpose. In dressed-down ceremonies between ten o'clock and noon on June 25, 1951, Lieutenant General Albert Wedemeyer laid a memorial wreath at the monument, while the remainder of the pro-gram took place before the rostrum in the national cemetery. Lakota Indian battle participants from Pine Ridge, South Dakota, attended, and one of them, eighty-nine-year-old Joseph High Eagle, reportedly "brandished a 7th Cavalry cartridge belt that he had taken from a trooper's body." Military brass from all branches included, besides Wedemeyer, Fleet Admiral William D. Leahy, Lieutenant General Howard A. Craig, and Colonel William A. Harris, former commander of the Seventh Cavalry in Korea. Others present included Montana governor John W. Bonner, U.S. senator Zales N. Ecton, U.S. represen-tative Wesley A. D'Ewart, Yellowstone National Park superintendent Edmund B. Rogers, and regional historian Merrill J. Mattes. Colonel Brice C. W. Custer represented the Custer family. A special guest was Master Sergeant Francis R. Riley, Seventh Cavalry, recently wounded in Korea. Troops present represented the army, navy, air force, and marine corps. Publicity preceding the anniversary came in articles and illustrations in *Life*, *Collier's*, and *Sports Afield*.

The anniversary proceedings scarcely distracted from the ongoing construction of the museum and visitor center (termed "Museum-Administration Building" in the dedication program). Designed by Omaha architect Daniel M. Robbins as an example of post–World War

II international style modernism and built between August 1, 1950, and July 2, 1951, initially under the overall direction of architect Albert R. Stocker of the Region 2 office and later of architects John B. Cabot and Francis R. Roberson of that office, the museum emerged as a valuable administrative and interpretive facility and collections repository that centralized both the cemetery and battlefield interpretation components of the national monument. Constructed about midway between the cemetery and the monument, the museum provided adequate space for accommodating visitors as well as an exhibits area where battle-related artifacts and information might be presented. The reinforced concrete and cinder block building, laid out on an east-west axis, included office space for Luce and his staff (Luce moved in in January 1952), a lobby area, an exhibit room, and a glass-walled orientation and observation room, as well as a finished basement containing work rooms, a furnace room, two public restrooms, a dark room (for photographic projects), and a walk-in vault for collection storage, all with forced hot air heating and cooling. (A storm vestibule with new doors was added to the north side entrance in 1955.) Component roofs were flat with steel trusses and had slight projecting eaves. That the museum had been constructed immediately below and west of the Custer monument and adjacent Last Stand grouping on otherwise pristine battlefield terrain (though close to the cemetery) apparently was not a major consideration in its planning beyond the fact that much of the primary interpretive resource would be visible from the observation room. The placement of the museum to bear so directly on the battlefield would lead to proposals for its removal in subsequent management plans. During the construction, mishaps occasionally took place. In December 1951, for example, a defective oil furnace spewed smoke and soot causing damage to the ceilings, walls, and exhibit space throughout and necessitating their repainting.

The completion of the museum in July 1952, including its initial exhibits (for which $31,200 had been appropriated in 1951), likely marked the height and supreme accomplishment of Luce's superintendency, a "Coronation Day," according to one observer. The dedication, scheduled on June 25 to correspond to the seventy-sixth anniversary of the battle, included an array of military and civilian officials. Luce coordinated the event, but rainy weather forced the planned outdoor festivities to be moved inside the new building, the number of anticipated attendees markedly diminished (although some twelve hundred people showed up). The dedication ceremony included remarks by several local and regional officials and by National Park Service staff from the park, region, and national headquarters. Among the National Park Service spokesmen were Luce, as master of ceremonies; Yellowstone National Park superintendent Edmund B. Rogers, who read an address from Assistant Director Ronald F. Lee, who was unable to attend; and Ned J. Burns, former chief of the service's museum branch, who had supervised completion of the exhibits (see chapter 7). General Jonathan Wainwright, hero of Corregidor and the Bataan Death March during World War II, and whose father had served at Fort Custer, donated to the museum a Model 1866 Winchester rifle that had been taken from a Crow Indian following the 1887 Sword Bearer insurgency, the gun, supposedly that of a Sioux or Northern Cheyenne warrior, having been picked up on the Little Bighorn battlefield in 1876. Colonel William A. Harris, formerly of the Seventh Cavalry, spoke of the tradition of the "Garry Owen" esprit that marked the history of the Seventh's old marching song. Colonel Brice Custer spoke of the family's interest in its completion and cut the ribbon to formally open the building. Observances took place at the monument, where General Wainwright laid a wreath honoring the dead, with proper attendance of the American Legion post from Crow Agency. Ever the publicist for Custer Battlefield, Luce made sure that the dedication was broadcast by radio and that it received regional and national tabloid coverage. Tribal attendance was small. Art Bravo represented the Crows and stood with Wainwright for a photo, but few, if any, other Indians attended, and none took part in the program.[9]

Other work completed during the early 1950s included the conversion into living quarters of Luce's old office in the stone house and the replacement of the water line in the cemetery. A house trailer, hauled in from Bismarck in 1954, was outfitted for use by seasonal employees. And in July 1953, lightning again damaged the flag pole in the cemetery, requiring its repair and repainting.

In terms of wildlife management in the park, Luce noted within a few years of his arrival that natural species were returning in considerable numbers. "Prior to 1940," he wrote,

dogs and cats were permitted to run loose in the area and wild game hunting was allowed. Since July 1940 we have noticed a continuous gain in the different species of birds. Last winter the robins remained in this area and to date they have hatched two broods. About two weeks ago we noticed three adult mule-ear deer within the reservation limits. This is the first time they have ever been seen here. We believe they are hiding out among the trees and brush along the river bank. Indians are permitted to hunt on their reservation through-out the entire year, and when these deer leave this area they will in all probability be killed. Cotton-tails and jack rabbits are slowly being reduced by disease. This has been especially true during the past two years.

In May 1947 Professor John W. Scott from the University of Wyoming arrived at the park to conduct a study of the mating and strutting behavior of the sharp-tailed grouse. Custer Battlefield National Monument was determined to be one of the few places west of the Black Hills where this species of grouse chose to dance and mate. In terms of the park's flora content, it was observed that it harbored original grasses, largely undisturbed because the acreage had never been intensively grazed over by cattle. In August 1948 Luce reckoned that several dozen sage hens (grouse) also frequented the battlefield tract, and he also spotted European partridges there. Still later, in 1952, the superintendent reported that pocket gophers were infesting the cemetery lawns and announced initiation of a trapping campaign.[10]

Memorial Day continued to be a major annual observance at the park, sponsored as before by the Hardin American Legion post, and was usually marked by a patriotic presentation by a visiting dignitary with appropriate musical performances by local bands or ensembles. For instance, in 1948 about two thousand people, many of them veterans from several veteran organizations in southeastern Montana, attended to hear a speech from Montana governor Sam C. Ford. The program ran as follows:

Overture "America"—Hardin High School Band
Welcome—Captain E.S. Luce
Patriotic Selection—Sextette, Hardin High School
Orders of the Day—Post Commander
Lincoln's Gettysburg Address—H.W. Hunston
Memorial Day Prayer—C.A. Bentley, Post Chaplain
Selections—Hardin High School Band

Presentation of Pin—Governor of Montana
Selection—Sextette, Hardin High School
Introduction of Principal Speaker—Dan W. Maddox
Address of the Day—Hon. Sam C. Ford, Governor of Montana
"Taps"
"Star-Spangled Banner"—Hardin High School Band

The events of the next year yielded a crowd that Luce reported as the second biggest in the history of the area, exceeded only by that of the fiftieth anniversary activities of 1926. Robert S. Yellowtail, agent of the Crow Reservation, read the "Gettysburg Address" during the proceedings.[11]

While most of the 1940s and early 1950s were dedicated to the processing and burial of World War II and Korean War dead, as well as to the campaign to win funding for the museum, the 1950s saw the beginning of other sustained development at the site. In 1953 Luce assumed direct administrative authority of the park when its "coordinated" status with Yellowstone National Park ended. The Reno–Benteen tract was finally fenced in 1954 (it had been partially fenced in 1947). Despite this and the new museum, Luce was sensitive to the need to not overdevelop the national monument. In that year, the Seventh U.S. Cavalry Association held its annual reunion at Billings, and Luce entertained a resolution of the body to erect on the battlefield a thirteen-foot-tall bronze equestrian statue of Custer mounted on a ten-foot-high granite pedestal. Balking at the proposal, Luce likened it to "placing the Empire State Building on the battlefield ridge. . . . It is our interpretive duty to keep this area in the plain, simple manner in which the battlefield was at the time of the battle." Moreover, he said, the development would offend Indians. "To put [up] a huge equestrian statue of General Custer . . . would be to pour salt into already unhealed Indian wounds. I am unalterably opposed." And in a remarkably insightful commentary for its time, Luce addressed the need to keep the site further unscathed by the intrusions of development: "We know when people come to the Custer Battlefield National Monument, they do not come to see what one person did. They want to know the part played by both Indians and the Army. They wish to visualize the conditions of the battlefield without any modernization. However, the true picture of the battlefield is disturbed by having living quarters, utility buildings and the National Cemetery encroaching on the picture. Even the museum is, in a way, exotic to the original pictures."[12]

Oddly, Luce's words cryptically presaged an era of unbridled development at Custer Battlefield National Monument, particularly that undertaken in accordance with the Mission 66 program of the National Park Service. Mission 66 was promulgated with the intent to upgrade the parks during the postwar period "to permit their wisest possible use," to provide "maximum enjoyment" for visitors and "maximum protection of the scenic, scientific, wilderness, and historic resources that give them distinction." Mission 66, inaugurated in 1956 with President Dwight D. Eisenhower's full support, brought radical change to the parks; carrying out the program meant wide-scale development, including construction of roads and trails, new utilities, picnic accommodations, and various administrative and public use buildings, and repair and rehabilitation of existing properties where necessary. The extensive service-wide agenda was to be completed by 1966, the fiftieth anniversary of the founding of the National Park Service.

At Custer Battlefield National Monument, the program accelerated after Luce's retirement in April 1956. Initial work began under his successor, John A. Aubuchon, who served as superintendent from 1956 to December 1958, and was completed during the term of Thomas A. Garry, next to Luce the longest tenured National Park Service superintendent at the park, who took over in March 1959 and remained until his retirement in January 1968. Mission 66 at the park embraced a $2 million building program that included improvements to the water system, with an above-ground enlargement of the reservoir atop the battle ridge, a remodeled irrigation system in the cemetery, and a new septic disposal system (Cop Construction Company). Southwest of the cemetery, three single-level, three-bedroom houses, planned as early as 1951, were constructed in 1961–62 for the superintendent, park historian, and administrative officer. At the same time, a multiple-unit apartment building was built for seasonal employees, along with a utility building with repair and maintenance facilities and storage space for cemetery supplies and motorized equipment (Herb Gruss Construction Company). (Much of this work lay outside of already compromised development areas, e.g., the cemetery and lodge area and early roads and trails, and thus directly affected virgin battlefield terrain.) Two World War II–vintage corrugated Quonset huts, each fifty feet long, acquired in 1947 and 1950 for maintenance and storage and situated on bluffs overlooking the Little Bighorn River near the west boundary of the park were slated for removal. The residence (former stable and garage remodeled in 1957) adjoining the rear of the superintendent's

lodge was also removed. With erection of a new home for the superintendent, the old lodge—following expressed concern from area preservation groups that it would be earmarked for demolition—was in 1963
converted into space for civic receptions and for a prayer room (the
building had variously served that function since 1948). Restrooms
for visitors were also located there. Landscaping for the construction
area and cemetery included the planting of nearly 100 deciduous and
conifer trees, besides nearly 150 shrubs.

Roads and trails were also to be improved under Mission 66. In
1957, a new entrance road was configured to enter the park near the
northwest corner of the cemetery rather than near the front of the
superintendent's lodge, and the next year part of the road and a new
parking lot was seal coated and spread with crushed rock. Meantime,
other construction entailed the raising of new masonry gateposts for
the iron gates, while a new parking area extended from the museum
to the cemetery pedestrian gate (Lalonde Construction Company). At
the museum and visitor center, the concrete slab floor in the observation room settled, requiring repair, and the doors to the room had to
be trimmed to fit accordingly. (A similar problem afflicted the floor of
the exhibit room, which was leveled and repaired early in 1959.) Inside
the lobby, the information desk and sales counter was redesigned to
separate interpretation from book sales. Later, a tree and several shrubs
were planted on the north and west sides of the visitor center to improve
the building's appearance.

Within the cemetery, the road from the west gate to the flagstaff
was rebuilt in 1957. And in April 1958, for the first time, the hedges,
trees, and lawn in the cemetery received fertilizer based on recommendations of a Bureau of Indian Affairs soil scientist. Other park
maintenance included planting trees along the river while dumping
forty-five cubic yards of rock there to form jetties to help retard bank
erosion. Meantime, the road leading to the Reno–Benteen site was
resurfaced, a new cattle guard installed at the south boundary of the
Custer field, and a trail built leading from the museum to the Custer
monument. Part of an old road extending south from the Reno–Benteen
parking lot was obliterated, while another trail was completed so that
visitors might better access the sites there. A series of interpretive
markers was erected between the Custer battlefield and the Reno positions. And in June 1963, with vandalism falling off, the tall iron fences
protecting the Custer monument and the Reno–Benteen monument
were removed so that visitors might gain unrestricted views of them.

Two years later, the Reno–Benteen parking lot was expanded; at that time the 1929 monument situated at the south end of the parking lot was moved to a point to the west, near the start of the self-guiding trail. An oil mat surface was applied to the trail.

The Mission 66 prospectus also entailed research-based projects, such as archeology to determine the location of entrenchments at the Reno–Benteen Defense Site, followed by their restoration (see chapter 8). At Custer's battlefield, a resurvey of the field was planned to locate unmarked grave sites and to identify some of those who died who were yet listed as "unknown." Additionally, documentary research would be conducted to help broaden the database of the Little Bighorn in relation to other episodes in the West, while acquisition of military and Indian artifacts would help augment interpretation of those facets of western life in the museum. Anticipated expenditures for the Mission 66 work stood at $385,000. Beyond its infrastructural components, however, Mission 66 as planned was rather one-dimensional and exclusive in its interpreted benefit respecting *all* Americans and rather typified societal and bureaucratic thinking of the time: "Mission 66 for Custer Battlefield National Monument means the provision of all the facilities and services necessary for each visitor to enjoy an informative and inspirational experience . . . [while promoting] greater understanding and appreciation of the difficulties *our forefathers* experienced in the westward advancement of the American frontier" (emphasis added).[13]

Visitation during the 1950s and early 1960s increased dramatically as the traveling public continued to frequent the national parks and monuments in greater numbers than ever before. In 1954 the annual number of visitors at Custer Battlefield reached nearly 120,000, while in 1966, twelve years later, the number had increased by nearly 100,000. (Among notables coming to the park were National Park Service director Conrad Wirth, who visited on August 4, 1960, and on August 31, 1962; First Lady Lady Bird Johnson, Secretary of the Interior Stewart Udall, and U.S. senator Mike Mansfield of Montana on August 14, 1964; National Park Service director George Hartzog on August 24, 1964; actor Walter Brennan in June 1965; and presidential daughter Lynda Bird Johnson, who camped overnight in three house trailers arranged in the Calhoun Road Loop on July 15–16, 1965.) A number of television programs filmed at the park, including one for the ABC series *Saga of Western Man* in May–June 1964, featuring Crow Indians portraying Sioux fighting The Westernaires, a riding club from Colorado. The segment aired in April 1965. An especially interesting visitor on August 9, 1962, was ninety-year-old Lucille Larrabee, from Eagle Butte, South Dakota; Mrs. Larrabee as a child had been in the Indian village at the time of the battle. A special event was the overstated publicity designation of the "one billionth" visitor on August 22, 1962—he was Al Stefanisin, of Roselle, Illinois, and he appeared in photographs published in the *Billings Gazette* and *Hardin Times-Herald*.

Occasionally, Luce commented on specific visits by bodies of people. During the summer of 1953, he was outraged at the presence of a group of Boy Scouts passing through en route to their Jamboree in California. "It was very evident," he wrote, "that many of the scouts, counselors, and scout-masters forgot their oaths. In the national cemetery grounds the scouts were lacking in due honor and respect to their country's dead. Many were caught playing leap-frog over the gravestones, breaking several of the water sprayers and using sling-shots against the head-stones, as well as trying to hit birds, grouse and rabbits." Less than a year later a group of 772 scouts traveling by train stopped in the valley and hiked up to the park. Luce, apprehensive after the earlier episode, likened their arrival to an "incursion" and "a parachute raid or attack."

Visitor accommodations likewise underwent modification, and in 1964–65 major changes in the battlefield visitor center were designed by architect Max R. Garcia of San Francisco and appropriate additions made to the original 1952 brick building. Stainless steel detailing high-lighted the changes, which included modifications to the entrance, the addition of restroom facilities, an observation deck extending beyond the glassed observation room on the building's east side, and struc-tural foundation repairs necessitated by the presence of bentonite in the earth. Soon thereafter, an architect from the regional office drew up plans for installing corrugated fiberglass projecting sunshade eaves on the outside of the observation room to cut back on sun glare, which was obstructing visitors' view and causing the room to overheat. Besides the observation deck, space in the visitor center was dedicated to a larger orientation lobby area for both book sales and an information desk. The exhibit room was reconfigured to permit better visitor circu-lation as well as new exhibits and was repainted with fabric murals installed on the walls. A new wing to include restrooms, a library room/historian's office, and a new superintendent's office was added on the west side of the building. This latter work was completed under contract by the Borgam Construction Company of Billings. Immediately outside, at the northwest corner of the building, a parking lot was constructed sufficient to accommodate sixty automobiles and six trailers. Cost for all the improvements totaled around half a million dollars.[14]

A recurring matter that appeared yet again during the Mission 66 period concerned encompassing land. It had long been obvious that the existing boundaries of the national monument did not take in the entire area of the historic Battle of the Little Bighorn, notably the ground in the valley west of the river where Major Reno had made his attack, as well as that enclosing the route of his withdrawal from the bottom to the heights east of the stream. Moreover, the area surrounding on all sides the 160-acre tract held significant actions and associations for the men besieged on the hilltop from midday June 25 until June 27, 1876. Likewise, it was conceded that many of the battle actions had occurred on the three-mile stretch of ground lying between the Reno–Benteen property and the originally designated tract where Custer's dead were found. Certainly, the acquisition of the Reno site in 1929 had been a major addition to aid in the protection and interpretation of the entire field. But to properly explain the whole story of the Battle of the Little Bighorn, as well as to protect the historic ground in its entirely, would require acquisition of a more expansive tract than that administered by the National Park Service.

In July 1956, Roy E. Appleman, a staff historian from the service's Washington office, toured the park with Park Historian Don Rickey, Jr. Appleman's report of his visit called for increasing the land base at the Reno–Benteen site to take in water carrier routes as well as Indian attack routes. Wrote Appleman, "It must not be forgotten that in this whole business the Indians were a necessary and important part of the action, and the ground they held and the positions from which they fought are as necessary as is the position held by the cavalrymen for a complete control of the historic grounds and the telling of the story." Appleman urged acquisition of "a reasonably small tract" west of the river and east of U.S. Highway 87, "representing Reno's northernmost advanced position eastward to the river and extending south to the ford of the Little Big Horn where his command . . . crossed to the bluffs east of the river." He recommended similar land acquisition in the 3-mile-long tract between the Reno–Benteen site and the Custer field, including that encompassing Medicine Tail Coulee and its ford, areas where Custer presumably had operated en route to his last battle. "All the land between the two areas should be acquired so that there is a solid block of land in the Monument east of the river." Acting on

Appleman's proposals, the National Park Service instituted a boundary adjustment study that projected acquisition of a 1.5-mile-wide enclosing swath that would run from Highway 8 on the north (present Highway 212) southeast to include all of the Reno–Benteen tract and cognate lands. Much of the recommended tract would touch on the east bank of the river. There was no provision for acquiring the land in the valley that Appleman had projected. Regardless, no further land acquisitions ever occurred, and the matter of acquiring requisite land to properly enhance and protect the resource, crucial to park planning, has remained one of befuddlement and consternation that has since defied solution.[15]

Acquisition of the extended property surrounding the National Park Service tracts would have protected it against degradation caused by its use for cattle grazing and farming and the establishment of buildings, stock ponds, and dirt roads and trails that have cumulatively torn the fabric and marred the historic landscape. In addition, beginning in 1953, the neighboring land, notably that lying between the battlefield tracts, experienced repeated seismographic testing through detonation of explosives in a search for petroleum that has gone on intermittently through the years into the 1970s. In 1955 heavy trucks bearing equipment illegally entered the target area, tearing down fences and crossing part of the Reno–Benteen site and leaving deeply rutted tracks in their wake. Early in 1958 as a result of action involving the U.S. attorney, the Stanolind Gas and Oil Company, responsible for the destruction, settled out of court for $3,000 to avoid prosecution. Another external threat to the park was the proposed placement "within fifty feet of our main entrance gate" of a hot dog stand, which caused the superintendent to lament not having purchased the land when he had the opportunity to do so for $3.50 an acre. The eatery, along with a souvenir stand, was indeed erected, and in 1961 a gasoline pump added another component. And in 1959 a would-be entrepreneur attempted to lease Indian property for a similar venture between the two battlefield tracts at the mouth of Medicine Tail Coulee.[16]

Concurrent with the Mission 66 program to upgrade existing physical facilities at Custer Battlefield and construct new ones, a new master plan for the park got underway in 1963, its purpose "to enrich the visitor's experience by providing an understanding of the conflict between red men and white during the period of westward expansion of which the Battle of the Little Bighorn, and the events leading to it, were a dramatic part." A key stated objective was "to acquire appropriate lands now separating the two existing battlefield areas . . . [and]

to acquire appropriate lands needed to facilitate improved protection, management, and interpretation of Monument resources and values." Other objectives of the plan included cooperating activities with the neighboring Crow Tribe, protection of other northern plains Indian war sites, improved interpretation and visitor use, expanded external programs, additional historical research, and training to ensure continued improvement of management skills and operational procedures. (By 1963 most of the proposed physical development at the park had been accomplished under Mission 66.) Beyond recommendations for improving overall interpretation, the plan called for interpretation of the cemetery in relation to the context of the Indian wars, continuation of existing conditions affecting traffic control, fire security, law enforcement, and first aid, and, following the boundary expansion, the addition of a picnic area "without intrusion on the Historic scene."

Permanent staffing at the park consisted of the superintendent, administrative assistant, historian, maintenance foreman, maintenance man, and one unfilled position for a ranger. (Luce had hired the first formal park historian at Custer Battlefield National Monument in 1953—James Bowers, a seasonal ranger from Fort Laramie National Monument whose appointment lasted little more than a year. Bowers was replaced in June 1955 by Don Rickey, Jr., a doctoral candidate at the University of Oklahoma and already viewed as an authority on military arms and equipment.) Temporary positions allowed for the seasonal hiring of a clerk-typist, five ranger-historians, one truck driver, two laborers, and one ranger. The new plan called for adding permanent positions for a clerk-typist, an assistant historian, and another laborer, besides a permanent ranger for resource management and visitor protection.

A major element of the plan dealt with the cemetery, which was increasing in interments at a rate of about one hundred per year. On May 1, 1961, sixteen remains exhumed from the Fort Mackenzie cemetery at Sheridan, Wyoming, were reinterred in the national cemetery. Requests from area veteran organizations for expansion of the cemetery increased. Because of the construction of the rostrum and assembly area at the northeast end of Section B, a planned 570 gravesites were withdrawn from that section; another 325 sites were withdrawn from Section E, adjacent to the stone lodge, for the purpose of maintaining distance from that historical property. Two new plots (originally three), Sections G and H, to be located south of Section A, would accommodate the approximately 900 withdrawn sites. According to the superintendent's report, "Each plot will be 12 rows of 25 sites each. The plots are spaced to repeat the pattern of the existing cemetery with a margin of grass outside the grave sites to the limits of the cemetery, which is enclosed with a hedge." Access to the new burial sections would be by way of a driveway from the maintenance area to the west. An automated piped irrigation system would provide water to the cemetery additions. In 1965, work completed in the cemetery involved the removal of the passageway and stable behind the stone lodge, as well as the adjacent garage, storeroom, and associated walks in Section E. Also, the old rostrum in the north corner of Section F, along with its collateral sidewalks, was removed and the cemetery in both sections restored for grave sites.

Other fixtures at the park by 1963, besides the Mission 66 structures, included a shallow well fixed with horizontal laterals located near the Little Bighorn in the southwest corner of the national monument from which water was drawn to the pump house for chlorination. From there water was pumped to the one-hundred-thousand-gallon reservoir atop Custer Hill near the monument. Water pressure for cemetery irrigation came from a pump in the maintenance building, where controls for the automated system were located. Sewage continued to be disposed through a recently installed septic and dosing tank unit fixed with a sand filter located south of the maintenance area. Electricity continued to be provided by the Big Horn Cooperative through an above-ground line running to a point along the south side of the cemetery. An underground cable then ran power to the visitor center, residences, and the maintenance facility. Telephone lines entered the area by way of power poles and were dispersed through the same trench as the electric power cable. And in 1962 the boundary fence was replaced by a firm in Gillette, Wyoming.[17]

Some of the development that occurred during the 1950s and 1960s would not have been permitted following passage of the National Historic Preservation Act of 1966. The legislation, which among other things created the National Register of Historic Places, combined existing and new legislation in a sweeping program to protect historic properties throughout the United States, requiring in federally owned areas strict adherence to policies to ensure that development such as had previously occurred at Custer Battlefield National Monument in no way affected the resource itself, that is, the battlefield proper. Under provisions of the Historic Preservation Act of 1966, it is likely that the construction of the museum directly on top of part of the principal terrain (to say nothing of the one-hundred-thousand-gallon reservoir atop Last Stand

Hill, buried electrical lines running through the Last Stand group, and adjoining asphalt parking lots) would have been prevented. In any event, Custer Battlefield National Monument, including the cemetery and the Reno–Benteen tract, as an existing National Park Service unit, was placed on the National Register in 1966 as comprising 926 acres, one building, eight structures, and fifty-six objects. Henceforth, technically and legally, all further development potentially affecting the historic property at the park was expected to comply with provisions of the 1966 law.[18]

A single reburial in the national cemetery drew international attention to Custer Battlefield National Monument in 1967. It was the reinterment there of the remains of Major Marcus A. Reno, Custer's second-in-command during the Battle of the Little Bighorn, whose performances in the valley action and subsequent occupation of the ridgetop position had likewise been rife with controversy. Although Reno had formally cleared his name in a court of inquiry convened in Chicago in 1879, his army career became shredded in the aftermath of Little Bighorn, and in 1880, following court-martial for "conduct unbecoming an officer and a gentleman," he was sentenced to be dishonorably dismissed from the service. He later contracted cancer, dying in 1889 in Washington, D.C., where he was buried in an unmarked grave. In 1966 Reno's great-grandnephew, Charles Reno, applied to the Army Board for the Correction of Military Records to show that the officer had been honorably discharged. With help from attorneys from the American Legion and others, Charles Reno succeeded in his case, and on May 5, 1967, the board directed correction of Reno's records to reflect his honorable discharge from the army. At the family's request, Reno's body was exhumed for transport and reburial with honors in—of all places— the national cemetery at Custer Battlefield National Monument, the scene of genesis of the very imputations that had hounded him through the last days of his army career and likely the last place on earth the major would have desired to rest. On the afternoon of September 9, 1967, Reno's flag-draped casketed remains arrived at the cemetery, where they were reburied with full military honors in Section C, near the flagpole and less than three hundred yards from Custer Hill. Montana governor Tim Babcock, members of the national leadership of the American Legion, and other dignitaries attended the event. As Charles Reno and other relatives looked on, traditionally attired representatives of the Northern Cheyenne, Crow, and Lakota tribes provided tributes, and the 163rd Armored Cavalry Regiment, Montana National Guard, served as pallbearers and delivered an eleven-gun salute. As final volleys resounded, Reno's bronze coffin was lowered into the earth and "Taps" reverberated in the late summer breeze.[19]

As stated, the posthumous reversal of Reno's dishonorable discharge and subsequent reburial in the cemetery at Custer Battlefield National Monument drew increasing public notice to the park. Visitation shot up from 218,062 in 1966 to 260,927 in 1967. While it dipped slightly in 1968, the number of visitors touring the park exceeded 250,000 the next year. Similarly, sales of books, pictures, and souvenir articles that took place at the information desk in the visitor center, jumped from just over $28,000 in 1968 to $37,000 two years later (see chapter 9). Although the Custer mystique contributed to the continually expanding popularity of the park, the postwar decades saw ever-increasing tourism as Americans and foreigners alike visited local, state, and national parks reflective of the country's past in far-flung but now easily accessible places.

In late 1963 and early 1964, Superintendent Garry participated in discussions with Big Horn County Montana Centennial Committee officials regarding the possibility of a battle reenactment as part of the upcoming Montana territorial centennial celebration. The park was considered to be the largest visitor attraction in the region. Garry initially offered reasons against such a reenactment but eventually consented on the condition that the event be held somewhere besides Custer Battlefield. Initially, there were problems recruiting enough participants, but the first reenactment, sponsored by the Crow Tribal Industrial Commission, with narration prepared by Joseph Medicine Crow, took place near the Crow Agency fairgrounds on June 27 and 28, 1964, and swelled visitation at the park by nearly seven thousand people. Garry reported that "we consider the reenactment narration very good and the various scenes extremely well done under the circumstances. Attendance and public reaction to the program certainly indicates . . . [that it] can be a worthwhile annual affair." In 1965 eight reenactments took place over two weekends in June, and in that year and 1966 the superintendent and park historian served as members of the board of directors for Big Horn County Special Events, Inc., which sponsored the events. In 1976, the centennial year of the battle, the event was discontinued because of "its potential for explosiveness"; it was reborn in the 1990s near Hardin. Along with another reenactment staged annually on Crow land adjoining the park, the affair has become a staple attraction for visitors each summer.[20]

Movies, television, magazines, and books, as well as newly founded study groups and associations, steadily promoted the interest in Custer and Little Bighorn. Walt Disney's fictional *Tonka* elicited attention when it played at movie houses across the nation in 1958. Thomas Berger's novel *Little Big Man* came out in 1964 and was turned into a popular movie by 1970, with parts filmed on battlefield terrain lying between the National Park Service tracts. A number of well-executed scholarly books about Custer and the Battle of the Little Bighorn promoted further interest. William A. Graham's compilation of army and Indian accounts in *The Custer Myth* garnered wide attention when it appeared in 1953. Graham, who decades earlier had served in the Judge Advocate Corps of the army, had personally known many officer participants in the battle. Similarly, Edgar I. Stewart's *Custer's Luck* provided the first comprehensive professional synthesis of data about the 1876 Sioux campaign and battle. Stewart, a college professor in Washington State, had served as a historical aide at the park in 1946. And in 1957 David Humphreys Miller's *Custer's Fall: The Indian Side of the Story* appeared, offering a freshly cohesive tribal perspective of the Little Bighorn (although much of its content was later questioned). Another work that drew notice in 1962, Robert M. Utley's *Custer and the Great Controversy*, dealt with the evolution of the various debates surrounding Custer's demise. It was likewise written by a former historical aide who served at the battlefield under Luce from 1947 to 1952 (Utley went on to become chief historian and assistant director for cultural resources in the National Park Service and in 1968 wrote a much-heralded [though controversial for its artwork] National Park Service handbook for the battlefield). All of these works contributed importantly during the 1950s and 1960s in stimulating and maintaining public interest in Custer, the Indians, and the Battle of the Little Bighorn.[21]

Although its effect was not immediate, another book had a profound influence on the course of events at Custer Battlefield. In 1970, Dee Brown's *Bury My Heart at Wounded Knee* appeared. Subtitled *An Indian History of the American West*, the volume became a runaway national bestseller. Although scholarly reviews rebuked its content as "old wine in new bottles" while citing its blatant lack of historical objectivity, the book nonetheless struck a discordant note that helped raise social consciousness about Indians generally and that in time translated into a direct and positive application affecting the park's interpretive programs, and, eventually, its administration and development. While change at the battlefield was promoted by the gradually increasing awareness and cumulatively changing attitudes toward Indians since the 1940s, probably *Bury My Heart at Wounded Knee* proved its overriding catalyst. Yet another volume that would similarly influence Custer Battlefield National Monument, symbolically and otherwise, in the years ahead, was *Custer Died for Your Sins: An Indian Manifesto*, by Vine Deloria, Jr.[22] The book, which properly voiced American Indians' frustrations with their historical treatment, would likewise one day inspire transcendent changes at the park.

ILLUSTRATIONS

Contemporary drawing titled *Custer's Last Fight*, by A. R. Waud, 1876. From Whittaker, *Complete Life of Gen. George A. Custer.*

Lieutenant Colonel George A. Custer

Major Marcus A. Reno

Captain Frederick W. Benteen

Principal Seventh Cavalry commanders at the Little Bighorn, June 25–26, 1876.

Sitting Bull, Hunkpapa Lakota

Gall, Hunkpapa Lakota

Crow King, Hunkpapa Lakota

Low Dog, Oglala Lakota

Two Moon, Northern Cheyenne

Leaders of the Indian coalition at the Battle of the Little Bighorn.

Lieutenant General Philip H. Sheridan, commander of the Military Division of the Missouri, whose postbattle activities perhaps most significantly influenced the establishment of Custer Battlefield National Cemetery in 1879. From the author's collection.

In August 1877 photographer John H. Fouch took the earliest image of the Little Bighorn battlefield and titled it *The Place Where Custer Fell*. The stake in the center indeed represents the spot where the officer's body was found on June 27, 1876. Courtesy of James S. Brust.

Sanderson's camp near the Little
Bighorn River.

Horse bones atop Custer Hill.

The fabricated grave for Lieutenant Sturgis.

Views of the battlefield by photographer Stanley J. Morrow, who accompanied
Captain George K. Sanderson's reburial detail in the spring of 1879.

Marker to Captain Myles Keogh (Sanderson stands at right).

Marking Lieutenant Crittenden's grave.

Flag-topped cordwood monument containing horse bones as erected on Custer Hill.

View to the west toward the Little Bighorn River, showing wooden stakes marking the sites of graves. Photo by David F. Barry, 1883.

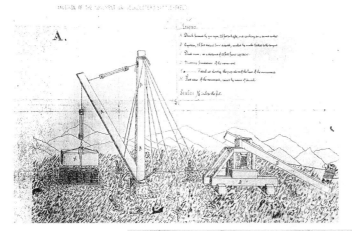

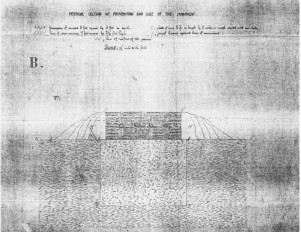

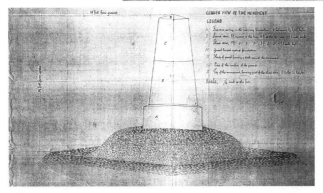

"Erection of the Monument on Gen. Custer's Battle-Field," three sketches showing the derrick crane employed, the foundation, and a view of the monument. National Archives.

The Custer Monument, Custer Memorial, or Seventh Cavalry Monument, as it has variously been called. This view, taken in the mid-1880s, clearly shows the souvenir chipping by early visitors that plagued the granite edifice. A soldier from nearby Fort Custer looks on at the right, while a dog relaxes in the shade afforded by the structure. Photo by David F. Barry

Two views of the battlefield in the 1890s. That at top was taken by photographer H. R. Locke in 1894 and shows the marble markers erected in 1890. A wooden cross denotes a revised position for where Custer fell. The bottom view reveals the effects of vandalism on the markers and Custer's cross. Such recurring damage eventually led to the appointment of an onsite superintendent and the further definition of the national cemetery (in the distance in this view) versus the battlefield proper.

No. 5. Custer's battlefield on Crow Agency, Montana, along the B. & M. R. R. Battle fought June 25th, 1876. Custer and all his men were killed. Photographed and copyrighted by H. R. Locke in 1894, Deadwood, S. D.

The Custer Monument and Last Stand group in the early 1890s (two views).

View south to north along Battle Ridge showing the rutted dirt road that traversed the ground between the monument and Calhoun Hill in 1910. The cemetery appears at the extreme upper left. Photograph by Roland Reed.

The dead from Fort Phil Kearny, Wyoming Territory, were buried atop the ridge near the Seventh Cavalry Monument from 1888 to 1934. Markers for these graves were placed in 1889, and this photograph was taken a short time later.

Aerial views of the battlefield and national cemetery in the 1930s, showing the superintendent's stone house complex, cemetery rostrum, flagstaff, and the fenced monument and Last Stand grouping on Custer Hill. Adjoining the monument was a fifty-thousand-gallon water reservoir that provided a gravity feed to the cemetery and existing facilities.

The Reno–Benteen Memorial was erected and dedicated in 1929, three years after Congress authorized acquisition of 160 acres of the site. Appearance of Major Reno's name in the inscription on the tapered granite shaft was specifically vetoed by Elizabeth B. Custer. This view is from 1974.

The gabled, two-story stone lodge and appurtenant stable/outbuilding, erected in 1894–95, served as the home for superintendents throughout most of the period of War Department administration and well into that of the National Park Service.

The rostrum was built in the national cemetery in 1934 and was demolished in 1965. It functioned as a speakers' platform during activities and ceremonial occasions, such as those on Memorial Day in 1948.

A 1951 view to the northwest of the seventy-fifth anniversary proceedings shows a large crowd in attendance, besides the stone house with added residential unit and garage, the privy with privacy screen, a network of unimproved roads and trails, and unrestricted parking on prime battlefield terrain.

Cemetery view looking toward the newly completed visitor center and the monument in 1952. At left front is the Fifth Infantry Monument, which arrived at the battlefield in 1908, while the obelisk standing in right rear is the Fort C. F. Smith Monument, moved to the national cemetery in 1892.

Graveside service for returned World War II dead at the national cemetery, July 1949.

Cemetery view in June 1980.

Stone House renovation in 1998, during which the former superintendent's lodge was converted into the White Swan Memorial Library. Photo by Douglas J. Kuhlman.

Battle survivors in front of the Seventh Cavalry Monument, June 25, 1886. Photo by David F. Barry.

A firing demonstration with troops from Fort Custer during the tenth anniversary observance in 1886.

Cavalry soldiers pose before the monument on Memorial Day 1897.

Attendees and their vehicles arrayed on the surrounding hills at the semicentennial observance in June 1926.

Retired Brigadier General Edward S. Godfrey, a battle participant, exchanges gifts and shakes hands with White Bull, also a participant, in a symbolic show of peace and amity during the 1926 commemorative activities.

Commemorative medal sold during the 1926
fiftieth anniversary proceedings.

At the ceremony to dedicate the new visitor center and museum on June 25,
1952, General Jonathan Wainwright of World War II fame joined Superintendent
Edward S. Luce and Crow representative Art Bravo to present a rifle reportedly
retrieved from the Little Bighorn battlefield in 1876.

General Wainwright paying homage to the dead of Custer's command during the 1952 dedication ceremony.

On September 9, 1967, the remains of Major Marcus A. Reno, Custer's second-in-command during the battle, were interred with full military honors in the national cemetery amid a throng of dignitaries and observers in a ceremony that brought international publicity to Custer Battlefield National Monument.

Compared to the 1926 activities, the proceedings of the centennial observance of the Battle of the Little Bighorn in 1976 were restrained and marked by controversy on the part of both the National Park Service and Indian activists who used the event to promote their objectives. As shown here, Harold G. Stearns addressed approximately eight hundred people while other speakers waited behind the lectern, among them Russell Means (*far left*), National Park Service assistant director Robert M. Utley (*fourth from left*), and Superintendent Richard Hart (*sixth from left*). Means later took the podium with Utley seated directly behind him. Photo by Mary Minton.

At the 111th anniversary of the battle in 1988, Indian activists led by Russell Means momentarily commandeered the event to emplace a steel plaque honoring Indian participants at the Little Bighorn. The incident ultimately influenced the name change to Little Bighorn Battlefield National Monument and set the course for establishment of the Indian Memorial in 2003. Photo by Michael Donahue.

The Indian Memorial was dedicated on June 25, 2003, acknowledging all tribes who took part in the Battle of the Little Bighorn. The bronze *Spirit Warriors* sculpture evinces the courage of the Indian people in defending their families and lifeways at the time of the victory over Custer's command. This view from the north depicts the Indian Memorial in the foreground with the Seventh Cavalry Monument in the distance.

Park Historian John Doerner championed the placement of red granite markers for Indian warriors who fell in the battle whenever the sites could be thoroughly supported by documentation. On June 26, 2003, the day following dedication of the Indian Memorial, Doerner helped dedicate a marker to Dog's Backbone, a Minneconjou Lakota killed near the Reno–Benteen Defense site.

Elizabeth B. Custer played an essential role in early promotion of the battlefield, even though she could not bring herself to visit the site where her husband died.

Elizabeth B. Custer supported the concept of a "memorial hall" where battle-related items might be deposited, and engaged an architect to sketch such a building. Until her death in 1933, Mrs. Custer worked with state and federal officials for legislation to make a museum a reality. Her posthumous donation of relics, letters, manuscripts, and photographs provided a significant early foundation to the park's artifact collections.

When completed in 1952, the Custer Battlefield National Monument Museum and Visitor Center also housed the offices of the superintendent and historian.

Dedication ceremonies for the museum took place on the seventy-sixth anniversary of the battle, June 25, 1952. Posing at the entrance were, left to right, Superintendent Edward S. Luce; Colonel Brice C. W. Custer; Ned Burns, National Park Service exhibits planner; and Colonel William A. Harris, who had commanded the Seventh Cavalry in Korea.

In 1964–65 the visitor center underwent modification to include the addition of an observation deck and extended eaves on the east side of the building to help offset sun glare.

A four-unit apartment building for seasonal employees was erected in 1961–62, along with a maintenance building, located at the far right of this picture. Completion of both structures comprised part of the Mission 66 program at the park.

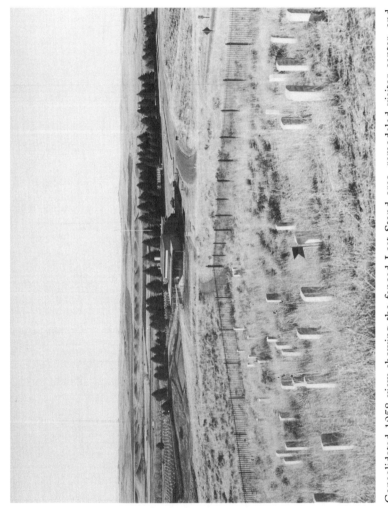

Consolidated 1958 view showing the fenced Last Stand area, remodeled visitor center, and parking area, together with the national cemetery interspersed with evergreen trees. Note the metal swallow-tailed flag denoting Custer's marker.

Among the many notable people who have visited the park over the years have been writers, government officials, religious leaders, foreign dignitaries, sports figures, and movie stars. In September 1949, novelist/historian Mari Sandoz (*Crazy Horse, Old Jules*) paid a visit and posed with Superintendent Luce amid the Last Stand grouping on Custer Hill.

The Little Bighorn battlefield has long drawn the notice of Hollywood, and many movies and television programs have been filmed either on site or in the immediate vicinity. In 1965 actor Walter Brennan posed with Superintendent Thomas Garry and two Crow youths during production of a documentary titled *End of the Trail*.

War Department guide William H. White stands before the superintendent's house in the 1920s.

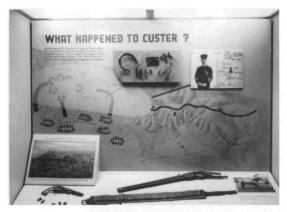

As indicated in these 1952 images, early exhibits in the museum and visitor center focused mainly on Custer, the battle story, and the history of the Seventh Cavalry, with few devoted to interpreting the presence of the "hostile" Sioux and Northern Cheyennes. Dioramas of Reno's retreat and the Last Stand proved especially popular and remain so today.

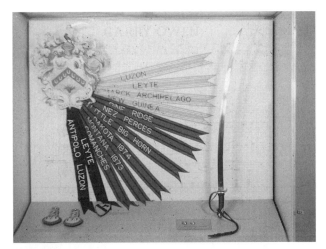

139

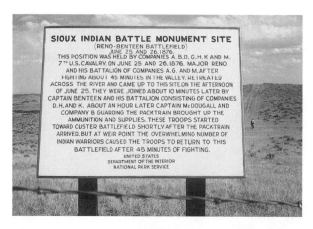

SIOUX INDIAN BATTLE MONUMENT SITE
(RENO-BENTEEN BATTLEFIELD)
JUNE 25 AND 26.1876.
THIS POSITION WAS HELD BY COMPANIES A. B.D. G.H. K AND M.
7TH U.S. CAVALRY. ON JUNE 25 AND 26.1876. MAJOR RENO
AND HIS BATTALION OF COMPANIES A.G. AND M.AFTER
FIGHTING ABOUT 45 MINUTES IN THE VALLEY. RETREATED
ACROSS THE RIVER AND CAME UP TO THIS SITE.ON THE AFTERNOON
OF JUNE 25. THEY WERE JOINED ABOUT 10 MINUTES LATER BY
CAPTAIN BENTEEN AND HIS BATTALION CONSISTING OF COMPANIES
D.H. AND K. ABOUT AN HOUR LATER CAPTAIN McDOUGALL AND
COMPANY B GUARDING THE PACKTRAIN BROUGHT UP THE
AMMUNITION AND SUPPLIES. THESE TROOPS STARTED
TOWARD CUSTER BATTLEFIELD SHORTLY AFTER THE PACKTRAIN
ARRIVED.BUT AT WEIR POINT. THE OVERWHELMING NUMBER OF
INDIAN WARRIORS CAUSED THE TROOPS TO RETURN TO THIS
BATTLEFIELD AFTER 45 MINUTES OF FIGHTING.
UNITED STATES
DEPARTMENT OF THE INTERIOR
NATIONAL PARK SERVICE

Early National Park Service interpretive markers. Those such as at the Reno–Benteen Defense Site in 1949 were replaced in 1953 with ten aluminum plaques attached to concrete bases that were installed at significant sites along the battlefield road. These remained for more than forty-five years, until replaced by porcelain enamel panels. A wooden marker denoting the area where Lame White Man fell was erected in 1956.

Interpretation in the late 1960s and early 1970s involved ranger tours and inter-action with visitors, such as at the Reno–Benteen Defense Site, as well as living history demonstrations wherein rangers donned period garb, fired weapons, and otherwise explained the dynamics of army–Indian warfare.

Living history afforded insights for park visitors into the lifeways of the Plains Indian tribes (1974), as well as perspectives of 1876 service in the U.S. Army (1995).

On July 21, 1949, Superintendent Luce oversaw relocation of the marker for First Sergeant James Butler. His assembly of Little Bighorn research students included, left to right, George G. Osten, Casey E. Barthelmess, Dan Bowman, Major George H. Zacherle, Floyd Cross, Lloyd C. Moss, and (Ret.) Colonel Elwood L. Nye).

In 1956 Park Historian Don Rickey, Jr., formalized the first significant research agenda for the park that included development of an administrative history, archeological recovery and restoration of the rifle pits at the Reno–Benteen Defense Site, and a reconnaissance survey of Nye–Cartwright Ridge.

Archeology at Reno–Benteen involved the excavation and restoration of rifle pits and trenches and included the recovery of soldier remains buried in them following the battle in 1876. This view shows the restored works, the numbered posts and interpretive markers, and, in the distance, the Reno–Benteen Memorial surrounded by an iron fence.

The grass fire that swept through the Custer battlefield area of the park on August 10, 1983, left a scorched and blackened landscape while damaging the foundations of some markers, yet paved the way for the first methodical archeological exploration of the battlefield terrain in 1984 and 1985. Bottom photograph by Daniel Martinez.

During the 1980s archeology dominated research at the park. In May and June 1984, volunteers working under archeologists Douglas D. Scott and Richard A. Fox, Jr., conducted a systematic metal detector survey of the seared ground, including the area of the Last Stand grouping. During a project in May 1994, archeologists unearthed a cavalry spur in the area between Deep Coulee and Calhoun Hill. Bottom photograph by Dick Harmon.

CHAPTER 6 | # National Park Service Administration, 1970–2000

With the departure of Edward S. Luce in 1956, Custer Battlefield National Monument lost a superintendent who had been steeped in the lore of the battlefield, intimately knew its ground, and intellectualized over its story. Thereafter, the National Park Service began a rotation of professional managers who, with a few notable exceptions, oversaw the park's administrative operations for relatively short periods before moving on to other assignments. Whereas Luce had provided a zeal for the story that the park conveyed, few others were so equipped by time and experience to follow his lead, although, fortunately, most proved to be capable stewards of the park resources. Yet a prevailing view in park service circles through much of the 1970s held that Custer Battlefield had become a training ground for novice superintendents or a pasturing zone for those on the brink of retirement. Daniel E. Lee, who succeeded Thomas Garry early in 1968, managed a park that attained national recognition for innovative interpretation, while it likewise wallowed in personnel issues. Lee became a victim of criminal assault by an irate seasonal employee and departed late in 1969. His successor, William A. Harris, brought administrative stability, although much of his time was diverted to scoping new areas along the Missouri River for the National Park Service.

Already in the Viet Nam era of the late 1960s and early 1970s the cumulative effects of best-selling books about Indians began to be registered. "Custer Had It Coming!" proclaimed bumper stickers adorning automobiles of the time. Antiestablishment Indian activist groups, such as the American Indian Movement, were gaining widespread public notice, and suggestions surfaced for changing the name of Custer Battle-field National Monument to something less personalized, more inclusive, and more in line with other units of the park system. In the years ahead, the issue of a possible name change, seeming to many a bow to political expediency, would generate longstanding controversy and debate on all sides of the matter. Such a recommendation formally appeared in the 1972 preliminary draft of the National Park Service master plan for the park: "Historians know the event as the Battle of the Little Bighorn—a well known title. Custer critics and many red Americans object to the present name of the National Monument. If impartiality and objectivity are to characterize future treatment of the battle story, to retain this name would be inconsistent."[1]

Meantime, visitation at the park topped 338,000 in 1971, an increase of more than 75,000 over the previous year. The 1972 plan, primarily driven by manifold interpretive changes recommended for the park partly to accommodate increased visitation, called for development to respond to what was in effect the physical reversal of the visitor experience and the enlargement of battlefield land mass in line with the previously discussed boundary expansion. Once the requisite land was obtained, a new visitor orientation facility would be located in the valley at Garryowen, and a new one-way access road would connect it with the road and parking area atop the bluffs at the Reno–Benteen Defense Site. According to the plan,

> The schematic route chosen for the new access road would roughly parallel the Reno retreat route to a point near the river where the visitor would leave his vehicle and walk a trail to the crossing site. . . . [The road] would continue up the river and cross it by bridge near Reno Creek. Swinging wide to the south and east of the entrenchment site to avoid marring the historic scene, . . . the road will top a ridge to the east from which a heavy concentration of Indian firing was directed. Here another stop would be made before dropping behind the ridge and moving up to the parking area at Reno Hill. The length of this new route would be approximately 5½ miles.

From that point, visitors would continue along the old park road through the remainder of the battlefield, moving with the historical flow of the action from south to north. Nearing the battle ridge and the monument, the road would diverge north from Calhoun Hill, circle north and west of the monument, and end at the parking lot adjoining the cemetery. Visitors would follow a walking path from there to the monument and, if desired, to Calhoun Hill. They would exit the park by backtracking to the north corner of the monument boundary and emerging on Highway 212. The former tour road leading along the battle ridge from Calhoun Hill to the monument was to be obliterated along with the parking area adjacent to the Last Stand area and the old entrance road. Anticipated increases in visitation based on trends called for adoption of "interpretive vehicles" at peak periods to shuttle visitors through the route.

Under the plan, the existing visitor center would be razed and all park administrative functions would be moved to the new facility. New maintenance buildings as well as employee housing would likewise be built at Garryowen, while the existing maintenance area would remain to serve cemetery needs. The old housing would remain for the use of law enforcement personnel, and the stone lodge, which was no longer used, would be operated as an interpretive building. Another question raised by the plan concerned cemetery expansion and expressed the belief that "expansion could [only] be made within existing Monument boundaries [and] would constitute a major intrusion upon the historic scene." (By late in the decade the cemetery would be temporarily closed to further burials except for those individuals with reserved spaces.)[2]

Although the 1972 plan envisioned grandiose changes based largely on interpretative concerns, its elements proved too radical and were perhaps too comprehensive and expensive to implement. In any event, the document was never approved, and its ultimate value lay in its original thinking about the interpretive configuration of battle-related resources that would influence all subsequent general management planning efforts at the park. In 1976 the parking lot at the Reno–Benteen area underwent reconstruction, and in 1978 modifications to the cemetery infiltration system permitted an increased water storage capacity for use during periods of extended drought. In addition, a new buried concrete reservoir was installed for domestic water use and fire protection, and a water treatment system and evaporation pond were built in the area bordering the northwest boundary of the park.[3]

An administrative change affecting management categorization of the national monument resources occurred in 1975, when two in-park historic districts were established. District 1 embraced the battlefield proper, consisting of the Custer and Reno–Benteen portions of the field and including the granite memorial monument atop battle ridge and that commemorating the activities at the Reno–Benteen Defense Site. It also embraced the two hundred plus stone markers designating the places where the members of Custer's command likely fell in the engagement. District 2 comprised the national cemetery, which in fact formed an enclave within the battlefield district, and included nearly four thousand graves plus the Fort Keough monuments and the Fort Smith marker, several ornamental markers, the historic 1908 flagstaff, and the stone lodge built in 1894. The rationale for creating the historic districts lay in the desire to create hierarchical levels of historic integrity (with District 2 having less integrity) so as to accommodate intrusive landscape issues like evergreen growth affecting the cemetery. Despite this, the district categorization proved fleeting and was evidently abolished or forgotten within a few years. During 1978 and 1979, restoration of the interior of the stone lodge in the cemetery took place, funded by the park's formal cooperating organization, the Custer Battlefield Museum and Historical Association (see chapter 9).[4]

In 1975 a "Statement for Management" was formulated and approved for the park (and reapproved with minor modifications in later years). Acknowledging the national cemetery, it articulated the primary purpose for the national monument: "to preserve and protect all historic resources pertaining to the Battle of the Little Big Horn and provide for a greater understanding of the battle, the events which led up to the encounter, and various effects it had on the future." Clearly stated management objectives included the management of "natural resources so as to continue to maintain the general environmental scene as it appeared at the time of the Battle of the Little Bighorn in 1876," as well as "the preservation and protection of historic structures, relics, artifacts, and museum collections" for public education, research, and enjoyment. The "Statement for Management" served to guide park administrators in the stewardship of the park's resources. In acknowledgement of the era-driven broadening of the interpretive story (discussed at length in chapter 7), the document noted that the "Battlefield represents more than Custer's engagement with 'Indians'; therefore, the story and all supporting facilities should in no way overshadow the pride and tradition associated with either force involved. There should be no psychological barriers to draw attention to any one particular individual or groups of individuals."[5]

While earnest park planning efforts in the early 1970s became reduced to a series of unapproved imaginative proposals and annually parroted bureaucratic statements for management, administrative focus at Custer Battlefield National Monument by mid-decade quickly turned to the upcoming centennial of the Battle of the Little Bighorn and appropriate commemorative activities at the park. Ironically, the centennial's arrival coincided with wide-scale upsurge in militant activity by several prominent American Indian activist groups. The most notable of these was the American Indian Movement (AIM). Founded during the politically turbulent 1960s, the group railed against perceived injustice against Indian people, both historical and contemporary, and advocated improvement of Indian conditions nationwide. It drew national publicity to its cause through such events as the nineteen-month occupation of Alcatraz Island in 1969–70, the takeover of Bureau of Indian Affairs headquarters in 1972, and the occupation of Wounded Knee, South Dakota, in 1973. The symbolism and anticipated publicity surrounding the upcoming one-hundredth anniversary observance of the Battle of the Little Bighorn made the event tailored for AIM interests and assured polarization preceding and during the event.

Anticipating possible trouble, the National Park Service planned scaled-down activities compared to the ceremonies respecting the fiftieth anniversary in 1926. Superintendent Richard T. Hart and Park Historian Richard Rambur coordinated the upcoming observance. Park service regional officials beefed up security at the battlefield, adding law enforcement personnel from other parks. Threatened archival and artifact collections were transported to Eastern Montana College of Education in Billings for safekeeping. Hoping to avoid confrontation with AIM, events scheduled to begin on June 25, 1976, were advanced to Thursday, June 24. The day was cool and rainy, and attendance was low, with fewer than one thousand people appearing. Music was provided by the Ninth Division U.S. Army Band, which also played the national anthem. As the ceremony began, members of AIM unexpectedly paraded into view to chants and drumbeats. "[They were] quickly welcomed by surprised officials," related one correspondent. Superintendent Hart quickly arranged a truce (thereby possibly avoiding confrontation) and allowed Russell Means, a director of the organization, time before the microphone. "As park rangers watched, the 150 men, women and children circled visitors seated before the speakers' platform while [Oscar] Running Bear, Means and others

mounted the platform carrying the United States flag upside down."
"We bear no ill will," said Means, who briefly addressed those present
on the current state of Indian affairs. The Indians soon departed,
moving up the ridge to the monument, which they danced around
while singing.

The speeches, meantime, continued at the podium. Superintendent
Hart delivered the formal opening remarks, calling on his listeners to
"honor all who died in the Battle of the Little Bighorn—civilian, soldier,
and warrior." The keynote address was delivered by Robert M. Utley,
the National Park Service's assistant director for cultural resources, as
well as a preeminent western historian, who as a young ranger had
worked at the park during the seventy-fifth anniversary in 1951. Utley's
measured remarks urged listeners to learn from the past but to not
interpret it in terms of modern morality. "My plea," he said,

> is that we temper our judgments with understanding, under-
> standing of the forces that caused essentially decent people to do
> what they did. We do not have the obligation, we do not even
> have the right, to indict these people—or to forgive them for that
> matter—for actions that may be offenses according to the stan-
> dards and perceptions of today but were not according to those
> of yesterday. . . . The injustice of the past did not necessarily
> spring from evil motives but rather from a set of values and
> assumptions that were entirely plausible in their time and place."

On June 25 the Indians conducted a sunrise ceremony near the
monument to honor their dead in the battle. The observance continued
at 10 a.m., the day dedicated to the fallen of all American wars. Cool
rainy weather mixed with sunshine as Harold G. ("Hal") Stearns of
Helena, Montana, state director of the American Revolution Bicentennial Administration, addressed some eight hundred attendees, many
huddled under umbrellas. In addition to Means, who appeared again,
spokesmen from the Northern Cheyenne, Lakota, and Crow tribes
made remarks, and the Lakota holy man Frank Fool's Crow joined
Stearns in laying a memorial wreath as the two joined hands in friendship. Fool's Crow, in addition, dedicated words ascribed to the Oglala
holy man Black Elk that had been placed in both Lakota and English
on the front of the visitor center: "Know the Power that is Peace."
Elsewhere in the vicinity, a group of Californians arrayed as 1876 soldiers

rode horses along Custer's route from the divide to the ford at the foot of Medicine Tail Coulee. Aged George Osten of Billings, who had erected the marker to scout Charley Reynolds in the valley thirty-eight years earlier, continued his annual tradition of placing a wreath at the site. While the centennial observance never approached in attendance or in variety of activities those of the semicentennial proceedings, the events, despite the weather and prevalent political undercurrents, were conducted in a spirit of dignity and inspiration. In its planning, however, the National Park Service had purposefully not extended formal invitations to the Custer family, a slight that angered many people present, and the last-minute granting of permission to Colonel George Armstrong Custer III to lay a family wreath at the monument appeared contrived and disingenuous at best.[6]

The National Park Service's handling of the proceedings for the centennial of the Battle of the Little Bighorn, notably its efforts to assure balance in the program as well as attaining security sufficient to protect against potential violence, reflected the uncertain temperament of the Vietnam postwar period. The event produced lingering rancor and alienated elements of various constituency groups for years thereafter, although its positive long-term influence on the park's interpretive program would be significant.[7]

Superintendent Hart retired from the government in May 1978. His replacement, James V. Court, brought an enthusiasm for historic preservation and a parallel fervor for a balanced Little Bighorn story. He would remain in the position for more than eight years, until late 1986, overseeing a spate of activities designed to improve interpretation and responsible development at the park. For most of Court's tenure, he was joined by Neil C. Mangum, an insightful and experienced Virginian with a passion for Indian wars history and who shared Court's zeal for promoting preservation management and evenhanded presentation. Both men would serve during particularly important periods in the battlefield's history, notably during a challenge to the park's interpretive program that arose in the mid-1980s (see chapters 7 and 9) and during and following the grass fire that swept the area during the summer of 1983, as well as during the resulting archeological projects that brought international attention to the park. Singly and together, Court and Mangum would leave longstanding imprints on the Little Bighorn battlefield. (Throughout the 1970s and 1980s, many of the park's interpretation-related efforts, including research projects, were augmented by dollars and support received through the sale of books and related products by the Custer Battlefield Museum and Historical Association [see chapter 9]).

Between 1982 and 1986 Court and Mangum worked with an interdisciplinary team of park planners and the public in formulating a new general management plan (formerly termed a master plan) to guide the future of Custer Battlefield National Monument. National Park Service management policies called for the completion of general management plans for every National Park Service unit to provide a guiding philosophy and management strategies for addressing park issues over a five- to ten-year period. Beyond the unapproved, interpretation-driven preliminary schematic of 1972, no comprehensive plan had been prepared and approved for Custer Battlefield since fulfillment of Mission 66 objectives in the 1960s. The effort of the early to mid-1980s to remedy that deficiency built upon the earlier proposals and necessarily reiterated the boundary expansion needs that had been formally proposed beginning in the 1950s.[8]

Throughout the period the plan was being formulated, Superintendent Court worked to build partnerships as well as to obtain land so that the requisite boundary expansion could occur. Fears existed that much private undeveloped land might be sold for vacation homes, motels, tourist businesses, convenience stores, and other endeavors. In 1982, in a move supported by some Crow tribal officials but that goaded his park service superiors, Court met as a private citizen with Secretary of the Interior Donald Hodel to express his concerns about the park. The secretary suggested formation of a nonprofit corporation to accept donations with which to purchase the land parcels needed to assure protection of the battlefield resources and view shed. Court thereupon established the Custer Battlefield Preservation Committee, with himself as executive director and Harold G. Stanton of Hardin as chairman and later president, and immediately began soliciting donations with which to purchase the requisite parcels of land. Years later, Court reminisced about this enterprise (which lasted well beyond his tenure as superintendent): "We set up a donation box in the visitor center. Custer groups were contacted and slowly money started pouring in; well, not exactly pouring in. In 1982 we took in $7, 837 while we needed about $500,000 for those first two parcels. We had a long way to go. In the intervening years other land was offered to us and by about 1990 we had raised nearly $3,000,000 and paid for about 2,200 acres of land. Most of these donations were small, but occasionally a nice size check would show up and surprise me."[9] The general management plan and collateral development concept plans, hinged as they were on the boundary adjustment/land protection zone, took several years to prepare. The document, with its range of alternatives, was released to the public in November 1985, and hearings were held in Billings, Sheridan, and Hardin. Following the review process, which included input from the Crow Tribe, the plan was approved on August 18, 1986. Important identified issues addressed in the document included the need to (1) identify the historic resources including the historic setting (natural resource) as they relate to the Battle of the Little Bighorn at Custer Battlefield and the surrounding area and set into motion methods of protection and preserving these resources for future generations; (2) reduce heavy visitor impact at Last Stand Hill, a prime national cultural resource, and improve visitor facilities; (3) provide the visitor with a better comprehension of the events and historic perspective of the Battle of the Little Bighorn.[10]

Under the preferred alternative, the projected park boundary would embrace a broadly encompassing view shed that expanded far beyond the original 1879 and 1929 tracts and bordered both U.S. Highway 212 and Interstate 90 to create a vaguely triangular swath some three miles wide by six miles long and adding more than twelve thousand acres to the monument grounds. Partly enclosing lands donated by the Land Preservation Committee, the area would take in all known and presumed battle terrain, including tracts on either side of the Little Bighorn, and incorporate the ground where the Indian village stood in 1876. Somewhat like its 1972 predecessor, the plan envisioned a wayside exhibit at the Garryowen area of Reno's first skirmish line and a shuttle tour road leading east toward the river, then skirting south, east, and north to gain the Reno–Benteen Defense Site and connecting with the existing tour road. The plan proposed a new visitor orientation/administration facility complete with 150-seat auditorium to be located one-quarter mile south of Highway 212, near the present entrance road and beyond view of Custer Hill and the monument. (The old visitor center and its adjoining parking area would be obliterated and the sites restored to their presumed 1876 appearance.) Other changes involved creation of a picnic area near the Highway 212 entrance/exit point, construction of an underground restroom at Reno–Benteen, and a new parking lot to accommodate oversized vehicles at the Garryowen location. Visitors might tour the site in their own vehicles or use the shuttle system (bus tours had been introduced in the early 1980s). While the plan would permit the continued pursuit of agriculture on lands recommended for inclusion within the revised boundary, "it would preclude industrial, commercial, residential, and other developments that may adversely affect the landscapes' historic association with the national monument." It would not permit plowing new prairie, construction of additional buildings or roads, or above-ground power lines. The plan required an increase in staffing for the park to include additional seasonal positions. Total anticipated cost of implementing the 1986 plan stood at nearly $8.5 million.[11]

Despite wide concurrence in the plan, it required a congressional appropriation to bring it to fruition, and that did not occur. The matter of boundary expansion required additional legislation from Congress, as well as approval from the Crow Tribe and local authorities. A National Park Service news release specified that "the added lands would be protected by a combination of zoning, easement, agreement or purchase with funds provided by the Custer Battlefield Preservation Committee, Inc." The reality was that the 1986 plan, broadly conceived, was aborted by an undercurrent of local and federal politics, compounded by economically recessive times, which practically assured that the required land base would never materialize. Without the land base—to be derived from Crow tribal and individual land holdings—the rest of the plan was bound to fail. Eventually, many tribal members came to oppose any transactions that they believed would remove their ultimate control over Indian-owned land; some feared condemnation of their lands. Under these circumstances, Superintendent Court's valiant efforts to acquire the needed property to effect boundary expansion went for naught, and late in 1986 he took early retirement to continue his preservation effort. The Crow Tribe passed a resolution in 1987 opposing the boundary expansion. (Over the next sixteen years, under Court's and Stanton's leadership, the Custer Battlefield Preservation Committee managed to acquire by lease or ownership more than thirty-two hundred acres, including critical property lying adjacent to the entrance road, in Medicine Tail Coulee, and surrounding the Reno–Benteen Defense Site, that, with congressional action, could be turned over to the park.)[12]

The land-protection interpretation-driven general management plan recommended for Custer Battlefield National Monument was not abandoned following Court's departure. Over the next several years legislative support packages went forward to the Washington office of the National Park Service for action, but little of substance resulted.

Meantime, for its land expansion needs and developmental concerns the National Trust for Historic Preservation added the park to its "most threatened" list, and Court's successor, Dennis L. Ditmanson, wrote that "one effect [of the designation] . . . will be to focus the attention of a wider audience on the situation here at the park." Superintendent Ditmanson commented within weeks after a contingent of AIM members accompanied Russell Means to the Custer monument on June 25, 1988, bringing into sharp focus the issues of evenhanded interpretation and bipartisan monumentation. The Indians reportedly desecrated the mass soldier grave, leaving behind a crudely fashioned steel plaque designed as a memorial to those Indians who had died in the battle. The plaque was later removed to the visitor center, where it was placed on exhibit. "Had the Service taken a more active part in the process in years past," wrote Ditmanson, "this incident could probably have been avoided." The episode nonetheless created a template by which an appropriate Indian memorial at the park was eventually realized (see chapter 10).[13]

In July 1989, doubtless partly in reaction to the attention to revising interpretation at the site generated by the centennial observance, National Park Service Rocky Mountain regional director Lorraine Mintzmyer appointed Barbara Booher, a Ute-Cherokee woman—a first in two categories—as park superintendent of Custer Battlefield National Monument. Cognizant of rising issues vis-à-vis modern Indian involvement at the site of the Sioux-Northern Cheyenne victory over Custer in 1876, Booher managed a park in flux both administratively and interpretively. The 1986 general management plan remained in effect but clearly had lost the support of the immediate Crow community as well as the Montana congressional delegation, and its implementation was altogether stymied. In 1990 the Crows resolved to support the concept of a new visitor center. Yet external threats, as outlined in the park's "Statement for Management" included the plan of "a private group of developers . . . [to build] a 60,000 square foot park visitor center, 65,000 square foot Crow cultural museum, and 65,000 square foot northern plains Indian museum, as well as a shrine to receive remains of Indian people." The proposal went clearly beyond the changes necessary as outlined in the 1986 plan.

Reflective of a growing national maturity regarding Indian–white history and Indian affairs, much of it inspired since the 1960s by groups such as AIM, by late 1990 several actions were underway to modify aspects of the park experience and make it more inclusive for

Indian people. In February 1991 the long-discussed and controversial name change issue was formally advanced in Congress, when Democratic Representative Ben Nighthorse Campbell, a Coloradoan of Cheyenne ancestry, introduced House Resolution 847 to change the name of the park to Little Bighorn Battlefield National Monument and to authorize construction of an appropriate Indian memorial there. The latter provision promised overdue recognition of all tribal sacrifices at the Little Bighorn and had accordingly been approved and a location tentatively selected by public involvement and an Indian Memorial task force. Despite considerable contention from Custer support groups who opposed the pending legislation, as well as proactive stances by AIM and other Indian activists, the measure, revised as House Resolution 848, won Senate concurrence and passed without opposition on November 22, 1991, and was signed into law by President George H. W. Bush on December 10, 1991. The Custer name was retained on the national cemetery. "We are relieved the process is over," said Superintendent Booher at the news. The legislation simultaneously authorized the design, construction, and maintenance of an Indian memorial at the site, funding for which was to come from donations. A ceremony recognizing the name change, attended by Lakota and Northern Cheyenne descendants of battle participants, was held at the park on Veterans Day 1992. However, further immediate changes involving implementation of the general management plan that would have showcased the new name and the Indian Memorial did not occur. An effort in 1992–95 to amend the 1986 plan included the addition of an alternate location for the visitor/administrative center west of Interstate 90 near Garryowen, besides enhanced exhibits reflecting recent archeological discoveries and an updated visitor circulation system. The revision was not approved, however, and the original 1986 plan, which had essentially been approved for more than a decade, went unimplemented.[14]

Although other matters competed for administrative attention during the 1990s, none drew more public notice than did events related to the name change, and especially the consequent Indian Memorial (see chapter 10), which brought a visit from Secretary of the Interior Manuel Lujan, Jr., in June 1990. Because of the national attention, moreover, Superintendent Booher found herself keynote speaker at various cultural awareness and equal opportunity events both regionally and nationally as word of the significant changes at Little Bighorn spread around the country. In an audacious planning move, the National Park Service secretly entered into a sixteen-month agreement in September 1992 with North Shield Ventures, Inc., a firm partially funded by a sub-sidiary of Time-Warner Communications, to explore the feasibility of undertaking a wide-scale partnership project that would reportedly produce an "enhanced living history experience near the [national] Monument." If carried out, the resulting development promised "a private sector partnership that would enhance the park's operating budget through donated funds, the private funding of a new visitor center, and resource protection."

Other matters concerned an incident of vandalism in the cemetery in July 1991 that caused significant damage to the flagstaff, and the theft from the museum exhibit in February 1992 of a prized battle-related relic, the diary carried by First Lieutenant Donald McIntosh, who was killed in Major Reno's valley action, which prompted FBI involvement and a major security and collections storage appraisal by the Rocky Mountain Regional Office. (The McIntosh diary was never recovered; it was later learned that the perpetrator of the crime, eventually appre-hended, had purposefully destroyed the artifact valued at $120,000.) And despite the conducive atmosphere generated by the name change and the forthcoming Indian Memorial, the battlefield remained a flash-point for Indian issues; on June 11, 1992, Russell Means and a group of AIM members attending a sun dance on private land near Medicine Tail Coulee Ford promoted confrontation with park service personnel by blocking the tour road at the south entrance/exit to the Custer battlefield tract in the interests of religious privacy. Park managers negotiated with the Indians, and Superintendent Booher, hoping to avoid conflict, agreed to close the route until the dance concluded four days later.[15]

But it was the North Shield Ventures project that brought continued attention to Little Bighorn Battlefield National Monument between 1992 and 1994. It was the height of the era of "partnerships" between government and private entities; such enterprises held promise with park service officials because they conceivably could help keep federal costs down while providing the public with greater benefits from a park experience. In the case of the North Shield Ventures proposal, National Park Service director James Ridenour looked to "tremendous economic advantages" for the Crow Indians and the State of Montana. In concept, the plan called for North Shield, through its president, Lawson S. Warren, to build a living history theme park a few miles from the entrance to the national monument. In somewhat convoluted fashion, Crow trust land would be purchased by Warren and his backers, given back to the tribe, and leased to the corporation, which would construct and operate the park. The National Park Service viewed its involvement as an opportunity to free up the logjam regarding land and the boundary proposed by the 1986 general management plan and to permit large-scale protection for property that conceivably could otherwise be opened to piecemeal development, thus impinging on the historic scene.

Opponents included several Battle of the Little Bighorn interest groups who believed that the National Park Service was, in effect, forsaking its responsibility by yielding control to private interests, thus jeopardizing the site. In fact, a memorandum of understanding signed by the National Park Service, the Crow Tribe, and North Shield sought only to explore the concept of a thirty-year partnership between government and private enterprise under which North Shield would construct and operate a visitor center and museum complex off park lands, build any required federal housing, and maintain the cemetery in return for exclusive rights to tours and concessions. Initially, North Shield would contribute funding to study a historic trail system, support related sites, archeology, and help finance the recently approved Indian Memorial (estimated total cost of the entire North Shield Ventures project: $65 million). "There seems to be a belief that the North Shield proposal is a sinister plot intended to destroy the battlefield," wrote Acting Superintendent Douglas C. McChristian. "Let me say for the record [that] there is no plot. There is no threat to the battlefield. The National Park Service has no intention of abdicating its responsibilities." McChristian assured critics that public meetings would ensue and that the plan would undergo rigorous scrutiny before any decision was reached. Yet the controversy continued, with figures like Robert M. Utley describing the proposal as "radical and potentially calamitous" and likening it to "turning over to a private entity part of the public trust. It must not happen."

Fifteen public hearings on the measure were held in Montana, Colorado, and Washington, D.C. Early in 1994 National Park Service director Roger Kennedy requested financial statements from the North Shield Venture partners and asked for a report on the consequences at Little Bighorn Battlefield National Monument should the project fail. Ultimately, inquiries over projections of annual gross sales and financial support, concerns from surrounding tribes, and the unending storm of controversy that swirled over the project joined to kill National Park Service involvement. The government formally withdrew its support, citing inadequate information on which to base a decision to proceed. North Shield continued planning discussions under its agreement with the Crow Tribe, however, and forecasted construction of its project by the spring of 1998. Yet it never happened, and the North Shield Ventures living history experience concept gradually melted away.[16]

The ambitious North Shield plan dominated news of Little Bighorn Battlefield National Monument throughout the early 1990s, even though management dealt with a host of other issues affecting the park. Superintendent Booher departed early in 1993 for a regional position, leaving McChristian as acting superintendent until September 1993, when Gerard Baker, a Mandan-Hidatsa raised on the Fort Berthold Reservation in North Dakota, arrived to succeed her. As superintendent, Baker welcomed various tribes that had historical associations with the Battle of the Little Bighorn. He also dealt with ever-controversial interpretation of the site, remaining more than four years before transferring to Chickasaw National Recreation Area in Oklahoma early in 1998. In the spring of 1999, Neil C. Mangum, who had served as historian and occasionally acting superintendent at the park from 1979 to 1988, returned as superintendent. Over the next three years, with park operating budgets now exceeding $700,000 annually, Mangum played major roles in improving interpretation and assuring resource protection while contending with increasing development issues. He coordinated with multiple groups the events that culminated in the 125th anniversary of the Battle of the Little Bighorn and helped pave the way for final realization of the Indian Memorial.[17]

Projects initiated in the 1990s included the rehabilitation of the museum, an attempt to maximize space given the limitations of the visitor center building while upgrading the existing room and adding exhibits. Admission fees, which had been instituted in 1987 ($3), were raised several times in the 1990s and early 2000s to support various projects, including the Indian Memorial. In compliance with the Native American Graves Protection and Repatriation Act, an inventory of human remains and funerary objects was completed at the park. (Appropriate remains were returned in 1997.) In 1995 Superintendent Baker contended with the prospect of a home and gift store being constructed on allotted reservation ground between the Custer and Reno–Benteen sites. Before it waned, the project scarred land bordering the Reno–Benteen site, and the tenant bulldozed land and drilled a well near the tour road.

On the 119th anniversary of the battle, Baker invited descendants of battle participants to attend ceremonies at the park. Crows, Lakotas, Northern Cheyennes, and Arapahos joined with members of the Seventh

Cavalry Memorial Association in presenting programs during the observance; similar activities continued in succeeding years. Cooperative and outreach activities became a mainstay of Baker's tenure.

In 1997–98, a visitor survey was conducted to help the park comply with the Government Performance and Results Act (GPRA); it showed that in all categories public satisfaction remained high. A strategic plan was inaugurated looking to long-range mission objectives of the park and the National Park Service, particularly yearly preservation of resources, public enjoyment, and organizational effectiveness. Visitor congestion, however, remained high at peak summer periods, and the park investigated alternative transportation systems in 1998–99, hoping to alleviate the problem. Although a guided bus tour operation begun in 1995 and conducted hourly each summer by Little Big Horn College (Crow Agency) helped alleviate the situation, the transportation study urged consideration of expansion of parking areas, widening the tour road, a reservation system, a remote parking and transit or shuttle system, and improved signage.

Visitation, after dipping slightly during the early 1990s, rebounded late in the decade, with more than 370,000 entrants to the park recorded in 1998. Although the park still awaited implementation of its long-suffering plan, its administration under Superintendent Mangum enjoyed improved relationships with park neighbors. Through cultivation of good community ties, the park staff, now 60 percent minority, with many from the local area, became more involved in civic programs, thus improving overall relationships with area tourism groups and private and public offices. In 1998 park staff opened discussions with the Crow Tribe to explore the concept of a visitor center/tribal cultural center in the vicinity of Garryowen, in line with the general management plan. In 1999–2000 the park worked with the Crows toward obtaining through purchase a vacated museum building in the valley close to the location conceived in the general management plan but finally backed away from paying an outstanding half-million-dollar debt on the facility in favor of developing conceptual plans for an entirely new structure. And in 2001 Senator Ben Nighthorse Campbell introduced a bill "to expand and enhance the Little Bighorn Battlefield National Monument." The measure, designed to permit inclusion of donated land held by the Custer Battlefield Preservation Committee, would protect the integrity of the site from development by appointment of an enhancement committee to maintain a registry of available land that might be conveyed to the national monument. The Crow

Tribe still resisted boundary expansion, however, leaving the bill fated to die in committee.

Throughout the 1980s and 1990s, the customary observances continued at the park and in the national cemetery, as well as in the surrounding communities. Each year since the 1980s, Little Big Horn Days in nearby Hardin continued to draw visitors for arts and crafts fairs, book sales, and related activities set around the locally arranged battle reenactments. At the park, Memorial Day activities continued, involving veteran groups and annual addresses. Each anniversary of the battle saw special recognition in ceremonies conducted at the monument. In 1986 the Northern Cheyennes celebrated a World Day of Peace there, preceding reburials in the cemetery for the remains of three dozen troopers uncovered during the archeological projects of 1983–84, a ceremony attended by John D. McDermott, representing the Advisory Council on Historic Preservation. Special events included the dedication of a marker for army scout Minton ("Mitch") Boyer in 1988 and the 1991 burial of a Seventh Cavalryman found two years earlier, attended by National Park Service chief historian Edwin C. Bearss. A special program in 1991 commemorated the fiftieth anniversary of Pearl Harbor. Beginning in 1995, when Gerard Baker was superintendent, members of all tribes that took part in the battle participated in the annual ceremonies; the observance of 1996, hosted by members of the Lakotas, Northern Cheyennes, Northern Arapahos, Crows, and Arikaras, highlighted a theme of "Peace, Unity, and Friendship."[18]

Worldwide interest in the Battle of the Little Bighorn was manifested early in 2001, when Superintendent Mangum traveled to Dresden, Germany, for the opening of a special exhibit on the battle at the Karl May Museum, named for the Saxonian author of historical novels of the American West. In June at the park, Mangum presided over the 125th anniversary of the Battle of the Little Bighorn, when more than six thousand visitors witnessed an extensive multicultural program comprising the observance, with descendants of soldiers and warriors and their families in attendance. (One was ninety-two-year-old Minnie Grace Mechling Carey, whose father, Private Henry W. B. Mechling, received the Medal of Honor for service with Reno and Benteen.) Guests read the names of the fallen in the battle, and a wreath-laying ceremony occurred at the mass grave of soldiers as F-16 fighters winged overhead. Later, the unveiling of a stone marker for Long Robe, a Sans Arc Lakota killed near the Reno–Benteen perimeter, concluded the events. The activities proceeded without disruption or incident.

Adding to the afterglow of the 125th anniversary and the inclusive-ness of that observance was receipt early in 2002 of word that Congress had approved $2.3 million for the Indian Memorial, finally moving that long-delayed project significantly toward completion (see chapter 10). Visitation, meantime, jumped from 365,000 in 2001 to nearly 430,000 in 2002.[19]

Except for the Indian Memorial, physical development at the national monument over the three-plus decades since 1970 has largely been confined to serving marginal needs and associated maintenance of the park and cemetery. Because of nonagreement over land matters, the site development outlined in the 1986/95 general management plan has remained stifled for lack for funds. As regards the broad battlefield domain, however, certain onsite development was required because of constantly increasing visitation through the decades. Since 1987 fee-demonstration monies, composed of a percentage of entrance fee dollars applied to essential park projects to enhance visitor services, have greatly facilitated progress. A major design and construction effort was a new two-lane electronically controlled main entrance gate and fee collection station patterned after the architecture of the old stone lodge in the cemetery. Final plans were approved in late 1992, with construction slated to start in the autumn of 1993. Other construction and mainte-nance involved the 1991 replacement of the roof on the visitor center, renovation of several rooms inside the building, including the restrooms, which were made handicapped accessible, remodeling of the entrance on the visitor center's north façade, removal of the west restroom entrance, and construction of a disabled access ramp that significantly altered the north side of the building. Also during the year the park employee residences received upgrades, including additional insulation. In 1995 a maintenance storage area was completed and a park road sealing project finished, while a water sewer rehabilitation project was completed two years later involving the establishment of a three-acre sewer drain field and appurtenant dosing and septic tanks and sewer lines. An addition was built on the pump house, and that structure was reroofed.

That same year also saw rehabilitation of the curator's office, storage area, and vault in the basement of the visitor center and installation of computer lines throughout the building. Within five years, major enhancements had been made to the sales area of the visitor center, necessitating the removal of the restrooms and the reconfiguration of the entire northwest portion of its north façade. Detached restrooms were erected on an island in the parking lot adjoining the building, the work partially funded by the Southwest Parks and Monuments cooperating association. Plans were also formulated to upgrade the visitor center's air conditioning system. In 2000 park maintenance joined with workers of the Montana Conservation Corps in replacing the barbed wire boundary fence, in the process extending the western fence line to its legally prescribed limit along the east side of the Little Bighorn River, thereby assuming control of approximately fifteen previously unfenced acres. A major development in 2003 was the conversion of an employee residence into an administration building complete with offices, permitting the superintendent to move and open needed administrative space for expansion within the visitor center. (The construction, while relieving cramped office accommodations, grossly modified a Mission 66 structure, while showing scant regard for longstanding aesthetic values.) Also, in June 2003, in anticipation of the dedication of the Indian Memorial, the Seventh Cavalry monument received a thorough cleaning, a project financially helped by battlefield supporters.[20]

The cemetery continued to receive routine maintenance attention in the form of interments, irrigation, and mowing through the period, and with park service efforts to highlight its historical role in the battle-field story it became a more integrated component of overall park interpretation. In 1997 a building addition to house a new iron removal system was completed; longtime buildup of iron deposits in the water discolored the marble grave markers, necessitating their cleaning by hand. New water lines were installed, and two supply pumps were rebuilt to facilitate the cleaning process. A major event regarding the cemetery was the rehabilitation of the stone house (former superintendent's residence) into the park library and historian's office administered by the park historian, a move that freed up space in the visitor center curatorial area. The work involved insulating the building, upgrading its basement, painting and refinishing woodwork, improving the floors, and installing a security system.

On September 4, 1998, the stone house was dedicated as the White Swan Memorial Library for one of the six Crow scouts in the battle (and whose remains repose in the cemetery). A descendant of White Swan, Scott Russell, spoke of the scout, while Joseph Medicine Crow provided some history of the old building. By the move, the library and research collection, previously housed in the visitor center, could better accommodate researchers in a secure and relatively quiet setting. Park Historian John Doerner and Park Curator Kitty Belle Deer

Nose together organized the new library, and Doerner became the first occupant of the facility in its new mission. In 2001 the building was repointed. A water shortage that year forced rationing, which resulted in the cemetery lawn and vegetation enduring considerable stress. The following year included beginning efforts in the cemetery to replace with a replica the weathered limestone Fort C. F. Smith marker, which would be dismantled and stored away securely (this project funded by battlefield support groups); installation of a touch-screen computerized registry of nearly five thousand interments in the cemetery; reconstruction of the road through the cemetery from the stone house to the flag staff and installation of handicapped accessible parking; reconditioning of the original War Department–era iron gates; and replacement of the outmoded cemetery irrigating system.[21]

At Little Bighorn Battlefield National Monument, development within the park has frequently coincided with resource management and protection. That part of the National Park Service mission at the site— protection and preservation of resources for the enjoyment and education of future generations—has not been accomplished easily through the years, with visitation continuing to rise since the 1960s. Periodically prepared resource management plans (one in 1991–92 another in 1998–99) have assured continuing balanced use and protection of park resources. The principal resources, of course, have remained the battle-field and cemetery complexes, and their appurtenances—the markers and monuments (and including all plants and wildlife)—and their care and preservation must always remain the utmost concern of management. By the 1990s, as the number of interments dropped significantly, work at the cemetery involved stabilizing graves, requiring the temporary removal of perhaps 80 percent of the headstones while mud-jacking the plots and releveling the terrain. As mentioned, discoloration of the markers in the cemetery from iron content in the irrigation water had been a longstanding problem that had defied easy solution until relatively recently, when a new water filtering system was installed. Likewise, the Seventh Cavalry monument atop Custer Hill has required cleaning to remove mineral staining from irrigating water, as well as stabilizing and periodic routine maintenance.

The markers on the battlefield have also received maintenance attention through the years. In 1978 Superintendent Court had the stones inventoried according to condition, and in 1984 the broken ones were replaced (along with some within the cemetery); some battlefield markers were stolen only to turn up in remote places across the country.

(At least one original marker went up for auction until the park intervened.) The bases of some of the original markers were bricked and set in concrete, and, as indicated, their care and continued maintenance has become a major effort. Some new markers have been added to the battlefield too. The steel plaque installed by AIM atop the mass grave on Custer Hill in 1988 was removed to be preserved in the visitor center museum (see chapter 10). Other Indian-raised markers, at least six stone cairns placed through the years by relatives of battle participants, remain in place on the Reno–Benteen and Custer fields. The site where Cheyenne leader Lame White Man fell was marked with a sign on the latter field in 1958. A nearby cairn has been ascribed to the spot where another Cheyenne, Noisy Walking, was mortally wounded. A tribal cairn was erected by 1998 at Reno–Benteen for the Lakota warrior Long Road killed there. In 2001, during the 125th anniversary observance of the battle, a formal red granite marker to Long Road was dedicated at that site.[22]

Another facet of battlefield protection has concerned trails, and there has been substantive change regarding them since the 1970s. Whereas during the 1950s and 1960s park policy dictated that visitors remain on established paths and trails, their mounting interest in key parts of the battlefield necessitated more compromise in that respect, especially as archeological research revealed data about areas like Deep Ravine and the so-called South Skirmish Line southwest of the battle monument. The issue was also tied to the material factors of creating the trails, and together they produced certain controversy through the 1980s and 1990s. During the late 1980s, part of the trail at the Reno–Benteen Defense Site was replaced with a beige-pink concrete, eliciting complaints from park service employees as well as from park visitors. In 1992 the park permanently closed an informal trail leading from the west side of the enclosed Last Stand area to the area of Deep Ravine, following years of a vacillating policy of having it opened or closed at the whim of the individual superintendent. According to one annual report, "resource degradation was clearly evident in the form of damage to vegetation, extreme widening of the pathway (up to 18 feet), compaction, erosion, threatened archeological resources, and greater danger of man-caused wildfire." (At one point, Superintendent Booher announced plans for an observation platform to be erected at the south side of the cemetery so that visitors might view Deep Ravine; it was not built.) Six years later, the Deep Ravine Trail and the trail to the Keogh group of markers east of the tour road reopened briefly for guided tours and an environmental assessment.

Results justified development of all-weather gravel trails to both areas and their permanent reopening late in 2000.[23] As important as the trail features appear to be for visitors and interpretation, however, their propagation nonetheless broadens the developmental footprint on the primary resource, a factor that must constantly be weighed by park managers concerned with the mounting specter of public overuse.

A constant threat to the resources at Little Bighorn Battlefield National Monument has been grass fire. Through the years of National Park Service management, small controllable blazes have occasionally blackened parts of the terrain. In 1947 a small fire burned about 7.5 acres at Reno–Benteen. In the late summer of 1958 a small human-caused grass fire consumed about two acres there. (These were the first fires under National Park Service administration.) Another there in 1968 was speedily quelled by a water truck reserved for such emergencies. Yet nothing prepared the park staff for the human-induced 600-acre inferno that raced across the Custer battleground on August 10, 1983. Driven by brisk winds, a smoldering fire believed previously extinguished erupted into a blaze that "burned like gasoline" as it swept through the thick grass and sagebrush of the site for ninety minutes, necessitating the evacuation of perhaps seven hundred people. Park service staff joined Bureau of Indian Affairs and Big Horn County fire-fighters in controlling the flames, which damaged neither the cemetery nor the visitor center but burned over virtually all vegetative ground cover, leaving charred terrain and many blackened stone markers. Yet the obvious aesthetic misfortune in fact presented the park with a historic opportunity, for the fire set the stage for a major archeological study that proceeded in 1984 and 1985, resulting in a plethora of new information to guide management and interpretation (see chapter 8). Likewise, the burn permitted initiation by the University of Colorado of a three-year plant succession study of sagebrush grassland to aid the National Park Service as well as rangeland management in eastern Montana's prairie ecology. In later years, other fires occurred. On August 20, 1991, a fast-moving wildfire scorched the entire Reno–Benteen Defense Site, as well as the ground lying between the park units. Within the Custer battlefield unit, it scarred nearly 125 acres along the northern slope of the battle ridge, including Calhoun Hill and the Keogh position, causing temporary closure of the tour road, and later brief evacuation of the park. Another fire on the evening of June 28, 1994, consumed perhaps 150 acres of the grass on Custer Hill near the monument before it was extinguished.[24]

Throughout recent decades, increasing public interest in the Battle of the Little Bighorn has correspondingly compounded the propensity of individuals to profit from the event. This has resulted in a boom of development beyond park boundaries but on documented battlefield terrain, to the further detriment of the primary resource lands embraced by the national monument. As a result, the historical view shed at Little Bighorn has in some respects been compromised, especially those areas fronting the west and north boundaries where traffic passes through Little Bighorn Valley and approaches the historic ground. Where during the 1950s and 1960s gas stations, cafes, and souvenir shops existed, by the early twenty-first century a panoply of tourist-related attractions proliferated. In 1993 a former motel operated by the Crow Tribe was renovated into the Little Bighorn Casino, proudly proclaimed as "the largest gambling hall in Montana," complete with a large computerized lighted sign visible in all directions. Several café/souvenir operations and retail shops, including a Kentucky Fried Chicken franchise, continued or were built near the junction of Interstate 90 and Highway 212 in the immediate vicinity of the entrance road. Another gas station and retail trading post complex, complete with a Custer Battlefield Museum, opened at Garryowen near another museum that started and failed. Even closer to the national monument was a sales venture near the Reno–Benteen Defense Site, stalled, at least, in 1995. Further, independent retailers intermittently set up shop in huts raised on Indian land in Medicine Tail Coulee; when they eventually abandoned their buildings, the landholder negotiated an agreement whereby the National Park Service cleaned up the site. All of this commercial development resulted from the proximity of privately held property to battlefield land, creating a mire of preservation ethic versus American capitalism and compromising all federal efforts in the 1980s and 1990s to embrace and protect the larger resource, to the long-range detriment of the historic ground. "We have development creeping in like bookends upon the battlefield view shed," concluded Superintendent Mangum. "It's hard to appreciate the solemness and mood of a place like this if there's a fast food franchise on the horizon." Because of the constant threat of external development, in 2003 the National Trust for Historic Preservation identified Little Bighorn Battlefield National Monument as one of the eleven most endangered historic places in the nation.[25]

CHAPTER 7 | National Park Service Interpretation

Since the 1940 transfer of Little Bighorn Battlefield National Monument from the War Department to the National Park Service, the site's interpretation has undergone inexorable change. The most noticeable difference has been the transition from a memorial shrine for Little Bighorn soldier dead to a national monument recognizing all the dead, soldiers and Indians. It was a metamorphosis born of evolving societal consciousness reflecting progressive social maturity in the nation as a whole, an understanding fostered by ever-narrowing physical proximity as technical improvements and burgeoning populations brought people together in greater mutual appreciation. When, in 1925, Mrs. Thomas Beaverheart, a Northern Cheyenne, wrote Superintendent Wessinger asking that a marker be placed on the battlefield to indicate the spot where her father, Lame White Man, had fallen in battle, her request drew no response. Seventy-eight years later, an Indian memorial was raised to honor the participation of all tribes involved.[1]

Interpretation in the National Park Service is grounded in a concept of educating the public about the natural and cultural resources at hand in any given park. The National Park Service today abides by the view of the National Association for Interpretation, which defines interpretation as "a communication process that forges emotional and intellectual connections between the interests of the audience and the inherent meanings in the resource." Such all-embracing views were seldom practiced during the early years of the park service–administered site, and through most of the park history since 1940 the commonly parleyed perspective was that from the military viewpoint and not from that of the Indians. Throughout the period of War Department administration, maintenance of the cemetery was the paramount duty, although by 1937 the department had issued an interpretive brochure dealing with the battle, and the Thomas Marquis booklets were offered for sale by local civilian guides.[2]

In essence, the National Park Service initially carried over the War Department perspective in its handling of the Little Bighorn story. Yet mounting numbers of visitors during the early 1940s foretold a rapidly growing public interest in the battle. As early as 1941, Superintendent Luce laid plans for initiating guide service at the site; he was aware that many visitors came away confused by the various groups of white markers scattered over the field. He planned for "suitable information markers placed at the proper places." He wrote, "As there has always been a deep interest in the Battle of the Little Big Horn River, . . . and that better than a hundred thousand visitors and tourists come to this place [each year], it is understood that a small pamphlet is soon to be issued covering the pertinent facts of this battle."[3]

The name change in 1946 to Custer Battlefield National Monument signified a major deviation from cemetery operations to historical interpretation of the battlefield by the National Park Service. From that point forward, the story of Little Bighorn evolved significantly. Early park service interpretative themes referenced Indian resistance to "the westward march of white man's civilization." The person of Custer remained a prime focal point, however, and the 1942 master plan stated that the "immediate influence of the Battle of the Little Big Horn on the policy of the Government towards its wards was more pronounced because it was an Indian victory over the ambitious and spectacular Custer. . . . The proposed museum will tell the story of the Battle of the Little Big Horn in relation to the removal of the Indians from the last frontier." In terms of interpreting the battlefield, the cemetery was viewed as an objectionable feature because its presence near the entrance distracted from "the historically important battlefield."[4] Even the 1949 master plan by Luce and his wife presented Custer and his soldiers as symbols of "traditional devotion to duty and love of country" and the battle as "the ultimate solution of the Indian problem." The first park service handbook appeared in 1949, and it presented Custer as the central figure, with Little Bighorn an epic of the westward movement, a concept continued in a 1956 brochure highlighting him as a "daring and gallant Indian fighter," with Indians portrayed as merely resisting the "march of civilization."

The view changed in the 1960s with the Civil Rights Movement, the Vietnam War, and the rise of the American Indian Movement provoking a major reassessment among the population. Movies like *Soldier Blue* and *Little Big Man* depicted a brutal side to the Indian wars, and many Americans' perceptions of Custer and his command turned negative, and he came to symbolize what was bad in the country. At the park, exhibits in place since the early 1950s that highlighted Custer were replaced by ones that downplayed his military career and sought to augment the Lakota and Northern Cheyenne side of the battle. By the 1970s, a value-neutral element had supplanted memorializing of the Seventh Cavalry and Custer, and the battle was interpreted, as reflected in exhibits, wholly in terms of "culture conflict" with the park committed to "memorializing one of the last armed efforts of the Northern Plains Indians to preserve their ancestral way of life." In the 1970s too came the first proposals for a name change that would further neutralize and broaden interpretation of the site. That objective was realized in the same 1991 legislation that authorized establishment of an Indian memorial to honor all tribes who participated in the battle. Thus, briefly put, has the tenor of the Little Bighorn story evolved at the park over the course of the past sixty years.[5]

As the first National Park Service superintendent at the park, Edward S. Luce forged and managed the first program of interpretation there. Aided by policy guidance received from Yellowstone National Park, the parent administrator for Custer Battlefield National Cemetery, Luce began work on a sixteen-page pamphlet, to be distributed to visitors in 1943, as well as on the first system of interpretive markers to be placed appropriately on the battlefield. Wayside exhibits and parking overlooks were planned along the tour road in conjunction with the 1942 master plan; three were produced in 1947, and a wayside exhibit plan for the Reno–Benteen site was drafted in 1948. When bids for six interpretive signs were opened in June 1948, it was discovered that funding was available for only three. "These will be placed as soon as they are received," reported Luce.

The first seasonal junior historical aide hired by Luce, William R. Tangney, reported for duty on June 11, 1941. When Tangney's successor arrived the following year, reported the superintendent, "a series of lectures and guided trips throughout the National Cemetery and the Custer Battlefield was immediately instituted." Until 1950, only one seasonal employee was hired; from 1950 to 1954 there were two historical aides; and after 1955 three or more aides assisted. During the off-season, Superintendent Luce and his wife, Evelyn, provided interpretation.

Free handout folders and leaflets were produced in 1941 to give visitors basic background on Custer and the campaign of 1876 and the ensuing battle. (These folders were increased in size in 1944 and were constantly revised to provide additional information.) The Luces' thirty-six-page booklet *Custer Battlefield* appeared to "favorable reception" following extensive review of the manuscript at Yellowstone and at National Park Service regional headquarters. It became the first publication in the agency's Historical Handbook Series. In 1952 the pages were revised to reference the new museum.[6]

One of the seasonal historical aides in 1946 was Edgar I. Stewart, who would author the monumental work *Custer's Luck*, published in 1955. Stewart recollected that "lectures were given from any vantage point at which a view of the Little Big Horn Valley was to be obtained. And they were given whenever there were enough people present to make it worthwhile. At least twice a day caravans were organized to follow the road up to Reno Hill." Stewart recalled two groups of visitors who were especially interesting: "One was a party of about 10 Cheyenne Indians whose relatives had participated in the battle. They knew personally many of the warriors who had taken part. . . . Another was a group of colored men and women who were especially interested in Isaiah Dorman, a colored interpreter with the troops who lost his life during Reno's retreat to the bluffs." He also remembered that the "markers outside the [Last Stand] enclosure and especially those closest to the road were badly chipped. People were always searching for arrowheads, cartridge shells, and so on, mostly with indifferent success. Small stones and even twigs from trees sometimes were carried away."[7]

Another historical aide, Robert M. Utley, interpreted the battle site for visitors for six summers, from 1947 through 1952. Utley recalled relating a primarily military story, with little emphasis on the Indians. "The Indians of course played a part in this story," he wrote years later, "—the Sioux and Cheyennes as the enemy who had wiped out Custer, the Crows and Arikaras as the scouts and auxiliaries in the war against their tribal enemies. But in our telling, these Indians emerged less as real people than as cardboard cutouts, impersonal foils in the battle of blue-coated frontiersmen to clear the way for sturdy westering pioneers. Our perspective was those who won the West, not those who lost the West." As Utley explained, "Later generations would look in contempt on the story we told and demand a 'balance' that easily strayed beyond to an opposite imbalance. I was part of those later generations and, endowed with new insights and perspectives, participated in the quest for balance. But I have never looked back in contempt or shame. We were products of our time and place, reflecting the larger society's time and place. We thought and behaved just as our later critics would have thought and behaved had they been our contemporaries."[8]

The museum added another dimension to evolving park interpretation by advancing a need for including exhibits in accordance with a museum prospectus completed by the Luces in 1947. Prior to 1952 Luce had prepared several small exhibits that were available to visitors in the front room of the superintendent's lodge. In the years leading to the construction of the museum, the park prepared an interpretive statement that received careful scrutiny to assure that the interpretation would be accurate, discerning, and comprehensive. These elements guided the exhibit planning that began under Harry B. Robinson, Region 2 museum planner, and Ned J. Burns, chief of the service's museum branch, early in 1948. A completed museum exhibits plan was approved in June 1950 by National Park Service director Newton B. Drury. Ralph H. Lewis, Harold Peterson, and Floyd LaFayette of the Washington office managed curatorial production of the displays.

The exhibits were organized under four major themes: (1) The Story of the Battle (including exhibit titles Why the Battle Was Fought, The Army Moves In, Cavalry Arms and Equipment, The Indian Encampment, Indian Weapons, Custer Divides His Forces, What Happened to Custer? The Beginning and End of the Battle, and After the Battle); (2) The Indian Exhibits (including The Hostile Indians, Indian Warriors, Indian Medicine, The Crow Indians, and Warriors Who Fought Custer); (3) General Custer (including Custer at West Point, Custer in the Civil War, Custer on the Plains, and Garrison Life); and (4) Seventh Cavalry Exhibits (three cases related to the history of the Seventh Cavalry). As indicated, the exhibits largely reflected Luce's interests and emphasized themes of army heroism and sacrifice and dealt primarily with the action on Custer's field, to the detriment of the Reno–Benteen episodes (although one diorama portrayed Reno's retreat). Exhibit cases were dedicated to Seventh Cavalry history and the personal history of Custer; save for a display of uniforms and weapons (and a Medal of Honor granted Sergeant Charles A. Windolph, who had been with Reno's command), there was little treatment of the enlisted men who served in the battle, nothing on the campaigns following the military disaster, and, although the Indians were reasonably well represented, the exhibits minimally detailed the cultural background of the Lakotas and Northern Cheyennes. Moreover, in layout design the twenty-nine jutting cases and panels in the exhibit room thwarted easy visitor flow and created bottlenecks to circulation. A relief map situated in the orientation and observation room at the east end of the exhibits room permitted views of Custer Hill, the monument, and the landscape south, east, and west and helped familiarize visitors with the layout of the battlefield.

Increased visitation following the opening of the museum necessitated the hiring of a full-time historian, and, as mentioned earlier, in 1953 James Bowers became the first permanent historian at the park. Most of his tenure coincided with the placement of ten aluminum interpretive markers attached to concrete bases along the road from the Custer monument to that at Reno–Benteen. Conceived by Luce, they constituted the first significant effort to provide a roadside interpretation program. Bowers was succeeded as historian by Don Rickey, Jr. Historian Rickey, as well as the Luces, added greatly to baseline research supporting park interpretation during the 1940s and 1950s through various research trips to federal repositories in Chicago, Washington, D.C., and other cities to gather microfilm and photostatic copies of pertinent archival materials. (After Rickey transferred to Jefferson National Expansion Memorial in 1960, his position was taken by Warren J. Petty, who was promoted from Fort Laramie National Historic Site. Petty himself transferred in 1963 and was succeeded by Andrew M. Loveless, reassigned from Fort Frederica National Monument.) In 1955 prior to their departure from Custer Battlefield National Monument, Superintendent Luce and his wife, Evelyn, were honored for their efforts to properly interpret the Little Bighorn Battlefield by presentation with a Westerners National Service Award by the Chicago Corral of the Westerners in Chicago.[9]

In 1954 in an effort to provide continuing interpretive talks to visitors during the off-season months when staff were unavailable, the park installed a repeating tape recorded message describing events preceding the battle and the encounter itself. (The message directed visitors to the Reno–Benteen battlefield: "We suggest that you drive directly to that area and read the interpretive signs as you return. The battle action unfolded from south to north, and the course of events is best understood by reading the signs on the return trip.") The tape system represented technological advance, especially when used in conjunction with the topographic relief map installed in the observation room; together the devices augmented the interpreter presentations.

When staff historian Roy E. Appleman of the Washington office visited the park in July 1956, he examined the program and reached several conclusions. He noted that "the present interpretive program turns largely on the museum and the recorded and personal talks given in the headquarters-visitor building. There is an excellent recorded talk which can be used as desired in the observation room [at the east end of the building] where orientation talks are given to groups of visitors. The seasonal historians deliver most of these talks but the recording is used whenever it is needed." Appleman observed that few interpretive markers stood on the battlefield and that "much remains to be done with this part of the interpretive program." He noted that "Superintendent Aubuchon personally greets each group of visitors as they enter the door or has one of the staff members do so, and gives them a resumé of what they can see and the assistance available. He makes everyone feel welcome and that is an excellent introduction to the Monument."

Appleman, however, called for a total revamping of the museum exhibits, believing that they represented "an extremely unbalanced story of the events that took place and contain many inaccurate statements of fact." Among his criticisms, he cited the dearth of information on Reno's actions, the overemphasis on Custer's personal history, a disjointed exhibit presentation of the battle, a failure to properly identify artifacts, including Indian items, factual problems with the dioramas, an irrelevant exhibit about the Seventh Cavalry, and problems with the relief map situated in the observation room (it was replaced by an upgraded one in 1963). He urged that the mounted remains of Comanche, Captain Keogh's horse that survived the battle, be acquired from the University of Kansas for permanent display: "I can think of no single exhibit that would excite and retain the public interest at Custer Battlefield as much as the display of this animal. . . . Comanche is unique as a display specimen."[10]

Appleman urged that the exhibits be modified under auspices of the Mission 66 program then underway. Other recommendations included those for constructing trails between the museum and the monument and a self-guiding trail at the Reno–Benteen Defense Site, as well as the placement of additional interpretive markers. Almost as an afterthought, and seemingly without application to battle interpretation, another objective sought "to interpret more fully the background of Indians such as the Crows and Cheyennes whose presence in adjacent and nearby reservations arouses considerable interest among many visitors."

Planning of the Reno–Benteen trail began in the autumn of 1956, and the gravel path opened the following year. A handout mimeographed brochure interpreted the site as of 1959, replaced the next year with a more substantial *Entrenchment Trail* booklet with text written by Rickey (later revised by Park Historian Mangum and ranger-historian Daniel Martinez in 1981 and 1983 and renamed *Reno–Benteen Entrenchment Trail*; the text was further revised in 1991 by Park Historian McChristian). Beginning in April 1957, a series of periodically rotating exhibits opened in the visitor center. They included a display about Fort Custer, Custer's Washita battle, the army and the Bozeman Trail, Cheyenne art and Crow beadwork, and the Custer battlefield, past and present. As an example of the interpretive offering, in July 1963, out of 34,505 persons visiting the park in that month, 20,367 received full interpretive talks, and another 6,474 received shorter talks. The Reno–Benteen self-guiding entrenchment trail tour was used by 6,729 people.[11]

In a master plan drafted for the park in 1964, the dedicated interpretive theme was "the significance of the Battle of the Little Bighorn and its role in the Indian–white conflict resulting from the westward expansion of the United States." Stated elements included events preceding the battle, the battle itself, events following the battle, the life of Custer, and the Indian wars army. A significant part of the story now, however, was the Northern Plains Indians, with emphasis placed on Indian culture, the Crow scouts, and the role of the people in defeating Custer's command. Since 1959 the self-guiding brochure describing the events at the Reno–Benteen Defense Site included accounts of Indian actions there. The master plan now called for the infusion of biographical data about significant Indian participants "so that more of the human element can be placed into the Indian story which has been largely depersonalized into tribal and ethnic considerations." In 1966, when members of the Oglala Sioux Ranger Corps visited the park, staff members invited them to perform a historical tribal victory song for visitors.

Evolving interpretation of the late 1960s also embraced the newly adopted concept of living history, wherein rangers, besides providing regular interpretive talks, dressed in period garb to explain aspects of enlisted soldier life at the time of the battle and to conduct firing demonstrations with weapons replicated after those used at the Little Bighorn. At Custer Battlefield National Monument, living history was championed by Park Historian B. William Henry, who succeeded Loveless in July 1967, and who soon introduced programs that became immensely popular with visitors and drew plaudits from within the National Park Service community for their accuracy and value. In 1970 and 1971 Superintendent William A. Harris and Park Historian L. Clifford Soubier, who succeeded Henry, authorized the hiring of Crow Indian youths to portray Sioux warriors in the living history sequences, including mock battle scenes—the first use of Indians in the park interpretive program. Subsequently, the programs were broadened to include aspects besides warfare of Plains Indian tribes' routine existence.[12]

During the 1960s, many of the earlier recommendations pertaining to interpretation were enacted. Additional markers and wayside exhibits were placed along the battlefield tour road, and in 1966 a new interpretive sign and box for the trail booklet was installed at Reno–Benteen. A major renovation in the visitor center in 1965 under Mission 66 while Andrew Loveless was historian involved enlarging the lobby to provide greater circulation room for visitors, besides the addition of new park service administrative offices. At the same time an attempt was made to reorganize exhibit elements to improve presentation as well as to correct the visitor flow problem by removing jutting showcases and panels. The latter was only partly successful, however, and bottlenecks remained. (The problem was not rectified, in fact, until the early 1970s when Superintendent Eldon G. Reyer and Chief of Maintenance Robert W. Hartung simply moved the offending dividers and panels.) Museum exhibits were revised to include mural art by artists Gayle Hoskins (*Custer's Last Fight*), J. K. Ralston (*Call of the Bugle* and *After the Battle*), and Kenneth Riley (*Fruitless Victory*). Among other things, the dioramas were dismantled and revised to correct inaccuracies (e.g., yellow neckerchiefs were removed). Some artifacts were consigned to the Eastern Museum Laboratory for cleaning and preservation treatment. Others, it was learned, were not correct; some displayed firearms post-dated the battle and were removed. Other battle relics in the displays were excised under a new minimalist policy of the National Park Service. Notably, materials related to Custer and the Seventh Cavalry were scaled back, because, according to one memorandum, "the objective of the area is not to memorialize either General Custer or the Seventh Cavalry." The Indian exhibits were enlarged, with emphasis given to the Indian scouts, while that formerly relating "Indian Warriors" expanded to one embracing "The Plains Indians," underscoring tribal cultures. Overall, many panel and showcase descriptions were rewritten. Improved lighting, lettering, coloring, and less clutter further characterized the revised exhibits. They were installed in October 1965, and the exhibit room reopened in November. Excess exhibit articles were placed in the large walk-in vault located in the basement, to be retrieved for future short-term displays. Historian Henry reported in 1968 that he was not authorized to change objects in the cases without approval from his superiors outside the park. Meantime, at Reno–Benteen concrete pedestals for the interpretive sign and pamphlet/cash box were installed along with numbered concrete posts for the self-guiding tour.

Two major additions to park interpretation were the appearance in 1967 of Don Rickey's *History of Custer Battlefield*, an administrative study written mostly during his tenure as park historian, and the 1969 publication of a new park service handbook, replacing the Luces' longstanding 1949 guide. Written by Robert M. Utley, then chief historian of the National Park Service, the well-executed handbook was at once controversial in its use of artist Leonard Baskin's darkly impressionistic fare. (One drawing of the dead and naked Custer lying on the battlefield caused commotion among support groups and was stricken prior to publication, leaving a blank page where it would have appeared; subsequent printings, however, carried the notorious illustration.) Nonetheless, the handbook offered a balanced view of the events leading to the battle, as well as Indian views of the action.[13]

Visitation at the park skyrocketed in the early 1970s, no doubt because of rising interest in the battlefield brought by the movie *Little Big Man* (1970), starring Dustin Hoffman and Faye Dunaway, parts of which were filmed in 1969 on Crow land between the Custer and Reno sites and east of the mouth of Medicine Tail Coulee. The first four years of the decade registered an average of 326,000 visitors annually, peaking in 1972 with 387,717 entering the park. Other national attention came by way of an article by western historian Alvin M. Josephy, Jr., which appeared in *Life* in July 1971. The article chastised the National Park Service for effectively marginalizing Indian people in its interpretation at Custer Battlefield National Monument and described the battlefield as "a sore from America's past that has not healed." Governor William L. Guy of North Dakota had previously complained following a visit that "I was disturbed by a feeling that history had been written and was still being interpreted by the white man for and from the white man's point of view." Midwest Regional Director J. Leonard Volz responded, pointing to Superintendent Harris's and Historian Soubier's realization of "the need to explain more of the Indian role in the battle and to present the Indian viewpoint rather than approaching the story from strictly a military standpoint," a view that would be registered in an interpretive prospectus being completed in 1972. Moreover, said Volz, the term "hostile," the government's designation for the nontreaty Lakota and Northern Cheyenne bands in 1876, by 1971 was deemed inappropriate and "we have eliminated its use in our interpretive program."[14]

Steadily rising concern for more balanced and inclusive interpretation continued throughout the early 1970s and, as noted, included recommendation for a name change to the park. The master plan that was drafted in 1972 stated as much, just as it proposed a revolutionary reconfiguration of the visitor access route from south to north—the way the battle action had unfolded—rather than from north to south, as it existed. The plan contained the following pronouncements:

> Approximately 60% of those who visit the [Seventh Cavalry] monument go on to Reno Hill [Reno–Benteen Defense Site]. . . .
> A few historical markers are found on the access road along the bluffs, but little continuity of the events can be effectively carried through from one unit to the other. In fact, due largely to the fact that the present sequence of the "average" visit is backwards, the trip to Reno Hill is perhaps more confusing than it is enlightening.
>
> In answer to frequent criticism of interpretation at the Monument, alleging that Custer was being glorified and that the Indian point of view was all but ignored, many changes have occurred in the program; but the criticisms persist. To the critics, for example, it seems odd that the site of one of the greatest Indian victories in American history be named for the loser.
>
> It would appear that it is difficult to give an objective account of such a symbolic event, dealing only with its specifics within restricted physical limits. We have told what happened there—but very little of the "why?"
>
> The complaints leveled at the Monument today are from a minority of its 300,000 annual visitors—the majority [are] seemingly content, and possibly thrilled at witnessing the site of one of the most exciting stories in American history. But if

interest and knowledge in frontier history and the Indian continue to increase at today's pace, many more critical voices will be heard in the future. It is not only Indians and the "bleeding heart" sympathizers who are voicing their disapproval. However imperfect the average visitor's knowledge of the battle, many are at least dimly aware that there are broad implications beyond the specific events. Finding scant treatment of these implications at the Monument, a sense of dissatisfaction ensues.

On the other side of the coin, there is an extremely large number of persons throughout the country and the world known as "Custer buffs." These individuals range from the zealous hero-worshipper to the serious scholar. Many have made a lifelong pursuit of studying the Battle of the Little Bighorn or some aspect of it. The reaction to the [past] outcry over Custer's glorification was to remove a great deal of material relating to the man from display in the visitor center. A forced move such as this could only serve to alienate Custer buffs and doesn't get to the root of the criticism anyway. Custer's stature either as a hero or a fool cannot be diminished by ignoring him. History and legend have made him loom large, and no attempt at de-emphasis can change that. Had Sitting Bull—a man of equal legendary eminence—been given equal treatment in the exhibits, objections to the Custer things probably would have been few.

In sum, the master plan presented "an interpretive program in need of a total overhaul; a visitor experience that is backwards, fragmented and incomplete; a visitor center that is ugly and too small; and development that is intrusive." The plan attempted to rectify these inadequacies, most of which appeared grounded in the interpretation.

Boldly stated, the plan was nonetheless never enacted, although some of its provisions would be addressed intermittently in subsequent years. Its promotion of a reconfiguration of the tour road, for example, heavily influenced later plans. In 1976 message repeaters were placed at the monument, the cemetery, and at the Reno–Benteen Defense Site, places where more extensive guided tours were also provided. More audio stations were planned in an interim interpretive prospectus prepared that year, along with a road tour publication guide recommended to interpret the battle action on the ground lying between the Reno tract and the Last Stand area. The existing interpretive markers, stated the interim plan, "do not work well; the information is sparse, and although they face away from the driver on his way to Reno–Benteen, there is a tendency to stop and look back, reading them in reverse order to the action." The document also proposed converting the old superintendent's lodge into an auditorium to accommodate audio-visual programs. Further, a 1980 draft interpretive plan called for the replacement of the 1953 topographic relief map in the observation room by one fitted with fiber optics to better show troop and warrior movements in conjunction with the audio recording.[15]

The appearance of Russell Means and his followers during the centennial program in 1976 was rife with meaning and ultimately had far-reaching consequences on the interpretive program at the park, although no one present at the time quite realized it. It brought into focus the matter of inclusiveness in the battle story. As Professor Edward T. Linenthal has observed, the Indians "made a frontal attack on the symbol of Custer and the Anglo-American interpretation of the battle. They understood completely the power of the Custer myth and carried out their form of symbolic guerrilla warfare where it would have the greatest impact—at the sacred site itself." Twelve years later, in 1988, Means and his people returned to punctuate that point with placement of an unauthorized plaque recognizing Indian involvement in the battle. While by that time the National Park Service interpretive program had become significantly overhauled to include more of the Indian version of events, the action impelled rapid change leading eventually to creation of an Indian memorial at the park.[16]

Meantime, during the late 1970s and early 1980s, park staff endeavored to broaden the appeal of the site to local constituencies as well as the public at large through a series of special topic temporary exhibits in the visitor center. Examples included displays about the weapons used during the battle; Curley, a Custer scout; a history of the Crow Fair (a community event on the Crow Reservation); Elizabeth Custer's devotion to her husband; Dr. Thomas Marquis, a historian of the Northern Cheyenne people; the American bison; development of the Springfield breechloading rifle; books on the Little Bighorn; and Indian scouts for the army. A major exhibit in the early 1980s was the dress helmet, Seventh Cavalry shoulder knots, and shoulder straps belonging to Custer's adjutant, First Lieutenant William W. Cooke, who had penciled the famous last message to Benteen near the outset of Custer's battle. Living history programs continued during the 1980s, including those titled "Horse Soldier, 1876: Army Life on the Frontier" and "Plains Indian Culture: Indian Life on the Plains." Guided tours included a cemetery walk, a battlefield walk relating sites on the Custer phase of the battle, and another walk relating Reno's valley fight and the experience atop the bluffs. A 1975 film, *Red Sunday*, narrated by actor John McIntire, had become a staple in the interpretive program by 1980. In 1983, Stella Foote of Billings loaned the park for exhibit a cased collection of military firearms, uniforms, and equipment, as well as Plains Indian artifacts and photographs, with purpose "to provide a clearer insight into the life of the frontier soldier, the Plains Indian and the Battle of the Little Bighorn."[17]

Despite the expansive interpretative agenda early in the decade, the program yet required fine tuning, as was apparent in the report of the five-member Custer Battlefield Publications and Interpretation Review Team, which visited the park in September 1984. The team had been generated on demands of a battlefield interest group enthusiast unhappy with the program. After three days of observation, the members concluded that the program, including exhibits, "should be strengthened by the inclusion of more information pertaining to the Indian side of the battle"; that the mid-1960s exhibits were "outdated" and needed "substantial modernization," including the removal of "offensive phrases and displays"; and that the interpretive film, *Red Sunday*, was "technically faulty, . . . unnecessarily critical of the U.S. Army, . . . lacking a central theme, . . . choppy in presentation, . . . confusing to the uninformed viewer," and needed to be replaced. The team also recommended that the "inappropriate" Black Elk quote on the front of the visitor center be removed. Administratively, the members advised that the superintendent and park historian positions be upgraded and that a museum curator be hired to properly care for the collections.[18] In the months and years following this review, many of its recommendations were enacted.

In 1983 the park began using a bus system to shuttle visitors between the visitor center and the Reno–Benteen Defense Site. Superintendent Court also expressed his desire to acquire a van with which to transport visitors with special interests to battle-related sites lying beyond the national monument boundaries. In 1985 the park offered thirty-two interpretive programs daily, including a two-and-one-half-hour guided van tour. (Occupants of oversized vehicles could also opt for the guided bus tour throughout the park or simply a shuttle from the parking area to the monument.)

That year saw the offering of a unique training course at the battlefield to aid in the interpretation of Plains Indian culture through living history. Devised by Park Historian Neil Mangum and Park Ranger Mardell Plain Feather, the course offered attendees experience in tepee living and eating native foods while learning such arts as tanning, bow-making, and quillworking. Recruits from the program conducted living history that articulated such elements as tribal social and structural organization and warrior development, with most participants coming from the Crow tribe.

A major addition to the program was a revised handbook prepared by Robert M. Utley to replace the one he wrote nearly two decades earlier. The new book contained broader interpretation, was more judgmental than its predecessor, and included more characterizations of battle participants. Utley's new handbook appeared in 1988 and has remained the official National Park Service publication since that time.[19]

Some changes also took place in the visitor center exhibit room, largely unaltered since the 1965 revision. These included the addition of temporary exhibits and art, including paintings and sculptures, which combined to produce a cluttered appearance. All of these additions were "bootlegged," that is, informally introduced and unauthorized by offices above the park, and consisted of materials loaned from public and private sources. Some, including the aforementioned uniform items belonging to Custer's adjutant, as well as some articles owned by Major Reno, were appropriate. But the large case loaned by Stella Foote contained a hodgepodge of poorly labeled soldier items and included mess equipment from World War I and a watch attributed to Custer that was, in fact, a modern creation used by actor Errol Flynn in the movie *They Died with Their Boots On*. The exhibit case remained in place over the objection of Park Historian Mangum.

By the latter years of the decade, the fruits of the 1984–85 archeological projects were appearing in revised battle assessments in academic publications, and these gradually made their way into onsite interpretation by way of battlefield marker replacement and revised maps and brochures. In 1986 a new brochure featured the artwork of Eric von Schmidt's spectacular *Here Custer Fell*, while two years later a slide show about the archeology was featured at the park, and soon new information about arms and tactics derived from the archeology infused the interpretation. By 1986 five new wayside exhibits along with pipe sight posts had been installed at Reno–Benteen, along with four others adjoining the audio message repeaters. And in 1986 the interpretation-driven general management plan appeared, directing a major reconfiguration of the visitor experience beginning in the area of

Garryowen, but frustrating park administrators from that time forward by hinging basic park improvement to land acquisition and concurrence from the Crow Tribe. In 1987 more multicolor wayside panels went up along the tour road, including one at the spot on the bluffs near the Reno–Benteen Defense Site where Custer had been last seen by Reno's men fighting in the valley. The archeology drew national attention, including coverage in *Time*, *Newsweek*, and *U.S. News and World Report* and on the network newscasts. *National Geographic* featured the digs in an issue of late 1986.

Meantime, interpretive talks by rangers continued much as before, and newly hired seasonals were advised to read the handbook and Stewart's *Custer's Luck*, as well as Don Rickey's *History of Custer Battlefield* for reference in forging their own presentations. In 1987 the summer program began on June 1, and seasonal historians were urged to attend a week of training and orientation immediately prior to that date. Two years later, a new video, *A Good Day to Die*, which promoted an Indian viewpoint in the destruction of Custer's command, commenced showing at the park. That same year featured the presentation in the visitor center of personal items belonging to Northern Cheyenne Laban Little Wolf, an exhibit arranged with the consultation of Little Wolf's descendants. The infusion of an increased Indian perspective continued into the 1990s following the passage of legislation authorizing the name change and the Indian Memorial. Although the museum still contained insufficient space, its exhibits reflected more balance, and one complete side was devoted to interpreting aspects of Plains Indian culture, including medicines and weapons.[20]

Accomplishments in the early 1990s included a new interpretive prospectus and resource management plan, while seasonal training now integrated the results of the archeological research to help interpret the battle story. Recommendations of the new prospectus comprised acquisition of property on the rising bench land opposite Reno's valley position for an interpretive overlook to better orient visitors. Significantly, the park created the position of chief of interpretation and visitor services, splitting away tasks formerly the province of the park historian. John Doerner occupied the position from 1994 until his appointment as park historian in 1999, when Kenneth Woody assumed the job. During the decade, a revised brochure for the battlefield also appeared, while a cemetery guidebook was published with assistance of the Custer Battlefield Historical and Museum Association. At the same time, a new tour bus was acquired with the help of the association.

A modified tour permitted visitors aboard the bus greater comprehension of Reno's valley fight and the retreat to the bluffs, while a new one-hour van tour combined visits of the Reno and Custer operations.

Inside the visitor center, new labeling described exhibits about Custer, the Indians, battle weapons, the dioramas, archeology, and even markers and memorials on the field. In 1991 with peaking interest emanating from a recent television mini-series based on the Evan Connell book *Son of the Morning Star*, the park received a loan from the Smithsonian Institution of the Model 1872 army dress helmet owned by Lieutenant Colonel Custer. Yet another exhibit highlighted the donated 1948 portraits by Rapid City photographer Bill Groethe of the last living Little Bighorn warriors.

Meantime, temporary non-battle-related exhibits featured the seventy-fifth birthday of the National Park Service and the fiftieth anniversary observance of Pearl Harbor. Outreach programs also involved the battlefield staff in activities like Career Days at Little Big Horn College at Crow Agency, presentations at the Hardin schools, and participation in the Native American Studies Program at Concordia College in Moorhead, Minnesota.[21]

In the early nineties, the North Shield Ventures educational park plan dominated attention. The plan looked to a likely revamping of the interpretation at the park, depending on (1) whether the concept was approved by the National Park Service, and (2) whether the entrance to the park was changed to the area below Reno–Benteen. But by early 1994 North Shield, at least so far as the government was concerned, was a dead issue, killed by a lack of confidence in its promoters, who had failed to back up their plan with sound financial footing (see chapter 6). Instead, the park focused on overhauling its exhibits to emphasize Indian participation and to improve circulation space in the visitor center.

The new exhibits, designed by the National Park Service's interpretative center in Harpers Ferry, West Virginia, together with a Georgia contractor, underscored displays of visual images and objects reflecting the peoples involved in the battle while highlighting mementos belonging to Custer. As well, from the 1960s through the early 1990s, book sales in the visitor center, an operation run by the Custer Battlefield Historical and Museum Association, had become a major profit center supporting those park operations considered peripheral and that could not normally be federally funded. The cooperating association offered an extensive array of titles dealing with military and Indian history concerning Custer, Lakota and Northern Cheyenne leaders, and the history surrounding the

Battle of the Little Bighorn. As visitation soared following the 1991 name change, so did sales in the book room.[22]

A major innovation in 1994 that fueled grist for much future interpretation at the park was the Little Bighorn Legacy Symposium, a public conference held August 3–6 at the Billings Sheraton. The meeting, broadly conceived by Park Historian McChristian, who believed that the battle and its results deserved modern examination and interpretation, was successively supported by superintendents Booher and Baker. An assemblage of historians, archeologists, anthropologists, writers, and filmmakers sought not to rehash details of the 1876 engagement but to explore fresh social, cultural, and historical perceptions about the action and its meaning and symbolism. It was the first park-sustained scholarly convention since Superintendent Luce's assembly of scholars in 1947. Speakers included Lakota, Crow, and Northern Cheyenne scholars, as well as those from government and academia, all participating in lectures and panel discussions. The event was sponsored by the National Park Service, the Montana Historical Society, Southwest Parks and Monuments Association, and the Wyoming/Montana Council for the Humanities, and the proceedings were later collected into a well-received publication, *Legacy: New Perspectives on the Battle of the Little Bighorn.*[23]

In 1995 Little Bighorn Battlefield National Monument revised and updated its earlier general management plan, again to no immediate avail. Meantime, the park presented twenty-eight interpretive programs during its summer schedule. A new film, *Brushing Away Time,* delineated the archeology and its significance in helping to explain what happened during the battle. Audio tours incorporating use of rental compact disc players utilizing a narrative written and edited by McChristian and Chief of Interpretation John Doerner, were available for use on the tour road. The audio station near the monument on Last Stand Hill was also updated using another piece prepared by McChristian and Doerner. Bus tours were managed by Apsaalooke Bus Tours under the auspices of Little Bighorn College, which had received a four-year exclusive concessions permit. Improvements to the interpretive program consisted of a new television monitor and video cassette recorder, inauguration of a junior ranger program, acquisition of a new tepee with furnishings to enhance the living history presentations, and preparation of revised text for the cemetery plaque. Of the six seasonal rangers hired to help interpret the site for the 1995 season, three were Indians.[24]

In spite of continuing efforts to include more of the Indian view-point, the 1990s saw increasing criticism of the battlefield's interpretation on other fronts. A historic trail proposal sought to improve background data by incorporating more information about Custer's route in approaching the Little Bighorn from the Yellowstone River. Further, it was believed that more context for the Little Bighorn story was needed in terms of adequate information about Indian tribal status, government administration of Indian affairs, and perspective in relating Little Bighorn to other events and military actions of the Great Sioux War of 1876–77. Particularly damning censure came in complaints that, after Historian McChristian had transferred from the battlefield, data inaccuracies and "egregious distortions" had crept into the interpretive program and that visitors were often fed nonsense by interpreters ill-equipped or ill-prepared to properly convey the facts. "Not only balance has gone down the drain, but also the most elementary factual content," wrote one critic. "Interpretation at Little Bighorn stands in urgent need of major overhaul."

The critique generated a response from regional headquarters, which sent a National Park Service team to evaluate the park's interpretive services and make recommendations. The team met at the park in April 1997, conducted a review, and devised a work plan to promote necessary changes. Almost simultaneously, the National Park Service requested the Organization of American Historians (OAH) to assess the quality of the current interpretive program at Little Bighorn and to report on its deficiencies. In May 1997 four distinguished historians of army–Indian affairs—Paul Andrew Hutton, executive director of the Western History Association, University of New Mexico; Edward T. Linenthal of the University of Wisconsin, Oshkosh; Frederick E. Hoxie of the D'Arcy McNickle Center for the History of the American Indian at the Newberry Library, Chicago; and R. David Edmunds of the University of Texas at Dallas—participated in an interpretation workshop at the park, then assessed the program and urged the park to, among other things, properly train and monitor its interpreters, review exhibits and ensure the use of collection materials (including a more tempered presentation of past archeology), and improve interpretation on the battlefield (including revision of the taped recordings). The reviewers also called for a new, better oriented visitor center located "on the lowland where visitors can see the entire site." "For all the hot air that has been expended on this site," observed Professor

Hoxie, "it is embarrassing to see how few resources my fellow citizens and I have allocated to its preservation and interpretation."[25]

In his report, Professor Hutton, while acknowledging a recent weighted trend toward Indian inclusiveness in the program, observed:

> interpretation at Little Bighorn is presently in an evolutionary stage—swinging from the shrine of Custer of over a generation ago to the obliteration of the Custer persona and the pro-Indian stance of today. The most recent past administration of the site has been marked by some rather severe 'shock treatment' as regards interpretation and this has led to howls of protest from many. In his [Superintendent Baker's] defense, this dramatic shift was probably essential to move interpretation far enough so that a true "neutrality" can be established in the near future.

An important development in 1997 was Baker's recruitment of Timothy P. McCleary, an instructor at Little Bighorn College, as interim park historian (the park historian position had been vacant since 1995). McCleary helped fulfill both Native American Graves Protection and Repatriation Act and legislative compliance mandates in that position.

During the summer of 1997, fifteen interpretive programs were presented daily. Living history stations showing aspects of both Plains Indian daily life and army life occupied the amphitheater adjoining the visitor center. In late June, the 121st anniversary of the battle saw representatives from the Crow, Arikara, Lakota, Northern Cheyenne, and Arapaho tribes, as well as the Seventh Cavalry, participate in relating history, singing, and prayer events at the park. Thousands of visitors attended the observance, the superintendent noting that "the anniversary programs greatly aid in the healing taking place between American Indians and Euro-Americans today. The interpretive themes of 'Peace, Unity, and Friendship' encourage and strengthen respect of diverse cultures in America and throughout the world."[26]

Almost simultaneous with the 1997 OAH evaluation of the park interpretative program came the appearance of two significant documents. The new "Interpretive Prospectus, Little Bighorn Battlefield National Monument," addressed many deficiencies noted in the OAH appraisal by developing primary interpretive themes. The prospectus endorsed the 1986/95 revised general management plan and made specific proposals for interpretation affecting prearrival orientation, the visitor center, the tour road, the Reno–Benteen unit, the Last Stand Hill unit, and the Indian village site, while encouraging personal services programs and initiation and expansion of partnerships to ensure the proper interpretation and protection of the resources. Interim suggestions advised better use of the present audiovisual program and fiber-optic map and reconfiguring existing visitor center space to better support interpretation. While recommending such new media as a theater, a wayside exhibit plan, and new brochures, the document concluded that "while all partnership agreements are important, the relationships between the park and the various Native American tribes associated with the battle deserve special note. . . . What should be interpreted regarding Native Americans and how such messages should be presented, must be done in consultation and partnership. . . . Such an effort at Little Bighorn could go far in continuing to improve relations, enhance the quality of interpretation, and increase multicultural ownership in the national monument." Beyond the interpretive prospectus, a schematic design plan for visitor center exhibits, prepared by the park staff, the Intermountain System Support Office, Harpers Ferry Center, and the Colorado Historical Society, presented viable concepts that with appropriate funding could be translated into a comprehensive new exhibit.[27]

Significant changes in the visitor center and along the tour road were announced in the late 1990s following the appointment of Neil C. Mangum as superintendent. Early in 1998, Mangum explained that donated funds would be used to design, produce, and install porcelain enamel wayside exhibit panels to replace cast aluminum and concrete markers dating to the 1940s and 1950s and to help better convey the Indian perspective. He also planned to upgrade visitor center exhibits to include a historic timeline, showing events leading to and following the battle, as well as a display dealing with Indian and civilian scouts in 1876. Mangum also projected funds to be spent on a new orientation film to replace *Last Stand at Little Bighorn*, deemed "too lengthy and comprehensive" for visitors, as well as on an electronic battle map featuring sound and light capabilities. Mangum further initiated what became a popular Friday night lecture series, bringing in noted authors and scholars to share their particular insights and expertise on the Indian wars and Little Bighorn. And he sought to forge partnerships with local communities and offices to promote a broad-based concept of Great Sioux War sites that would, in turn, enhance visitor experience at the park. Visitors still had the option of touring the field by way of buses operated through Little Bighorn College. Through an early seasonal training program and proper mentoring and feedback, the superintendent could report that "the park is telling a balanced history—that is, from a multicultural perspective . . . and . . . the park themes are appropriate and achieve a high degree of accuracy."[28]

Indeed, Mangum's tenure as superintendent coincided with an increasing realization of inclusiveness that Little Bighorn Battlefield National Monument had not known before the 1990s and the beginning of the transition that accompanied the name change, authorization for an Indian memorial, and the ground-breaking tenures of superintendents Barbara Booher and Gerard Baker. The neutrality and balance forecasted in Paul Hutton's evaluation of the interpretation at Little Bighorn reached fruition under Mangum and continued with the help of a staff of both Indian and non-Indian personnel dedicated to the place and its story.

Working with Chief of Interpretation Kenneth Woody and other park staff, and in consultation with members of the Northern Cheyennes, Park Historian John Doerner with Mangum's concurrence undertook a project to locate Indian casualty sites to be appropriately dedicated with red granite markers. Two sites honoring Lame White Man and Noisy Walking were thus marked on Memorial Day 1999, and a third honoring a Lakota, Long Road, was so marked in 2001. This project is especially difficult and may be brief, for there is little precise and documented information about where Indian fatalities occurred on the field. For the battlefield to retain credibility, evidence of location must be clear, valid, and convincing. Nonetheless, with inclusiveness instead of exclusiveness as the norm, the Little Bighorn experience has broadened yet moderated and taken on greater meaning.

The largesse would culminate in creation and dedication of the Indian Memorial, the planning and design for which continued through most of the 1990s. "Everyone feels more welcome now," said long-term Park Curator Kitty Belle Deernose, "for the story now includes comments from those who won rather than by just those who lost." At the anniversary program in 2000, a bevy of tribal representatives attended from among the Crows, Northern Cheyennes, Sioux, and Assinniboins.[29]

Major interpretive additions to the Little Bighorn program came early in 1999 with preparation of an environmental assessment for walking trails to the Keogh marker group and to Deep Ravine. The trails, which had been intermittently closed due to erosion during previous years, could provide visitors with insights into the battle action.

The results of the assessments allowed for the establishment of all-weather gravel trails permitting their permanent reopening by late 2000. The debut of the Deep Ravine Trail was accompanied by development of a revised guide book (initially prepared in the 1980s) correlated to sites along its route. A revised trail guide also appeared to better interpret to visitors the sites associated with the action at the Reno–Benteen Defense Site, along with a revised guide to the Custer National Cemetery.

The first of the new wayside exhibits, meantime, were ready for installation in the early summer of 2000; highly detailed in their color illustrations, they conveyed the appearance of the Indian village in 1876, the movement of troops into Little Bighorn Valley, Reno's initial engagement and retreat from the valley, and the movement to and from Weir Point. Also, the park's new orientation film, a seventeen-minute presentation titled *Their Shots Quit Coming*, neared completion. A handout published in 2000 by the Southwest Parks and Monuments Association, moreover, provided visitors with background of the battle together with complete information about the park's interpretive program from Memorial Day through Labor Day.[30]

Yet serious problems remained with the interpretation program, many of them grounded in the continuing physical constraints afforded by long-outdated facilities, as faithfully described in the park's 2000 scope of collections statement:

> The Visitor Center, built in 1952 when visitation was extremely low, . . . is inadequate and too small to accommodate visitors and staff. Inside, the lobby, the bookstore/sales area, and information desk are cramped together. . . . During the summer visitors are literally packed into a tiny, un-air-conditioned museum that has changed little since the 1960s. Outdated displays and exhibits attempt to tell the story of the battle from both the soldier and Indian point of view. . . . Recent exhibit upgrades, which were museum object oriented, failed to meet the park's primary interpretive goals. The standard NPS "Mission 66" exhibit design style is outdated for the current staffing and visitation levels. . . . Interpretive movies are shown in a makeshift basement auditorium that is too small for summer crowds. . . . The theater is totally inaccessible for the mobility impaired, and is potentially a fire and safety hazard due to insufficient emergency egress.[31]

Regardless, as the new century brought continuance of balanced interpretation at the Little Bighorn, ranger presentations embraced discussions of Indian village life, while the museum introduced temporary exhibits relating to the broader aspects of the Great Sioux War and to Custer's Civil War career. By 2000 annual visitation averaged approximately 375,000. In 2001 the interpretive staff gave more than one thousand programs to nearly 95,000 attendees. Superintendent Darrell J. Cook, who replaced Mangum in 2002, reported on the continuing upgrade of the wayside exhibits and additions to the museum exhibits, as well as preparations for the dedication of the Indian Memorial during the summer of 2003.

The park, furthermore, continued to provide an important vehicle for the study of guerilla-style warfare during the post-9/11 period with occasional visits and "staff rides" by officers in training at the Army Command and General Staff College at Fort Leavenworth, Kansas. Indeed, in its 127-year history, Little Bighorn battlefield, while thus possessing relevance in the modern world, by 2003 had come to reflect in its interpretation a transcendent force that far surpassed its history as an shrine to Custer and his dead command and embraced a public site reflective of once past conflict between cultures that is at long last truly owned by all Americans.[32]

CHAPTER 8 | # Research and Collections

Since the transfer of Custer Battlefield National Cemetery from the War Department to the Department of the Interior in 1940, research has been an abiding component of park interpretation. In contrast to the period of War Department administration, through the years of National Park Service stewardship numerous projects have been conducted that have advanced knowledge about the course of Custer's defeat and the Indian victory at the Little Bighorn. Research during the War Department period had more to do with ascertaining the proper placement of markers on the field, with administrative attention primarily devoted to maintenance of the national cemetery.

While the number of markers ultimately placed on the field exceeded the number warranted, there remains yet confusion over the placement of some of them. For example, the remains of First Sergeant James Butler were retrieved from Deep Coulee in 1905, although his marker, according to the 1891 Geological Survey map, should have been located several hundred yards southeast on the slope of the ridge between Deep Coulee and Medicine Tail Coulee. Throughout the years of National Park Service administration, the markers have continued to be a subject for research with the hope of clarifying issues of grave location, identification, and correct marker placement.[1]

As the charge of the National Park Service shifted from administration of the cemetery to interpretation of battlefield components of the park after 1940, research activity increased. Because of Superintendent Luce's background and his knowledge and interest in the site, he brought appropriate credentials to promote scholarly inquiry leading to enhanced interpretation. His friends came to include avocational students like Fred Dustin and Charles Kuhlman, among others, who turned out important chronicles on the Battle of the Little Bighorn. Luce's own *Keogh, Comanche, and Custer* became a widely regarded source for its time. It contained new information about Captain Myles W. Keogh and his horse, Comanche, which survived the Custer engagement, together with compilations of previously unpublished statistical material drawn from official Seventh Cavalry records. Luce managed to get many of the regimental records deposited at Custer Battlefield National Monument where they formed the nucleus of a burgeoning collection of study materials there.

An important research development during Luce's tenure involved what became known as Nye-Cartwright Ridge, a high gentle crest located south of Deep Coulee on the ground rising between that drainage and Medicine Tail Coulee, a mile or so southeast of the southeast corner of the battlefield boundary. During the 1920s, a local rancher named Joseph A. Blummer began finding expended army cartridges on the ridgetop. In 1943 two of Luce's confederates, R. G. Cartwright, a South Dakota schoolteacher, and Army Lieutenant Colonel Elwood L. Nye, picked up more than one hundred more casings there, indicative of the place having been the scene of significant action in 1876 by men of Custer's battalion. More cartridge cases and other artifacts were found there subsequently, and the ridge informally took the name Nye-Cartwright Ridge.

Within three years of his arrival, Luce himself had examined much of Custer's route from Medicine Tail Coulee to the Last Stand area, found artifacts, and drawn significant conclusions about an area immediately south of Nye-Cartwright Ridge, along a spur running at right angles to Nye-Cartwright and comprising part of the north rim overlooking Medicine Tail Coulee. "Eureka!" he wrote. "I have just lately found evidences of expended carbine cartridge shells at a different place or places. To me, the most probable route if I had been commanding the troops. The placing of these shells definitely shows a mounted rear guard action, and also a stand on a ridge overlooking Medicine Tail Coulee, about 2 miles from the battlefield proper." His enthusiasm impelled Luce to call for a professional archeological study of the battlefield, although that did not occur immediately.[2]

Over the next several years, Luce's quest to learn Custer's route mounted. In July 1946, with concurrence from the National Park Service directorate, he hosted several students of the battle in a three-week field conference to examine sites to assess the new data and divine its possible meaning. At the same time, the group attempted to identify the locations of the "Crow's Nest," the point in the Wolf Mountains where Custer's scouts first discerned the location of the Indian village; the sites of the "morass" and the "burning tepee" during the march of the troops from the divide; and the various troops' positions at the Reno–Benteen Defense Site. They also excavated the burial pit of horse bones previously located near the Seventh Cavalry monument and briefly examined in 1941.

Attending the seminar were Nye, then a veterinarian and associate professor from Fort Collins, Colorado; Kuhlman, from Billings; R. G. Cartwright from Lead, South Dakota; and Joseph A. Blummer from Absher, Montana. In an apparent attempt to keep relic hunters away from the new site after the attendees returned home to formulate their conclusions, Luce announced that a fence had been erected and guards placed around the area. Luce filed an official report of the proceedings, noting in his cover letter his hope that "further study may result in positive identification of these points."[3]

Luce's interest in the new finds led him to project an expansion of the park to include lands lying between Reno–Benteen and Custer's battlefield, a concept reenvisioned in planning for the park ever since. He prepared a large grid map, blueprint copies of which he distributed to his research colleagues. In the late 1940s, he began scouring the ground with an unwieldy army mine detector. "So far, I have been able to locate a few expended cartridge shells with it," he wrote. "With this machine I hope to establish the length and locations of the skirmish lines." Luce's work in the area adjoining Nye-Cartwright Ridge, at a spot since designated Luce Ridge, significantly initiated an ever-growing body of base information that has continued to the present regarding the movements of Custer's battalion to and from the Little Bighorn River.

Luce and his wife also undertook a study of Major Reno's actions in the valley. In July 1949 Luce convened another assembly of Little Bighorn students, who again pondered the evidence and attempted once more to locate the Crow's Nest. The principal event of this meeting, however, was the relocation of the Butler marker, which Luce believed had been erroneously placed, based upon azimuth readings he took with a transit. As one of the party recalled, "We all took part in digging up the marker [in Deep Coulee] and moving it to the correct location. While digging the hole for relocating the marker, several empty cartridge cases were discovered showing that Luce's deductions were correct." (In all likelihood, the marker placed in 1917 at Deep Coulee properly designated the place where Butler's remains were found.) In addition, the attendees urged the relocation of Captain Keogh's marker to the southeast, to a position indicated in the 1879 Stanley Morrow photograph (the move was accomplished years later in 1983), while advising the removal of markers for lieutenants Sturgis and Harrington and Dr. Lord.[4]

Besides his on-field research, Luce and his wife labored to assemble copies of pertinent archival materials for the park. They compiled a bibliography of books and articles pertaining to Custer and the battle, and their off-season travels to the National Archives and other repositories helped increase the park's information base. (In October 1947 Luce took the opportunity to travel to Lead, South Dakota, where he interviewed ninety-five-year-old Charles Windolph, one of the last living white survivors of the Battle of the Little Bighorn.)

By the early 1950s, while Luce sporadically continued his research as time allowed, the National Park Service called on Custer Battlefield National Monument and other parks to complete unit administrative histories. When Don Rickey, Jr., joined the staff as park historian, he began work on that study, which explained federal governance of the park since 1876 through War Department administration and including the brief period of National Park Service oversight. Rickey finished a draft of the study early in 1957; a revised draft was submitted to management in September 1958. (Although he transferred from the park in 1960, Rickey updated the manuscript for publication in 1967 by the Custer Battlefield Historical and Museum Association.)[5]

In 1956 under Superintendent John A. Aubuchon and within the framework of the National Park Service's Mission 66 program, Rickey tailored a carefully measured research agenda for the park. Rickey projected six priorities, as follows:

1. Completion of the manuscript for the administrative history.
2. Preparation of numbered markers to be used with a self-guiding leaflet at the Reno–Benteen Defense Site.
3. Archeological restoration of rifle pits and trenches at Reno–Benteen.
4. Completion of a reconnaissance survey of the Nye-Cartwright Ridge area, lying between the Reno–Benteen Defense Site and Custer's battlefield "to locate the positions of battle relics (especially empty

cartridges) connected with Custer's first contact with the hostiles. This facet of the battle has never been researched, and is essential to our interpretive development."

5. Research trip to the National Archives and Library of Congress to examine and gather Indian and military data, including materials from the files of the Order of Indian Wars.

6. Continue to seek out persons and repositories owning letters, diaries, photographs, journals, and papers owned by soldiers who served during the Sioux Campaign of 1876, copies of which might be added to the park historical research files.

Rickey's program received endorsement from both the regional and national offices of the National Park Service.[6]

The emphasis on field research at Reno–Benteen responded to a need to properly interpret that part of the Battle of the Little Bighorn to the visiting public, whose attention heretofore had been focused largely on the Custer phase of the action. Rickey's priority in this endeavor was certified by Washington, D.C., staff historian Roy E. Appleman, who evaluated the park's research and interpretation activities during a visit in July 1956. He concluded that the exhibits contained "an almost complete absence of information on the Reno fight in the valley, which opened the battle, and the extremely important two day and one night fight at Reno–Benteen Hill. . . . Actually, the Reno–Benteen Hill phase of the battle is virtually ignored. By no sound historical analysis can this be justified."

Rickey's research on that area was well underway. With assistance from Jesse W. Vaughn, an attorney and history sleuth from Windsor, Colorado, Rickey used modern metal detectors to locate groupings of cartridge cases to identify major points of occupation of the army perimeter on Reno Hill. (Vaughn had earlier pioneered the use of metal detectors at Indian wars sites, notably at the Rosebud battle-field.) At Reno–Benteen, Rickey posited stakes to mark these locations and transcribed the information on large-scale topographic maps. He and Vaughn also found approximately eight hundred cartridges from Indian guns fired from the surrounding ridges. From the configuration thus revealed, he was able to develop interpretive strategies for the site, and during the summer of 1957 the stakes planted there were charted. Following construction at Reno–Benteen in 1965, the positions were to be resurveyed and permanent marker stakes established. From buttons, small bones, and other debris, he also located at least one possible burial site among the entrenchments. Rickey and Vaughn also found materials at the mouth of Medicine Tail Coulee and along Deep Coulee during their field work, which continued sporadically between 1956 and 1960 and promoted the need for readjusting the park boundary. (Additional discovery of Indian positions east and southeast of the Reno–Benteen site occurred in 1969.) Beyond the metal detector survey, Rickey called for intensive archeology at Reno–Benteen to help locate and then reestablish trenches and rifle pits to aid knowledge and interpretation at the park.[7]

Rickey's metal detection projects were fundamental to the future holistic interpretation of Custer Battlefield National Monument. In 1958 his request for archeological investigation at Reno–Benteen was approved. Robert T. Bray, a National Park Service archeologist assigned to Effigy Mounds National Monument in Iowa, arrived in June to undertake the work. The month-long endeavor was profoundly significant. During the work, Rickey and Bray located and excavated parts of four sets of soldier remains that had been buried in the trenches and rifle pits at Reno–Benteen. Moreover, in the course of excavating approximately 630 lineal feet of earth averaging 5 feet wide and 1 foot deep, the team restored three trenches and four rifle pits to their original 1876 appearance. As Bray explained, "There was a full awareness at all times of park values concerning the preservation of the natural scene, and in all the excavation work, sod was carefully stripped and later replaced and tamped down so as to leave the least possible evidence of the exploratory trenching." Throughout the effort, the earlier metal detection work of Rickey and Vaughn proved instrumental in defining locations where defensive actions had occurred and where the archeological work proceeded. Based upon Rickey's calculations and Bray's field work, the location of the hospital area was determined to be in a swale south of the memorial marker and east of the bluff top. Altogether, the archeological investigation helped define the perimeter of action and brought forth new and extensive knowledge of the features of the Reno–Benteen Defense Site that translated into improved and meaningful interpretation of Entrenchment Trail. On August 1, 1958, the human remains recovered during the archeology were interred with honors in a single grave in the national cemetery.[8]

During the late 1960s and early 1970s, historical research was irregularly conducted pertaining to the markers and to the action of Custer's battalion north of the Reno–Benteen site. In 1969 additional materials surfaced regarding discrepancies over the 1947 relocation of the Butler marker. Soon after, Superintendent William A. Harris directed a comprehensive research effort to compile information from the park historical files regarding all artifact finds, including bones, recovered on the ground north of Weir Point and through the Custer battlefield unit and to plot their locations on a large aerial survey map of the area. Completed more or less informally during the summer of 1970, the project represented the first park-sponsored initiative since Luce's inquiry to correlate information from assembled reports of cartridge and other artifact finds and deduce army and Indian movements on the field in 1876. Another initiative undertaken in 1979 dealt with examining the original placement of markers on Custer's battlefield for the purpose of possibly correcting any placement errors.[9]

Thus, with few exceptions, battlefield research operated haphazardly under National Park Service administration. Until the 1970s, only Historian Rickey had foreseen the need for a broad and sustained research effort, and with administrative support he succeeded in accomplishing much of what he had proposed. Part of the problem subsequently was that until the late 1990s park historians were required to serve also as chiefs of interpretation in their parks, and increasing responsibilities in that discipline, including ever-mounting visitation, the profusion of government regulations, and expanded off-site programs, thus competed for their attention.

All that changed on August 10, 1983, when a large range fire swept over the ground of the Custer battlefield unit, burning away sagebrush and accumulated thickets of dried buffalo grass leaving a scorched, barren plain dotted with blackened markers. While lamenting the fire and seared acreage left in its wake, Superintendent James V. Court saw a silver lining in the possibilities it afforded for archeological exploration. The blaze had consumed a vast tract of heavy grass that had seldom been grazed, removing it to terrain level. Both Court and Historian Neil C. Mangum recognized potential advantage in the circumstance. A preliminary archeological survey conducted by archeologist Richard A. Fox, Jr., then a graduate student at the University of Calgary, confirmed the possible location of burial sites in Deep Ravine and recovered human skeletal remains on Calhoun Hill, along the south end of the battle ridge. More remains turned up along a foot trail approaching Deep Ravine, while various cartridge casings likely fired from army and Indian firearms were also retrieved. Fox's preliminary findings spurred a formal request from Court and Mangum to the Rocky Mountain Regional Office in Denver for more intensive and systematic survey and testing of the entire singed battlefield land-scape while verifying the locations of markers on the field. While the regional office approved the project in principle, it authorized no funding for the work. Fox's report together with the project request, relayed to the National Park Service Midwest Archeological Office in Lincoln, Nebraska, won the support of Douglas D. Scott, chief of the Rocky Mountain Division. He quickly structured a two-year project to be codirected by himself and Fox. The Custer Battlefield Historical and Museum Association provided the necessary dollars for completing the work.[10]

Work got underway in May 1984. The field team consisted of one hundred volunteers who assisted over a five-week period with metal detecting, flagging of finds, excavating, photographing sites, assigning numbers, computerizing data, and otherwise recording archeological findings. Under the direction of Scott and Fox, the team proceeded with announced objectives to determine locations and movements of the soldier and Indian forces and to discover the variety of weapons employed by the Lakotas and Northern Cheyennes. The battlefield tract was divided into one-hundred-meter grids, each of which was systematically combed by a team of volunteers who retrieved and recorded all artifacts encountered. Materials excavated were individu-ally bagged for shipment to the Midwest Archeological Center for later analysis and documentation.

In May and June 1985, the project continued. (The 1985 work included an inventory of the Reno–Benteen Defense Site.) Over the course of the two field seasons, more than five thousand artifacts were retrieved, varying from thousands of expended cartridge casings and bullets to pieces of soldier uniforms and equipment, iron arrowheads, pocket knives, coins, bits of government horse gear, even a wedding ring; together, they formed a large data base that additionally incor-porated information from a variety of other sources and combined to permit judgments about the findings as a whole.[11]

The archeological project of 1984–85 constituted the first large-scale research effort to occur on Custer's field and brought forth a plethora of new data promoting conclusions about the manner of demise of his battalion. Together and separately, Scott and Fox analyzed the findings and based on artifact patterning reached several notable ver-dicts concerning the flow of the battle, among them, the governance of military discipline throughout most of the struggle; the existence of strong Indian positions on Greasy Grass Ridge conforming to the route of withdrawal of soldiers from the mouth of Medicine Tail Coulee at the Little Bighorn; army defensive positions at Calhoun Hill and the possible movement of some troops from there to the Keogh position; a strong Indian position east of Calhoun Hill that, together with similar sites on Greasy Grass Ridge, suggested that Company L troopers died in an intense cross-fire from two warrior groups. Another Indian position was located northeast of Custer Hill, while soldier skirmish positions were verified near the head of Deep Ravine and positions southwest of the Last Stand group.

Other findings confirmed Custer Hill as indeed the likely last stage of the battle, signified by a clustering of cartridge and bullet evidence. Findings relative to Deep Ravine suggested that that feature might have harbored the final desperate fighting by soldiers, likely men of Company E, until well-armed warriors overwhelmed them, although repeated attempts to locate bodies purported to be there, including the use of a power augur to penetrate the soil, proved unsuccessful. In addition to new information helping to interpret army and Indian movements during the Custer phase of the action, the archeology project identified various types of Indian guns (including repeaters), confirmed the use of bows and arrows by many of the warriors, made significant observations about soldier life and death based upon osteological study of recovered skeletal remains (including tentative personal identifications of some men), and employed forensic analysis of firing pin impressions to show movement of weapons (and presumably individuals) over the field. (All human remains discovered in the course of the 1984–85 field surveys were interred in the national cemetery on June 25, 1986.)

The innovative use of metal detectors, recording, and recovery, in fact, inaugurated a new model for the discipline of battlefield archeology as a whole. Chronicled in various media, the project drew worldwide attention to the park and promoted increased interest and visitation during succeeding years. Yet the survey work did not escape criticism from those who believed it inappropriate to dig up the site. Retired National Park Service chief historian and assistant director for cultural resources (and former park historical aide) Robert M. Utley opined that the results of the archeology were but "modest" when compared to the loss of dignity borne by the site and the loss of credibility on the part of the park service, which "violated its own [historic preservation] canons to embark on a fishing expedition of predictably rich publicity yield and highly doubtful . . . data yield." On another front, the projects encouraged some cases of artifact looting by trespassers entering the monument at night with metal detectors and digging up historical turf.[12]

The archeology project of 1984–85 effectively commenced a spate of collateral inquiries of limited and more direct scope that have intermittently transpired at the park since that time. These have included forensic evaluations of specific discoveries, such as that of a soldier's skull, humerus, and clavicle found at the Reno retreat crossing in 1989 (later buried in the national cemetery) and of the disinterred remains of ten individuals variously found on the battlefield between 1905 and 1925 and buried in seven graves in the cemetery, as well as archeological surveys of parts of the perimeter and adjacent lands of the Custer battlefield unit and the Reno–Benteen unit, including parts of Deep Coulee and tracts bordering the entrance road, which have brought forth new information regarding the possible movements of Custer's command, the Reno retreat, and the movement of the Reno and Benteen forces to and from Weir Point during the battle. More exploratory work was performed in Deep Ravine, including the use of ground-penetrating radar, in a continuing search for evidence of the soldier bodies purportedly buried there, and the postbattle equipment dump of the Reno–Benteen contingent was located and examined. The latter project provided more information about army equipment and soldier cultural behavior in combat conditions. And in 1996 work proceeded to reexcavate and re-restore the rifle pit entrenchments at Reno–Benteen originally studied in 1958.

More recently, clearance archeology was necessitated by the construction of the Indian Memorial, and the horse cemetery originally discovered by Superintendent Luce in 1941 near the cavalry monument was thoroughly excavated in 2002. All told, archeology generated by the initial survey of 1983 resulted in three major inventories, two excavation projects, and more than a dozen projects in the park or on adjacent lands. As before, many of the projects were funded by the Custer Battlefield Historical and Museum Association.[13]

In addition to the archeology, other research projects have been completed since the early 1980s either to benefit interpretation or to compile basic data on park resources. Attempts to gain insights into the battle action from Indians were not significant until the 1960s, when Park Historian Rickey initiated contact with Northern Cheyennes to determine where some of them fell during the battle. In the course of this effort, Rickey pursued interviews with John Stands In Timber, the Northern Cheyenne tribal historian, who provided much new information about battlefield sites gained in earlier years from his informants. These links, unfortunately, were not sustained after Rickey left, and it was only during the 1980s that the quest for this data resumed. It included the collection and transcription of modern Northern Cheyenne oral histories about the Battle of the Little Bighorn, undertaken on contract in 1985–86.

Other studies involved a survey of plant life on the battlefield following the 1983 fire, contracted for in 1984 and completed in 1987; an inventory of reptiles and amphibian species present in the park, conducted in 2001–2002; and a vegetation survey undertaken in 2000–2001. Unusual experiments in psychometry, not sponsored by the National Park Service, occurred between 1980 and 1986 and involved retired park historian Rickey's employment of a psychic to help determine incidents of personal trauma at the battle. While the experiments were seemingly successful, they were unconventional and lacked authority in professional circles, and the results have largely been viewed as interesting yet unverifiable asides to the battle history.[14]

Since National Park Service administration of the battlefield began in 1940, the park has acquired a large inventory of artifacts and manuscripts together comprising perhaps the single most important repository of historic objects, art, and documentary materials relating to the Battle of the Little Bighorn and the Indian wars of the trans-Mississippi West. There is also a respectable collection of natural history articles. These materials support the mission of the park in interpreting (through exhibition of objects and support of scholarly research) the Battle of the Little Bighorn to the public. Few accessions beyond occasional battlefield relics had been acquired during the years of War Department administration, and these had been used as display items in the stone house by early superintendents. It remained for the aggressive Luce to undertake the first conscious national effort to gather materials that would benefit both research and exhibitry needs at the park, a process initiated with his appointment and that endured throughout his tenure as superintendent. As a result of his early contacts, the park acquired through a donation from Dr. Verne A. Dodd, of Columbus, Ohio, the diary and letters of Dr. James M. DeWolf (Accession No. 7), killed during Reno's retreat from the valley. In August 1942 Luce finessed the indefinite loan of Seventh Cavalry records, manuscripts, photographs, and relics spanning the period from 1866 to 1916 from the regimental commander at Fort Bliss, Texas. The Seventh Cavalry

Collection (Accession No. 11), held in the park's safe deposit vault in an old bank at Crow Agency, served as a cornerstone for the park's archival collection.[15]

In November 1942 Luce engineered the acquisition of the important assemblage of paper and relic items that had belonged to Dr. Thomas B. Marquis (Accession No. 12). A dentist on the Northern Cheyenne Reservation, Marquis had accumulated a large number of artifacts from his Cheyenne friends. Later, as a resident of Hardin, he had exhibited many of them in a small museum. Marquis was an avid researcher and student of both the Indians and the Custer battle, and he generated a large number of manuscript items. Following his death in 1935, Marquis's collection was placed in storage in the Big Horn County Library in Hardin. Luce's contacts with Marquis's daughters, Minnie Hastings and Anna Heil, resulted in the donation of his artifact items to the National Park Service. In December 1942 Luce also succeeded in acquiring the papers, photographs, and relics of Captain Francis Gibson, a battle participant, through his daughter, Katherine Fougera (Accession No. 15).[16]

A premier cornerstone acquisition was the Elizabeth B. Custer Collection (Accession No. 19), consisting of thousands of artifacts, letters, manuscripts, and photographs that were bequeathed by the widow to a museum at the battlefield when one was finally built there. With the 1939 museum approval legislation in hand, Luce at first utilized the storage vault in Crow Agency; then in 1948 he had a coal bin converted into a fireproof steel-doored concrete vault in the park maintenance building. Mrs. Custer's collection arrived in May 1943 for safekeeping, at which time Luce and his wife, Evelyn, began inventorying its contents. Because of the probate process, the park did not receive final legal title to the Elizabeth B. Custer Collection until 1951. Following construction of the museum, many of the objects and papers it contained became a permanent part of the exhibits.

Luce facilitated the donation of yet another body of artifact materials in the spring of 1946, when a collection of battlefield relics and Fort Custer guns—as well as an authenticated Custer buckskin suit—held by the Big Horn County Library was presented to Custer Battlefield National Monument (Accession No. 25). More materials in the form of books, newspaper clippings, papers, and glass slides that had belonged to Colonel William C. Bowen (Accession No. 30), who had served in the Yellowstone region as a young Fifth Infantry officer in 1876–81, were donated by his daughter, Gladys Bowen, in 1949. Other important acquisitions for exhibit purposes were the Medals of Honor awarded to Private James Pym and Charles Windolph for service with the water party during the battle.[17]

Another important early acquisition was the Anson Mills material (Accession No. 44) donated by Mills's granddaughter, Mrs. R. E. Cotter. A career soldier, Mills had served in the Third Cavalry under Brigadier General George Crook in 1876 and had taken part in the fighting at Powder River in March of that year, at Rosebud Creek in June, and at Slim Buttes in September. His collection contained army and Indian items recovered at Slim Buttes, Dakota, including a Company I, Seventh Cavalry, silk guidon previously stripped from Keogh's command at the Little Bighorn. Mills had loaned the guidon to another institution, which had returned it to him in a decrepit state, and it arrived at the park in 1951 in like condition. At approximately the same time, Luce effected the donation of a number of Indian items—Sioux arrows, a war club, lance, pipe, and eagle feather war bonnet, among other items—from the Sioux Indian Museum in Rapid City, South Dakota (Accession No. 41). These articles reached the park in time to be integrated into the exhibits for the new museum.

Although not directly associated with the battle, a historically significant collection of firearms and Indian objects related to the 1876 period belonging to career officer George H. Harries was donated by a descendant, Edith M. Jenkins (Accession No. 52). Included were a .45-caliber Colt single action army revolver, as used by soldiers in the battle; a likely warrior-used .50-caliber Springfield rifle; a commercially available .44-caliber revolver, pattern of 1875; a "Green River" knife; a Plains war club; and a gun-shaped club bearing three striking blades.[18]

Since the early 1950s, the Custer Battlefield Historical and Museum Association has purchased various objects and collections, which were then donated to the museum. A singular contribution of the association was the Fred Dustin Collection (Accession No. 81), acquired in 1957, comprising the research materials, including books and maps, related to the Great Sioux War and the Little Bighorn collected by the author of *The Custer Tragedy* and representing virtually a lifetime of study of those topics. The association variously bought several uniforms and small arms for donation to the park. Another important contribution of the association was a collection of letters (Accession No. 127) belonging to photographer David F. Barry from Mrs. Custer, Frederick W. Benteen, and former Seventh Cavalry trumpeter John Martin. Later, the body commissioned Montanan J. K. Ralston to produce the oil painting, *Call of the Bugle*, which was added to the museum exhibits in 1965.[19]

In 1959 a major research component was added to the park with acquisition of the Hammer File, an exhaustive collection of biographical data about members of the Seventh Cavalry, together with accompanying civilian employees, in 1876, prepared by Dr. Kenneth Hammer of the University of Wisconsin at Whitewater. Hammer also donated a body of valuable research materials during the late 1980s (Accession No. 671). Meantime, through the years since 1940 the Custer Battlefield National Monument library collection had grown due to the diligence of the Luces and Historian Rickey in acquiring pertinent volumes, and by the early 1960s it contained several hundred books and monographs, many of them rare, devoted largely to the battle, the campaign, the army, and the Indians, as well to Custer and other personalities involved. In addition, several file drawers of research information had been assembled over the years and more or less segregated by topic. By 1964 many of the books and manuscript items had not yet been formally catalogued or properly curated, and during a visit to the park Regional Chief of Interpretation and Visitor Services Edwin C. Alberts noted the need to treat these materials, "some of which are probably of priceless value to scholars." Because of donation stipulations, the collections could not be permanently transferred to larger repositories more capable of managing them, and Alberts proposed a two- to three-month program to ensure their "proper curatorial and preservative treatment."[20]

A formal plan for treating the library and manuscript items at the park was submitted early in 1965, and inventorying and cataloging ensued preparatory to a National Archives microfilming project that got under way that summer. Acting Museums Coordinator Nan V. Carson explained the process introduced at the park to categorize and protect its archival acquisitions:

> Our goal was to establish a classification system and file plan for all of the . . . [documentary] collections at the park and to fully process a sufficient amount of the material contained in the [Elizabeth B.] Custer Collection to provide the park with a fully structured file and procedural plan. To achieve this, we sorted, collated, cataloged and filed a substantial amount of this particular collection, working, ordinarily, 14 hours of each day from Tuesday, January 26 through Saturday, January 30.

Some time was spent explaining procedures and the file plan to Historian [Andrew] Loveless, as well as working with other personnel at the park to train them in the mechanics of cataloging. When we completed work on Saturday evening, all appropriate basic files were begun, into which the remaining material in the Custer Collection, as well as all of the other substantial and important research and documentary collections at the area (with the exception of the official records of the 7th U.S. Cavalry), could be processed and incorporated.

Although by mid-June 1965 Historian Loveless reported that the cataloging project was nearly complete, it lasted into 1971, when the last of the materials were microfilmed. While most artifact items were by that time housed in the walk-in fireproof vault in the basement of the museum, many of the documentary items were kept in a locked non-fireproof file cabinet. Regional specialists urged the park to obtain a fireproof cabinet for those materials. In addition, during the late 1960s cataloging of the library books was completed by volunteer labor.[21]

In October 1975, fearing potential violence at the battlefield from Indian activist organizations during the upcoming centennial observance, park service officials determined that the archival and object collections should be protected by temporarily relocating them to Eastern Montana College in Billings (Custer's uniforms went into storage at the park service conservation laboratory in Harpers Ferry, West Virginia), and in 1979 a cooperative agreement was effected to that end. Later renewals with Eastern Montana College specified that until September 1984 that institution would continue curating the correspondence, manuscripts, books, and documents related to the Battle of the Little Big Horn. The arrangement, however, ultimately proved detrimental to the collection, and its return from Eastern Montana College coincided with recommendation for the establishment of one full-time park position to ensure its professional management.

Beginning in 1979 part of the photographic collection still housed at the battlefield was cataloged and indexed under the supervision of Historian Mangum; five years later, Mangum compiled the first comprehensive register of all photographs in the various collections at Custer Battlefield National Monument. Original images included tintypes, cartes-de-visite, cabinet cards, magic lantern slides, and stereograph cards by such well-known photographers as David F. Barry, Orlando S. Goff, John H. Fouch, Frank J. Haynes, and Stanley J. Morrow. Besides the photographs, the battlefield collections include a number of art works, such as J. K. Ralston's *Call of the Bugle* and another by the same artist, *After the Battle*, which depict the battlefield on the late afternoon of June 25, 1876. Another famous painting, one by Gayle Hoskins that adorned the dust jacket and end papers of William A. Graham's *The Custer Myth*, had been donated to the park by the Stackpole Publishing Company of Harrisburg, Pennsylvania. In 1975 the four-by-five-foot rendering titled *Custer's Last Fight* was sent to the National Park Service conservation laboratory in Harpers Ferry, West Virginia, for preservation treatment and was returned to the park in 1980.

In 1977 (and again in 1989) the park considered and rejected solicitations to acquire through purchase seventy-two portraits of Lakota survivors of the Battle of the Little Bighorn reportedly rendered by artist and author David Humphreys Miller between 1935 and 1941. A significant addition in 1979 was the 1885-pattern dress blouse owned by Custer's trumpeter, John Martin (Giovanni Martini), who carried the pivotal message to Benteen during the battle. And in the mid-eighties the park obtained Custer's personal photograph album, besides another gun that had been used in the battle.[22]

Throughout the 1980s, the collections increased in size as well as in value. Whereas a 1980 appraisal valued the museum holdings at $1 million, another completed just seven years later placed their worth at $5 million. (Historian Mangum used that figure and the consequent need for protection to argue for hiring a full-time curator at the park.) A major manuscript addition consisted of an important body of correspondence from Indian wars and Little Bighorn student Walter Mason Camp (Accession No. 312), donated to the park in 1986.

Mangum's successor as park historian, Douglas C. McChristian, meantime sought to improve the park's database, and thus enhance its research capability, with the addition of microfilm copies of army records and other pertinent materials related to the Seventh Cavalry. As McChristian explained, he hoped "to consolidate here at the battlefield pertinent record groups now held by other institutions, particularly the National Archives." Accordingly, the park acquired copies of the Register of Enlistments, 1866–93; the Seventh Cavalry Muster Rolls, 1866–84; and the Seventh Cavalry Regimental Returns, 1866–81. In the interest of preserving the unique manuscript items deposited in the various battlefield collections, McChristian also sought to have microfilmed many original documents, including those in the Camp Collection, to ensure their long-term protection. Further insurance came in the formulation of the park's first "Museum and Archival Use Policy," a guideline to aid the increasing numbers of researchers seeking information from the collections.[23]

Experienced curatorial attention for the varied collections at the park followed the 1990 appointment of Kitty Belle Deernose as museum curator, a position initially funded in the 1980s by the Custer Battlefield Historical and Museum Association. Deernose brought academic training in museum studies coupled with professional experience with Indian collections and archival materials, and during her tenure the treatment of collections at Little Big Horn Battlefield National Monument measurably improved. Moreover, her appointment coincided with an upsurge in research requests by the public, including those of several documentary film producers seeking historical images. Mail research requests likewise surged to several hundred per year in 1991–92.

Meantime, the park collections continued to multiply. In 1991 a new accession comprised a series of photographs of nine aged Sioux battle survivors taken by photographer Bill Groethe at a reunion in Custer State Park, South Dakota, in 1948. And in 1993 the park received by donation the Medal of Honor of Little Bighorn participant Henry W. B. Meching, together with his Indian wars campaign medal and other battle-related items. Included too were several period Sioux Indian artifacts, notably a necklace and bow and arrows purportedly acquired at the time of Sitting Bull's surrender in 1881.

A traumatic artifact loss was the February 1992 theft from a plexiglass case of First Lieutenant Donald McIntosh's bullet-scarred notebook, which had been on his person when he was killed during Reno's fight in the valley. Some time after the battle, it had been retrieved from a Lakota woman. The notebook had reposed in the museum exhibit for forty years. Although the culprit was eventually arrested, he unfortunately had seemingly destroyed the virtually irreplaceable artifact. The loss of the piece, however lamentable, nonetheless prompted a security-conscious rehabilitation of the museum gallery beginning in 1993.[24]

By the late 1990s the growing number of collections at the park presented manifold challenges, inviting professional review by the National Park Service archivists at the Western Archeological and Conversation Center (WACC) in Tucson, Arizona. Many of the older bodies of photographs and archival holdings needed evaluation relative to their organization, long-term preservation treatment, and accessibility. Many collections lacked finding aids, essential cataloging data, and adequate storage. In 1996–99 an archival assessment by WACC examined the needs of the Elizabeth Bacon Custer Collection, the Walter Mason Camp Collection, and the Seventh Cavalry Collection. One serious problem was the past intermingling of materials from different collections. Recommended treatment specified reorganizing the archival holdings to reestablish their provenance, and then microfilming them, while long-range plans envisioned their being scanned onto CD ROM to ensure better and more secure access. At the same time, Superintendent Mangum envisioned scanning the artifact collections for three-dimensional accessibility.

In 1998–99 several more collections, including the Thomas B. Marquis and David F. Barry collections, were recataloged, and work shortly began on others. In all, thirty-six accessioned groups were treated. These needs, meanwhile, corresponded to major improvements in the physical repository recommended in earlier storage plans. In 1997–98 store room and curatorial space (needed to accommodate the growing archeological collection and related records stemming from the various field projects) was significantly renovated and reoutfitted with appropriate cabinetry and flooring, and security and fire protection equipment, including cameras, was installed. Moreover, a survey of collection conditions was necessary for the large-format art works, paper documents, and photographs. At the same approximate time, the park historian's office, along with the basic park library exceeding three thousand volumes (minus certain rare volumes held in the downstairs vault), microfilm collections, data files, and diverse bodies of blueprints, maps, and plats, along with audio-video materials, was relocated to the old stone house (former superintendent's residence) to form the White Swan Memorial Library, dedicated in 1998.

Fee-demonstration funds, together with grants from Special Emphasis Program Allocation System (SEPA) funds, supported much of the work in 1997–98. A temporary museum technician position was added that year to aid in the overhaul, and the park was able to revise its scope of collections statement.

Another important project completed in 1997 dealt with policy development affecting the repatriation of human remains to appropriate tribes in accordance with the Native American Graves Protection and Repatriation Act, as well as with the actual return of remains variously recovered on the battlefield. Through 2000–2001, backlog cataloging continued, again with the help of WACC personnel, who also succeeded in reproducing several Indian ledger art drawings from the Thomas B. Marquis and Mary Jane Colter collections for exhibiting in the museum and scanning on CD-ROM. A museum disaster plan was formalized, along with comprehensive access and use policies governing patron use of the collections. Future projects anticipated computerized linkage to the Automated National Catalog Record System, further transfer of collection materials to microfilm and CD-ROM, and internet access to the library and museum collections.[25]

In sum, the efforts dedicated to collections management in 1996–99 represented the most comprehensive evaluation and treatment in the park's history and went a long way to correctly preserving the priceless national heritage that they compose. The Little Bighorn Battlefield National Monument collections are today broadly classified as cultural in nature. The Cultural Collection incorporates archeology, history, ethnology, and archives, although a natural history collection exists to incorporate data related to studies in biology, geology, and paleontology. As of 2003, the cultural component encompassed archeology holdings of 6,102 items; ethnology, 184; and history, 849, while archives documents totaled 34,730 pieces.[26]

CHAPTER 9

Nonprofit Support Groups and Interest Groups

Since the 1950s, several groups have contributed, both officially and informally, to support administrative and interpretive development at Custer Battlefield National Monument, renamed Little Bighorn Battlefield National Monument in 1991. Among these are cooperating associations, organizations acting under formal agreement with the National Park Service to serve as nonprofit partners in promoting enhancement of the visitor experience. Cooperating associations provide quality educational publications, related merchandise, and even learning programs to help visitors appreciate thematic values of a given park area, be it cultural or natural. Revenues generated from the sale of books, videos, and other products go to support park interpretation and visitor services programs. Earnings from sales help fund publications, scientific research programs, artifact acquisition and conservation, library purchases, and other educational activities. Cooperating associations are governed by boards of directors composed of individuals elected to the positions. Beyond cooperating associations, interest groups consist of organizations of persons sharing common identifying interests generally related to the subject matter that a park conveys in its interpretation and that often serves as a focus of action for the group.[1]

In the case of the several organizations related to the subject of Custer and the Battle of the Little Bighorn, many members (including officers) of one association also belong to others, and individual member loyalty to the subject matter sometimes transcends specific group purpose. At the park, the result of this multifarious and somewhat incestuous reality has, as a matter of course, historically instigated confusion and has in the long term affected park-group cooperation.

Historically, the single most influential and longest enduring cooperating association serving the park has been the Custer Battlefield Historical and Museum Association (CBHMA), a body whose early tranquil relationship with the monument in time turned tumultuous. Founded in January 1953 by virtue of a memorandum of agreement (MOA) initiated by Luce with the expressed purpose of augmenting park operations through sales of books and related publications, the CBHMA adopted a constitution and bylaws and formed a board of directors composed of "local men of prominence and special interest." Board and members worked aggressively to provide funds to facilitate the acquisition of important artifacts and collections, subsidize publication of brochures and monographs (as well as full-length books), and underwrite research, including that involved with the large archeological projects of the 1980s. The association variously purchased important art works for donation to the park, made available funding to create necessary summer positions, and contributed generously to the organization, cataloging, preservation, and microfilming of the extensive manuscript holdings. It also made several financial loans to other park areas, with substantial benefits to Custer Battlefield National Monument.[2]

The initial board of directors numbered seven individuals, with Judge Ben Harwood as president, George G. Osten, treasurer (Osten would be reelected for twenty-five years), and Edward S. Luce, executive secretary. At their initial meeting, the board drafted a constitution and bylaws, later approved by the regional directorate of the National Park Service. Membership in the association was elective but purposefully restricted from the general public: "It was the opinion of the board that for the present a compact organization composed of members vitally interested in the Custer Battlefield could best carry out the purposes and intent of the Association." Later, provision was made for limited expansion in membership to include "genuinely interested" persons. When Don Rickey, Jr., assumed the park historian position, he was elected to the group, and in July 1955 he succeeded Evelyn Luce as a director. At the time Superintendent Luce retired from the government in 1956, he resigned from the association, and Rickey took over as its executive secretary; thereafter, until the late 1970s, either the superintendent or the park historian formally functioned in that role. (Thereafter, the park historian served as "association coordinator.") Nine new members were elected that year, including artist J. K. Ralston and authors Charles

Kuhlman and J. W. Vaughn, boosting the body to seventeen people. Three years later, on December 14, 1959, the organization was incorporated and new bylaws were adopted.[3]

Through the early years, the CBHMA sales steadily increased. The first important acquisition and donation of the association was the 1956 purchase for $2,500 of the Fred Dustin Collection, followed by funding for its proper cataloguing. Two years later, Rickey asked for and received $3,000 to fund the archeology at Reno–Benteen. Although the body manifested continued interest in acquiring or controlling the land between Reno–Benteen and Custer's field, landowners resisted all overtures. Meantime, selective recruitment brought the membership of the body to thirty by early 1963. In that year the association approved spending $3,500 for Ralston's painting *Call of the Bugle* and the next year acquired the David F. Barry Collection for $1,200 for donation to the park.

In 1964 the association opposed the projected National Park Service demolition of the stone superintendent's home in the national cemetery in accordance with Mission 66 objectives, and its efforts went a long way to saving the historically significant building. By this time too, the CBHMA was involved in producing flyers and brochures to aid in interpreting the park to visitors, including the trail at Reno–Benteen. Sales in 1963 reportedly netted approximately $12,000; by 1965, the figured had exceeded $18,000.[4]

Throughout the 1960s, the association thus functioned as a small body augmenting the local programs of the National Park Service. Member Michael J. Koury recalled the yearly routine: "Once a year we met in the stone house, about twenty-five or thirty of us. We conducted a two-hour business meeting, usually comprising . . . a treasurer's report and the report by the battlefield historian (at that time a member of the board). When the meeting was adjourned, we all were invited to the superintendent's house . . . for a potluck picnic." With the increases derived from books sales, the CBHMA continued an able benefactor to park ventures. In 1967 the association funded artwork for the new park handbook written by Robert M. Utley, but the final outrage of members over the inclusion of the Leonard Baskin illustrations, particularly one showing a nude Custer in death, forced the first printing to appear with a blank page in place of the offending graphic, and soured relations between the group and the National Park Service. The association also backed publication of Rickey's administrative history, which appeared in 1967 as *History of Custer Battlefield*.

When it was determined that National Park Service policy precluded cooperating associations from involvement in land acquisition, the CBHMA made $14,000 previously earmarked for that purpose available to the park's interpretive program. In 1968 the association opened a branch outlet at nearby Bighorn Canyon National Recreation Area (it became independent in 1975), and total sales surpassed $28,000. Two years later, anticipating the upcoming centennial in 1976, the body designated a steering committee along with several subcommittees in readying for the event. Objectives included the production of a commemorative coin, issuance of a centennial stamp, and replication of a Springfield carbine as a commemorative item. A scholarship of $500 was made available for a student intent on attending college in Montana. The committee also tried unsuccessfully to gain loan of Comanche from the University of Kansas.[5]

As the association succeeded in its sales program in 1972, it employed eight people to handle its operations. Sales continued to rise, exceeding $58,000 during the year. Annual meetings continued to be held on the lawn of the old stone house, and in 1973 saw a record turnout with thirty-four members in attendance. A major donation in 1974 was $4,000 to subsidize Kenneth Hammer and the Brigham Young University archive collections in readying certain of the Walter Mason Camp Papers for publication. The book, comprising a significant addition to battlefield history, appeared in 1976 from Brigham Young University Press as *Custer in '76: Walter M. Camp's Notes on the Custer Fight* and was an instant hit among Little Bighorn aficionados.

Beginning in 1975, the association began publication of a bimonthly newsletter, which eventually evolved into *The Battlefield Dispatch* and has continued as a valuable chronicle of CBHMA affairs as well as park-related activities. As the battle centennial approached, the association sponsored "Artists, Authors, and Historians," a seminar in Billings, although most planning ultimately devolved on the park staff.

A significant change came in 1975 when an amendment to the bylaws proposed by the executive secretary and approved by the board permitted membership to any person interested in the battle—a profound departure from the previous elective system and a move that opened the association to Custer and battle enthusiasts from all over. Perhaps significantly for the course of future National Park Service–association relations, the switch to open membership coincided chronologically with the ongoing interpretive thrust begun in the 1960s to include more of the Indian perspective of the event in addition to that of Custer and the military.[6]

Concerns over funding by the centennial committee at length brought its dissolution by the National Park Service, and in 1975 the focus of the organization turned more directly to aiding cultural resources preservation in the park (e.g., donating $20,000 for refurbishment of the stone house). Most of CBHMA's centennial goals were scuttled, although plans for the carbine reproduction and commemorative medal came to fruition.

During the period of the centennial observance, several issues appeared that produced contention between the association and the park administration, many of them related to the National Park Service's conduct during the formal ceremonies. Criticism arose over the service's seeming solicitude at the presence of Indian activist Russell Means and his followers, as well as over the internal decision to largely ignore members of the Custer family who were present. Another postcentennial issue that repeatedly arose concerned a proposed name change for the park (and thus possibly for the CBHMA) removing the Custer name, while yet another questioned the executive secretary's perceived mishandling of the association's business activities. In the wake of the disagreements, the National Park Service drafted a document, signed by CBHMA, spelling out specific responsibilities to be adhered to by each signatory. A casually formed association book review committee that had monitored potential sales items was terminated and that function turned over to the park staff. Following completion of the work on the stone house in 1980, a large bronze plaque listing the founding members of the association was mounted on the exterior wall of the structure.[7]

Among beneficial accomplishments by the association during the early 1980s (when book sales profits generally exceeded $100,000 per annum) were its contributions to support the cataloging, microfilming, photographing, and indexing of park collections held at Eastern Montana College in Billings, as well as its disbursements to non-park-related groups. A committee was established to assist Superintendent James Court's Custer Battlefield Preservation Committee in the matter of land acquisition. These projects drew praise from National Park Service Rocky Mountain regional director Lorraine Mintzmyer, who addressed the membership at the annual meeting at the stone house in 1982. In 1984–85, the association generously underwrote the archeology project, the largest combined research endeavor yet undertaken at the park. The body further subsidized appointment of a staff curator for several years until the park service funded the position after the arrival of Superintendent Booher. Meantime, by late 1982, membership in the CBHMA, actively promoted by the park staff to bolster available funds for its programs, had climbed to 377, or about 300 more than in 1976 following the introduction of open membership; by late 1987 there were more than 2,500 members.[8]

Yet during this period accounting problems plagued the association. Early in 1984 the group's business manager was dismissed for mismanagement of funds, and a follow-up Department of the Interior Office of the Inspector General audit of CBHMA urged that board members provide more oversight to financial matters and that new accounting and reporting principles be established. At approximately the same time, a review panel assessing park publications and interpretation cited the need for "a better working relationship" between the association and superintendent and observed that "the demonstrated interest of this group might be channeled in a number of productive directions by the Superintendent."

In 1985 the park turned the book review function back to the association, which formed a six-member committee to consider and approve new titles. Throughout the 1980s, association members partook of area field trips to battle-related sites during the week of the annual meetings. As sales increased to $247,000, donations in support of park projects continued, with $25,000 in 1985–86 directed to produce a new interpretive film for screening in the visitor center, as well as to rehabilitate the dated relief map in the observation room (some funding was later withdrawn from the film project). In 1985 the first issue of *Greasy Grass*, a research annual, appeared, and in 1987, to promote further Little Bighorn research, the CBHMA sponsored its first annual symposium at Hardin Middle School, a perennially successful fixture ever since. In 1988–89, CBHMA donations to the park topped $100,000, and by 1991, when it moved its headquarters to Hardin and opened a new sales location, the body ranked high among cooperating associations in its support of the National Park Service. Associate Regional Director for Park Operations Homer Rouse lauded CBHMA: "I don't know of any association that has a bigger heart and greater interest in what's going on within their park than this one."[9]

While it matured and continued donations to support park enterprises, however, the changing and escalating association membership likewise became more independent in challenging park service views, as well as more strident in its complaints about park service administrative actions. The group's liberal funding of certain park positions, including that of curator, arguably created within its leadership a sense of investment and entitlement that was unjustified. Too, conflicted employee loyalty of CBHMA-funded employees supervised by park service staff often promoted unsettled working arrangements.

Moreover, while the group munificently extended its dollars to park projects, its ever-burgeoning membership through its board more overtly committed to an agenda promoting the sanctification of Custer and his men in its support of park affairs—this as the National Park Service sought to balance interpretation at the site. The CBHMA wrote a terse letter to National Park Service director William Penn Mott in 1988 after Indian activists placed an inflammatory marker on the mass grave at the base of the monument, an act that many members condemned as desecration. Exacerbating the incident, Russell Means appeared unexpectedly and spoke at the 1989 annual meeting. Later, the group publicly voiced objection to the "political" appointment of Barbara Booher as superintendent and to that of her successor, Gerard Baker, based on what members perceived as their insufficient credentials for the position. When Congress formally deliberated over changing the name of Custer Battlefield National Monument, the CBHMA membership voted three to one to oppose the measure ("revisionist history," penned one affiliate), and President Ron Nichols later conveyed the organization's position in hearings conducted in Billings. And in 1991, when the legislation was approved, the CBHMA decided against changing its longtime title to conform to the new park name, Little Bighorn Battlefield National Monument.

In the months following passage of the legislation, which also contained provision calling for establishment of an Indian memorial at the park, relations between CBHMA and the National Park Service further deteriorated. A prolonged dispute regarding sale of the Dee Brown book *Bury My Heart at Wounded Knee*, which the association book review committee, as well as the board of directors, had disapproved over the objection of Superintendent Barbara Booher, only heightened the growing estrangement. A similar dispute in 1992 regarding the non-scholarly book *Soldiers Falling Into Camp* added to the furor.[10]

The relationship did not improve. The National Park Service pronounced the growing lack of cooperation of the CBHMA as being beyond the tenets governing performance of a cooperating association. In the agency's view, CBHMA had evolved into an advocacy—even watchdog—group. Although park service officials applauded the CBHMA's internal operations, it believed that many of its members possessed "behavioral patterns that result in attacks on the park staff by letter, through the media, through congressional representatives, and by the membership directly." The Time-Warner North Shield Ventures, Inc., proposal in 1992–93 fueled the ongoing dispute, with the association squaring up in firm opposition to a plan that most members (as well as many National Park Service employees) believed jeopardized primary park resources and subordinated site interpretation from the park service to private enterprise (see chapter 6). In 1992 the park dissolved the CBHMA book review committee. The National Park Service renewed its MOA with the association for a one-year term, rather than the customary five years. Despite efforts of the CBHMA leadership to reach accord with Regional Director Robert M. Baker, the relationship faltered altogether when in August 1993 Baker suddenly terminated the MOA, directing the four-decades-old organization to cease operating at the park and to remove its property by late October. National Park Service director Roger G. Kennedy approved Baker's decision, and an appeal by the association board of directors to the secretary of the interior proved futile. At the park, the Southwest Parks and Monuments Association (later Western National Parks Association), a venerable partnering institution based in Tucson, Arizona, replaced CBHMA as the new cooperating association. In 1994 Superintendent Gerard Baker directed the removal of the bronze plaque dedicated to the founding members of CBHMA from the front of the stone house in the cemetery.[11]

Dennis Ditmanson, who had served at the park as a seasonal ranger in the 1970s—before the CBHMA membership expansion—and later as superintendent in the 1980s, offered the following assessment of the break:

> When I first encountered CBHMA in the early 1970s, it was still a small operation managed by park staff. . . . Contact with the Board was limited to a single visit each summer when an employee cookout was held in connection with what I recall was the annual meeting. When I returned as superintendent in 1986, I found a very active, very aggressive group that was both defensive about its role at the park and suspicious of Service actions relating to its operation. . . . The crux of the problem . . . [was] one of power and influence as well as perception. The

association board saw itself in a variety of roles: historical society, advocacy group, friends group, consultant, protector of the legend, etc., but I don't believe they ever made the connection that the Service viewed associations in yet another category. . . . They could never accept the fact that the park story had, over time, become inclusive of all points of view. They could talk the talk about seeking the "truth" and "telling the Indian side of the story," but I never perceived that they really meant it. In the end, they simply could not accept the notion that the park's mission encompassed all peoples.[12]

Thereafter, as the North Shield Ventures project failed, CBHMA functioned from afar and in later years sought to rebuild its affiliation with Little Bighorn Battlefield National Monument. In 1995 a Friends of the Little Bighorn Battlefield Committee of the CBHMA attempted a détente with the park, but the effort failed, and the liaison committee disbanded. Nonetheless, the association persevered in its endeavor to establish a conciliatory bond, in 1997 contributing funds to the park to purchase a photocopier in memory of longtime ranger-historian Clifford L. Nelson, who had been murdered at Seeley Lake, Montana, the previous year. In 1998, the return of Neil Mangum as superintendent promised a new beginning between the National Park Service and the CBHMA, and regular monetary donations to support park activities subsequently resumed, including a sum to benefit construction of the Indian Memorial as well as interpretive waysides. Through 2003, Mangum and his successor, Superintendent Darrell Cook, worked to once again include the association in a positive interest-group collaboration, thus assuring its future benevolence to park programs. Meantime, the Southwest Parks and Monuments Association became a valued partner, its gross annual sales consistently exceeding half a million dollars as it continued to support the park interpretive program with significant donations.[13]

Many members of the CBHMA also belonged to the preeminent Custer interest group, the Little Big Horn Associates (LBHA), "a non-profit society formed for the preservation of information and truths pertaining to the peoples and times of the Battle of the Little Big Horn, June 25, 1876 [sic]." While interested in the scholarly pursuit of information, the LBHA is also the heart of the Custer buffs—individuals whose avocational (and for some, emotional) lives revolve around the Custer persona and the Battle of the Little Bighorn.

Founded in early 1967 by several battle and Custer devotees mostly in Montana, Washington, and California, the small body printed a mimeographed newsletter that was disseminated among the incipient group. Following the appearance of an Associated Press story about the LBHA, membership increased rapidly. While associates came from all walks of life, their consuming interest in, and commitment to, Custer and the Little Bighorn ensured the group's proliferation.

In 1969 LBHA elected a board of directors and an editorial board to monitor the newsletter and the new *Research Review* journal dedicated to sharing research results generated by members. The organization continued to grow; in 1974 the group's first membership meeting was held in Louisville, Kentucky, an event presaging popular yearly convocations of lectures, exhibits, tours, and banquets all eliciting broad media coverage. Current membership exceeds eight hundred. The group publishes ten newsletters and two research journals per year; four hardbound volumes published in 1981, 1984, 1987, and 2002 carried original member contributions in the *Custer and His Times* series.[14]

For most of the first decade of its relationship with Custer Battlefield National Monument, the LBHA followed its governing credo. Members visited the park, researched in its holdings, and generally supported the park as they pursued their interests. Following the opening of membership in the CBHMA in the early seventies, many members of the LBHA also joined that body and after the conclusion of the National Park Service's centennial commemorative activities, widely perceived as inadequate, many in the LBHA membership aligned themselves with that of the CBHMA in disapproving the events and castigating park service officials for appeasing Russell Means and his followers and for affronting the Custer family. When the recurring matter of the name change appeared in the seventies and eighties, most members opposed it.

In the early summer of 1983, CBHMA and LBHA each held their annual meetings in the proximity of the park, and the cross-fertilization continued. During the LBHA meeting in Billings, however, prolific researcher/military historian and ardent Custerphile John M. Carroll, a prominent member of both groups and a member of the board of directors of the LBHA, who had previously (and independently) leveled a series of charges at park management, including one of "pro-Indian bias" in the interpretive program as represented in the quotation from Black Elk on the exterior front of the visitor center, called for the removal of Superintendent Court and Historian Mangum (both of whom had become LBHA members and active participants in the organization's conferences). Carroll lobbied LBHA members for support. His accusations brought Assistant Secretary of the Department of the Interior G. Ray Arnett to the park to attempt a resolution. In Billings, Carroll's sortie finally collapsed when the LBHA board meeting in executive session rejected his allegations and censured him for inappropriate use of the organization's name.[15]

LBHA leadership, however, soon had its own rifts with the battlefield administration over the existing book review selection process (which Carroll had also opposed) and pursuit of a balanced interpretive program, with the CBHMA over its board of directors nomination process, as well as with members of its own organization who disapproved of the board's conduct toward the park. Of particular import to some in the LBHA besides Carroll was the Black Elk quotation, which the leadership desired removed from the front of the visitor center. The October 1984 report of a Carroll-demanded independent review team examination of the interpretive program and other components of park service administration at the battlefield (see chapter 7), however, while sustaining the quotation, also obviated most other concerns of the LBHA board of directors.

In an attempt to further resolve differences and reconcile with the park, LBHA leadership imposed a six-month moratorium on communication by the board with the park service administration. The suspension period seemingly improved the working relationship on both sides, and since that time, the LBHA has more or less steered clear of controversy by reverting to an apolitical agenda respecting most park issues. At the 112th anniversary, however, when members of AIM placed the plaque honoring the victors atop the mass grave, some in the LBHA strenuously objected to this latest example of what they viewed as park service appeasement. (Other members, however, felt that, while such a monument to the warriors was indeed warranted, it should not be placed on a whim.) And when the North Shield Ventures proposal to develop a theme park at the site appeared in the early 1990s, LBHA adopted a broadly based position seeking to ensure the preservation of the historical integrity of Little Bighorn battlefield and to oppose commercial development seemingly inherent in the plan that might threaten the property. Members of the LBHA, as well as other battlefield interest groups, became riled when Superintendent Baker invited tribal groups associated with the battle to take part in a war honors tradition—known as "counting coup"—on the cavalry monument atop Custer Hill during the 120th anniversary proceedings.[16]

Another significant interest group is the aforementioned Custer Battlefield Preservation Committee (CBPC), organized by Superintendent Court and Hardin attorney Harold Stanton in 1982 with the sole intent of preserving the battlefield property from diverse commercial intrusions and continued with Court as executive director for more than two decades (see chapter 6). According to its promotional literature, the park included but one-tenth of the land fought over in 1876 and the committee needed to raise more than $8 milliion to acquire additional acreage, which following congressional authorization could be conveyed to the National Park Service. Moreover, the potential for wide-scale off-park development concerned Court ("Once this land has been altered, the personal interpretation of the montage of fact and conjecture will be unattainable. . . . This place must be preserved as is, as it has always been.") Since that time, land acquisition through purchase or exchange supported by tax-deductible donations has targeted some 9,000 acres surrounding and connecting parts of the battlefield terrain (Reno–Benteen and Custer's battlefield), as indicated in the park's languishing 1986 General Management Plan, and by the late 1990s garnered more than 3,500 acres. The transfer of the acquired property to National Park Service administration yet awaits donation and congressional sanction and legislation, but the political reality is that the Crow Tribe generally continues to oppose an action that its leaders feel might negatively restrict its land base. (In 1987 some of the Crows demonstrated against the park service's land protection plan, which called for enlarging the land base and was thus seemingly aligned with the objectives of the CBPC. National Park Service director William Penn Mott personally assured the Crow Tribe that their land was secure.) Despite the positive intentions of the CBPC, its efforts have been occasionally stymied by the park administration, which in 1993, for example, removed its lucrative donation box from the visitor center on grounds that the committee did not formally account for the money received from it.[17]

Other interest groups exist, but most are either too remote geographically or more topically diverse to be constant influential factors at the park, although their membership rosters often mirror those of the CBHMA, LBHA, and the CBPC. At least one group, the Custer Association of Great Britain, lies more than an ocean away (although its members frequently visit), while another, the Order of the Indian Wars, reflects a consuming interest in the Indian conflicts of the trans-Mississippi West as a whole, not just the Battle of the Little Bighorn. Most all of these groups are interconnected, and members remain knowledgeable on issues affecting the park, partly at least through various newsletters published periodically by the organizations as well as by concerned individuals.

Meantime, out of the wake of the demise of the CBHMA at the park, another group emerged to actively support park programs through donations and volunteerism. The Friends of the Little Bighorn Battlefield, a nonprofit fund-raising body, signed an MOA with the National Park Service in March 1998. President Bob Reece, ever-cognizant of the recent past, let it be known that the group was "not a 'Custer' organization. We are non-political and we do not favor one particular side of the conflict (cavalry or Indian). Instead we promote diversity at the battlefield with our projects and in assisting with interpretation at the battle site." Since its organization, the Friends of the Little Bighorn Battlefield, through sponsoring various activities, has aided staff interpretive visits to Deep Ravine, helped host the dedication of White Swan Library, and raised funds to assist in the placement of warrior casualty markers on the battlefield, as well as helped preserve the Fort C. F. Smith marker in the national cemetery and donated funds to pay for park interpretive wayside exhibits.[18]

As the work of the Friends of the Little Bighorn Battlefield proceeds, its members uphold the important service tradition that past support and interest groups have maintained and still maintain in the park's history, while testifying to the continuing high interest in the Battle of the Little Bighorn among the general public. Despite the controversies that foreshadowed its demise as a cooperating association, the CBHMA led the way in providing quality publications and related materials to augment and enhance the interpretive experience for millions of park visitors, and the organization survives as an interest group whose members still seek to serve the park's needs. Indeed, members of all of these groups are extremely knowledgeable—often expert—in the history of the Battle of the Little Bighorn. Finally, together or separately, the several associations enthusiastically carry on as important partners whose efforts can significantly benefit Little Bighorn Battlefield National Monument today and in the future.

CHAPTER 10 | # Indian Memorial

Recognition of Indian participation in the Battle of the Little Bighorn has been a long time coming. Beyond basic acknowledgement of their historical presence during the event, the government during the years of War Department administration and well into the period of National Park Service administration viewed the Indians largely as faceless people without historical investment in the struggle that had occurred there, even though the short-term aftermath had proved cataclysmic to their traditional existence. Removed to the reservations, the Lakotas and their Cheyenne compatriots and their descendants thereafter passed uneasy lives as they subsisted on government doles, forgotten by most Americans—symbolically fleeting impediments to white civilization, a momentary backlash in the course of American imperialism.

During the years since 1876, relatives had occasionally placed stone cairns on the field to indicate where warriors had been killed or wounded in the fighting. These contrivances constituted the first Indian monumentation on the site. Yet federal recognition of Indian valor was not a consideration, and in 1925 Mrs. Beaverheart's letter requesting help in formally marking where her father had died in the battle went unanswered.[1]

As mentioned, War Department oversight of Custer Battlefield National Cemetery between 1879 and 1940 provided little interpretation of the site, and what existed promoted the role of Custer and his soldiers above that of the warriors who had defeated them in mortal combat. Although by this time individuals like ethnologist George Bird

Grinnell, Judge Eli S. Ricker, Walter M. Camp, and Dr. Thomas B. Marquis had interviewed Indian participants of the Little Bighorn and other conflicts for several decades, Indian accounts of the engagement were not widely circulated and, moreover, were viewed by white historians as conflicting, confusing, and irreconcilable to the presumed course of events. While interpretation increased following transfer of the site to the National Park Service, it remained the military perspective—chiefly that dealing with Custer and his soldiers—that garnered the most attention and was conveyed to the public, enabled by the presence of Superintendent Edward S. Luce, himself a former Seventh Cavalry soldier with a manifested interest in army history.

That interpretation continued with negligible change to what one historian has termed a theme of "patriotic orthodoxy," wherein the heroic Custer and his troops fell sacrificially—and thus symbolically—to an overwhelming horde of savages.[2] By the 1960s through the early 1970s, however, white Americans were beginning to reassess their historical treatment of Indian people, with books like *Bury My Heart at Wounded Knee* and *Custer Died for Your Sins* promoting social awareness respecting Indians historically as well as in the modern population. As a result, interpretation at Custer Battlefield National Monument during the 1970s gradually transformed to include more Indian perspectives and thus more balance (see chapter 7). (As early as 1956 a wooden marker had been placed on battle ridge denoting where Chief Lame White Man fell.)

Already, North Dakota governor William L. Guy had suggested the need "to memorialize the Indian Americans . . . in a way at least equal to the memorials already lavished on the white Americans of Indian war fame," a view that drew congressional support in that state's delegation. Secretary of the Interior Rogers C. B. Morton also received letters from citizens desirous of seeing a monument at the park dedicated "to the warriors who fought so valiantly to preserve their land." In 1972 Superintendent Eldon Reyer refused to permit AIM members to erect a plaque dedicated to the warriors who fought "the hostile aggression of the United States government." And when in the next year the group Indians for Equality appealed to Morton for a memorial, Chief Historian Utley responded that the battlefield, in fact, already served as a "memorial to the participants of both sides" and that installing another monument would lessen the site's historical integrity and detract from "the honor done to the victorious Indians and defeated Cavalrymen and Indian scouts."

Simultaneous with the rising attention to the Indian side of events was budding opinion for a park name change that would more properly reflect neutrality at the battle site. In 1971 Superintendent William A. Harris proposed changing the name to Little Bighorn National Battlefield to "demonstrate that the National Park Service, the Federal Government, and the American public recognize both sides of the issue equally." As it stood, wrote Harris, to the Indians the park was but "another example of [the] white man's oppression of their culture and heritage." Harris's recommendation received endorsement from the Washington office and was later included in the park's 1975 Statement for Management.[3]

The change did not become reality, however, for another sixteen years. During the interim Indian activist groups seeking inclusiveness demonstrated at the park several times. In October 1972 AIM members of the Trail of Broken Treaties, including Russell Means, conferred with Superintendent Reyer unsuccessfully seeking to install a plaque at the park honoring "our heroic warriors," although Reyer acknowledged the need "to have the battlefield viewed from the Indian standpoint as well as from Custer's." Four years later, Means and his followers appeared during the centennial observance with the same request. Superintendent Hart told them that the National Park Service would support a proposal for a monument initiated by the Indians and of a design approved by the agency director. In 1988 the Indians renewed their quest, appearing at the park on the anniversary of the battle to boldly assert a history of abuse of their people at the hands of the federal government. As the speeches proceeded, Means's followers produced shovels, stripped sod from the mass grave atop Custer Hill, mixed cement, and installed a three-foot-square steel commemorative plate with a welding rod inscription reading, "In honor of our Indian Patriots who fought and defeated the U.S. Calvary [sic] In order to save our women and children from mass-murder. In doing so, preserving rights to our Homelands, Treaties and sovereignty. 6/25/1988 G. Magpie Cheyenne." Throughout the events, Superintendent Ditmanson and park rangers stood by amid "palpable tension," wisely opting to allow the action to continue rather than to risk violent confrontation that would possibly harm park visitors and threaten other park resources. Ditmanson told Means that his request for the plaque to remain would be forwarded to the director of the National Park Service, and "with that, the activity broke up fairly quickly."[4]

The plaque remained atop the grave for more than two months. It was eventually relocated for exhibit to the visitor center, as the National

Park Service committed to providing an appropriate alternative, and in May 1989 an Indian Memorial task force was formed to evaluate possible sites on the battlefield for a future permanent memorial.[5] Among four tentatively identified locations based on visibility and visitor accessibility, a site perhaps seventy-five yards north of the mass grave and monument atop Last Stand Hill was generally favored as most suitable. The theme for the memorial, "Peace through Unity," was adapted from statements of Enos Poor Bear, elder of the Oglala Sioux, and Austin Two Moons, elder of the Northern Cheyennes.

The successive appointments of Barbara A. Booher and Gerard Baker as superintendents in 1989 and 1993 opened dialogues long missing with the Indian community, hastening changes that had been evolving slowly at the park. Booher's appointment besides gave impetus to the park name change as well as to the movement for a lasting memorial.

While initial congressional efforts to authorize the memorial stalled in the 101st Congress in 1990, subsequent legislation (House Resolution 848) introduced in the 102nd by Representative Ben Nighthorse Campbell (Dem.-Colo.) to effect the name change as well as authorization for the Indian Memorial succeeded through hearings in the designated House and Senate subcommittees, where most opposition was registered to the name change. Subsequently, the measure passed both bodies by November 1991, and on December 10, 1991, President George H.W. Bush signed it into law.[6]

Specifically, the first part of the act decreed that the former Custer Battlefield National Monument would henceforth be known as Little Bighorn Battlefield National Monument, and that the national cemetery would be known as Custer National Cemetery. The second part of the act dealt with the Indian Memorial, acknowledging the monument raised to Custer and his men in 1881 and noting the lack of comparable recognition to commemorate the Indians "who gave their lives defending their families and traditional lifestyle and livelihood." The act authorized establishment by the secretary of the interior of an eleven-member advisory committee composed of six individuals (including a chairperson) representing tribes that took part in the Battle of the Little Bighorn "or who now reside in the area," two individuals being artists of national stature, and the remaining three "being knowledgeable in history, historic preservation, and landscape architecture." Members of the commission were charged with ensuring the design, construction, and maintenance of the memorial, to include the selection of a site "on the ridge in that part of the Little Bighorn

Battlefield National Monument which is in the vicinity of the 7th Cavalry Monument." The design of the memorial would be selected from a national design competition, with criteria including compatibility in form and scale with existing park resources as well as sensitivity to history and artistic merit.[7]

Despite some early thought that construction of an Indian memorial would destroy pristine battlefield terrain, the proposed site had previously been disturbed during the years of army administration, and the project complied with National Park Service management policies. Therein, such a memorial as was proposed was categorized as a commemorative work "designed to perpetuate in a permanent manner the memory of a . . . group, event, or other significant element of history." In compliance with policy, the memorial would, moreover, be located to "avoid disturbance of natural and cultural resources and values" and sited "in surroundings that are relevant to the subject of commemoration and where it will not encroach upon any existing commemorative work and not interfere with open space and existing public use." Ethnographically, National Park Service policies acknowledged tribal needs to pursue traditional religious and cultural practices, and the Indian Memorial would thereby require the park to plan and execute programs "reflecting informed concern for the contemporary peoples and cultures traditionally associated with them." Finally, management policies permitted a cultural landscape to be "rehabilitated for contemporary use if . . . rehabilitation will retain its essential features and will not alter its integrity and character or conflict with park management objectives."[8] In the tenor of political correctness, however, little consideration apparently was given the fact that placement of any new memorial would further degrade the primary resource. Technically, the cavalry monument had been installed soon after the battle and was considered part of the historic scene. Erection of any other memorial, Indian or otherwise, more than one hundred years later would only compromise the site and threaten the integrity of an already jeopardized cultural landscape.

On Veterans Day 1992, a large group of tribal representatives gathered at Little Bighorn Battlefield National Monument to acknowledge the new name of the park and the authorization for the Indian Memorial. Meantime, the first steps following passage of legislation involved drafting a charter and selecting the eleven-member Indian Memorial Advisory Committee (six of them tribal representatives) to advise and consult with the secretary of the interior regarding the memorial, its site, and the national design competition, with seven serving as jurors in the competition. The charter was approved by Secretary of the Interior Manuel J. Lujan late in 1992. In the spring of 1994, Secretary of the Interior Bruce Babbitt appointed the members, and at their first meeting in Billings on August 2–3, 1994, the appointees were sworn in and initiated their work. Dr. Leonard Bruguier was selected chair of the committee. For the next three years, the members donated several days each quarter to meet and fulfill their assignment. As Linda Pease recalled, "We never saw things eye to eye, yet we all . . . would compromise, putting our emotions aside. The National Park Service would regularly advertise our meetings in the *Federal Register* and the *Lakota Times*, hoping we would gain input from the tribal communities that could attend freely. Rarely did anyone attend."[9]

The competition to seek an appropriate conceptual design for the Indian Memorial began on August 1, 1996, when the advisory committee announced a call for entries and began distribution of program packets. The announcement encouraged submissions from amateurs, students, and design professionals based on the "Peace through Unity" theme and declared awards of $30,000 for first place, $15,000 for second place, and $5,000 for third place for the winners, as well as six honorable mention certificates, following evaluation by the jury of all tendered designs.

A symposium at the park September 7–9 provided background for entrants and prospective entrants. The registration deadline was September 24, and contestants were permitted to ask questions through the following week. Design submissions were required to be postmarked by January 13, 1997, and winning entries (out of more than five hundred) were announced on February 17, 1997 following a week-long deliberation by the jury in Billings and public exhibition of the submitted designs in Denver. First prize went to John R. Collins and Allison J. Towers of Philadelphia, Pennsylvania. Their winning submission consisted of a circular stone and earthen structure subtly rising from the surrounding prairie and graced with openings facing the cardinal directions, reflecting tribal spirituality distinct to the nearby army monument. Two decorated lodge poles stood on either side of an axial gap bisecting the enclosure as a "Spirit Gate" aligned as counterpoint to the army monument. Inside, a weeping wall symbolized the tears of American Indians whose lives were uprooted, while adjoining marble panels acknowledged all tribes who participated at the Little Bighorn, including those who scouted for the army, and accommodated year-round ceremonial use as a living memorial. Prominently adorning a platform at north center of the interior stood an open bronze glyphic sculpture denoted "Spirit Warriors," equestrian tribesmen silhouetted against the sky and distant landforms as to symbolize the ethereal reality of human existence.[10]

In September 1997 the Roybal Corporation, a Denver architectural and engineering firm, received a contract from the National Park Service to transpose the winning design into construction documents. And in 1998 a required archeological survey of the projected site mitigated any potential compliance problems in placing the Indian Memorial. Yet funding for building the structure was not immediately forthcoming; the 1991 legislation provided only for donations "from individuals, foundations, corporations, or public entities for the purpose of providing for the memorial," and the anticipated cost exceeded $2 million. Impetus for the fundraising drive came on Veterans Day 1999, when tribal representatives, Indian Memorial Advisory Committee members, veterans of several wars, and National Park Service officials assembled at the park for a groundbreaking ceremony at the designated site for the memorial. Regional Director Karen Wade addressed the need for completing the memorial, and Jay Vestal of the National Park Foundation spoke of his office's ongoing efforts to initiate a national fundraising campaign. Former Superintendent Barbara Sutteer (formerly Booher), now of the Intermountain Regional Office's Office of American Indian Trust Responsibility, unveiled a sign denoting the location, while Chairman Leonard Bruguier symbolically spaded the earth with a "gold-plated" shovel. Afterward, Superintendent Mangum remarked that "the focus now is raising the $2 million. . . . The commitment is there."[11]

Donations, however, barely trickled in. The National Park Foundation's efforts stalled for lack of funding and only managed $70,000 by mid-2001. Although the Northern Cheyenne Tribe contributed $5,000, and the Friends of the Little Bighorn sponsored an Indian Memorial Run that yielded $2,000, other offerings, including raised entrance fees to help build the memorial and donations through the park web site, were not enough. For one thing, members of the tribal communities believed that support should come from both Indian and non-Indian sources, and, moreover, the federal government should principally fund the project; historical precedent for that view existed in the funding of the army monument in 1881 and its maintenance ever since. Early in 2001, Superintendent Mangum concluded that "after eight months of intensive solicitation activity, it appears that achieving the goal will be more difficult than expected. Indian tribe [contributory] prospects have not been forthcoming with lead gifts as planned. It is proving difficult to make a strong solicitation argument to non-Indian sources when those groups with a close relationship to the project have not committed first." The inaction and delay proved frustrating. "I think it's time to build it," observed Mangum. "It's been way too long. . . . Otherwise it looks like another government promise to a people that will be broken." He had come to believe that, although the enactment legislation had specified donations to raise the memorial, the law did not preclude the use of federal dollars. In the end, Mangum took his case directly to the Montana congressional delegation in Washington, D.C., impressing the members with his argument for federal dollars to build the memorial. With support from U.S. senator Ben Nighthorse Campbell, the delegation responded favorably, in October 2001 adding $2.3 million for line-item construction to complete the project to the Department of the Interior's 2002 appropriation.[12]

Funding thus assured, the park proceeded with plans to begin construction as soon as possible. Early in 2002, with construction documents prepared and compliance issues resolved, the superintendent announced that a contract would be awarded before the end of March, with construction starting in April, the Indian Memorial completed by August (later rescheduled for November and, ultimately, into 2003), and dedication ceremonies tentatively to occur on Veterans Day 2002 (later rescheduled for June 25, 2003). Mangum, who had previously extended his tour at the park, now accepted reassignment, and Darrell J. Cook, superintendent of nearby Bighorn Canyon National Recreation Area, assumed the added responsibility of stewarding Little Bighorn Battlefield National Monument with the commitment of seeing the memorial finished. Architect Rudolph B. Lobato of the Intermountain Region Office in Denver served as project manager of the construction. Accordingly, under Lobato's overall guidance, on April 12, 2002, work got underway by the general contractor, CCM, Inc. (Cain Construction Management, Inc.), of Billings. Colleen Cutschall, an Oglala Lakota artist and professor at Brandon University in Manitoba, was selected to produce the "Spirit Warriors" sculpture in bronze. On recommendations from the advisory committee and park staff, the earlier design was refined to include a woman figure, and the Christopher S. Collins Studio, of Glenside,

Pennsylvania, began preparation of the full-size preliminary artwork model from which the final bronze sculpture would be cast. Another contract would obligate funds to complete the tribal messages on the integral stone interpretative panels inside the memorial.[13]

Construction delays in the base structure caused by changed orders, along with misinterpretations of design drawings, time extensions, and contract modifications, combined to impede completion of the Indian Memorial until late April 2003. Inside the embedded walls of the structure, the marble adjoining panels remained incomplete, the spaces occupied by temporary masonite sheets dedicated to the assorted tribes represented in the battle. Meantime, the model "Spirit Warriors" sculpture, was transported by the Collins brothers of the designer/artist team from Pennsylvania to Lander, Wyoming, where Eagle Bronze Foundry used it to produce wax molds for casting the final sculpture. The completed piece received a final chemical wash chosen by the artists for a patina finish. Installation of the sculpture took place on April 17, following which the general contractor completed grade and surface treatments, walkway reconstruction, and began revegetation of the surrounding ground.

A final assessment of the project occurred on May 29, 2003, and CCM agreed to complete closing tasks by early July and following the dedicatory proceedings. On Superintendent Cook's recommendation, installation of the Spirit Gate lodge poles, originally designed to "celebrate the axis connecting the Indian Memorial with the Cavalry obelisk, thereby enhancing their relationship and the 'Peace through Unity' message" was indefinitely delayed because of aesthetic concerns registered by the tribes. While all of this proceeded, Superintendent Cook and the park staff, with the help of former superintendent Barbara Sutteer, hosted several planning and consultation meetings with the historically affiliated tribes to formulate the dedication ceremony. In the end, the tribes prepared the agenda and invited speakers and participants, while the park served only to host the event and to participate in planned activities.[14]

In what was the most broadly meaningful observance in the park's history, dedication ceremonies for the Indian Memorial took place on Wednesday, June 25, 2003, the 127th anniversary of the Battle of the Little Bighorn. Tepees once more intermixed with the cottonwoods bordering the Little Bighorn River, harboring visitors and participants in the proceedings. Ponies grazed nearby. The day started cold and damp with the sky partly overcast, though sunshine and warmth steadily increased. Anticipating large crowds (an estimated nine to ten thousand people attended the daylong activities), the park waived all admission charges and arranged with the Crow Tribe for parking space in lots close to Crow Agency. Buses continually shuttled visitors to and from the park, with only handicapped accessible spaces designated near the visitor center.

Echoing the conciliatory theme "Peace through Unity" that had guided creation of the Indian Memorial, the day's activities led off with a daybreak Prayer for World Peace service atop the battle ridge, followed by tribal pipe ceremonies at the new memorial that included meditation, songs, and drumming. At 8 a.m., riders in traditional dress from among the Crows, Northern Cheyennes, Lakotas, Arikaras, and Arapahos moved along Battle Ridge to the Indian Memorial, then passed on to the amphitheater west of the visitor center. An hour later, Indian members of several veterans' posts, preceded by members of the Second Battalion, Seventh Cavalry, from Fort Hood, Texas, marched in procession from the old stone house through the cemetery to the amphitheater, en route lowering the flag to half staff and initiating the formal activities. Following the playing of the National Anthem, the units posted colors at the Indian Memorial, thereby formally dedicating the new park addition.

Then, at about 10:20 A.M., came programmed speeches by invited dignitaries and guests, introduced to the audience by former superintendents as hosts—all key players in the development of the Indian Memorial—Barbara Sutteer, Gerard Baker, and Neil Mangum. (Superintendent Darrell Cook, who oversaw construction of the memorial, modestly deferred his own contributions to those of his predecessors throughout the event.) Among the dignitaries were Montana governor Judy Martz, Secretary of the Interior Gayle Norton, Senator Ben Nighthorse Campbell and former Montana representative Pat Williams (both of whom had helped pass enabling legislation for the memorial in 1991), Northern Cheyenne tribal president Geri Small (the Northern Cheyenne Tribal Council had passed a resolution supporting the dedicatory ceremony), Crow tribal chairman Carl Venne, Standing Rock Sioux tribal vice chairman Tom Iron, Cheyenne River Sioux tribal chairman Harold Frazier, Rosebud Sioux tribal president William Kindle, and Fort Peck Sioux tribal councilman Leland Spotted Bird. Honored guests included the Hopi family of Iraqi War victim PFC Lori Piestewa, the first American Indian woman to die in combat as a member of U.S. forces. Campbell, chairman of the Senate

Committee on Indian Affairs, whose efforts led to the name change as well as the memorial's authorization, told the throng that "one hundred and twenty-seven years is a long time to wait." During the proceedings, a war-bonneted Russell Means, whose actions years earlier in many ways precipitated the day's activities, briefly commandeered the podium, presenting an impromptu, largely conciliatory, address. (AIM members meantime retrieved the plaque installed near the monument in 1988 and thereafter exhibited in the visitor center, moving it to the Indian Memorial for the day before removing it from the battlefield for their own museum; the park deaccessioned the piece).

Following a barbecue luncheon, the presentations continued with remarks by representatives of the Arapaho Tribe, Oglala Sioux Tribe, Southern Cheyenne and Arapaho Tribes, and Three Affiliated Tribes (Arikara, Mandan, and Hidatsa). In the afternoon, a flyover of the Battle Ridge by Montana Army National Guard Black Hawk helicopters honored American veterans of all wars. An open forum later proceeded at the amphitheater and the Indian Memorial, followed by dedication by Park Historian John Doerner near the memorial of a marker for an unknown Lakota warrior killed near Last Stand Hill on June 25, 1876. The next day Doerner conducted a ceremony dedicating a similar marker for Dog's Backbone, a Minneconjou Lakota warrior killed during the fighting at Reno–Benteen on June 26, 1876. On June 29 the historian unveiled a marker and wayside exhibit east of the cavalry monument at the site of the Seventh Cavalry Horse Cemetery, where the remains of army horses had been discovered during construction of the Indian Memorial.[15]

The dedication of the memorial to their fallen held great significance to the people of the tribes involved in the Battle of the Little Bighorn. At long last their achievement at arms was recognized. Their stories of the battle, once ignored or considered irreconcilable, had been increasingly validated—even confirmed—by scholars and battle students (much of the archeological work over the previous twenty years bolstered and/or verified many Indian accounts of the action) so that their testimony now comprised an important reservoir to enrich interpretation at the park. But beyond this redemption of human credibility, the people's ownership of place was acknowledged and their dignity respecting it affirmed.

Commentary from attendees at the dedication was mostly conciliatory, with much of it devoted to the propriety of regaining long lost recognition. Tim Lame Woman, a Northern Cheyenne who in 1988 had marched with Russell Means to place the impromptu plaque, said that the idolization of Custer and his monument "was a continued insult." "We wanted America to recognize our contributions, but nothing was up there, and it hurt. . . . We finally have something, a place for our children to go and see." Emmanuel Red Bear, a descendant of Sitting Bull and Crazy Horse, noted that "there will never be a day when everything will be made up to us, but coming back here is like a healing to us." Ernie LaPointe, likewise a descendant of Sitting Bull, also saw the Indian Memorial as "a long overdue memorial to the victors." And William C. Hair, a Northern Arapaho, believed that "this memorial is the first time in the history of the United States of America that aboriginal people are being recognized through governmental processes. This is the closest we'll ever come to acknowledgement from the government of the atrocities we have suffered."

Yet others viewed the structure as symbolizing the strength and survivability of the Indian community. "It took 127 years to get this," observed Northern Cheyenne Geofredo Little Bird, a participant in the daybreak ceremony. "They were trying to exterminate all the tribes from the face of the earth. But we are still here. . . . The memorial shows us as we are today, [and] . . . we belong here now." His tribesman Clifford Long Sioux addressed the cruel irony inherent in the Indian victory: "Even though the battle was won, our way of life completely changed forever." Beyond honoring the Indians, Long Sioux saw the memorial as a means of reconciliation between Indians and whites: "It's time for healing, and this is part of the healing process." George Amiotte, an Oglala Lakota healer, wearing the four purple hearts and bronze star awarded him as a marine in Vietnam, prayed at the memorial: "Today is a beautiful day to be alive in the great circle of life. Remember the beauty of their deaths. Make the warriors who laid down their lives proud of you." And Northern Cheyenne Donlin Many Bad Horses remarked on the crowd: "This is the most beautiful day I ever saw. . . . I'm very glad so many people came out—came out to see what kind of people we are, the proud people we are."[16]

Former superintendent Barbara Sutteer believed that the moment was ripe for change. "People say it was just done because it was politically correct, but I don't think so. It goes back to timing and thinking at the time, and the people wanted to see something done." She also saw the breaking down of communication barricades as propitious for history and believed that the presence of the memorial would "bring out new accounts, sharing, and new learning." Even initial opponents of the memorial evinced optimism through the temperance of their remarks. Kevin J. Connelly, president of the Custer Battlefield Historical and Museum Association, which had contributed funds to the memorial project, acknowledged the appropriateness of the structure: "Some think there could have been a better place for it, but for the most part our members accept it. The fight is over." Father Vincent A. Heier, a long-time Custer student and an officer in several of the various interest groups, concluded, "All in all, I found the Indian Memorial a very moving site and a good addition to the battlefield."[17] Even a perennial critic of the establishing memorial waxed appeasingly: "Our worst fears were not realized. . . . The monument's earthen berm was not too obtrusive, nor did it vulgarly compete for attention with the mass grave monument erected in 1881. . . . The construction of the new monument and its attendant access paths affect the actual battlefield of 1876 far less drastically than did the erection [there] of the 1881 obelisk, which was prefaced by a radical landscaping of the very ridge on which Custer died."[18]

In the final analysis, the Indian Memorial is in the correct place at the correct time. While it certainly exemplifies contemporary political adroitness, it just as definitively mirrors the attitudinal changes in an American society that, however slowly, is prone to increasingly readjust itself to recognize and accommodate the differences that compose it, and that alone should justify the memorial's existence. Finally, it represents the manifestation of equality, sacrifice, and conscience, qualities of principle on which the nation was founded. Historian Paul Andrew Hutton termed it "a living memorial to triumph, loss, and renewal," and therein perhaps lies its true meaning. The one-time shrine to Custer and his command had completed its transformation into an inclusive and vibrant national historic site.[19] While the Indian Memorial was indeed a long time in coming, with its establishment Little Bighorn Battlefield National Monument would never be the same again.

Afterword

It is clear that events at Little Bighorn battlefield have come full circle since 1876. The presence of the victors, once relegated intellectually and interpretively at the site, and all but physically gone but for rare anniversary and ceremonial appearances, has at last been validated for all time, their enduring contributions to its history legitimized. That, in itself, represents the most contextual transformation in the history of the cemetery/park since its inception as a government-designated reserve in 1879.

Other changes have likewise been significant, though perhaps less overwhelmingly positive to the future well-being of the historic site. Of major concern since the 1940 transfer from War Department to National Park Service administration has been the proliferation of development both within and beyond park boundaries that continues to threaten the integrity of the historic ground as well as its inclusive setting. Overall, Little Bighorn has become highly and perhaps irretrievably affected by the handiwork of multiple custodians and audiences through the years. In-park improvements have been directed to facilitate ever-increasing public use (roads, sidewalks, buildings, and assorted infrastructural changes) and interpretation (signage, wayside exhibits, and interpretive trails) in an ongoing effort to ensure resource preservation. Yet given the reality of the constricted land base composing the site, and with realization that that condition might well continue for decades to come, vigilant park stewards must guard against further developmental intrusions on pristine battlefield terrain. For the future of the park and its resources, it is essential that physical development, beyond maintenance, be minimized and that federal historic preservation policies, at all events, are observed *to the letter*. Moreover, future superintendents must be properly trained and sensitized respecting historic preservation law and policy, as well as in the responsibilities that that knowledge assumes, while their own superiors must more carefully monitor and recognize potentially damaging activities in the park. Superintendents and staff members must overcome the urge to make additions directly on the field, whether they be new trails or monuments or interpretive waysides. Managers at all levels must implement developmental change cautiously and wisely, with the welfare of the park and its irreplaceable land resources ever uppermost in mind.

Similar vigilance must monitor external development too, ensuring that the view shed for battlefield resources is protected as much as possible and, to that end, that dialogue with park neighbors remain open and sustained. By the early twenty-first century, the presence of the Little Bighorn battlefield has generated a commercial center whose very existence conversely and perversely threatens the park's greater well-being. Indeed, the plains of 1876 Montana have through succeeding decades been consumed by modern expansion. A four-lane interstate highway running between Sheridan, Wyoming, and Billings now dominates Little Bighorn Valley and is joined near the park's northwest perimeter by U.S. Highway 212, a major route connecting Yellowstone National Park and the Black Hills. Close to the park, tourism fairly governs the arteries, with obtrusive private museums, shops, and gas stations bordering Interstate 90, while a casino complex, trading posts and gift shops, and fast-food eateries crowd the I-90–Highway 212 intersection to mar the historical view from the battlefield while infringing on terrain outside park boundaries where important battle action occurred in 1876.

"The next few years," admonished Edward T. Linenthal in 1997, "are . . . the battlefield's 'last stand.' Either some solutions to the [encroachment] problem will be found, or the Little Bighorn will join the growing list of battlefields lost to commercial development."[1] The challenge for park administrators must be to achieve developmental balance within and without park boundaries, assuring that this eternally stricken field will survive for the edification and enjoyment of generations to come.

APPENDIX 1 # National Cemetery/ National Monument Legislation

1. Establishment, 1879

Source: *Index of General Orders, Adjutant General's Office, 1879* (Washington, D.C.: Government Printing Office, 1880).

General Orders   HEADQUARTERS OF THE ARMY,
     No. 78   ADJUTANT GENERAL'S OFFICE,
     Washington, August 1, 1879.

The following orders have been received from the War Department:

I. The ground known as the Custer Battle-field, on the Little Big Horn River, Montana Territory, is announced as a National Cemetery of the fourth class.

II. Upon the completion of the survey of the site, and after the order of the President of the United States has been obtained declaring and proclaiming the same a military reservation, the boundaries thereof will be announced in General Orders from the Headquarters of the Department of Dakota.

BY COMMAND OF GENERAL SHERMAN:
R.C. DRUM,
Assistant Adjutant General.

OFFICIAL:

Assistant Adjutant General.

2. National Cemetery Reservation, 1886

Source: *Executive Orders Relating to Indian Reserves Issued Prior to April 1, 1890* (Washington, D.C.: Government Printing Office, ca. 1890). Microfiche copy in University of Colorado Law Library, Boulder. Also, manuscript copy exists in Presidential Executive Orders and Proclamations, 41-12, Congressional Information Service, Microfiche.

EXECUTIVE ORDER OF DECEMBER 7, 1886

War Department,
Washington City, November 27, 1886.
[To The President,]

SIR: Upon the recommendation of the Lieutenant-General commanding the Army, I have the honor to request that the following-described tracts of land, in the Territory of Montana, embraced within the limits of the Crow Indian Reservation, created by treaty dated May 7, 1868, Executive orders dated respectively October 29, 1875, and March 8, 1876, and act of Congress approved July 10, 1882, may be duly declared and set apart by the Executive for military purposes, in connection with the post of Fort Custer, viz:

1.—*Post reservation.*
Commencing at the center stone of the parade ground of Fort Custer, Mont., and running thence due south 3 miles to the place of beginning on the southern boundary; thence due east 3 miles; thence due north 6 miles; thence due west 6 miles; thence due south 6 miles: thence due east 3 miles to the place of beginning. Area: 36 square miles.

2.—*National cemetery of Custer's battle-field.*
Reservation.—Commencing at a point 1,200 feet north 35 degrees west of Custer's monument, and running thence north 35 degrees east 1,200 feet; thence south 35 degrees east 1 mile; thence south 55 degrees west to the right bank of the Little Big Horn River; thence along said right bank to the prolongation of the western boundary; thence along said prolongation to the place of beginning. Area: 1 square mile.

3.—*Limestone reservation, near old Fort C. F. Smith, Mont.*
Commencing at a point 1,772 feet due north and 700 feet due east of the site of the flag-staff of the old post of Fort C. F. Smith, and running

thence due south 1 mile and 5,206 feet; thence due west 2 miles; thence due north 1 mile and 4,470 feet to midstream of the Big Horn River; thence down said midstream to its intersection with the prolongation of the eastern boundary; thence along said prolongation to the place of beginning. Area: 3.48 square miles.

Tracings of the propose reservations are inclosed herewith.

It appears that about thirteen Indian families have received allotments of land within the limits of the proposed reservation for the post of Fort Custer (No. 1), and the Department of the Interior reports that, with the distinct understanding "that these thirteen families shall not be disturbed, but shall be allowed to remain where they are now located, and to retain their present allotments of land and be permitted the free and unrestricted enjoyment thereof, unless they shall voluntarily release or abandon the same," that Department will interpose no objection to the declaration of the proposed reservation as herein requested.

I have the honor to be, sir, with great respect, your obedient servant,

WM. C. ENDICOTT,

Secretary of War.

The PRESIDENT.

EXECUTIVE MANSION, *Washington, December 7, 1886.*

The within request is approved and the reservations are made and proclaimed accordingly; *Provided,* That the thirteen Indian families herein referred to shall not be disturbed, but shall be allowed to remain where they are now located and to retain their present allotments of land, and be permitted the free and unrestricted enjoyment thereof unless they shall voluntarily release or abandon the same.

The Secretary of the Interior will cause the proper notation to be made in the General Land Office.

GROVER CLEVELAND.

3. Reno–Benteen Battlefield, 1926

Source: *United States Statutes at Large, December 1925 to March 1927*, vol. 44, part 2 (Washington: Government Printing Office, 1927), 251.

CHAP. 138.—An Act Authorizing the Secretary of the Interior to acquire land and erect a monument on the site of the battle with the Sioux Indians in which the commands of Major Reno and Major [*sic*] Benteen were engaged.

Be it enacted by the Senate and House of Representatives of the United States of America in Congress assembled, That the Secretary of the Interior is hereby authorized and directed to acquire, by condemnation or otherwise, such land as may be deemed appropriate, not exceeding one hundred and sixty acres, on the site of the battle with the Sioux Indians in which the commands of Major Marcus A. Reno and Major Frederick W. Benteen were engaged, and to erect thereon a suitable monument and historical tablet.

SEC. 2. That there is hereby authorized to be appropriated, out of any money in the Treasury not otherwise appropriated, the sum of $2,500, or so much thereof as may be necessary, to carry out the provisions of this Act.

Approved April 14, 1926.

4. Reno–Benteen Battlefield, 1928

Source: *United States Statutes at Large, December 1927 to March 1929*, vol. 45, part 1 (Washington: Government Printing Office, 1929), 225.

EXCERPT FROM ACT OF MARCH 7, 1928 45 STAT. 225

ERECTION OF MONUMENTS

The unexpended balance of the appropriation of $25,000 from tribal funds of the Osage Indians, made in the Act of March 3, 1925 (Forty-third Statutes at Large, page 1162), for the erection of a monument as a memorial to Indians of that tribe who gave their lives in the recent war with Germany, is hereby made available for the same purpose until June 30, 1929.

For acquiring not to exceed one hundred and sixty acres of land on the site of the battle with the Sioux Indians in which the commands of Major Marcus A. Reno and Major Frederick W. Benteen [*sic*] were engaged, and the erection thereon of a suitable monument and tablet, as authorized by the Act of April 14, 1926, $2,300: *Provided,* That the reservation and monument provided herein shall be maintained by the Quartermaster Corps, United States Army, in conjunction with the Custer Battle Field Monument.

For the purchase and erection of a monument to Quanah Parker, late chief of the Comanche Indians, as provided by the Act of June 23, 1926, $1,500.

5. Compensation of Crow Indians, 1930

Source: *United States Statutes at Large, April 1929 to March 1931*, vol. 46, part 1 (Washington, D.C.: Government Printing Office, 1931), 168–69.

CHAP. 169.—An Act Providing compensation to the Crow Indians for Custer Battle Field National Cemetery, and for other purposes.

Be it enacted by the Senate and House of Representatives of the United States of America in Congress assembled, That a sum not to exceed $3,045 is hereby authorized to be appropriated, out of any money in the Treasury not otherwise appropriated, for the purpose of compensating the Crow Indians and their successors in interest for the appropriation of certain tribal and allotted lands from the reservation established by treaty dated May 7, 1868 (Fifteenth Statutes, page 649), for cemetery purposes as a site for the Custer Battle Field National Cemetery by Executive order dated December 7, 1886.

SEC. 2. That out of the money herein authorized to be appropriated there shall be deposited in the Treasury of the United States to the credit of the Crow Indians the sum of $2,965, and that the Secretary of the Interior is hereby authorized to withdraw from such sum any amounts found to be due to individual allottees, said amounts to be subject to disposition in accordance with existing law and regulations of the Interior Department: *Provided,* That the deposit of said sum to the credit of the said Indians shall constitute full satisfaction to the said Indians for the taking of their lands comprised within the Custer Battle Field National Cemetery and shall forever bar any legal or equitable claim that the Indians may have to said lands or to the payment of compensation therefore. That the Secretary of the Interior is further authorized to make payments, out of the money herein authorized to be appropriated, the sum of $80 to the successors in interest under allotment numbered 423 of White Goose, which allotted lands were subsequently patented to S.G. Reynolds on August 26, 1912: *Provided,* That the acceptance of such sum by the successors in interest under the said allotment and patent shall constitute full satisfaction for the taking of that portion of the allotted and patented lands comprised within the Custer Battle Field National Cemetery and shall forever bar any legal or equitable claim that such successors in interest shall have to said lands or to the payment of compensation therefore.

SEC. 3. That there is hereby granted to the United States, and its assigns, for use for cemetery and other governmental purposes, all right, title, and interest of the Crow Indians or their successors in interest to the tribal and allotted lands comprised within the said Custer Battle Field National Cemetery as set apart by Executive order of December 7, 1886.

Approved, April 15, 1930.

6. Reorganization, 1933

Source: Thomas Alan Sullivan, comp., *Laws Relating to the National Park Service*, Supplement 1 (July 1933–April 1944) (Washington, D.C.: Government Printing Office, 1944), 205–207.

EXECUTIVE ORDER
of July 28, 1933, No. 6228
ORGANIZATION OF EXECUTIVE AGENCIES

WHEREAS executive order No. 6166 dated June 10, 1933, issued pursuant to the authority of Section 16 of the Act of March 3, 1933 (Public No. 428—47 Stat. 1517) provides in Section 2 as follows:

"All functions of administration of public buildings, reservations, national parks, national monuments, and national cemeteries are consolidated in an office of National Parks, Buildings, and Reservations in the Department of the Interior, at the head of which shall be a Director of National Parks, Buildings, and Reservations; except that where deemed desirable there may be excluded from this provision any public building or reservation which is chiefly employed as a facility in the work of a particular agency. This transfer and consolidation of functions shall include, among others, those of the National Park Service of the Department of the Interior and the National Cemeteries and Parks of the War Department which are located within the continental limits of the United States. National Cemeteries located in foreign countries shall be transferred to the Department of State, and those located in insular possessions under the jurisdiction of the War Department shall be administered by the Bureau of Insular Affairs of the War Department."

and;

WHEREAS to facilitate and expedite the transfer and consolidation of certain units and agencies contemplated thereby, it is desirable to make more explicit said Section 2 of the aforesaid executive order of June 10, 1933, insofar as the same relates to the transfer of agencies now administered by the War Department:

NOW, THEREFORE, said executive order No. 6166, dated June 10, 1933, is hereby interpreted as follows:

1. The cemeteries and parks of the War Department transferred to the Interior Department are as follows:

NATIONAL MILITARY PARKS
Chickamauga and Chattanooga National Military Park, Georgia and Tennessee.
Fort Donelson National Military Park, Tennessee.
Fredericksburg and Spotsylvania County Battle Fields Memorial, Virginia.
Gettysburg National Military Park, Pennsylvania.
Guilford Courthouse National Military Park, North Carolina.
Kings Mountain National Military Park, South Carolina.
Moores Creek National Military Park, North Carolina.
Petersburg National Military Park, Virginia.
Shiloh National Military Park, Tennessee.
Stones River National Military Park, Tennessee.
Vicksburg National Military Park, Mississippi.

NATIONAL PARKS
Abraham Lincoln National Park, Kentucky.
Fort McHenry National Park, Maryland.

BATTLEFIELD SITES
Antietam Battlefield, Maryland.
Appomattox, Virginia.
Brices Cross Roads, Mississippi.
Chalmette Monument and Grounds, Louisiana.
Cowpens, South Carolina.
Fort Necessity, Wharton County, Pennsylvania.
Kenesaw Mountain, Georgia.
Monocacy, Maryland.
Tupelo, Mississippi.

NATIONAL MONUMENTS
White Plains, New York.
Big Hole Battlefield, Beaverhead County, Montana.
Cabrillo Monument, Ft. Rosecrans, California.
Castle Pinckney, Charleston, South Carolina.
Father Millet Cross, Fort Niagara, New York.

Fort Marion, St. Augustine, Florida.
Fort Matanzas, Florida.
Fort Pulaski, Georgia.
Meriwether Lewis, Hardin County, Tennessee.
Mound City Group, Chillicothe, Ohio.
Statute [sic] of Liberty, Fort Wood, New York.

MISCELLANEOUS MEMORIALS
Camp Blount Tablets, Lincoln County, Tennessee.
Kill Devil Hill Monument, Kitty Hawk, North Carolina.
New Echota Marker, Georgia.
Lee Mansion, Arlington National Cemetery, Virginia.

NATIONAL CEMETERIES[1]
Battleground, District of Columbia.
Antietam, (Sharpsburg) Maryland.
Vicksburg, Mississippi.
Gettysburg, Pennsylvania.
Chattanooga, Tennessee.
Fort Donelson, (Dover) Tennessee.
Shiloh, (Pittsburg Landing) Tennessee.
Stones River, (Murfreesboro) Tennessee.
Fredericksburg, Virginia.
Popular Grove, (Petersburg) Virginia.
Yorktown, Virginia.

1. Pursuant to Section 22 of said executive order it is hereby ordered that the transfer from the War Department of national cemeteries other than those named above be, and the same is hereby postponed until further order.

2. Also pursuant to Section 22 of said executive order it is hereby ordered that the transfer of national cemeteries located in foreign countries from the War Department to the Department of State and the transfer of those located in insular possessions under the jurisdiction of the War Department to the Bureau of Insular Affairs of said Department be, and the same are hereby postponed until further order.

FRANKLIN D. ROOSEVELT.
THE WHITE HOUSE,
July 28, 1933.

7. Museum, 1939
Source: *United States Statutes at Large, 1939*, vol. 53, part 2 (Washington, D.C.: Government Printing Office, 1939), 1337.

[CHAPTER 634]
AN ACT

To provide for the erection of a public historical museum in the Custer Battlefield National Cemetery, Montana, approved August 10, 1939 (53 Stat. 1337)

Be it enacted by the Senate and House of Representatives of the United States of America in Congress assembled, That the Secretary of War is authorized and directed (1) to select a site within the Custer Battlefield National Cemetery, Montana; (2) to erect and maintain thereon, as a memorial to Lieutenant Colonel George A. Custer and the officers and soldiers under his command at the Battle of Little Big Horn River, June 25, 1876, a public museum suitable for housing a collection of historical relics; (3) to accept on behalf of the United States for exhibit in such museum the collection of relics now a part of the estate of Mrs. George A. Custer, deceased, the wife of such Lieutenant Colonel George A. Custer; and (4), in his discretion to accept such other historical relics as may deem appropriate for exhibit therein.

SEC. 2. The Secretary of War is authorized and directed, notwithstanding any provision of law to the contrary, to do all things necessary to carry out the provisions of this Act, by contract or otherwise, with or without advertising, under such conditions as he may prescribe, including the engagement by contract of services of such architects, sculptors, artists, or firms, and such other technical and professional personnel as he may deem necessary, without regard to civil-service requirements and restrictions of law governing the employment and compensation of employees of the United States.

SEC. 3. There is hereby authorized to be appropriated the sum of $25,000, or so much thereof as may be necessary to carry out the provisions of this Act.

8. Revocation, 1940

Source: Thomas Alan Sullivan, comp., *Proclamations and Orders Relating to the National Park Service* (Washington, D.C.: Government Printing Office, 1947), 331.

EXECUTIVE ORDER
[No. 8428—June 3, 1940—3 CFR, Cum. Supp., 664]
REVOKING EXECUTIVE ORDER NO. 6228 OF JULY 28, 1933, AS TO CUSTER
BATTLEFIELD NATIONAL CEMETERY

By virtue of the authority vested in me by Executive Order No. 6166 of June 10, 1933, entitled "Organization of Executive Agencies," section 2 of Executive Order No. 6228 of July 28, 1933, interpreting the said order of June 10, 1933, is hereby revoked insofar as it pertains to or affects the transfer of the Custer Battlefield National Cemetery in the State of Montana.

This order shall become effective on July 1, 1940.

FRANKLIN D. ROOSEVELT.
THE WHITE HOUSE,
June 3, 1940.

9. Redesignation, 1946

Source: Hillory A. Tolson, comp., *Laws Relating to the National Park Service*, Supplement 2 (May 1944–January 1963) (Washington, D.C.: Government Printing Office, 1963), 402.

An Act to change the designation of Custer Battlefield National Cemetery, in the State of Montana, to "Custer Battlefield National Monument," and for other purposes, approved March 22, 1946 (60 Stat. 59)

Be it enacted by the Senate and House of Representatives of the United States of America in Congress assembled, That the area now within the Custer Battlefield National Cemetery, in the State of Montana, shall hereafter be known as the "Custer Battlefield National Monument," under which name this national monument shall be entitled to receive and to use all moneys heretofore or hereafter appropriated for the Custer Battlefield National Cemetery.

10. National Park Service Functions and Activities, 1946

Source: *United States Statutes at Large, 1946*, vol. 60, part 1 (Washington, D.C.: Government Printing Office, 1947), 885–86.

[CHAP. 788]
AN ACT

To provide basic authority for the performance of certain functions and activities of the National Park Service.

Be it enacted by the Senate and House of Representatives of the United States of America in Congress assembled, That appropriations for the National Park Service are authorized for—

(a) Necessary protection of the area of federally owned land in the custody of the National Park Service known as the Ocean Strip and Queets Corridor, adjacent to Olympic National Park, Washington; necessary repairs to the roads from Glacier Park Station through the Blackfeet Indian Reservation to the various points in the boundary line of Glacier National Park, Montana, and the international boundary; repair and maintenance of approximately two and seventy-seven one-hundredths miles of road leading from United States Highway 187 to the north entrance of Grand Teton National Park, Wyoming; maintenance of approach roads through the Lassen National Forest leading to Lassen Volcanic National Park, California; maintenance and repair of the Generals Highway between the boundaries of Sequoia National Park, California, and the Grant Grove section of Kings Canyon National Park, California; maintenance of approximately two and one-fourth miles of roads comprising those portions of the Fresno-Kings Canyon approach road, Park Ridge Lookout Road, and Ash Mountain-Advance truck trail, necessary to the administration and protection of the Sequoia and Kings Canyon National Parks; maintenance of the roads in the national forests leading out of Yellowstone National Park, Wyoming, Idaho, and Montana; maintenance of the road in the Stanislaus National Forest connecting the Tioga Road with the Hetch Hetchy Road near Mather Station, Yosemite National Park, California; and maintenance and repair of the approach road to the Custer Battlefield National Monument and the road connecting the said monument with the Reno Monument site, Montana.

(b) Administration, protection, improvement, and maintenance of areas, under the jurisdiction of other agencies of the Government, devoted to recreational use pursuant to cooperative agreements.

(c) Necessary local transportation and subsistence in kind of persons selected for employment or as cooperators, serving without other compensation, while attending fire-protection training camps.

(d) Administration, protection, maintenance, and improvement of the Chesapeake and Ohio Canal.

(e) Educational lectures in or in the vicinity of and with respect to the national park, national monuments, and other reservations under the jurisdiction of the National Park Service; and services of field employees in cooperation with such nonprofit scientific and historical societies engaged in educational work in the various parks and monuments as the Secretary of the Interior may designate.

(f) Travel expenses of employees attending Government camps for training in forest-fire prevention and suppression and the Federal Bureau of Investigation National Police Academy, and attending Federal, State, or municipal schools for training in building fire prevention and suppression.

(g) Investigation and establishment of water rights in accordance with local custom, laws and decisions of courts, including the acquisition of water rights or of lands or interests in lands or rights-of-way for use and protection of water rights necessary or beneficial in the administration and public use of the national parks and monuments.

(h) Acquisition or rights-of-way and construction and maintenance of a water supply line partly outside the boundaries of Mesa Verde National Park.

(i) Official telephone service in the field in the case of official telephones installed in private houses when authorized under regulations established by the Secretary (16 U.S.C.s17j-2.)

11. Name Change and Indian Memorial, 1991
Source: *United States Statutes at Large, 1991,* vol. 105, part 2 (Washington, D.C.: Government Printing Office, 1992), 1631–33.

Public Law 102-201
102d Congress

An Act

Little Bighorn Battlefield National Monument

Be it enacted by the Senate and House of Representatives of the United States of America in Congress assembled,

TITLE I

SEC. 101. REDESIGNATION OF MONUMENT.

The Custer Battlefield National Monument in Montana shall, on and after the date of enactment of this Act, be known as the "Little Bighorn Battlefield National Monument" (hereafter in this Act referred to as the "monument"). Any reference to the Custer Battlefield National Monument in any law, map, regulation, document, record, or other paper of the United States shall be deemed to be a reference to the Little Bighorn Battlefield National Monument.

SEC. 102 CUSTER NATIONAL CEMETERY.

The cemetery located within the monument shall be designated as the Custer National Cemetery.

TITLE II

SEC. 201. FINDINGS.

The Congress finds that—

a monument was erected in 1881 at Last Stand Hill to commemorate the soldiers, scouts, and civilians attached to the 7th United States Cavalry who fell in the Battle of the Little Bighorn;

while many members of the Cheyenne, Sioux, and other Indian Nations gave their lives defending their families and traditional lifestyle and livelihood, nothing stands at the battlefield to commemorate those individuals; and

the public interest will best be served by establishing a memorial at the Little Bighorn Battlefield National Monument to honor the Indian participants in the battle.

SEC. 202. ADVISORY COMMITTEE.

(a) Establishment.—The Secretary of the Interior (hereafter in this Act referred to as the "Secretary") shall establish a committee to be known as the Little Bighorn Battlefield National Monument Advisory Committee (hereafter in this Act referred to as the "Advisory Committee").
(b) Membership and Chairperson.—The Advisory Committee shall be composed of 11 members appointed by the Secretary, with 6 of the

individuals appointed representing Native American tribes who participated in the Battle of the Little Big Horn or who now reside in the area, 2 of the individuals appointed being nationally recognized artists and 3 of the individuals appointed being knowledgeable in history, historic preservation, and landscape architecture. The Advisory Committee shall designate one of its members as Chairperson.

(c) Quorum; Meetings.—Six members of the Advisory Committee shall constitute a quorum. The Advisory Committee shall act and advise by affirmative vote of a majority of the members voting at a meeting at which a quorum is present. The Advisory Committee shall meet on a regular basis. Notice of meetings and agenda shall be published in local newspapers which have a distribution which generally covers the area affected by the monument. Advisory Committee meetings shall be held at locations and in such a manner as to ensure adequate public involvement.

(d) Advisory Functions.—The Advisory Committee shall advise the Secretary to ensure that the memorial designed and constructed as provided in section 203 shall be appropriate to the monument, its resources and landscape, sensitive to the history being portrayed and artistically commendable.

(e) Technical Staff Support.—In order to provide staff support and technical services to assist the Advisory Committee in carrying out its duties under this Act, upon request of the Advisory Committee, the Secretary of the Interior is authorized to detail any personnel of the National Park Service to the Advisory Committee.

(f) Compensation.—Members of the Advisory Committee shall serve without compensation but shall be entitled to travel expenses, including per diem in lieu of subsistence, in the same manner as persons employed intermittently in Government service under section 5703 of title 5 of the United States Code.

(g) Charter.—The provisions of section 14(b) of the Federal Advisory Committee Act (5 U.S.C. Appendix; 86 Stat. 776), are hereby waived with respect to the Advisory Committee.

(h) Termination.—The Advisory Committee shall terminate upon dedication of the memorial authorized under section 203.

SEC. 203. MEMORIAL.

(a) Design, Construction, and Maintenance.—In order to honor and recognize the Indians who fought to preserve their land and culture in the Battle of the Little Bighorn, to provide visitors with an improved understanding of the events leading up to and the consequences of the fateful battle, and to encourage peace among people of all races, the Secretary shall design, construct, and maintain a memorial at the Little Bighorn Battlefield National Monument.

(b) Site.—The Secretary, in consultation with the Advisory Committee, shall select the site of the memorial. Such area shall be located on the ridge in that part of the Little Bighorn Battlefield National Monument which is in the vicinity of the 7th Cavalry Monument, as generally depicted on a map entitled "Custer Battlefield National Monument General Development Map" dated March 1990 and numbered 381/80,044–

(c) Design Competition.—The Secretary, in consultation with the Advisory Committee, shall hold a national design competition to select the design of the memorial. The design criteria shall include but not necessarily be limited to compatibility with the monument and its resources in form and scale, sensitivity to the history being portrayed, and artistic merit. The design and plans for the memorial shall be subject to the approval of the Secretary.

SEC. 204. DONATIONS OF FUNDS, PROPERTY, AND SERVICES.

Notwithstanding any other provision of law, the Secretary may accept and expend donations of funds, property, or services from individuals, foundations, corporations, or public entities for the purpose of providing for the memorial.

SEC. 205. AUTHORIZATION OF APPROPRIATIONS.

There are authorized to be appropriated such sums as are necessary to carry out this Act.

TITLE III

SEC. 301. EXTENSION OF ALIENABILITY RESTRICTIONS ON SETTLEMENT COMMON STOCK.

Section 37(a) of Public Law 92-3, the Alaska Native Claims Settlement Act (43 U.S.C. 1629c(a)) is amended to striking "December 18, 1991." And inserting in lieu thereof "July 15, 1993: Provided, however, That this prohibition shall not apply to a Native Corporation whose board of directors approves, no later than March 1, 1992, a resolution (certified by the corporate secretary of such corporation) electing to decline the application of such prohibition."

Approved December 10, 1991.

Little Bighorn Battlefield National Monument Park Visitation Totals, 1940–2003

1940 (July–December): 60,450
1941: 67,989
1942: 25,258
1943: 14,046
1944: 15,571
1945: 18,976
1946: 51,039
1947: 56,576
1948: 66,876
1949: 73,725
1950: 73,771
1951: 93,091
1952: 109,261
1953: 109,972
1954: 119,159
1955: 132,556
1956: 115,808
1957: 130,278
1958: 130,818
1959: 130,865
1960: 146,537
1961: 150,308
1962: 179,661
1963: 175,025
1964: 188,753

1965: 190,289
1966: 218,062
1967: 260,927
1968: 238,779
1969: 253,354
1970: 263,237
1971: 338,598
1972: 387,717
1973: 312,171
1974: 259,880
1975: 235,238
1976: 294,837
1977: 330,550
1978: 272,996
1979: 205,854
1980: 185,546
1981: 255,548
1982: 207,661
1983: 223,634
1984: 250,218
1985: 278,233
1986: 278,233
1987: 267,725
1988: 228,795
1989: 227,523
1990: 233,222
1991: 265,252
1992: 331,404
1993: 446,052
1994: 403,230
1995: 408,141
1996: 367,114
1997: 361,432
1998: 370,045
1999: 397,518
2000: 333,281
2001: 365,182
2002: 429,826
2003: 426,344

Source: "Visitation Records—Custer Battlefield," in Superintendent's Annual Reports, Little Bighorn Battlefield National Monument Administrative Files.

War Department and National Park Service Superintendents and National Park Service Historians at Custer Battlefield National Monument/Little Bighorn Battlefield National Monument, 1893–2003

War Department Superintendents

Andrew N. Grover	July 1893–April 1906
W. H. H. Garrett	April 1906–March 1909
Oscar Wright	March 1909–July 1910
G. W. Thomas	July 1910–June 1912
James McGowan	June 1912–July 1912 (Acting)
Daniel Dommit	July 1912–December 1913
Eugene Wessinger	December 1913–August 1929
Joseph Morrow	December 1929–January 1930
Alex Naylor	January 1930–August 1930 (Acting)
Victor A. Bolsius	August 1930–June 1934
Harvey A. Olson	June 1934–July 1938
William O. Mickle	July 1938–April 1939
Fulton Grigsby	April 1939–November 1939
Harold Montague	December 1939–November 1940

National Park Service Superintendents

Edward S. Luce	January 1941–May 1956
John A. Aubuchon	May 1956–December 1958
Thomas K. Garry	March 1959–January 1968
Daniel E. Lee	February 1968–December 1969

A Gallery of Superintendents
War Department

Andrew N. Grover,
first superintendent,
1893–1906.

Eugene Wessinger,
longest serving superin-
tendent, 1913–29.

Harvey A. Olson,
1934–38.

National Park Service

Edward S. Luce, 1941–56

John A. Aubuchon,
1956–58

Thomas A. Garry,
1959–68

Daniel E. Lee, 1968–69

William A. Harris,
1970–72

Eldon G. Reyer, 1972–74

A Gallery of Superintendents

Richard T. Hart, 1974–78   James V. Court, 1978–86   Dennis L. Ditmanson, 1986–89

Barbara Booher, 1989–93   Douglas C. McChristian (Acting), 1989, 1993   Michael D. LeBorgne (Acting), 1989

Gerard Baker, 1993–98   Neil C. Mangum, 1998–2002   Darrell J. Cook, 2002–

William A. Harris	January 1970–July 1972
Eldon G. Reyer	September 1972–July 1974
Richard T. Hart	September 1974–May 1978
James V. Court	May 1978–December 1986
Dennis L. Ditmanson	December 1986–March 1989
Douglas C. McChristian	March 1989–April 1989 (Acting)
Michael D. LeBorgne	April 1989–May 1989 (Acting)
Barbara Booher	July 1989–February 1993
Douglas C. McChristian	February 1993–September 1993 (Acting)
Gerard Baker	September 1993–January 1998
Neil C. Mangum	March 1998–July 2002
Darrell Cook	July 2002–

Park Historians

James Bowers	July 1953–August 1954
Don Rickey, Jr.	June 1955–February 1960
Warren J. Petty	August 1960–September 1963
Andrew M. Loveless	September 1963–January 1967
B. William Henry, Jr.	July 1967–November 1969
L. Clifford Soubier	November 1969–October 1971
J. D. Young	October 1971–June 1974
Richard Rambur	July 1974–March 1977
S. Paul Okey	1977–October 1979
Neil C. Mangum	October 1979–May 1988
Douglas C. McChristian	August 1988–August 1995
Timothy McCleary	June 1996–December 1997 (Non-NPS interim)
John A. Doerner	June 1998–

Notes

1. Signal Event

1. For the changing meanings and purposes of the Little Bighorn battlefield through the years, as well as government accommodation of them, see the following by Edward T. Linenthal: *Sacred Ground*, 129–71; "From Shrine to Historic Site"; and "Transformation."

2. Fenneman, *Physiography*, 61–79, 86–91; Thornbury, *Regional Geomorphology*, 287–93; C. Hunt, *Natural Regions*, 12, 63, 91; Thom, Hall, Wegemann, and Moulton, *Geology of Big Horn County*, 12–15; Abbott, *Montana in the Making*, 14–21. The plesiosaur discovery is chronicled in Alan R. Tabrum, "Report on the Plesiosaur Collected at Custer Battlefield National Monument," January 1978, Research Files, Little Bighorn Battlefield National Monument, Crow Agency, Montana. During the years preceding the battle along its banks, the Little Bighorn River was often referred to as the Little Horn River because of its status as a subordinate affluent of the Bighorn River, itself named after the bighorn sheep inhabiting the mountains in which the river has its source.

3. Beck and Haase, *Historical Atlas*, maps 3, 4, 5, 7, 10; Abbott, *Montana in the Making*, 23–28; Rickey, *History of Custer Battlefield*, 1–3.

4. The best overview of Crow history and culture is in Voget, "Crow," 695–717. See also Hoxie, *Parading through History*; Lowie, *Crow Indians*; Frey, *World of the Crow Indians*.

5. Rickey, *History of Custer Battlefield*, 4–5. For the Lakotas, see Hassrick, *Sioux*. For the Northern Cheyennes, see Moore, *Cheyenne Nation*. For the Arapahos, see Trenholm, *Arapahos*; Fowler, *Arapaho Politics, 1851–1978*. As well, see the following articles in Sturtevant, *Handbook*: "Arapaho" (by Loretta Fowler): 840–62;

"Cheyenne" (by John H. Moore, Margot P. Liberty, and A. Terry Strauss): 863–85; "Crow" (by Fred W. Voget): 695–717; "Teton" (by Raymond J. DeMallie): 794–820.

6. Fur trade activities are explicated in Wishart, *Fur Trade of the American West*, and Barbour, *Fort Union*.

7. Rickey, *History of Custer Battlefield*, 7–11, 15–16.

8. Contextual background for the Great Sioux War, 1876–77, is derived from material contained in the following sources: Utley, *Frontiersmen in Blue*; Utley, *Frontier Regulars*; Utley, *Indian Frontier*; Anderson, "Early Dakota Migration"; McGinnis, *Counting Coup*; Ewers, "Intertribal Warfare"; J. A. Hanson, *Little Chief's Gatherings*; R. White, "Winning of the West"; Vestal, *New Sources of Indian History*; Anderson, *Kinsmen of Another Kind*; Utley, *Lance and Shield*; Hyde, *Life of George Bent*; Hafen and Hafen, *Powder River Campaigns*; Paul, *Autobiography of Red Cloud*; Larson, *Red Cloud*; Doyle, "Indian Perspectives"; Hebard and Brininstool, *Bozeman Trail*; Brown, *Fort Phil Kearny*; Fritz, *Movement for Indian Assimilation*; C. Robinson, *Good Year to Die*; Athearn, *William Tecumseh Sherman*; Hutton, *Phil Sheridan*; Wooster, *Indian Policy, 1865–1903*; Rickey, *History of Custer Battlefield*, 17–18. The various treaties referenced appear in Kappler, *Indian Affairs*.

9. Early army operations against the Lakotas and Northern Cheyennes in 1876–77 through the Rosebud encounter are detailed in the following works: McDermott, "Crook's 1876 Campaigns"; Bourke, *On the Border*; Finerty, *War-Path and Bivouac*; Gray, *Centennial Campaign*; Gray, *Custer's Last Campaign*; Greene, *Battles and Skirmishes*; Greene, *Lakota and Cheyenne*; Hedren, *Fort Laramie in 1876*; Hedren, *Traveler's Guide*; Mangum, *Battle of the Rosebud*; Marquis, *Warrior*; Powell, *People of the Sacred Mountain*; Utley, *Frontier Regulars*; Vaughn, *With Crook at the Rosebud*; Vestal, *New Sources of Indian History*; and Vestal, *Warpath*.

10. There exists a plethora of studies describing the Battle of the Little Bighorn. The following titles include the most comprehensive and authoritative accountings: Sklenar, *To Hell with Honor*; Gray, *Custer's Last Campaign*; Greene, *Lakota and Cheyenne*; Hardorff, *Lakota Recollections*; Hardorff, *Cheyenne Memories*; Marquis, *Warrior*; Michno, *Lakota Noon*; Powell, *People of the Sacred Mountain*; Rankin, *Legacy*; Utley, *Frontier Regulars*; Utley, *Lance and Shield*; and Vestal, *Warpath*. On-terrain movements of Custer's battalion, based upon Indian sources and early archeological finds, are considered in Greene, *Evidence and the Custer Enigma*, but are thoroughly chronicled and analyzed in relation to more recent archeology in Scott and Fox, *Archaeological Insights*; Scott, Fox, Connor, and Harmon, *Archaeological Perspectives*; and Fox, *Archaeology, History*.

11. Post–Little Bighorn operations of the Great Sioux War are considered in McDermott, "Crook's 1876 Campaigns"; Bourke, *Mackenzie's Last Fight*; Bourke, *On the Border*; Finerty, *War-Path and Bivouac*; Greene, *Battles and Skirmishes*; Greene, *Lakota and Cheyenne*; Greene, *Slim Buttes, 1876*; Greene, *Yellowstone Command*; Greene, *Morning Star Dawn*; Hedren, *Fort Laramie in 1876*; Hedren, *First Scalp for Custer*; Hedren, *Traveler's Guide*; Hedren, *We Trailed the Sioux*; C. King, *Campaigning with Crook*; Marquis, *Warrior*; Powell, *People of the Sacred Mountain*;

S. Smith, *Sagebrush Soldier*; Utley, *Frontier Regulars*; Utley, *Lance and Shield*; and Vestal, *Warpath*.

2. Recognition

1. The *Worcester (Mass.) Daily Spy*, August 23, 1877, enclosed in Samuel E. Staples to Representative William W. Rice, November 9, 1877, National Archives (NA): Record Group (RG) 94, copy in Little Bighorn Battlefield National Monument Administrative Files (hereafter cited as LBAF); Gibbon to Captain Daniel W. Benham, Seventh Infantry, June 28, 1876, copy in the Manuscripts Department, Montana Historical Society, Helena; Quote of veteran Seventh Infantryman Joseph Sinsel in a clipping from the *Billings Gazette*, April (no day indicated) 1925, contained in Vertical File M, "Custer Battle," Parmly Billings Public Library, Billings, Montana. Other quoted material is in Lieutenant Colonel (Assistant Adjutant General) George D. Ruggles to Lieutenant General Philip H. Sheridan, Telegram, July 8, 1876, NA, copy in LBAF; J. M. Hanson, *Conquest of the Missouri*, 378–79; and Clifford, *Captain Walter Clifford*, 104. The classic description of the discovery of the dead on the battlefield is in First Lieutenant James H. Bradley's letter to the *Helena Herald*, July 25, 1876, reprinted in Stewart, *March of the Montana Column*, 171–74. Godfrey's remembrances are reprinted from his 1892 article in *The Century* in Graham, *Custer Myth*, 376–77. Other contemporary accounts are in Marquis, *Two Days*, 7; and Marquis, *Which Indian Killed Custer?* 5–10. See also Dustin, "Some Aftermath," and, for the matter of the burials as a whole, Kuhlman, *Legend into History*, xi–xvii. For the condition of Custer Hill in the aftermath of the fighting, as well as the most comprehensive treatment of the initial burials and after, see Hardorff, *Custer Battle Casualties*, and its sequel, *Custer Battle Casualties, II*. Perhaps the most descriptive panorama of the entire ground and burials, utilizing extensive first-person data, appears in Taunton, *Custer's Field*, 22–41 (including notes).

2. Gibbon to Benham, June 28, 1876; First Lieutenant Thomas W. Lord to the Adjutant General (AG): U.S. Army, August 14, 1876, with endorsements, and Captain Otho E. Michaelis to Lord, September 29, 1876, with endorsements (including Terry's of October 3, 1876), NA, copy in LBAF.

3. For the caste system and discussion of the commissioned-enlisted reality of army life, see Rickey, *Forty Miles*, 62–78; Foner, *United States Soldier*, 66–71; and Coffman, *Old Army*, 200–205.

4. Terry to Sheridan, March 26, 1877, NA, copy in LBAF; Sheridan to Sherman, April 4, 1877, with Sherman's endorsement, NA, copy in LBAF. The project was initially turned down by Secretary of War George W. McCrary because there was no appropriation "applicable to the purpose, and the accounting officers do not allow accounts for such expenses." AG to Sheridan, April 8, 1877, NA, copy in LBAF. On April 28, 1877, the adjutant general wrote Sheridan: "I have now the honor to inform you that upon a reconsideration of the subject the Secretary of War has decided to pay from the Contingent fund of the Army, for the

expenses of bringing in the bodies of General Custer and the officers who fell with him. . . . The Secretary of War requests that the expenses may be made as small as possible." NA, copy in LBAF.

5. Sheridan to Secretary of War, May 7, 1877, NA, copy in LBAF.

6. Special Orders No. 40, Headquarters, Military Division of the Missouri, May 16, 1877, NA, copy in LBAF.

7. Sheridan to Lieutenant Colonel Michael V. Sheridan, May 16, 1877, NA, copy in LBAF.

8. *Worcester (Mass.) Daily Spy*, August 23, 1877, citing a correspondent who accompanied Sheridan's party; *Bozeman Avant Courier*, July 19, 1877; *New York Herald*, July 15, 1877, reprinted in *Bighorn Yellowstone Journal* 1 (Spring 1992): 2–6. See also Superintendent Eugene Wessinger to AG, July 26, 1928, NA, copy in LBAF.

9. Comment of Philetus W. Norris, first superintendent of Yellowstone National Park, who apparently arrived at the battlefield the day after Sheridan departed. *Bozeman Avant Courier*, July 19, 1877.

10. J. M. Hanson, *Conquest of the Missouri*, 380; Map, "Custer's Battle–Field (June 25th, 1876): Surveyed and drawn under the personal supervision of Lieut. Edward Maguire, Corps of Engineers U.S.A. by Sergeant Charles Becker, Co. 'D' Battalion of Engineers," NA, RG 77, copy in LBAF. A hearsay account reported by a Little Bighorn participant allowed that "there was a dispute about the remains of Custer, as to whether the bones were Custer's. The first two sets of bones were taking [*sic*] from the box and the third put in. Michael Sheridan . . . made the remark: Nail the box up, it is all right as long as the people think so." Henry P. Jones to Walter M. Camp, January 5, 1919, Camp Papers, Robert Ellison Collection, Western History Department, Denver Public Library. Scout Thomas LeForge, who witnessed the disinterment of Custer's remains, reported that "they gathered up nothing substantial except one thigh bone and the skull attached to some part of the skeleton trunk. Besides these, the quantity of cohering and transferable bodily substance was not enough to fill my hat." Marquis, *Memoirs*, 284. In regard to Custer's remains, years later a veteran soldier stated that he "knew very well the man who sewed his body up in a saddle blanket [on June 28, 1876]. To identify the body later a small piece of alder about three inches long in which the pitch was pushed out and his name in ink was written on paper rolled up, and put in the hole, both ends were plugged up tight, and that was sewed on the breast of the corpse [*sic*]. That man was saddler of B Troop. Baily [John E. Bailey] by name." *Winners of the West*, March 1938. Sheridan's remarks regarding Cooke's remains are in Sheridan to "Mr. Cook," July 16, 1877, NA, copy in LBAF. For the likely recovery of Boston Custer's remains at this time, see Hardorff, *Custer Battle Casualties*, 48.

11. Philetus Norris in *Bozeman Avant Courier*, July 19, 1877. Crittenden's father had written General Sheridan: "It would be vandalism to dig up and scatter widely the bones of those who have been buried as they died, shoulder to shoulder.

They all perished together, fighting without hope, and comradeship thus cemented should never be sundered." Qtd. in Page, "Where Custer Fell," 8.

12. Sheridan's report of July 20, 1877, from which these quotes, as well as much descriptive information, have been borrowed, is reproduced in Graham, *Custer Myth,* 375 and passim. Scott's quote is in H. Scott, *Some Memories,* 48. Sheridan told the *Chicago Times* (July 25, 1877): perhaps exaggeratedly, that the remains of more than two hundred soldiers were reinterred in the same trenches, "but rather more decently than before. Three feet of earth, tastefully heaped and packed with spades and mallets, was put upon each set of remains, and the head marked by a cedar stake." Qtd. in Hardorff, *Custer Battle Casualties,* 39.

13. Ibid., 41–42. With Hodgson's body previously casketed, the boxes with the remains were numbered one through ten as follows: Cooke, Keogh, Captain Custer, Riley, Smith, Calhoun, Lieutenant Colonel Custer, Yates, DeWolf, McIntosh. "Remains of Officers taken up on Custer's battle-ground and brought to this Fort by the Steamer *Fletcher,* July 12, 1877," NA, copy in LBAF. See also Dr. W. A. Turner to David Hilger, Montana Historical Society, July 12, 1934, relating Turner's memories (some faulty) of the Sheridan expedition, Item SC 863, Manuscript Department, Montana Historical Society. Shipping information for Cooke and Riley is in Sheridan to "Mr. Cook," July 16, 1877, and endorsement, NA, copy in LBAF; and N. Johnson to AG Edward D. Townsend, May 14, 1877, NA, copy in LBAF.

14. Brust, "Fouch Photo"; Brust, "Little Big Horn"; Brust, Pohanka, and Barnard, *Where Custer Fell,* 131–33.

15. Sheridan to AG, April 8, 1878, NA, copy in LBAF; Diary of John G. Bourke, Manuscripts Collection, U.S. Military Academy Library, West Point, New York, entry of July 17, 1877, microfilm, vol. 21, roll 2, as excerpted in Boyes, "Visit to Custer Battlefield," and cited in Hardorff, *Custer Battle Casualties,* 54–55; *Winners of the West,* August 30, 1932 (quote of veteran Fifth Cavalryman A.W. Shannehan); Brust, Pohanka, and Barnard, *Where Custer Fell,* 12–13; *Reports of Inspection,* 14, 20, 44, 89–90; D. Dixon, *Hero of Beecher Island,* 140. Forsyth's report, in Forsyth to Sheridan, April 8, 1878, NA, RG 94, copy in LBAF, is reproduced in Fred Dustin, "Dustin Describes the Re-Burials," 371. Second Lieutenant Homer W. Wheeler, Fifth Cavalry, with Generals Sheridan and Crook at the battlefield, noted that "a few days before our arrival, a severe hail storm had devastated the whole valley, washing out several of the bodies which had been buried near a ravine." *Frontier Trail,* 210. During the visit, Bourke and Wheeler—as apparent souvenir hunters—took the opportunity to cut off the hoofs of the skeleton of a horse in the "Last Stand" area speculated to have been ridden by Custer. "Bourke had his pair made into inkstands, and gave one of them to a Philadelphia museum. I placed mine in a grain sack, and being ordered out against the hostile Nez Perces in 1877, I left the sack, with some other property, in our wagons, which was lost." Ibid., 219. The Keogh site (Company I) disclosed to Wheeler "a slight depression in the ground. Evidently at one time it had been a buffalo wallow, and the wind had blown out the dirt, forming a semi-circular depression covering several yards. The

graves were around this depression. . . . This was the only position we found where it looked as if a defense had been made, for the men had fallen all over the battle-field, here and there." Ibid. Sheridan's comment about "graves nicely raised" might have been but a verbal placebo in case his letter was made public. It certainly did not square with Bourke's and Wheeler's observations. Although some writers have stated that Sherman visited the battlefield in July 1877 (e.g., Kuhlman, *Legend into History*, xiii): the official documents in no way support the assertion and, more-over, suggest by way of omission of mention that time constraints prevented him from going there, even though he was at Post No. 2. See, e.g., Colonel O. M. Poe's diary in *Reports of Inspection*, 89–91.

16. *New York Sun*, July 25, 1877; Sheridan to AG, April 8, 1878, NA, copy in LBAF. The national military cemetery concept was inaugurated in 1862, when Congress appropriated funds for the purchase of lands at Civil War sites for the interment of the soldier dead. By 1870 there were seventy-three such cemeteries containing nearly three hundred thousand burials, many of which went uniden-tified. *Army Almanac*, 486. See also *National Cemetery Regulations*, 1.

17. Staples likely saw the remarks of a reporter who had visited the battlefield the day before General Sheridan arrived there: "So scandalous is it [the lack of proper burials] that I will not write the details." Qtd. in Hardorff, *Custer Battle Casualties*, 52.

18. The *Sun* piece was datelined July 25, 1877. It is reproduced in Hardorff, *Custer Battle Casualties*, 58–61. Sheridan to Sherman, April 8, 1878; Staples to Rice, November 9, 1877, enclosing clipping from the *Worcester (Mass.) Daily Spy*, August 23, 1877; Rickey, *History of Custer Battlefield*, 28–29. The attempted secrecy of Colonel Sheridan's mission is borne out at the head of Philetus Norris's article in the *New York Herald*, July 15, 1877, reprinted in *Bighorn Yellowstone Journal* 1 (Spring 1992): 2–6.

19. Hardorff, *Custer Battlefield Casualties*, 63–66; diary of an unidentified man, July–August 1878, Montana Historical Society Archives, SC 1312, entry for August 13, 1878 (quote); *Army and Navy Journal*, September 21, 1878; Fleming's comments in *St. Paul (Minn.) Pioneer Press*, October 10, 1877, reprinted in *Big Horn–Yellowstone Journal* 2 (Spring 1993): 15.

20. *New York Herald*, October 23, 1877. This reporter's statement was evi-dently crafted to refute criticism that the battleground was in deplorable condi-tion: "It is unseemly for people to say that these men's bones lie bleaching in the sun and without decent burial." The graves, he stated, were "in good condition" and "only one was dug up."

21. Hedren, "Holy Ground," 197; Hoyt, "Roughing It Up," 29; *Army and Navy Journal*, February 15, 1879; F. Hunt, "Purposeful Picnic"; Rickey, *History of Custer Battlefield*, 66–67; Brust, Pohanka, and Barnard, *Where Custer Fell*, 115; McChristian, "Burying the Hatchet," 4. In 1924 an unidentified scribe to a tabloid devoted to the interests of Indians war veterans wrote: "I was told by an old lady who frequently visited the battlefield, one year after the battle, that she would go up

there on Sundays and find skulls lying around on the ground, which she would try to place in the grave from which she thought they had come." The same writer noted that well into the twentieth century human remains continued to surface on the field: "I, myself, one day picked up a section of a rib which I found by the marker of Mark Kellogg, who was the correspondent for the *New York Herald*. To whom it belonged I do not know, but it was a human rib. In 1923 one of the business men of the town of Hardin found under a sagebrush, directly above the spot where Custer was first buried, a perfectly preserved ulna." *Winners of the West*, December 1924.

Miles's first visit is described at length in his autobiographical *Personal Recollections*, 283–93. The visit of Mrs. Samuel D. (Jerusha) Sturgis and her two daughters, Ella M. Lawler and Nina L. Dousman, besides a Miss Boyle, an apparent family friend, took place on August 19, 1878. The detachment from Fort Keogh, commanded by First Lieutenant William P. Clark, was to help Mrs. Sturgis "search for the remains of her son." Although Miles accompanied the party to the battlefield, he simultaneously scouted the area along the Yellowstone River and Rosebud Creek for routes for a wagon road and telegraph line. Another detachment from Fort Custer met the Sturgis party at the battlefield, ultimately accompanying the visitors to Terry's Landing on the Yellowstone, where the ladies boarded a steamboat headed downstream. Calendar for Samuel D. Sturgis Papers, State Historical Society of Wisconsin, in author's files; First Lieutenant Frank D. Baldwin to Clark, August 13, 1878, Baldwin to Lieutenant Colonel George P. Buell, August 13, 1878, and Miles to Buell, August 18, 1878, in Letter Book, District of the Yellowstone, from August 6, 1878, to August 8, 1879, NA, RG 393, Part 3, Entry 889.

22. AAG to Buell, October 29, 1878, NA, copy in LBAF.

23. Sanderson to Post Adjutant, Fort Custer, April 7, 1879, with endorsements, NA, RG 94, copy in LBAF; Brust, "Stanley J. Morrow's 1879 Photographs"; General Order No. 78 in *Index of General Orders, 1879*; "Report of the Quartermaster-General," October 10, 1879, in *Report of the Secretary of War, 1879*, 229; Rickey, *History of Custer Battlefield*, 29–30. In late August 1880, Lieutenant Clark, Second Cavalry, visited the field and described Sanderson's monument as "a crib of the bones of men and horses, a pyramid about five feet high and four feet [square] at the base." Clark to AAG, Department of Dakota, October 7, 1880, NA, RG 98, copy in LBAF; L. L. Garrison, "List of Legislative Enactments, Custer Battlefield National Monument (CBNM): January 17, 1985," copy in the National Park Service (NPS) Library, Denver, Colorado. National cemeteries had been authorized by Congress in 1862 as a means of ensuring a repository of the nation's war dead. Accordingly, in 1867 it was decreed that such cemeteries be enclosed with "good and substantial stone or iron" fences and that "each grave . . . be marked with a small head–stone, or block, with the number of the grave inscribed thereon." By 1879 there were eighty national cemeteries containing approximately 350,000 graves, all under the administration of the Quartermaster Department. Ingersoll, *History of the War Department*, 380–82; *Army Almanac*, 486–90.

24. Sanderson to AAG, Department of Dakota, undated, NA, U.S. Army Commands, Letters Sent, Fort Custer, 1879–82, copy in LBAF. In June 1880 Second Lieutenant Hunter Liggett, Fifth Infantry, passed over the battlefield, noting that "many mementos of the bloody tragedy here enacted still cover the ground." "Report on the Itinerary of Lieutenant W. P. Clark's Reconnaissance of the Big Horn Mountains," undated, NA, RG 98, copy in LBAF.

25. Frederick Whittaker's poem "Custer's Last Charge" in *Army and Navy Journal*, July 15, 1876; "The Custer Monument," *Army and Navy Journal*, July 29, 1876; *New York Herald*, July 11, 1876, cited in Rickey, *History of Custer Battlefield*, 27; "Widow's Relief Fund," in Microfilm Roll 17, Records of the War Department, Little Bighorn Battlefield National Monument (LBBNM). For in-depth discussion of the fund, see Hedren, "Holy Ground," 191–92; Stewart, "Custer Battle and Widow's Weeds," 53–55; *New York Herald*, May 30, 1877, qtd. in Rickey, *History of Custer Battlefield*, 27. Elizabeth Custer's interest in removing a graveside statue of her husband at West Point that she disliked is discussed in Leckie, *Elizabeth Bacon Custer*, 223–27. For the West Point statue and its unveiling, see ibid. and *Army and Navy Journal*, August 30 and September 6, 1879.

26. Meigs to the Secretary of War, October 16, 1878, NA, RG 94, copy in LBAF; "Report of the Quartermaster-General," October 10, 1879, 229–30; Meigs to AG, July 28, 1879, with endorsements, NA, RG 94, Microfilm Roll 17, Records of the War Department, LBBNM; Rickey, *History of Custer Battlefield*, 60, 140 (citing Meigs to Elizabeth B. Custer, October 26, 1881, Package 44, Elizabeth B. Custer Collection, LBBNM); Hardorff, *Custer Battle Casualties*, 69.

27. "Battle Monument to Genl Custer and Others," December 29, 1878, Custer National Cemetery Correspondence, Letters Received (LR) and Letters Sent (LS): 1890s–1930s, LIBI Acc. No. 381; "Inscriptions for Custer Monument," NA, RG 92, Office of the Quartermaster General, Cemeterial File, copy in LBAF; Colonel John W. Davidson to AAG, Department of Dakota, February 25, 1881, NA, RG 94, copy in LBAF; Hardorff, *Custer Battle Casualties*, 70–71. An undated document (ca. early 1894) titled "Custer Battlefield, Montana, National Cemetery (Fourth Class)" stated that the monument cost $1,089.43, NA, copy in LBAF. See also Rickey, *History of Custer Battlefield*, 60–61.

28. Roe to AAG, Department of Dakota, August 6, 1881 (copy): with endorsements, NA, RG 94, copy in LBAF; Diagrams, "Erection of the Monument on Gen. Custer's Battlefield," "Vertical Section of Foundation and Base of the Monument," and "Corner View of the Monument," NA, RG 94, copy in Map Drawer 1, Nos. 12, 13, and 14, LBBNM; *Army and Navy Journal*, September 17, 1881; Hardorff, *Custer Battlefield Casualties*, 69–70. (A snippet in the *Army and Navy Journal*, July 7, 1883, termed the stone "Montello granite.") The plan to place the remains "in a trench around the base of the Monument, which will be sodded" had been previously announced by Colonel Davidson. Davidson to AAG, Department of Dakota, February 25, 1881, NA, RG 94, copy in LBAF. Roe's detail returned to Fort Custer on July 30, 1881. Sanderson to AAG, Department

of Dakota, July 31, 1881, NA, LS, Fort Custer, 1879–82, copy in LBAF; Hedren, "Holy Ground," 200–201. A formal description of the monument reported that it "consists of three sections of smoothed light granite resting on a one-foot high concrete base. The first stone section is square, the second two are square, but tapering towards the top. The overall height is about 16½ feet. One side at the base is approximately seven feet, and 2½ feet at the top. The entire monument is bordered around by 10 feet of grass, then a low wall of granite slabs. Inscribed on the monument are the names of men directly under Custer's command (including Custer himself) who lost their lives in the vicinity. Most are buried beneath the monument in a mass grave." Custer Memorial, Classified Structure Inventory Report, September 6, 1975, LBBNM. The monument was placed on the National Register of Historic Places on October 15, 1966, ibid. See also Rickey, *History of Custer Battlefield*, 61–62.

29. The account of the finding of a skeleton in August 1884, appeared in the *Weekly Yellowstone Journal* (Miles City, Mont.): September 13, 1884, as reproduced in *Bighorn Yellowstone Journal* 1 (Summer 1992): 21–22. Sanders's report is in Sanders to AAG, Department of Dakota, May 30, 1882, with endorsements, NA, RG 92, copy in LBAF. See also Rickey, *History of Custer Battlefield*, 51.

30. *Billings Gazette*, June 28, 1886; Upton, *Fort Custer*, 106–12, 191–92, 196–97; Rickey, *History of Custer Battlefield*, 72–74; Mills, *Harvest of Barren Regrets*, 341–42; Robert A. Murray, "Ghost-Herders on the Little Big Horn: The Custer Battlefield Story," 33–34, unpublished manuscript dated February 20, 1981, in the files of LBBNM; *Army and Navy Journal*, June 18, 1887; Upton, *Participants*, 18, 21; "Wyoming Druggist Collects Custer Relics," *Tile and Till* (November 1939):4, reprint in Vertical Files—"Custer Battle," Sheridan County Fulmer Public Library, Sheridan, Wyoming; McChristian, "Burying the Hatchet," 4–5. Memorial Day exercises in 1901 were cancelled after Burlington officials failed to provide railroad cars to run from Sheridan and Billings to the battlefield. *Anaconda (Mont.) Standard*, May 26, 1901.

31. Rickey, *History of Custer Battlefield*, 38–39, 43–44; Marquis, *Memoirs*.

32. "National Cemetery on the Site of Custer's Battle Ground, June 25th 1876, Surveyed by First Lieutenant Edward Maguire, 1879, Office Chief Engineer, Mil. Div. Mo. 1881," copy in Walter M. Camp Collection, LBBNM, Folder 2, Document 13361; Secretary of the Interior Kirkwood to Secretary of War Robert Lincoln, September 13, 1881, and "Transcript from Endorsement Book," Interior Department Reservation Files, with endorsement, September 13, 1881, NA, RG 94, copy in LBAF; Commissioner of Indian Affairs John D. C. Atkins to Secretary of the Interior, September 26, 1885, NA, RG 94, copy in LBAF; Colonel Nathan A. M. Dudley to AAG, Department of Dakota, November 25, 1885, NA, RG 94, copy in LBAF (quotes); "In the Matter of Proposed Military Reservations at and near Fort Custer, M.T.," enclosing related documents, 1879–83, and dated 1886, NA, RG 94, Reservation File, Microfilm Roll 17, "Records of the War Department," LBBNM; "Map of Military Reservation of

Fort Custer, M.T.," 1879 (showing original and revised tracts of national ceme-
tery): NPS Technical Information Center (TIC) drawing 381 5307, "Military
Reservation Boundary," Lakewood, Colorado; *Executive Orders Relating to Indian
Reserves*, microfiche copy in University of Colorado Law Library, Boulder; General
Order No. 90, Headquarters of the Army, December 15, 1886 (which revoked
paragraph 2 of General Order No. 78): in *Index of General Orders, 1886*; *Military
Reservations* (1898): 121–23; *Military Reservations* (1910): 221 (see also 1916,
231); "An Act Providing compensation to the Crow Indians for Custer Battle
Field National Cemetery, and for other purposes," in Garrison, "Legislative
Enactments"; Rickey, *History of Custer Battlefield*, 29–31; National Register of
Historic Places Inventory—Nomination Form, "Custer Battlefield National Mon-
ument (Partial Inventory: Custer Battlefield Historic District)," dated May
1985, copy in the files of LBBNM; B. Smith, "Politics and the Crow Indian
Land Cessions," 33. See also the following survey materials in Map Drawer 2,
White Swan Memorial Library, LBBNM: Maps of Township No. 3 South,
Range No. 35 East of the Principal Meridian, M.T., editions of 1884, 1902, and
1914; "Supplemental Plat of Township No. 3 South Range No. 35 East of the Principal Meridian, Montana"; and Transcript of the Field Notes of the Subdivision
Lines of Fractional Township No. 3 South, Range No. 35 East, July 1883, 404–26.

3. War Department Years: National Cemetery, 1880s–1920s

1. Utley, *Lance and Shield*, 266–67.
2. Brigadier General (Quartermaster General) Rufus Ingalls to Chief Quartermaster, Department of Dakota, June 15, 1883, NA, copy in LBAF; *Report of the
Secretary of War, 1884*, 688–90; *Report of the Secretary of War, 1885*, 684–87; *Report
of the Secretary of War, 1887*, 570–71; Nichols, "Capt. Owen J. Sweet," 31. Contemporary description of the fence around the monument is in Lieutenant Colonel
Jacob Ford Kent to Inspector General, August 4, 1891, NA, copy in LBAF. For
the Fetterman Fight ("Massacre") of December 21, 1866, see Brown, *Fort Phil
Kearny*. A detailed plat of the Fort Phil Kearny reburials is "Ground Plan Showing
Location of Remains of Officers, Soldiers and Citizens, Removed from Cemetery
at Old Fort Phil Kearney [*sic*], and Burried [*sic*] on the Custer Battle Field, Little
Big Horn River, M.T., Oct. 24th 1888 under Supervision of Capt. J.M.J. Sanno,
7th Infantry," NA, copy in LBBNM Map files, Drawer 1, No. 10. Erection of
headstones in 1889 for the Fort Kearny dead is described in Captain John W.
French to Post Adjutant, Fort Custer, November 3, 1889, NA, RG 92, copy in
LBAF. It is referenced in *Report of the Secretary of War, 1890*, 721. See also Rickey,
History of Custer Battlefield, 51; Murray, "Ghost-Herders," 39–40. For the Crow
insurgency, see Rickey, *History of Custer Battlefield*, 39–40; *Billings Gazette*, November 18, 1934; Calloway, "Sword Bearer"; Upton, *Fort Custer*, 117–67.
3. Dandy to Brigadier General Samuel B. Holabird, Quartermaster General, September 6, 1889, NA, RG 92, Microfilm Roll 17, Records of the War

Department, LBBNM; *Report of the Secretary of War, 1889*, 353–55; French to Post Adjutant, Fort Custer, November 3, 1889. A survey of the plat considered by Dandy was as follows: "Beginning with a line from the Custer Monument to Lieutenant Crittenden's grave, 3172 feet. Magnetic course North 45° West; Station C. Reference 58.5 feet North, 28°30' East of corner stone of iron fence; Station 31+72. Reference 15 feet South, 45° East of Lieutenant Crittenden's monument (Headstone); Station 31+72, angle 90°. Point established 300 feet South west; Station A, angle 90°. Point established 65 feet S,W; Station A. Magnetic reading of center of monument South 25° West. (Center of monument means about perpendicular line of N.E. Corner of upright stones.); Station O, Station 31+72, and point established at angle 20° from station 31+72, S.W., 300 feet, are marked by iron pins driven flush with ground; Point established at angle of 90° to station O, 65 feet S.W., is marked with wooden pin with iron tack in head." Dandy added: "It will be noted that the plat described is a rectangular figure containing a little less than twenty-five acres, and allowing for undulations and inequalities in the ground will require about 7,600 feet of fencing for its enclosure." Dandy to Holabird, September 6, 1889. See "Plot of National Cemetery at Custer's Battle Field on the Little Big Horn River, Mont.," undated, ca. 1889, NPS TIC 381 5308 12–1–31, "Plot of National Cemetery." See also Rickey, *History of Custer Battlefield*, 30–31.

4. Rickey, *History of Custer Battlefield*, 68, 141 (citing *New York Herald*, January 21, 1895). The stones were likely crafted by the firm of Sheldon and Sons, West Rutland, Vermont, under a contract made August 21, 1888, for twenty thousand stones. *Report of the Secretary of War, 1890*, 719–20.

5. General Order No. 70, April 29, 1890, Fort Custer, Montana Territory, NA, copy in LBAF; *Report of the Secretary of War, 1890*, 721; Murray, "Ghost-Herders," 34; Nichols, "Capt. Owen J. Sweet," 32–35, which reproduces Sweet's entire report.

6. *Report of the Secretary of War, 1890*, 721; Kent to Inspector General, August 4, 1891; Rickey, *History of Custer Battlefield*, 116–17, 147, citing Walter M. Camp to Elizabeth B. Custer, January 10, 1921, Elizabeth B. Custer Collection, LBBNM; Brust, Pohanka, and Barnard, *Where Custer Fell*, 13. The number of spurious markers on the battlefield has been determined to be at least forty-two and possibly as many as seventy-two. Ibid., 31–32. For a well-rounded discussion of the bogus stones, see ibid., 119–21.

7. First Lieutenant James B. Aleshire to Chief Quartermaster, Department of Dakota, September 24, 1891, NA, RG 92, copy in LBAF; Lieutenant Colonel Marshall I. Ludington to Chief Quartermaster, Department of Dakota, October 22, 1891, NA, RG 92, copy in LBAF.

8. Ludington to Grover, June 2, 1892, NA, RG 92, copy in LBAF; Grover to Ludington, June 23, 1892, NA, RG 98, copy in LBAF; First Lieutenant John B. McDonald, Tenth Cavalry, to Ludington, June 24, 1892, NA, RG 92, copy in LBAF. For the various reinterments from regional forts, see, for Fort C.F. Smith, Second Lieutenant William T. Johnston, Tenth Cavalry, to Lieutenant Colonel

David Perry, commanding Fort Custer, June 11, 1892 (which describes in detail the individual remains removed from Fort C. F. Smith): NA, RG 92, copy in LBAF; for Fort Abraham Lincoln (including Fort Stevenson): Major John V. Furey, Department of Dakota, to Post Quartermaster, Fort Abraham Lincoln, North Dakota, August 22, 1891, with endorsements, NA, RG 92, copy in LBAF; *Report of the Secretary of War, 1891*, 483; *Report of the Secretary of War, 1892*, 360; *Billings Gazette*, May 25, 1947. See also Milner and Forrest, *California Joe*, 319–20. For the Hayfield Fight of August 1, 1867, see Greene, "The Hayfield Fight." For discussion of relocation of the Fort C. F. Smith graves, see Brust, Pohanka, and Barnard, *Where Custer Fell*, 163–65. It is likely that a dedication for the national cemetery took place between 1889 and 1894, for which Wyoming state senate president Franklin Mondell made a dedicatory address. Rickey, *History of Custer Battlefield*, 74, 142 (citing *Sunday Call*, June 24, 1900).

9. Furey to Ludington, January 30, 1893, NA, RG 92, copy in LBAF; Ludington to Chief Quartermaster, Department of Dakota, February 8, 1893, NA, RG 92, copy in LBAF.

10. Ibid.; Campbell to Furey, June 30, 1893, NA, RG 92, copy in LBAF; *Report of the Secretary of War, 1893*, 221, 325, 328, 330.

11. Ludington to Chief Quartermaster, Department of Dakota, February 8, 1893; Grover to Brigadier General (Quartermaster General) Richard N. Batchelder, July 11, 1893, NA, RG 92, copy in LBAF; manuscript journal, Custer Battlefield National Cemetery, entry for July 11, 1893.

12. Ludington to Depot Quartermaster, July 5, 1893, NA, RG 92, copy in LBAF.

13. Owen to Hand (unidentified in the correspondence): July 16, 1893, NA, RG 92, copy in LBAF; "Report of the Survey of the Custer Battlefield National Cemetery Reservation," in Owen to the Quartermaster General, August 3, 1893, NA, RG 92, copy in LBAF.

14. Ibid.

15. Ibid.; manuscript journal, entry for August 23, 1893; Grover to Lieutenant Colonel George H. Weeks (Deputy Quartermaster General): October 31, 1893, enclosing drawings for "Temporary House for Sup't Custer Battle–Field National Cemetery." NA, RG 92, copy in LBAF; "Custer Battlefield, Montana, National Cemetery (Fourth Class): undated, ca. early 1894, NA, copy in LBAF; *Report of the Secretary of War, 1894*, 293.

16. Ibid.; *Report of the Secretary of War, 1895*, 225, 361, 362, 364, 366; manuscript journal, entries for June 27, November 12, 1894; "Articles of Agreement" for lodge, May 18, 1894, NA, RG 92, copy in LBAF; "Specifications for labor and materials for a stone lodge for Superintendent of National Cemetery at Custer Battlefield, Mont.," including drawings, NA, RG 92, copy in LBAF; "Superintendent's House," September 12, 1949, in Administrative Research Collection, LBBNM, Accession No. 738; "Superintendent's Lodge, Custer Battlefield National Monument, Big Horn County, Montana," Historic American Building Survey (HABS No. MON–7): copy on file in White Swan Memorial Library, LBBNM.

17. Manuscript journal, entries for April 1, June 22, June 29, August 7, August 20, August 23, and October 29, 1895, February 1, March 27, April 7, April 28, May 21, May 23, June 24, July 3, October 29, and November 20, 1896, and June 3, 1897; "The Custer Battle Field, as It Is Today," in *Chicago Sunday Times-Herald*, September 13, 1896; *Report of the Secretary of War, 1897*, 385; Rickey, *History of Custer Battlefield*, 47, 53 (citing, for relocating the Fort Phil Kearny dead, Grover to Depot Quartermaster, Washington, D.C., February 11, 1896, in LS, 7/11/93–2/14/25, LBBNM): 57 (citing, for Grover's recommendations, Grover to Depot Quartermaster, September 29, 1897, LS, 7/11/93–2/14/25, LBBNM): 63; Brust, Pohanka, and Barnard, *Where Custer Fell*, 110, 141–45; Moss, "Military Cycling"; Schmitzer, "Wheels of War," 28. See also Dollar, "Putting the Army on Wheels."

18. Manuscript journal, entries for December 12, 1893, and November 12, 1896 (affecting Crow timber issues); Rickey, *History of Custer Battlefield*, 31, 47, 48, 136, citing Superintendent Edmund B. Rogers, Yellowstone National Park, to Regional Director, NPS, Region 2, September 8, 1943, "Lands, 1930–41," File 601, Custer Battlefield National Monument (CBNM).

19. *Annual Reports of the War Department, 1903*, 455. This comment was perhaps one of the first signifying onset of a longtime debate, mostly generated by visitors, over whether the battlefield should retain its natural appearance or be manicured in the manner of the cemetery. The issue continued intermittently into the late twentieth century. Former superintendent Neil C. Mangum to author, February 1, 2005.

20. Manuscript journal, entries for May 16, 1900, May 18, 1903, and February 25, May 24, and June 20, 1905; *Report of the Secretary of War, 1900*, 341; Greene, *Nez Perce Summer* 448n71; Rickey, *History of Custer Battlefield*, 51, 53. For the fight at Canyon Creek, see Greene, *Nez Perce Summer* 206–30. Recent exhumations and analysis of battle remains interred in the cemetery do not support the identification of Sergeant Butler; it is possible that the wrong body was recovered from Deep Coulee. Scott, Willey, and Connor, *They Died with Custer*, 178–82.

21. Manuscript journal, entries for March 16, April 5, and April 28, 1906. *Report of the Secretary of War, 1900*, 341; *New York Times*, February 16, 1908.

22. Ibid.

23. Manuscript journal, entries for June 21, July 16, and September 13, 1907, April 20, June 28, August 3, August 25, October 17, October 22, November 5, November 16, and December 15, 1908, and February 12 and March 24, 1909; Richard J. Cronenberger, "Classified Structure Field Inventory Report," for "Iron Flag Pole," November 15, 1982, copy in the White Swan Memorial Library, LBBNM. Miles's campaigns are presented in Greene, *Yellowstone Command*. For White Bird Canyon see Greene, *Nez Perce Summer* 34–48.

24. Manuscript journal, entries for March 25, May 3, May 17, June 18, August 19, October 5, October 19, and October 28, 1909, and January 11, February 28, April 15, May 10, June 2, June 13, July 25, and July 27, 1910; Rickey, *History of Custer Battlefield*, 57, 69–70 (citing Wright to Quartermaster General, June 13, 1910), LS, 1/11/93–2/14/25, CBNM; Brust, Pohanka, and Barnard, *Where Custer Fell*, 117.

That Wright's marker placements further muddled things on the battlefield is registered in a letter to General Godfrey from Walter M. Camp, a serious avocational
student of the Little Bighorn, who solicited the aged officer's assistance in rectifying
the situation:

> In 1908, I discovered that there were 254 government markers . . . [on
> Custer's field], whereas the number of bodies found there on June 27,
> 1876 was 207 (or 206?). I think I was, perhaps, the first person to discover
> this mistake, for the Custodian there then told me I did not know what I
> was talking about when I acquainted him with the facts. I at once sus-
> pected that markers sent for Reno's killed had been planted on Custer
> Ridge, and this opinion I was able to confirm a year or two later, when I
> met the officer of the 25th Infantry who set the markers in 1894. He was
> a Lieutenant Burkhardt [Second Lieutenant Samuel Burkhardt, Jr.]. . . .
> A captain of the 25th Inf. [Sweet] . . . had charge, but Burkhardt . . . did
> the work. He admitted to me that, being unable to locate the places
> where Reno's men had fallen (Lieut. Roe . . . having gathered up all the
> remains in 1881), he set all of the markers on Custer Ridge. Historically,
> this was, of course, a bad piece of business. . . . In 1910, four more markers
> were placed by Custodian Oscar Wright (for Porter, Lord, Sturgis and
> Harrington): so that there are now 258 markers there, or 51 too many.
> There are 17 or 18 too many markers in the group at the monument, too
> many in the group around Keogh's marker, too many between the monu-
> ment and the river, and none in the big gully where about 28 ought to be.
> I discovered these [missing?] dead in the gully with Capt. McDougall in
> 1909, and he was clear that there were only 9 dead between the end of
> the ridge and the gully (not counting the group that lay around the body
> of Gen. Custer)—only 9 dead between the end of the ridge and the gully,
> and 28 in the gully. As the markers now stand, there are more than 50
> where there should be only 9, on that side, and not enough at or in the
> gully. The marker for Lieut. Hodgson (placed in 1910) down at Reno hill
> is in the wrong place—about 2000 feet from where it ought to be. There
> is no marker for Sergt. Butler of L Co., none for Vincent Charlie of D. Co.,
> and none where Mitch Bouyer's body was found, which lay near the river
> north of the Cheyenne village—that is, on the opposite side of the river
> from the Cheyenne village. I have authentic information of the location
> of Bouyer's body from an officer of the 2nd Cavalry and from the son of
> Lamedeer, who was fighting with the Sioux. These two independent
> sources of information are so clear and plausible that I have accepted
> them as correct. Bouyer's body was never buried and neither was Vincent
> Charlie's [sic]. The latter fell on Weir's retreat from his most advanced
> point toward Gen. Custer, and Gen. Edgerly gave me the location of the
> body. I have been on the battlefield with four enlisted men who helped
> bury the dead, and all my sources of information are equally authentic.

Col. Mathey gave me important information which could be used to correct some of the mistakes that were made in the planting of these markers in 1894. I will not go into further details here. Your interest and influence would go further toward having something done to correct these mistakes than would the intervention of any other man, and I wish the War Dept. would sent you out there with authority to straighten out the mistakes. The number of markers on the Custer ridge should, by all means, be made to correspond with the number of dead found there, which is a matter of official record. The names on the monument which include those for the dead of Reno's command, are a further check on the number of markers that should be on Custer Ridge. The presence of the Fetterman markers are a further incongruity—the intermingling of markers for soldiers killed on battlefields more than 100 miles apart. I would suggest that of the surplus markers on Custer ridge, some 27 (if that is the correct number) might be removed and placed in a group or circle on Reno hill, and 29 more might be placed in a circle around the McIntosh marker, if land could not be set aside on which to string them out on the line of Reno's retreat out of the bottom. I may not be doing right by proposing to work you like this in your old age, but unless something is done before many years, it will likely never be done, and people will come to lose confidence in the accuracy of the marking of that historical spot.
[Camp to Godfrey, November 6, 1920, Edward S. Godfrey Papers, 344–45, Library of Congress.]

25. Manuscript journal, entries for September 6, September 17, September 24, October 7, and October 15, 1910, and January 18, 1911; Special Order No. 136, June 22, 1917, cited in manuscript journal; Rickey, *History of Custer Battlefield*, 53 (citing Superintendent Daniel Dommitt to Quartermaster General, October 31, 1912, LS, 7/11/93–2/14/25, LBBNM); "Ft. Assinniboine, Mont. Reburial at Custer Battlefield National Cemetery," roster of names in File "Bear Paw Battlefield—Jim Magera Research," in the library/archives of Nez Perce National Historical Park, Spalding, Idaho. The Battle of the Bear's Paw Mountains is treated in Greene, *Nez Perce Summer*, 271–324.

26. Rickey, *History of Custer Battlefield*, 48–49, 57, 63, 111, 112, and 138–39 (citing Wessinger to Elizabeth B. Custer, January 30, 1924, Package No. 44, Elizabeth B. Custer Collection; and Wessinger to Depot Quartermaster, Washington, D.C., February 8, 1916, LS, 7/11/93–2/14/25, LBBNM). The pump house was built in about 1912. "Old Pump House," September 12, 1949, in Administrative Research Collection, LBBNM, Accession No. 738. There is no archeological evidence for Wessinger's reported salting of the site with expended cartridge casings. Scott, Fox, Connor, and Harmon, *Archeological Perspectives*, 183–86.

27. *Chicago Sunday Times-Herald*, September 13, 1896; Rickey, *History of Custer Battlefield*, 40, 41, 138 (citing *Sheridan Post*, October 1, 1903); Murray, "Ghost-Herders," 41, 42–43; McChristian, "Burying the Hatchet," 5. The 1902

Sheridan reenactment took place at five in the afternoon. A reporter described it as including "the charge by the troops, the attack by the howling mob of painted fiends from every glen and canyon, the Redskin in white with hell written in his every act of vengeance, the rapid firing of volley after volley like continuous thunder, the slow but forced retreat of the soldiers and the rapid thinning of the lines by the circling, howling hordes of feathered savages, the retreat of the colors to the brow of the hill and the determined stand taken by the brave boys until all were dead and the standard fell to the dust." *Sheridan Enterprise*, July 5, 1902, as reprinted in *Sheridan Press*, May 20, 1957. See also *Sheridan Press*, July 13, 1955. The film of the Dixon–Wanamaker reenactment reposes in the National Anthropological Archives of the Smithsonian Institution. A detailed account of the 1909 reenactment is in Rickey, *History of Custer Battlefield*, 74–75 (citing *Billings Daily Gazette*, September 26, 1909). See 1910 photo by Photographer Roland Reed in Hathaway, *Native American Portraits*, 112–13. For the road, see Rickey, *History of Custer Battlefield*, 111, 146 (citing Wessinger to Depot Quartermaster, Omaha, Nebraska, July 8, 1915, LS 7/11/93–2/14/25).

28. Rickey, *History of Custer Battlefield*, 115–16, 147 (citing Godfrey to Elizabeth B. Custer, June 2, 1916, Elizabeth B. Custer Collection, CBNM; and Wright to Depot Quartermaster, Washington, D.C., May 10, 1909; Dommitt to Depot Quartermaster, Washington, D.C., July 7, 1913; Dommitt to Depot Quartermaster, Washington, D.C., August 28, 1913, all in LS, 7/11/93–2/14/25, CBNM).

29. Rickey, *History of Custer Battlefield*, 41–42, 84–85. Many results of the Dixon expedition appear in J. Dixon, *Vanishing Race*. Godfrey's complaints are chronicled in Rickey, *History of Custer Battlefield*, 45 (citing Godfrey to Elizabeth B. Custer, May 21, 1916, Package No. 43, Elizabeth B. Custer Collection, CBNM).

30. Account of the fortieth anniversary in *The Custer Story*, supplement to the *Billings Gazette*, May 27, 1961, 55; description of events in Elizabeth B. Custer's hand in undated note, ca. 1916, Elizabeth B. Custer Collection, LBBNM; Microfilm Roll 4, "Other Correspondence, Orders, and Miscellaneous Documents," frames 3756–59; McChristian, "Burying the Hatchet," 6; Rickey, *History of Custer Battlefield*, 77–79, 143 (citing *Sheridan Post*, June 27, 1916, *Detroit Free Press*, July 12, 1916, and *Billings Gazette*, June 26, 1916); *Hardin Tribune*, May 26, 1916; *Billings Gazette*, November 10, 1920; Murray, "Ghost-Herders," 48–49; Brust, Pohanka, and Barnard, *Where Custer Fell*, 22, 158–59. A typed copy of Godfrey's 1916 speech, accompanied by his handwritten transmittal letter, is in the collections of the Parmly Billings Public Library.

31. Whiteley and Whiteley, *Playground Trail*, 73; Brochure, "Custer Battlefield Highway" (quote); Kinsley, "Custer Memorial Highway," copy in Sheridan County Fulmer Public Library, Sheridan, Wyoming; Rickey, *History of Custer Battlefield*, 42; Roe, *Custer's Last Battle*, map inside back cover and opposite p. 40, titled "A Great Interstate Route Named After a Famous General"; Brochure, ca. 1920, "Custer Battlefield Hiway: The Historical Hiway to the West"; Rickey, *History of Custer Battlefield*, 42.

4. War Department Years: Transitions, 1920s–1940

1. Classified Structure Field Inventory Report, Battlefield Stone Markers HS-33, copy in the White Swan Memorial Library, LBBNM; Rickey, *History of Custer Battlefield*, 56, 58–59, 70, 139 (citing Montana Adjutant General E. H. Williams to Superintendent, Custer Battlefield, January 19, 1932, Historical Research Files, CBNM, which relates Montana Governor John E. Erickson's opposition to removing Crittenden's remains); Manuscript journal, last page; "Proposed Entrance Gates, Custer Battlefield Cemetery, Crow Agency, Mont. A. H. Brodkey Co., Omaha, Nebr., June 8, 1931," NPS TIC 381 6000 5-1-32, "Entrance Gates/Battlefield," NPS, Denver Service Center; "Location Plan U.S. National Cemetery in the Custer Battlefield, Montana U.S. National Cemetery Reservation." "Retraced [apparently in 1932] from Map Prepared by Depot Quartermaster, Washington, D.C., April 10, 1916," NPS TIC 381 5319 10-1-32, "Cemetery Location Plan," NPS, Denver Service Center; see also NPS TIC 381 5318 9-1-32, "Layout Plan of Cemetery," and NPS TIC 381 5318A 10-1-34, "Layout Plan of Cemetery," NPS, Denver Service Center; Information sheet, Custer Battlefield National Cemetery, Montana, January 16, 1929 (revised September 21, 1934), copy in LBAF; "Rostrum" File, September 12, 1949, Administrative Research Collection, LBBNM, Accession No. 738; "Comfort Station," Administrative Research Collection, LBBNM, Accession No. 738; Brust, Pohanka, and Barnard, *Where Custer Fell*, 100–101, 160–61; Obituary of Dave Manning, http://www.geocities.com/chippewahogans/obitdavemanning.html. A detailed account of the rostrum dedication appears in *Winners of the West*, June 30, 1935. The cricket infestation is described in Swisher, "Controlling Mormon Crickets," 63. In 1941 NPS superintendent Edward S. Luce mentioned that the cricket fence had "served its purpose" in his monthly report but that "box elder insects" were "beyond control." "They are here the year around and are very obnoxious in that they dirty the woodwork, fall into food, crawl over the floors and ceilings and the walls and ordinary insect control methods seem to have no effect." Superintendent's Monthly Report, Memorandum to the Director, January 31, 1941, Administrative Research Collection, LBBNM, Accession No. 738 (hereafter cited, with dates, as SMR). The reburials of Fort Logan dead are referenced, citing War Department records, in Milner and Forrest, *California Joe*, 320. The quote regarding available space is in Information sheet, Custer Battlefield National Cemetery, Montana, January 16, 1929 (revised September 21, 1934): copy in LBAF.

2. Major General Benjamin F. Cheatham to Assistant Secretary of War, June 8, 1927, re: "Boundary of Custer Battlefield National Cemetery," QM 600.93, NA, copy in LBAF; Attorney General to Secretary of War, March 26, 1928, NA, copy in LBAF; Cheatham to Assistant Secretary of War, April 12, 1928, QM 600.93, NA, copy in LBAF; Lieutenant Colonel Hugh C. Smith to Assistant Secretary of War, April 24, 1928, NA, copy in LBAF; Major S. M. Williams and Crow Reservation Superintendent C. H. Asbury to Commissioner of Indian Affairs, November 5, 1928, NA, copy in LBAF; United States, *Statutes at Large*, 46:168–69;

War Department, *Military Reservations, Montana*, October 25, 1937, Section 2, 2–3 (respecting 46 Stat. 876), copy in LBAF; Department of the Interior, "Right of Way for Poles and Lines," Act of February 15, 1901, with date of initiation, April 19, 1932, NA, copy in LBAF; Rickey, *History of Custer Battlefield*, 30. The inquiry into allotment claims disclosed that, because of the meandering west boundary formed by the east bank of the Little Bighorn River, the Custer Battlefield National Cemetery Reservation actually contained but 583 acres (including the Indian claims) instead of 640. Williams and Asbury to Commissioner of Indian Affairs, November 5, 1928. The January 28, 1937, revocable five-year lease to Vincent Nipper is noted in Information sheet, Custer Battlefield National Cemetery, Montana, January 16, 1929 (revised September 21, 1934): copy in LBAF.

3. Rickey, *History of Custer Battlefield*, 86.

4. Quote is from a typed brief titled "Anniversary of the Custer Massacre" in the Elizabeth B. Custer Collection, LBBNM, Microfilm, Roll 4, frames 3754–55. For forty-fifth anniversary activities, see undated typescript by Mrs. Custer, ibid., frames 3703–04; random notes by Mrs. Custer, 1921 in ibid., frames 3736–44, 3745–53; typescript by Mrs. Custer titled "A Noteworthy Anniversary," ibid., frames 3721–25. In one missive, she wrote, "A monument is to be unveiled to my husband's memory. . . . I was so sorry to disappoint them, but I could not get courage to meet the crowds of enthusiastic & wonderful western people." Random notes, May–June 1921, ibid., frame 3734. In another letter, she wrote, "I was so moved to have Montana and the West do so much to celebrate the forty-fifth anniversary of the battle. It was a great three days. I had not nervous strength to go through the ordeal." *Winners of the West*, February 1924. See also McChristian, "Burying the Hatchet," 6.

5. Veterans and former civilian employees who registered at the Seventh Cavalry Camp at Crow Agency, including some who participated in the Battle of the Little Bighorn, were Anthony L. Barron, Theodore W. Goldin, A. C. Rallya, John C. Lockwood, Daniel Newell, Lawrence J. Henry, Steven Elwood, John Burri, A. F. Loeffing, William E. Morris, Jacob Horner, John C. Creighton, Charles A. Smith, Lansing A. Moore, and William C. Slaper. Names list dated January 25, 1934, William Carey Brown Papers, Box 21, Folder 16, Western History Collections, Archives, University of Colorado at Boulder Libraries.

6. The primary narrative on semicentennial activities is McChristian, "Burying the Hatchet," 50–65. The article has been reprinted in *Greasy Grass* 18 (May 2002): 2–15. See also Rickey, *History of Custer Battlefield*, 81–83; *Billings Gazette*, June 15, 18, 22–27, 1876; *Hardin Tribune-Herald*, June 25, 1926; *Helena Independent Record*, July 26, 1926; *Winners of the West*, December 15, 1925, and May 30, July 31, and August 30, 1926; Brust, Pohanka, and Barnard, *Where Custer Fell*, 114–15. General Godfrey's report to the National Custer Memorial Association is reprinted in Koury, *To Consecrate This Ground*, 12–16. The remains of the man encrypted near the Garryowen store were exhumed by the NPS in May 1957 to facilitate highway improvements. The tomahawk entombed in 1926 was not

found. Park Historian Don Rickey, Jr., noted that it was possible that the remains were of someone besides a cavalryman, because certain identification had been impossible. *Billing Gazette*, May 18, 1957. For the 1926 festivities, see various articles and clippings from the Hardin and Billings newspapers in the "Custer Scrapbook," as well as Vertical File M, "Custer Battle Anniversaries," Montana Room, Parmly Billings Public Library. See also the thorough compilation of photos and articles in Upton, *Participants*, 42–207. The "Free Official Program" of the three-day anniversary proceedings is in ibid., 207.

7. McChristian, "Burying the Hatchet," 65; Rickey, *History of Custer Battlefield*, 83. A full account of the 1936 observance is in *Winners of the West*, July 1936.

8. Senate Joint Memorial No. 3, Fifteenth Legislative Assembly of the State of Montana, March 1, 1917, typescript copy in LBAF.

9. Unknown party in *Winners of the West*, December 1924.

10. Wagner, *Old Neutriment*, 201–202.

11. The complete inscription reads, "This area was occupied by troops A, B, D, G, H, K, and M, Seventh U.S. Cavalry, and the pack train when they were besieged by the Sioux Indians June 25th and 26th 1876."

12. United States, *Statutes at Large*, 44:251, 45:225; Leckie, *Elizabeth Bacon Custer*, 297–98; Rickey, *History of Custer Battlefield*, 64; McChristian, "Burying the Hatchet," 16; "Classified Structure Field Inventory Report," for "Reno–Benteen Memorial," November 15, 1982, copy in the White Swan Library, LBBNM; Colonel C. C. Reynolds to the Judge Advocate General, May 28, 1941, Subject: "Transfer of title papers and data relating to Reno Battlefield Reservation, Montana," NA, copy in LBAF; Upton, *Participants*, 178–82, including Mrs. Custer's anti-Reno letter to James Shoemaker of March 19, 1925(?). The attempt to have Reno's name added was led by Custer/Little Bighorn researcher Fred Dustin. See Major General Henry Gibbins to Dustin, August 3, 1939, copy in LBAF. The Reynolds site had been marked in 1908 by a pipe and brass plate, replaced by a cross attached to another pipe in 1926. The marker placed by Osten and a group of battle scholars in 1938 was some time later moved to a point adjacent to an irrigation ditch because it interfered with plowing. It was returned to its proper location in the 1990s. McIntosh's marker likewise was moved, apparently for the same purpose, but has since been restored to its likely original location. Brust, Pohanka, and Barnard, *Where Custer Fell*, 36–39.

13. Commissioner of Indian Affairs John Collier to Acting Superintendent Richard B. Millin, May 4, 1936; Crow Reservation Superintendent W. L. O'Hara to Collier, May 14, 1934, with attached "Map of Proposed County Road"; Collier to Colonel James H. Laubach, Quartermaster Corps, May 25, 1934, with enclosures; Major T. Otis Baker to Collier, May 26, 1934; "Copy of Field Notes 'Custer Battlefield' Road, Big Horn County, Montana, Road Number 81"; Laubach to Collier ("Chief, Bureau of Indian Affairs"), March 19, 1934; "Description of Right of Way Leading to Custer Battlefield Reservation, Montana," March 21, 1934; Collier to Millin, March 23, 1934; Millin to Collier, April 3, 1934; Collier to

Laubach, April 12, 1934; Colonel John T. Harris to Superintendent, Crow Indian Agency, November 2, 1937; Superintendent Robert Yellowtail to Harris, November 17, 1937; Yellowtail to Harris, January 3, 1938; Petition for "Grant for Right-of-Way from Custer Battlefield to Reno Battlefield, June 28, 1938"; "Grant for Right-of-Way Custer Battlefield to Reno Battlefield" including allotment numbers, undated, ca. 1938; Major General Henry Gibbins to Yellowtail, January 20, 1938, copy contained in Memorandum, Superintendent Edward S. Luce, Custer Battlefield National Cemetery, to Superintendent, Yellowstone National Park, Wyoming, April 19, 1941. See also Richard A. Young, Chief, Land Resources Division, Rocky Mountain Region, to Superintendent, Crow Indian Agency, May 21, 1987; "Plat Showing Route of a Proposed Highway Between the Custer and the Reno Battlefields, Big Horn County, Montana," January 1932; "Map of the Route of a Proposed Highway Between the Custer and the Reno Battlefields in Township 3 South, Range 35 East, Mont. P.M., Big Horn County, Montana," June 28, 1938. (All of these documents, from appropriate War Department [RG 92], Bureau of Indian Affairs [RG 75], and NPS [RG 79] records in the NA, have been copied and are variously on file in the LBAF and in map drawers at White Swan Library, LBBNM.) Copies of pertinent maps are in NPS TIC 41902 ("Map of the Route of a Proposed Highway. . . ."): NPS TIC 381 5328 (undated "Base Line Profile of Proposed Battlefields Highway"): NPS TIC 381 5330 ("Proposed Battlefields Highway"): NPS TIC 381 5301 ("Road to Reno Monument Layout Plan," November 26, 1938): and NPS TIC 381 2009 ("General Development Plan," January 1, 1942). The proposed alignment passed through parts of Sections 20, 29, 28, 33, and 34, Township 3 South, Range 35 East, and Section 3, Township 4 South, Range 35 East. The Manning Construction Company contract is referenced in Dave Manning tribute, http://www.geocities.com/chippewahogans/articlesdavetribute7.html. Legal authority for constructing the road to the Reno–Benteen site rested with Public Law 310, March 4, 1915 (38 Stat. L 1188, Sec. 2): which permitted the opening of "public roads within any of the said Indian reservations in conformity to and in accordance with the laws of the State of Montana" with approval of the Indian superintendent. United States, *Statutes at Large*, 38:1188. The 1930 rough-cut road is referenced in Rickey, "Myth to Monument," 215. For likely terrain changes resulting from the construction, see W. King, "Tombstones for Bluecoats," 17; NPS TIC 381 5330, "Crossing of Medicine Tail Creek/Proposed Battlefield to Battlefield," July 1, 1935; NPS TIC 5304 "New Channel & Road Sections—Road to Reno Monument," November 1, 1938; Brust, Pohanka, and Barnard, *Where Custer Fell*, 66–67. The Ellison role in the Reynolds Marker placement is described in SMR, August 31, 1945. Others in attendance at the Reynolds Marker dedication were Earl A. Brininstool, Fred Dustin, Albert W. Johnson, and Dr. Charles Kuhlman. Remarks by R. C. Dillavou, president of the Billings Lions Club, preceded the unveiling by Brininstool and his wife. Clipping from an unidentified source in the Vertical Files, Montana Room, Parmly Billings Library. See also *Billings Gazette*, August 17, 18, 1938.

14. Much of the quoted material is from assorted undated notes kept by Elizabeth B. Custer, ca. 1919–1923, copies in the Elizabeth B. Custer Collection, LBBNM; Miles to "The Honorable Senators and Members of Congress," December 19, 1923, copy in LBAF; Custer to David Hilger, May 2, 1923, in Elizabeth B. Custer Collection, LBBNM.; U.S. Congress, Senate, *Bill to Provide for Building*, 1, copy in LBAF; Rickey, *History of Custer Battlefield*, 31–33. In February 1924 a letter from Mrs. Custer appeared in *Winners of the West* in which she stated, "I am trying to have some kind of a memorial hall on the battlefield where souvenirs, pictures, and relics of the old days of the Seventh Cavalry could be kept. It will, I fear, be a long struggle to get anything built, but I have courage to wait." She and General Miles apparently also joined forces to promote the erection of a monument to Custer in the Big Horn County town of Custer, Montana. Edmond G. Toomey, March 8, 1924, copy in LBAF.

15. Case to Dixon, October 8, 1924, copy in LBAF; Walsh to Case, December 20, 1923, copy in LBAF. Mrs. Custer's will stipulated that "My husband's portraits and photographs, his arms and accoutrements, uniforms, souvenirs of war or frontier, books and illustrations, trophies of the chase, and each and every article of personal property owned by me . . . I give . . . to the Public Museum or Memorial which may be erected on the battlefield." Qtd. in Hart, "Changing Exhibitry and Sensitivity," 34.

16. Clipping regarding the Billings Commercial Club dated June 10, 1933, in Vertical File M, Montana Room, Parmly Billings Public Library; Mangum, "Popular Reaction to Custer," 55; Rickey, *History of Custer Battlefield*, 45–46, 50; W. White, *Custer, Cavalry, and Crows*, 11, 180, 182 (citing the *Hardin Tribune*, January 20, 1938); *Winners of the West*, January 30, 1935. O. F. Wheaton, trust officer for Mrs. Custer's estate, let it be known that "the relics cannot be disposed of during the lifetime of two relatives of the widow. With their passing the mementoes may be donated to any memorial or association, with the battlefield receiving preference." *Winners of the West*, May 30, 1934. Regarding White, one observer wrote, "Tourist visitors to the battlefield are intensely stirred by the stories of Mr. White. Interest is accentuated by reason of his having been on the original scene in 1876, and by his being now one of the very last survivors of that era. He knows, for he was there. Although he has strong views concerning the affair, he is quite mild in expressing his views. He is not in the least boastful, and his hearers accord to him the full accrediting to which he is entitled. It is almost pitiable to think that here is one Montana man whose position never can be filled suitably after he is gone." *Hardin Tribune*, March 29, 1935. See also *Hardin Tribune*, June 25, 1933.

17. U.S. Congress, Senate, *Act to Provide for the Erection of a Public Historical Museum*, 1–2, copy in LBAF.

18. Woodring's letter is enclosed in U.S. Congress, House, *Custer Battlefield Historical Museum*. See Public Law 362, Chap. 634, U.S., *Statutes at Large*, vol. 53, pt. 2, 1337, also contained in Sullivan, *Laws*, 199. See also Rickey, *History of Custer Battlefield*, 34–36. For the continuing endeavor to create the museum, see

also H. Robinson, "Custer Battlefield Museum"; the article was reprinted as a pamphlet as H. Robinson, *Custer Battlefield Museum*, 42–45.

19. Public Law 428, 74 Cong., Section 16, Statute No. 1517, Act of March 3, 1933; Executive Order No. 6166, June 10, 1933 (5 U.S.C. secs. 124–32) and Executive Order No. 6228, July 28, 1935 (5 USC secs. 124–32): in Sullivan, *Laws*, 203–207; Executive Order No. 8428, June 3, 1940 (3 CRF. Cum. Supp., 664); *Report of the Secretary of the Interior, 1933*, 16–17; "The National Park Service," in *Report of the Secretary of the Interior, 1940*, 186; Rickey, *History of Custer Battlefield*, 88. Background of the consolidation movement, including alternating opposition and cooperation between the NPS and the War Department, is detailed in Unrau and Willis, *Administrative History*, 34–37, 43, 47, 53–60. Transfer of jurisdiction of Forest Service properties to the NPS took place in 1934. Ibid., 64. As late as 1937, the War Department referenced the cemetery reservation as the Sioux Indian Battle Monument Site. General Order No. 6, War Department, August 4, 1937, copy in LBAF. The last superintendent under War Department administration was Harold A. Montague, who served from December 1939 through November 1940. (He had been preceded by William O. Mickle, July 1938–April 1939, and Fulton Grigsby, April 1939–November 1939). Rickey, *History of Custer Battlefield*, 131.

5. National Park Service Administration, 1940–1969

1. Rickey, *History of Custer Battlefield*, 88, 90. Superintendent Luce arrived on January 6, 1941. SMR, January 31, 1941.

2. Utley, "'Cap' Luce," 6. Luce, from Massachusetts, had served in the Seventh Cavalry in 1907–10. He had been a headquarters clerk and had been discharged but then reenlisted, serving in the coast artillery and Twelfth Cavalry. In World War I, he was commissioned a captain and served in France until gassed. Thereafter he pursued civilian work until joining the War Department as a civilian employee at Arlington National Cemetery. In the 1920s and 1930s, Luce had labored with Elizabeth Custer and General Miles, as well as with Senators Walsh and Wheeler, on behalf of the museum project. Ibid., 6–7; Rickey, *History of Custer Battlefield*, 88–89. See also Utley's well-drawn reminiscent portrait of Luce in *Custer and Me*, 24–26. A contemporary review of Luce's book is in *Winners of the West*, December 1939.

3. SMR, June 30, 1941; SMR, July 31, 1941; SMR, September 30, 1941; Rickey, *History of Custer Battlefield*, 98, 99, 104. In 1941 Luce reported that many markers had been "chipped and destroyed." He wrote, "It is believed that if some other kind of marker could be substituted for the white marble historic markers, preferable metallic, much of this desecration could be done away with." SMR, January 31, 1941. Cemetery data is in SMR, February 29, 1944. The power outage is mentioned in SMR April 30, 1941. The power line from Crow Agency remained a problem. Wrote Luce, "There has been considerable trouble with the river washing out its banks causing the extension of the wire span between the poles." A lightning

strike in August 1941 necessitated the replacement of transformers there. Eventually, Big Horn County Electric Cooperative took over maintenance of the facility. SMR, November 30, 1941; SMR, February 29, 1944. Flooding was a perennial problem. In March 1943 Luce reported that "in 3 days the river . . . rose about 16 feet and flooded the Bighorn and Little Bighorn valleys, washing out the roads at several places. Several of the nearby towns were under water. Ice jams occurred in this area and the waters backed up the valleys from the town of Hardin." The flooding damaged the pump house, located near the river, and also the power line at Crow Agency. SMR, March 31, 1943. In 1947 the flooding caused the Little Bighorn River to rise twenty-one feet, halting highway traffic and nearly destroying the pump house. SMR, March 31, 1947.

4. NPS TIC 381 5339, "Topography—Custer Section," July 1, 1941; NPS TIC 381 5340, "Base Map," January 1, 1942; "New Pump House," September 12, 1949, in Administrative Research Collection, LBBNM, Accession No. 738. Septic tank–related problems occurred intermittently. A new system was installed in 1951, but the drainage lines and disposal field were "completely clogged with sludge" in late 1957 and early 1958. SMR, January 6, 1958; SMR, February 10, 1958.

5. Luce to Nathalie C. Gookin, October 3, 1943, in LBAF; "Visitation Records—Custer Battlefield," 1940–83, in LBAF; SMR, October 31, 1943; Public Law 332, 60 Stat. 59, in Tolson, *Laws*, 402; SMR, March 31, 1946; Rickey, *History of Custer Battlefield*, 90.

6. SMR, October 31, 1941; SMR, November 30, 1941; SMR, August 31, 1942; NPS TIC 381 5342, "Land Ownership," January 1, 1942; NPS TIC 381 6975, "Property Line Study," April 1, 1942; "The Master Plan, Custer Battlefield National Cemetery, Montana," unpublished document, ca. 1944, in the NPS Intermountain Regional Office Library, Lakewood, Colorado; NPS TIC 381 2009, "General Development Plan," January 1, 1942. Interpretive features of the plan are presented in chapter 7, this volume. In 1944 a land dispute affecting ground in the southwest portion of the Reno–Benteen tract was resolved through "equitable agreement." SMR, November 30, 1943; SMR, September 30, 1944. For Luce's projections of battlefield expansion based on new findings, see SMR, April 11, 1945.

7. Luce believed that "many battlefield artifacts in the possession of individuals are being lost or destroyed for the want of a battlefield museum. The collection and preservation of authentic artifacts is one of our goals, lest these visual aids be lost completely. At such time when facilities are available they can then be displayed and appreciated by the visiting public." SMR, July 1, 1946.

8. Public Law 633, 60 Stat. 885, in Tolson, *Laws*, 16–17; State of Montana, House Joint Memorial No. 6, 31st Legislative Assembly, State of Montana, copy in LBAF; NPS, Synopsis of Congressional Record, entry for February 25, 1949, 1555, copy in LBAF; Luce to Mr. Miller, March 16, 1948, copy in LBAF; SMR, March 31, 1942; SMR, August 31, 1948; "Custer National Cemetery, Crow Agency, Big Horn County, Montana," *Interment.net*, http://www.interment.net/data/us/mt/bighorn/custernatl/custer.htm; SMR, August 31, 1947; Rickey, *History of Custer Battlefield*,

99. Robert M. Utley, who served there as an historical aide, recalled that in one instance fourteen reburials took place on a single day in the summer of 1948. Utley assumed the role of playing "Taps" at every burial, besides helping to dig the graves and then filling them back in. Utley, *Custer and Me*, 29.

9. "Visitation Records—Custer Battlefield," 1940–1983, in LBAF; SMR, August 4, 1948; SMR, September 1949; SMR, April 30, 1950; SMR, May 31, 1950; SMR, July 31, 1950; SMR, August 31, 1950; SMR, April 1, 1951; SMR, December 31, 1951; SMR, January 31, 1952; SMR, April 30, 1955; NPS Chief of Information Herbert Evison to Luce, June 18, 1952, copy in LBAF; Telegram, Hillary Tolson to Luce, June 20, 1952, copy in LBAF; Luce to Rogers, June 21, 1952, copy in LBAF; Utley, "'Cap' Luce," 7; "Museum & Administrative Offices," and photographs, in Administrative Research Collection, LBBNM, Accession No. 738; SMR, May 31, 1952; SMR, June 30, 1952; Luce, "Custer Battlefield Museum Dedicated"; Rickey, *History of Custer Battlefield*, 91, 93–94, 101–102; Robert M. Utley, e-mail message to author, April 22, 2005. Important contemporary information about the museum and visitor center appears in H. Robinson, *Custer Battlefield Museum*, 38, 45–47, but see especially the "Montana Historic Property Record for Little Bighorn Battlefield National Monument Visitor Center" prepared in February 2006 by architect Rodd Wheaton. The 1951 seventy-fifth anniversary events are described in SMR, June 30, 1951. See also O'Keane, "Band Played Garryowen," 21–23; "It Was Only 75 Years Ago" (quote); Burleigh, "Little Big Horn." Other publicity was generated by the Lewiston, Montana, Chamber of Commerce, which suggested during an ongoing controversy regarding the status of Sitting Bull's bones that the remains of the Hunkpapa leader be removed to Custer Battlefield National Monument. SMR, March 31, 1953; SMR, April 30, 1953. The relocation never happened.

10. SMR, June 30, 1945; SMR, May 31, 1947; SMR, August 31, 1947; SMR, August 31, 1948; SMR, March 8, 1952; SMR, March 31, 1952.

11. SMR, May 31, 1948; SMR, May 31, 1949.

12. Qtd. in Frost, "Custer Battlefield Monuments," 100, 101. See also SMR, June 30, 1954. Regional Director Howard Baker supported Luce: "It would seem that the proposal to erect such a monument or statue would throw out of line the whole simplicity of the battlefield and the museum. I would agree that the battlefield and museum should commemorate all of those who were killed there, and not just the one man." SMR, November 30, 1954. Luce's views of historic Indians did not gel with his view of some respecting liquor consumption after President Dwight D. Eisenhower signed the measure permitting them to purchase alcohol in state saloons. At the battlefield, he wrote in the summer of 1953, "We have been chasing the drunken Indians out of here in pairs. Hope that things will quiet down." Luce to George Osten, August 22, 1953, in LBAF. For the fencing at Reno–Benteen, see SMR, July 3, 1947.

13. SMR, December 31, 1947; SMR, March 31, 1948; SMR, July 1953; "Quonset Hut," September 12, 1949, in Administrative Research Collection,

LBBNM, Accession No. 738; "Equipment Shelter," in ibid.; SMR, March 8, 1952; SMR, June 30, 1954; NPS TIC 381 D28, "Mission 66 for Custer Battlefield National Monument," no date (quotes); SMR, March 5, 1958; SMR, May 1, 1958; SMR, July 3, 1958; SMR, September 5, 1958; SMR, October 6, 1958; SMR, December 11, 1958; SMR, April 7, 1959; SMR, June 8, 1959; NPS TIC 381 2009A, "General Development Plan," 1952; NPS TIC 381 2009 B, "General Development Plan," January 1, 1953, and February 1, 1953; NPS TIC 381 2009 C, "General Development Plan," January 1, 1953; NPS TIC 381 2009 D, "General Development Plan," July 1, 1956; NPS TIC, Midwest Region, Master Plan Narrative, vols. 1–3, 1964; Edwin C. Alberts, memorandum to Associate Regional Director, November 2, 1964, copy in LBAF; "CBNM Chronology," copy in LBAF; SMR, November 30, 1955; SMR, January 31, 1956; SMR, March 31, 1956; SMR, June 8, 1956; SMR, April 3, 1957; SMR, May 2, 1957; SMR, August 8, 1957; SMR, October 8, 1957; SMR, July 6, 1961; SMR, September 5, 1961; SMR, March 6, 1963; SMR, July 2, 1963; Rickey, *History of Custer Battlefield*, 98–99, 100, 113; Utley, *Custer and Me*, 57.

Luce's retirement was effective on May 1, 1956, although he departed on leave on April 19. SMR, May 8, 1956. In 1955–56, all park employees took part in the Ground Observer Corps program of the U.S. Air Force to identify aircraft spotted in the vicinity of the battlefield. SMR, October 31, 1955; SMR, January 31, 1956; SMR, February 29, 1956. The demolition threat to the stone lodge is addressed in *Great Falls Tribune*, April 1, 1962. Cost estimate for the Mission 66 work is in *Billings Gazette*, November 18, 1965.

For the residences (apparently originally planned to be two-story buildings) and four-unit seasonal quarters, see NPS TIC 381 2023 (two sheets): "Interior Changes of Residence, Headquarters Area, Custer Battlefield National Mon.," July 9, 1956; NPS TIC 381 3007B, "Site Development, Headquarters Area, Custer Battlefield National Monument," "As Constructed Drawing," April 18, 1961. For earlier proposed configurations of the residence area, see NPS TIC 381 2007E, "Headquarters Area, Part of the Master Plan, Custer Battlefield National Monument," July 29, 1949; and NPS TIC 381 2007H, "Headquarters Part of Master Plan, Custer Battlefield National Monument," August 24, 1959. The latter plat provided for two additional houses "for expansion if ever required." Another show four residences posited directly south of the west half of the cemetery. NPS TIC 381 2007G, "Headquarters Area, Part of the Master Plan, Custer Battlefield National Monument," September 23, 1949. Trees planted in 1962–63 were green ash, hackberry, Rocky Mountain juniper, cottonwood, English hawthorn, and honey locust; shrubs were shrubby potentilla, staghorn sumac, clove currant, pearhip rose, common snowberry, chokecherry, and American plum. NPS TIC 381 3014B, "Planting Plan, Headquarters Area, Custer Battlefield National Monument," August 1962.

14. "Visitation Records—Custer Battlefield," 1940–83, in LBAF; "CBNM Chronology," copy in LBAF; SMR, July 31, 1953, and SMR, April 30, 1954 (Luce

quotes); SMR, April 10, 1962; *Hardin Tribune-Herald*, June 18, 1964; SMR, September 5, 1962 (contains a photograph of Mrs. Larrabee outside the entrance of the visitor center); SMR, July 6, 1964; SMR, September 2, 1964; "Site Plan," Drawing No. NM Cus 2013-E, Max Garcia, December 1964, Map Drawer, White Swan Memorial Library, LBBNM; SMR, May 6, 1965; SMR, August 4, 1965; "Little Bighorn Battlefield National Monument, Montana," *Mission 66*, http://www.mission66.com/libi/index.html; NPS TIC, Midwest Region, Master Plan Narrative, vols. 1–3, 1964; *Billings Gazette*, October 31, 1965; *Billings Gazette*, November 18, 1965. Other major influxes of scouts occurred in May 1958, when, on separate occasions, 2,516 girl scouts and 745 boy scouts descended on the park. SMR, June 6, 1958. Detailed assessment of structural changes to the visitor center under Mission 66 appears in Rodd Wheaton, "Montana Historic Property Record form for Little Bighorn Battlefield National Monument Visitor Center," February 2006.

15. Roy E. Appleman, "Report of Visit to Custer Battlefield National Monument—Montana, July 12, 1956," September 25, 1956, copy in LBAF; NPS TIC 381 7101, "Land Ownership and Recommended Boundary Adjustment," November 1, 1960; SMR, August 6, 1956. Two small boundary adjustments, similar in their details to the 1928–30 cases involving three Crow allotments, occurred in 1944 and 1947. In each case, lands assigned had been erroneously granted, and in each adjustments were made to rectify the errors and to compensate claimants. For details, see Rickey, *History of Custer Battlefield*, 96–97. In April 1963 Superintendent Garry met with landowners at Crow Agency seeking input and, most likely, approval of the park's boundary adjustment plan. Instead, he heard objections to it. SMR, May 6, 1963. Further land acquisition would require approval of the Crow Tribe, besides an act of Congress, to complete.

16. SMR, March 31, 1953; SMR, April 30, 1953; SMR, July 31, 1953; SMR, August 31, 1955; SMR, March 1, 1957; SMR, December 8, 1959; SMR, July 6, 1961; Rickey, *History of Custer Battlefield*, 97.

17. SMR, June 30, 1953; SMR, August 14, 1954; SMR, June 30, 1955 SMR, April 3, 1961; SMR, June 6, 1961; SMR, November 6, 1961; SMR, January 8, 1963; SMR, August 4, 1964; SMR, January 8, 1965; NPS TIC, Midwest Region, Master Plan Narrative, vols. 1–3, 1964; Luther T. Peterson, Jr., to Superintendent, February 10, 1964, copy in LBAF; NPS TIC 3020, "Restoration of Cemetery Grounds," July 1, 1964; NPS TIC 3026, "Topography–Proposed Cemetery Extension," November 1, 1966; "CBNM Chronology."

18. National Register of Historic Places, http://www.nationalregisterofhistoric places.com. For background on the Historic Preservation Act of 1966, see Murtagh, *Keeping Time*, 62–77.

19. SMR, July 3, 1967; *Rapid City Journal*, June 1, 1967; Nichols, *In Custer's Shadow*, 355–69; A. Day, "Marcus A. Reno." The book that influenced Charles Reno to proceed with clearing Major Reno and having his remains removed to Montana was Terrell and Walton, *Faint the Trumpet Sounds*, with coauthor and retired army colonel George Walton playing a defining role in the actions.

20. "Visitation Records—Custer Battlefield," 1940–83, in LBAF; Neil C. Mangum to Historian, Fort Larned National Historical Site, February 23, 1983, copy in LBAF. For NPS involvement in the initial reenactments, see SMR, December 5, 1963; SMR, February 5, 1964; SMR, March 4, 1964; SMR, May 4, 1964; SMR, July 6, 1964; SMR, April 5, 1965; SMR, May 6, 1965; SMR, July 7, 1965. An account of the 1964 reenactment, together with a complete roster of participants, appeared in the *Hardin Tribune-Herald*, July 2, 1964. For 1968, see the *Hardin Tribune-Herald*, July 4, 1968; for plans for 1973, see *Hardin Tribune-Herald*, July 5, 1973. In 1976, the centennial year of the battle, the event was cancelled because of "its potential for explosiveness." *Hardin Tribune-Herald*, February 13, 1975. For the reenactments, see also Linenthal, *Sacred Ground*, 139–40, 142.

21. Graham, *Custer Myth*; Stewart, *Custer's Luck*; Miller, *Custer's Fall*; Utley, *Great Controversy*.

22. Brown, *Bury My Heart at Wounded Knee*; DeLoria, *Custer Died for Your Sins*.

6. National Park Service Administration, 1970–2000

1. Superintendent William A. Harris to Jerome A. Greene, February 29, 1972, author's personal files; NPS TIC 381 D11, "Master Plan," October 1, 1972 (quote).

2. The *Hardin Herald* reported on February 7, 1975, that "only 254 of some 4,500 burial plots remain available." One plan, never enacted, was to acquire land at the site of old Fort Custer near Hardin for a new national cemetery. *Hardin Herald*, November 6, 1975. Throughout the period there was pressure from veterans' groups, as well as from the Crow Tribe, to expand the cemetery. Despite formal closure of the cemetery in 1978, veterans and dependents with reserved plots are still being interred there on an average of three to five per year. Neil Mangum to author, February 6, 2005.

3. NPS TIC 381 D11, "Master Plan," October 1, 1972; NPS TIC 381 80006, "Reconstruction of Parking Lot/R-B Area," April 1, 1976; Memorandum, "Environmental Assessment," re: Water System, recommended August 15, 1976, copy in NPS Intermountain Regional Office Library, Lakewood, Colorado; L. Clifford Soubier, telephone interview, May 5, 2004.

4. "Classified Structure Field Inventory Report," September 6, 1975; L. Clifford Soubier, telephone interview, May 5, 2004; Mangum to author, February 6, 2005; Nichols, "CBHMA," 6–7.

5. NPS TIC 381 D7, "Statement for Management," April 1, 1979 (quotes); NPS TIC 381 D7-A, "Statement for Management," February 20, 1981 (includes initial park and regional approvals dated November 14 and December 15, 1975).

6. Laura Waterman Wittstock and Elaine J. Salinas, "A Brief History of the American Indian Movement," http://www.aimovement.org/ggc/history.html; *Billings Gazette*, June 25, 1976 (quote); Utley, *Custer and Me*, 152–53; *Great Falls Tribune*, June 26, 1976; *Billings Gazette*, June 26, 1976; NPS, press release, June 24, 1976 (Utley quote); program, Custer Battlefield National Monument Commemorative Ceremony, June 25, 1976, copy in LBAF; *Little Big Horn Associates Newsletter* 10

(August 1976): 14 (hereafter cited as *LBHA Newsletter*); *Custer/Little Bighorn Battlefield Advocate* 1 (Winter 1994): 1; Koury, *Custer Centennial Observance*, 7–24; Koury, *To Consecrate This Ground*, 21–45; Linenthal, *Sacred Ground*, 141–44. Superintendent James V. Court later acknowledged that the park's 1976 installation of the Black Elk quotation was "partly to placate some Indian groups, including the American Indian Movement, which was threatening to burn the place down." *Rocky Mountain News*, July 15, 1985. Russell Means maintained that Superintendent Hart "promised to put up a monument to honor the Indian dead of Greasy Grass." For Means's memories of the moment, see Means, *Where White Men Fear to Tread*, 357–58. For Utley's recollections of the events and their immediate aftermath, see Utley, *Custer and Me*, 151–56.

7. For a concise account of the criticism, including that of newspapers, directed toward the NPS during the aftermath of the centennial observance, see Linenthal, *Sacred Ground*, 145–46.

8. Court to Jay Smith, *LBHA Newsletter* 18 (June 1982): 5–6; Mangum, "Confessions," 4. The planning process for the 1980s is outlined in U.S. Department of the Interior, National Park Service, *Management Policies, 1988*; general management plans are discussed in chapter 2, pp. 6–9. See also U.S. Department of the Interior, National Park Service, *Planning Process NPS-2*, 1–9. A statement for management for the park was prepared in 1982. NPS TIC 381 D7-B, May 11, 1982. A fully revised and expanded statement for management appeared in 1984–85. NPS TIC 381 D7-C, May 1, 1985.

9. Court, "Battlefield Preservation Complete."

10. NPS, press release, November 20, 1985.

11. NPS TIC 381 D16c, "Final General Management and Development Concept Plans, August 1986" ("EA/GMP/DCP"): December 1, 1987; NPS TIC 381 80041, "Draft General Management Plan," April 1, 1986; NPS TIC 381 80043, "Proposed Boundary," April 1, 1986; *Billings Gazette*, November 30, 1985; *Sheridan Press*, December 11, 1985; *Hardin Herald*, June 4, 1986. It was anticipated that the planned visitor center would, in fact, combine into a single complex three facilities: a Paul Dyck Plains Indian Museum, a Crow tribal museum/information center, and the NPS visitor center. Court, "Battlefield Preservation Complete."

12. NPS, press release, November 18, 1986; Court, "Battlefield Preservation Complete." For background and achievements of the Custer Battlefield Preservation Committee, see ibid.; NPS TIC 381 D7-D, "Statement for Management, Custer Battlefield National Monument," December 1, 1990; *Rocky Mountain News*, July 21, 1985; *Denver Post*, July 21, 1985; *LBHA Newsletter* 20 (October 1986): 3; *Billings Gazette*, May 17, 1987; *Billings Gazette*, June 29, 1987; *LBHA Newsletter* 22 (April 1988): 2; *LBHA Newsletter* 23 (April 1989): 8; *Billings Gazette*, January 21, 1989; *The Battlefield Dispatch* 8 (Fall 1989): 3; *The Battlefield Dispatch* 11 (Winter 1992): 5; *The Battlefield Dispatch* 13 (Fall 1994): 4; *The Battlefield Dispatch* 17 (Fall 1998): 6; *LBHA Newsletter* 35 (February 2001): 3; *LBHA Newsletter* 35 (October 2001): 3. The donation box in the visitor center was authorized on November 6,

1985. Deputy Regional Director Jack W. Neckels to Harold Stanton, November 6, 1985, copy in LBAF. In June 1985, a $500,000 appropriation to accommodate land purchase was included in the Department of the Interior's budget proposal for fiscal year 1985 but was eventually dropped. *Billings Gazette*, June 21, 1984. Several significant donors, at least one of whom remained anonymous, contributed to the Custer Battlefield Preservation Committee. The project through the years produced a number of donated items for sale or auction to raise funds, including a lock of Custer's hair, his field desk, and a replaced marker from Captain George W. Yates's grave site at the Fort Leavenworth National Cemetery. *Billings Gazette*, December 6, 1985; *Billings Gazette*, November 30, 1991; *Billings Gazette*, January 23, 1992; *LBHA Newsletter* 34 (February 2000): 8. An account of a demonstration by Crow Indians against planned battlefield expansion in which they disrupted a speech by NPS director William Penn Mott, Jr., appears in the *Billings Gazette*, June 29, 1987.

13. Ditmanson to Earl Harmon, August 12, 1988 (quotes): copy in LBAF; *LBHA Newsletter* 22 (July 1988): 2. For Ditmanson's appointment, see NPS, press release, November 6, 1986; *LBHA Newsletter* 20 (November 1986): 2. Means's reminiscence of this incident, which he apparently believed took place in 1987, appears in *Where White Men Fear to Tread*, 491. He claims, regarding an Indian memorial, that Ditmanson told him, "'I'll personally put it through the system and make sure it happens.' I said, 'Not good enough. . . .' We marched to the monument area atop a low hill. . . . While I gave a speech about Custer, several AIMsters began to dig near it. Others began to mix cement. In a few minutes, they erected a new monument, an innocuous slab of iron with an inscription." Ibid.

14. Rouse, "Custer Battlefield Up-date", 87–88; *Billings Gazette*, June 19, 1991; *Denver Post*, July 14, 1991; *Rocky Mountain News*, July 26, 1991; *Billings Gazette*, July 27, 1991; *The Progressive*, September 1991:11; *Denver Post*, August 26, 1991; *Lakota Times*, September 4, 1991; *Billings Gazette*, November 24, 1991; *Denver Post*, November 28, 1991 (Booher quote); *Billings Gazette*, December 11, 1991; *LBHA Newsletter* 26 (February 1992): 3 (citing *Lakota Times*, December 18, 1991); *Big Horn County News* (Hardin, Mont.): November 4, 1992; *Denver Post*, November 15, 1992; program, Oglala Sioux Tribe, Little Bighorn Dedication Ceremony, Crow Agency, Montana, November 11, 1992, copy in LBAF; U.S. Congress, House, *To Redesignate Custer Battlefield National Monument*; U.S. Congress, House, Committee on Interior and Insular Affairs, *Authorizing the Establishment of a Memorial*; Public Law 102-201, December 10, 1991, 105 Stat. 1631; Davenport, *Laws*, 362–64; *LBHA Newsletter* 27 (March 1993): 3–4. Despite earlier consideration, as recently as the spring of 1987, the park historian could write that "there is currently no move afoot to change the name of Custer Battlefield National Monument." Mangum to Kevin C. Miller, April 7, 1987, copy in LBAF. Former NPS chief historian Robert M. Utley, noted for his even-handed analysis of historical Indian–white relations, endorsed the name change because he believed that the present name "has become deeply offensive to the Indian community. . . . They

look upon Custer as a personification of all that was wrong in American Indian policy, all that was brutal, all that was unjust." *Billings Gazette*, October 26, 1991. For political setbacks affecting the 1991 legislation, see *Billings Gazette*, October 30, 1991. Opposition to the name change legislation from the Custer family appears in "Letters," *Montana:The Magazine ofWestern History* 41 (Autumn 1991): 93. A report by Booher is in *The Battlefield Dispatch* 9 (Fall 1990): 2. For examples of the controversy the name change generated, see *LBHA Newsletter* 21 (August 1987): 4; *LBHA Newsletter* 21 (October 1987) 2–3. For a brief balanced overview of the issue and its meaning, see Linenthal, "From Shrine to Historic Site," 310–13.The proposed and approved general management plan revisions appear in NPS TIC 381 D23, SAR 1991–92" (hereafter cited as SAR); NPS TIC 381 D7-D, "Statement for Management, Custer Battlefield National Monument," December 1, 1990; NPS TIC 381 D16D, "Final General Management and Development Concept Plans, August 1986, Updated May 1995, Little Bighorn Battlefield National Monument," 12–14.

15. NPS TIC 381 D23, SAR, 1990; NPS TIC 381 D23, SAR, 1991–92; *LBHA Newsletter* 26 (August 1992): 2, 3; *The Battlefield Dispatch* 12 (Winter 1993): 4; *The Battlefield Dispatch* 14 (Spring 1995): 1; Linenthal, "From Shrine to Historic Site," 316. Booher drew national attention to the park with press notices and an interview in *People*. Plummer, "General Custer Loses"; *Time*, July 17, 1989:65; *Denver Post*, June 29, 1989; *Rocky Mountain News*, June 30, 1989; *Washington Post*, July 3, 1989; *Milwaukee Journal*, September 11, 1989.

16. For details of the North Shield plan and specific reactions to it, see Lawson Stowe Warren to Secretary of the Interior Manuel Lujan, Jr., December 18, 1991; Lujan to Warren, January 16, 1992; Warren to NPS Director James Ridenour, March 16, 1992; Assistant Solicitor, Parks and Recreation, August 28, 1992. Copies in Associate Regional Director Michael D. Snyder to Michael J. Koury, July 8, 1993; "Memorandum of Understanding Between National Park Service, The Crow Tribe, and North Shield Ventures, Inc.," September 1992; Paul C. Pritchard, National Parks and Conservation Association, to Roger Kennedy, February 9, 1994; CBHMA to membership, February 1993; Michael J. Koury to Robert M. Baker, undated (early 1993); Baker to Koury, February 10, 1993; Robert M. Utley to Peggy Lipson, NPS, Rocky Mountain Regional Office, June 7, 1993; Utley to NPS Director Roger Kennedy, November 1, 1993 (Utley quote); Rod Greenough, National Parks and Conservation Association, to James V. Court, Custer Battlefield Preservation Committee, March 14, 1994, all in Michael J. Koury Files, Johnstown, Colorado (hereafter cited as Koury Files). See also *Denver Post*, October 8, 1992; *Denver Post*, January 25, 1993; *LBHA Newsletter* 27 (February 1993): 4, 6, 8; *Big Horn County News*, March 10, 1993; *LBHA Newsletter* 27 (April 1993): 2; *Billings Gazette*, May 12, 1993; *The Battlefield Dispatch* 12 (Spring 1993): 10–11 (McChristian quote); *LBHA Newsletter* 27 (May 1993): 2, 5 (Utley quote); *Big Horn County News*, June 2, 1993; *Custer/Little Bighorn Battlefield Advocate* 1 (Fall 1993): 1, 4, 5, 7; *Rocky Mountain News*, November 18, 1993; *Big Horn County*

News, December 1, 1993; *The Battlefield Dispatch* 13 (Winter 1994): 5; *Billings Gazette*, January 8, 1994; *Denver Post*, May 2, 1994; *LBHA Newsletter* 28 (March 1994): 4; *LBHA Newsletter* 28 (July 1994): 3, 4; *The Battlefield Dispatch* 14 (Winter 1995): 2, 3; *Billings Gazette*, March 13, 1996.

17. *The Battlefield Dispatch* 12 (Winter 1993): 4; *LBHA Newsletter* 27 (February 1993): 5; *LBHA Newsletter* 27 (October 1993): 3; *Rocky Mountain News*, December 30, 1997; *The Civil War News* (February/March 1998): 8; *Big Horn County News*, January 28, 1998; *Little Big Horn Associates* 32 (February 1998): 3; *The Battlefield Dispatch* 17 (Winter 1998): 1.

18. *Billings Gazette*, June 26, 1992; Memorial Day 1991 program; Custer Battlefield National Monument, 110th Anniversary Ceremonies, June 25, 1986; NPS, press release, May 1, 1986; McDermott, "Remarks on the 110th Anniversary"; *Time*, July 7, 1986; *Billings Gazette*, May 2, 1986; Marker dedication for Mitch Boyer, scout, Custer Battlefield National Monument, August 25, 1988; Reburial ceremony, Custer Battlefield National Monument, June 23, 1991; *LBHA Newsletter* 25 (August 1991): 3; *The Battlefield Dispatch* 10 (Summer 1991): 1; Little Bighorn Battlefield National Monument, 120th Anniversary of the Battle of the Little Bighorn, 1996, program; *Billings Gazette*, June 25, 1996; Little Bighorn Battlefield National Monument, 122nd Anniversary of the Battle of the Little Bighorn, 1998, program; Little Bighorn Battlefield National Monument, 123rd Anniversary of the Battle of the Little Bighorn, June 25–26, 1999, program; 124th Anniversary Battle of the Little Bighorn, Sunday June 25th, 2000, program; 50th Anniversary Pearl Harbor Day, December 7, 1991, Custer Battlefield National Monument, program; *Big Horn County News*, October 2, 1991; *Billings Gazette*, June 23, 1996.

19. *The Battlefield Dispatch* 12 (Winter 1993): 10; *The Battlefield Dispatch* 14 (Spring 1995): 1–2; U.S. Department of the Interior, National Park Service, "Notice of Inventory Completion for Native American Human Remains and Associated Funerary Objects from the Little Bighorn Battlefield National Monument, MT in the Possession of the Little Bighorn Battlefield National Monument, National Park Service, Crow Agency, MT," http://www.cast.uark.edu/other/nps/nagpra/DOCS/nic0262.html; *LBHA Newsletter* 24 (April 1995): 3; *The Battlefield Dispatch* 14 (Winter 1995): 1–2; NPS TIC 381 D39 "Superintendent's Annual Report for 1997"; NPS, "Little Bighorn Battlefield NM 1998 Visitor Survey Card Data Report," LBBNM; *Little Bighorn Battlefield National Monument 1999 Annual Performance Report, October 1, 1998–September 30, 1999*, LBBNM; NPS TIC D56, *Field Report*, 2001; NPS TIC 381 D43 "Superintendent's Annual Narrative Report, Fiscal Year 1998"; NPS TIC 381 D47, SAR, 2000; "Little Bighorn Battlefield National Monument Enhancement Act of 2001," http://www.theorator.com/bills107/s1338.html; NPS TIC 381 D48, SAR, 2001; *The Battlefield Dispatch* 20 (Fall 2001): 5; *The Battlefield Dispatch* 20 (Winter 2001): 1; *Custer/Little Bighorn Advocate* (Summer 2001): 3–4; John A. Doerner, "A New Warrior Marker Dedicated for Long Road, Sans Arc Lakota," ibid., 6, 15; *LBHA Newsletter* 35 (August 2001): 6–7; *LBHA*

Newsletter 36 (February 2002): 4. For the 125th anniversary observance, the park published a brochure keepsake titled *125th Anniversary* that listed the interpretive events of June 25 and 26, 2001.

20. *The Battlefield Dispatch* 6 (Spring 1987): 4; NPS TIC D23, "Superintendent's Annual Narrative Report, 1991–1992"; Wheaton, Montana Historic Property Record form; *LBHA Newsletter* 28 (February 1994): 7; NPS TIC 381 D23, SAR, 1995; NPS TIC 381 D39, SAR, 1997; NPS TIC 381 D47, SAR, 2000; *LBHA Newsletter* 36 (February 2002): 4–5; NPS TIC 381 D48, SAR, 2001; *The Battlefield Dispatch* 20 (Fall 2001): 15; *LBHA Newsletter* 35 (April 2001): 6; *Friends of the Little Bighorn Battlefield* 3 (September 2003): 3. One cannot overestimate the importance of fee-demonstration monies to the maintenance and building effort at the park since 1987. As one former superintendent explained, "fee-demo [dollars have] . . . opened up financial doors heretofore closed for LIBI [Little Bighorn Battlefield National Monument]," permitting the funding of numerous projects once considered nearly impossible. Neil Mangum to author, February 6, 2005.

21. NPS TIC D23, "Superintendent's Annual Narrative Report, 1991–1992"; *The Battlefield Dispatch* 10 (Spring 1991): 2; NPS TIC 381 D39, SAR, 1997; *The Battlefield Dispatch* 17 (Summer 1998): 6; *Billings Gazette*, September 2, 1998; *The Battlefield Dispatch* 17 (Fall 1998): 1, 4; NPS TIC 381 D47, SAR, 2000; NPS TIC 381 D48, SAR, 2001; *LBHA Newsletter* 35 (November 2001): 3; NPS TIC 381 80076–3, "Rebuild Cemetery Street," January 1, 2002; *Custer/Little Bighorn Advocate* (Fall/Winter 2002): 14; *The Battlefield Dispatch* 22 (Spring 2003): 1, 16; *Friends of the Little Bighorn Battlefield* 3 (September 2003).

22. NPS TIC 381 D23, "Superintendent's Annual Narrative Report, 1991–1992"; *The Battlefield Dispatch* 10 (Fall 1991): 3; *LBHA Newsletter* 36 (February 2002): 5; *LBHA Newsletter* 37 (February 2003): 7; R. E. Doran to Neil Mangum, July 19, 1987, copy in LBAF; Mangum to files, August 28, 1987, copy in LBAF; Michael Donohue, "Interview with Cliff Arbogast," *LBHA Newsletter* 27 (August 1998): 4–5; *LBHA Newsletter* 22 (September 1988): 8; McCleary, "Stone Cairn Markers"; *The Battlefield Dispatch* 21 (Winter 2002): 15.

23. Ditmanson to Richard C. Hellhake, October 20, 1987, copy in LBAF; *Billings Gazette*, March 17, 1988; *Billings Gazette*, May 2, 1990; *LBHA Newsletter* 24 (August 1990): 8; NPS TIC 381 D23, SAR, 1990; NPS TIC 381 D23, "Superintendent's Annual Narrative Report, 1991–1992," March 19, 1993 (quote); *LBHA Newsletter* 25 (March 1991): 3; *The Battlefield Dispatch* 10 (Fall 1991): 3; *The Battlefield Dispatch* 10 (Winter 1991): 4; *The Battlefield Dispatch* 11 (Spring 1992): 4; *LBHA Newsletter* 26 (September 1992): 2; *The Battlefield Dispatch* 17 (Summer 1998): 6; *The Guidon* (February 1999); *The Battlefield Dispatch* 19 (Spring 2000): 5; NPS, "Environmental Assessment, Deep Ravine and Keogh/Crazy Horse Trails, Little Bighorn Battlefield National Monument," February 1999, LBBNM; NPS TIC 381 D47, SAR, 2000; *Battlefield Dispatch* 19 (Fall 2000): 14. For an explanation of early policy precluding indiscriminate walking off established trails, including on the then-informal Deep Ravine Trail, as well as providing special

access to the battlefield, see the letter of Superintendent Ditmanson in *LBHA Newsletter* 21 (October 1987): 4.

24. SMR, August 31, 1947; "CBNM Chronology," copy in LBAF; SMR, October 6, 1958; "Master Plan of Custer Battlefield National Monument," July 1964, entry for "Fire History"; *Billings Gazette*, August 11, 1983; *Billings Gazette*, March 6, 1984; Bock and Bock, "Ecology and Evolution," 560; Mangum to Director, NPS, November 7, 1985, copy in LBAF; NPS TIC 381 D23, "Superintendent's Annual Narrative Report, 1991–1992"; *Billings Gazette*, August 24, 1991; *Billings Gazette*, August 21, 1991; *LBHA Newsletter* 25 (October 1991): 5; *LBHA Newsletter* 25 (November 1991): 3; *The Battlefield Dispatch* 13 (Summer 1994): 4; *LBHA Newsletter* 28 (October 1994): 4.

25. *The Battlefield Dispatch* 13 (Winter 1994): 4; *The Battlefield Dispatch* 14 (Summer 1995): 1, 6; NPS TIC 381 D47, SAR, 2000; *LBHA Newsletter* 18 (May 1984): 3. A visionary scenario, wherein a park ranger twenty years into the future addresses site visitors about the battle, went like this: The ranger would tell them, "Well, down there, where that restaurant is, is where the Indians charged, then where you see the gas station is where the soldiers tried to cross the river. Now over there, where that apartment complex is, that was the site of the famous Sioux village. The 'Crazy Horse Disco' is the site of the major battle and up there on the hill, just about where the 'Custer Slept Here Motel' is, is where the final stand took place. It used to be much nicer." *Valley (Mont.) Tribune*, July 23, 1984, cited in *LBHA Newsletter* 18 (August 1984): 8; *Christian Science Monitor*, July 11, 2000 (Mangum quote); National Trust for Historic Preservation, http://www.nationaltrust.org/11Most/index.html. The park had in 1988 been placed on a list of "endangered nationally significant historic places." Linenthal, *Sacred Ground*, 157. In 1997 Professor Linenthal recommended that "given the centrality of the battle, the figure of Custer, and the recent attention paid to the site as a place of intense cultural negotiation, the Little Bighorn Battlefield National Monument should be placed at the top of 'endangered' historic sites in the nation." "OAH Site Visitation, May 24–25, 1997," submitted June 16, 1997, copy provided by William P. Wells.

7. National Park Service Interpretation

1. Mrs. Thomas Beaverheart to Superintendent, Custer Battlefield National Cemetery, July 27, 1925, cited in Rickey, *History of Custer Battlefield*, 70. Mrs. Beaverheart's letter read, "My father Vehoenxne [Lame White Man] was among the Cheyennes who was killed at the Custer Battle. He was a Cheyenne Chief, and there are two Cheyenne men living yet who know where he fell and where he was buried. We would be glad if you could help us get the place marked, so that the place might be remembered on the next anniversary." Qtd. in ibid., 141.

2. The National Association for Interpretation definition of interpretation appears on the association web site: http://www.interpnet.org/. The six-page brochure,

written by Superintendent Harvey A. Olson, was titled *The Custer Battlefield National Cemetery*. Rickey, *History of Custer Battlefield*, 118.

3. SMR, January 31, 1941 (quote); SMR, February 28, 1941 (quote); SMR, June 30, 1941; SMR, July 31, 1941; SMR, August 27, 1941; SMR, September 30, 1941. The 8 x 10½ inch sixteen-page publication, titled *Custer Battlefield National Cemetery*, appeared in 1943. Other smaller brochures were issued intermittently through the 1950s.

4. U.S. Department of the Interior, National Park Service, *Master Plan*, 1942 (quotes).

5. Mangum, "Popular Reaction to Custer." The dichotomy of views regarding Indians and soldiers, together with the evolving history of those views by the 1970s, is rationally expressed in Utley, "Frontier Army", reprinted with minor changes as *Good Guys and Bad: Changing Images of Soldier and Indian* (N.p.: Custer Battlefield Historical and Museum Association, ca. 1978).

6. SMR, April 30, 1948; SMR, November 30, 1941; SMR, June 30, 1942 (quote); SMR, June 30, 1948 (quote); SMR, December 31, 1948; SMR, January 31, 1949; SMR, May 31, 1950; SMR, June 30, 1950; Rickey, *History of Custer Battlefield*, 120–21, 123; U.S. Department of the Interior, National Park Service, *Master Plan*, 1942; NPS TIC 381 2009, "General Development Plan."

7. SMR, July 31, 1946; *Billings Gazette*, May 27, 1961.

8. Utley reported for duty on June 4, 1947. SMR, June 30, 1947; Utley, *Custer and Me*, 44 (quote). See also "Robert Utley Reflections," http://www.friends littlebighorn.com/utleyreflections.htm.

9. Utley, *Custer and Me*, 42–43; SMR, April 30, 1947; SMR, July 3, 1947; SMR, February 29, 1948; SMR, April 30, 1950; H. Robinson, *Custer Battlefield Museum*, 1–36; SMR, January 11, 1954; SMR, February 9, 1960; SMR, September 9, 1960; SMR, October 8, 1963; Hart, "Changing Exhibitry and Sensitivity," 35–37; Rickey, *History of Custer Battlefield*, 121–22, 125, 129–30; SMR, September 30, 1955.

10. Rickey, *History of Custer Battlefield*, 128; "Tape Recorded Talk Battle of the Little Big Horn," recorded January 17, 1957, Washington, D.C. (quote), copy in author's files; Roy E. Appleman, "Report of Visit to Custer Battlefield National Monument—Montana, July 12, 1956" (quote), copy in LBAF. The relocation of Comanche to the park had been proposed as early as 1947, when General Jonathan Wainwright suggested as much. It was recommended as a possible temporary centennial feature in 1969 by Park Historian B. William Henry, Jr. Memorandum, Henry to Superintendent, November 12, 1969, copy in LBAF. Frequent references to Comanche as the "sole survivor" of the Little Bighorn are inaccurate, since many soldiers as well as Indians survived the overall battle. Park Historian L. Clifford Soubier wrote that the "lack of official witnesses [to the battle] forms the basis of much of the Custer mythology, and in turn, Comanche's aura. The Custer buff stands glassy-eyed before the mounted hide muttering 'if only he could speak!' Since many Indian accounts of the battle exist, the implication is that the testimony of an Army horse would be more credible than an Indian's." Regarding

the propriety of exhibiting Comanche at the park, Soubier concluded that "it would represent an object of curiosity out of proportion to its significance. It would be a pity if a visitor left Custer Battlefield with his strongest impression that of a stuffed horse." "L'Affaire Comanche, or Flogging a Dead Horse," unpublished manuscript, ca. 1970, copy in the LBAF. The relief map comprised an important interpretive device by which visitors were enabled to familiarize themselves with the battlefield landscape fairly quickly. Its significance to the interpretive program can be measured by its relatively frequent mention in the monthly reports. SMR, August 31, 1956; SMR, April 3, 1963; SMR, August 9, 1963. See SMR, May 2, 1957, and SMR, June 6, 1957, regarding the tape player ("Mohawk Message Repeater"), which was not trouble free. Acting Superintendent Don Rickey, Jr., wrote, "There seems to be sufficient footage at each end of the tape to add a recorded chorus of 'Garryowen,' and we have sent our reserve tape and a recording of 'Garryowen' to the manufacturers, requesting this service." SMR, July 6, 1957.

11. Ibid.; NPS TIC 381 D28, "Mission 66 for Custer Battlefield National Monument," undated, ca. 1956, 2, 3; Memorandum, Superintendent Aubuchon to Regional Director, Region 2, October 15, 1956, copy in LBAF; "CBNM Chronology," copy in LBAF; SMR, August 6, 1957; SMR, September 3, 1957; SMR, January 6, 1958; SMR, August 1, 1958; SMR, July 6, 1959; SMR, December 8, 1959; SMR, January 6, 1960; SMR, February 9, 1960; SMR, August 9, 1963. The initial trail at Reno–Benteen was fraught with problems because visitors using it often embarked onto other terrain. In 1960 an asphalt trail was proposed. Wrote Superintendent Garry, "We shall attempt to plant out the side trails and set up several signs, . . . requesting users not to leave the trail, and providing better direction for following the system of numbered posts. Also, next season a greater effort will be made to have a Ranger–Historian at the site during periods of heavy use." SMR, November 7, 1960.

12. SMR, May 4, 1967; Rickey, *History of Custer Battlefield*, 122; "Master Plan of Custer Battlefield National Monument" (July 1964); SMR, August 10, 1966; "CBNM Chronology," copy in LBAF. A thorough assessment of the 1969 living history program is in Memorandum, Superintendent Daniel E. Lee to Regional Director, September 10, 1969, copy in LBAF; Memorandum, Soubier to Superintendent William A. Harris, September 28, 1970, copy in LBAF. The Crow youths hired were Sharon Old Elk, Garret Door, and Paul Spotted Horse. Soubier noted, "The only complaint came from a woman who objected to our showing grown men shooting at children." Ibid. In 1960 the Custer Battlefield Historical and Museum Association, the park's cooperating association, purchased fifteen items of Indian medicine for the exhibits at an expense of twenty dollars. SMR, March 4, 1960. Robert L. Hart indicated that early park exhibits reflected a ratio of three to one in ethnocentric military themes over Indian themes, but by the mid-eighties interpretation "had changed from a simple military engagement to a complex clash between two cultures." "Changing Exhibitry and Sensitivity," 46–47.

13. NPS TIC 3016, "Interpretation," January 1, 1963; SMR, October 8, 1963; Memorandum, Ray H. Mattison to Associate Regional Director, August 21, 1964, copy in LBAF; Hart, "Changing Exhibitry and Sensitivity," 37–42; SMR, May 6, 1965; SMR, November 3, 1965; *Billings Gazette*, October 31, 1965; SMR, April 7, 1966; *LBHA Newsletter* 2 (November 1968): 3; Koury, "A Bit of CBHMA History," 99–100; "CBNM Chronology"; Utley, *Custer and Me*, 114–17; Linenthal, *Sacred Ground*, 153, 168.

14. "Visitation Records: Custer Battlefield," 1940–1983, in LBAF; *LBHA Newsletter* 5 (August 1971): 3; Josephy, "Custer Myth"; Linenthal, *Sacred Ground*, 156; Governor William L. Guy to Midwest Region Director J. Leonard Volz, January 20, 1971 (quote), copy in LBAF; Volz to Guy, February 9, 1971 (quotes), copy in LBAF.

15. NPS TIC 381 D11, "Master Plan," October 1, 1972, 39–41, 43 (see also the general development map on p. 58); NPS TIC 381 D7-C, "Statement for Management," May 1, 1985, 14; U.S. Department of the Interior, National Park Service, *Interim Interpretive Plan*, 1, 4 (quote); NPS TIC 381 D16c, "Final General Management and Development Concept Plans," August 1986, 12–13; Linenthal, *Sacred Ground*, 154.

16. Ibid., 130–31.

17. NPS, press releases, January 10, May 5, and December 15, 1980, July 27, September 11, and December 21, 1981, and June 7, 1983; "Custer Battlefield First Annual Press Day," undated, ca. 1980, copies in LBAF.

18. "Report of Custer Battlefield Publications and Interpretation Review Team," October 8, 1984, copy in LBAF. See also Mangum, "Confessions," 4–5.

19. *LBHA Newsletter* 18 (February 1984): 4; Acting Superintendent Mangum to Director, NPS, November 7, 1985, copy in LBAF; Mangum to Chief Historian, Fossil Butte National Monument, September 10, 1986, copy in LBAF; Utley to Court, April 4, 1985, copy in LBAF; NPS TIC 381 D16c, "Final General Management and Development Concept Plans," August 1986, 13; Mangum, "Confessions," 5.

20. Acting Superintendent Mangum to Associate Regional Director, Rocky Mountain Region, November 26, 1986, copy in LBAF; Superintendent Ditmanson to Regional Director, Rocky Mountain Region, February 5, 1987, copy in LBAF; Mangum to Robert L. Hart, February 13, 1987, copy in LBAF; Hart, "Changing Exhibitry and Sensitivity," 43; author's observations of exhibits, ca. 1986; "Statement for Interpretation (SFI) and Annual Interpretive Programs Reports (AIPR)," January 27, 1988, copy in White Swan Memorial Library, LBBNM; Mangum to Robert Krick, April 10, 1987, copy in LBAF; Mangum, "Popular Reaction to Custer," 60–61; Superintendent Booher to Edith Stuart Phillips, September 27, 1989, copy in LBAF; *The Battlefield Dispatch* 8 (Fall 1989): 1; Linenthal, *Sacred Ground*, 168; NPS TIC 381 D23, SAR, 1990. Among the publications based on the recent archeological findings were Scott and Fox, *Archeological Insights*; Fox, *Archaeology, History*; and a video, *History Recovered*, produced by Michael W. Parks (1987). See also Jordan, "Ghosts on the Little Bighorn."

21. *The Battlefield Dispatch* 10 (Fall 1991): 3; Douglas C. McChristian, e-mail message to the author, January 31, 2005; NPS TIC 381 D23, SAR, 1990; *The Battlefield Dispatch* 9 (Fall 1990): 6; "LIBI Phase Two Label Text Completion Project," copy in LBAF; NPS TIC 381 D23, SAR, 1991; exhibit text for Markers and Memorials at Little Bighorn Battlefield, Museum Rehab, Phase 3, copy in unnumbered box in maintenance building, LBBNM. The nine Groethe portrait subjects were Dewey Beard, Nicolas Black Elk, Comes Again, Little Soldier, Iron Hawk, John Sitting Bull, Little Warrior, High Eagle, and Pemmican. *The Battlefield Dispatch* 10 (Fall 1991): 1.

22. *Denver Post*, October 8, 1992; *Big Horn County News*, November 4, 1992; *Denver Post*, November 15, 1992; *The Battlefield Dispatch* 11 (Fall 1992): 6; *LBHA Newsletter* 28 (July 1994): 3; *Billings Gazette*, March 3, 1995.

23. *LBHA Newsletter* 28 (July 1994): 3; Rankin, *Legacy*. Presenters at the Legacy Conference included Dan Flores, Alvin Josephy, Jr., Joseph C. Porter, Colin G. Calloway, Jerome A. Greene, John D. McDermott, Joseph A. Marshall III, Margot Liberty, Richard A. Fox, Jr., Douglas D. Scott, Paul L. Hedren, Brian W. Dippie, Paul A. Hutton, John P. Hart, Richard S. Slotkin, and Edward T. Linenthal.

24. NPS TIC 381 D23, SAR, 1995; *The Battlefield Dispatch* 14 (Summer 1995): 1.

25. NPS TIC 381 D16D, *Final General Management and Development Concept Plans, August 1986 updated May 1995, Little Bighorn Battlefield National Monument*; Greene, "A Battle among Skirmishes," 90; Robert M. Utley to Intermountain Field Area Director John C. Cook, October 8, 1996 (quote), copy in LBAF; NPS TIC 381 D39, "Superintendent's Annual Report for 1997"; Memorandum, Program Leader, Education and Interpretation, to Superintendent, Rocky Mountain System Support Office, undated, enclosing "Little Bighorn Battlefield Interpretive Upgrade Work Plan," copy in Koury Files; Paul A. Hutton, "Little Bighorn Battlefield, OAH Committee Site Visit, May 24–25, 1997," http://members.aol.com/Custerfact/hutton.htm; OAH report of Frederick E. Hoxie, undated, ca. June 1997, 5, LBBNM (quote). The arrangement by which OAH provides such assistance for NPS interpretive programs resides in "Agreement between the National Park Service and the Organization of American Historians, 1443CA000193013," dated October 1994, copy in LBAF. For the OAH evaluation, see also Linenthal, "OAH Site Visitation, May 24–25, 1997," submitted June 16, 1997, and R. David Edmunds, "Little Big Horn Site Visit, May 24–25, 1997," June 12, 1997. Copies provided to the author by William P. Wells.

26. Hutton, "Little Bighorn Battlefield, OAH Committee Site Visit, May 24–25, 1997" (first quote); NPS TIC 381 D39, "Superintendent's Annual Report for 1997" (second quote). See also *The Civil War News* (February/March 1998): 8–9.

27. U.S. Department of the Interior, National Park Service, *Interpretive Prospectus*, 9–13, 21–26, 29, quote on 37; "Little Bighorn Battlefield Visitor Center Exhibit Schematic Design Plan Proposal," November 1997, copy in LBAF.

28. Memorandum, Mangum to Tim Priehs, Executive Director, Southwest Parks and Monuments Association (SMPA), March 5, 1998, copy in SPMA file in

unnumbered box in maintenance building, LBBNM; *The Battlefield Dispatch* 17 (Summer 1998): 6; *Bighorn County News*, August 19, 1998; *The Battlefield Dispatch* 17 (Fall 1998): 4; NPS TIC 381 D43, "Superintendent's Annual Narrative Report, Fiscal Year 1998," April 1, 1999. Speakers at the Friday Night Lecture Series, which continued during the summers of 1999 and 2000, included Leonard Bruguier, Sandy Barnard, Richard A. Fox, Jr., Tom Bullhead, Ben Pease, Paul A. Hutton, Douglas D. Scott, and Robert M. Utley. "Little Bighorn Battlefield National Monument Friday Night Lecture Series, 1998," copy in LBAF; Little Bighorn Battlefield National Monument, press release, August 14, 2000, copy in LBAF.

29. *Billings Gazette*, May 30, 1999; Doerner, "So That the Place Might Be Remembered," 6–10; Bert Gildart, "Two Sides of Little Bighorn," http://away .com/primedia/military/two_sides_of_bighorn_1.html (quote); NPS TIC 381 D47, "Superintendent's Annual Narrative Report, 2000."

30. *The Battlefield Dispatch* 18 (Winter 1999): 4; *LBHA Newsletter* 34 (May 2000): 3; *The Battlefield Dispatch* 19 (Spring 2000): 5; *The Battlefield Dispatch* 19 (Fall 2000): 14; NPS TIC 381 D47, "Superintendent's Annual Narrative Report, 2000"; Southwest Parks and Monuments Association, *Little Bighorn Battlefield National Monument*. See the following brochures by the Western National Parks Association: *Deep Ravine Trail, Reno–Benteen Entrenchment Trail, Custer National Cemetery*.

31. Scope of Collection Statement, 2000, 8, 9, LBBNM.

32. *LBHA Newsletter* 35 (November 2001): 3; NPS TIC 381 D48, "Superintendent's Annual Narrative Report, 2001"; *The Battlefield Dispatch* 21 (Fall 2002): 6, 7; *LBHA Newsletter* 36 (February 2002): 5; *The Battlefield Dispatch* 21 (Winter 2002): 5; *Custer/Little Bighorn Advocate* (Fall/Winter 2002): 14; *LBHA Newsletter* 37 (February 2003): 7; Mac Greeley, "From the Bighorn to Baghdad: The Indians Wars Staff Ride," *Assembly* (May/June 2003): 43–46, available online at http://www.aog .usma.edu/PUBS/assembly/030506/baghdad.htm; Linenthal, "Transformation," 40.

8. Research and Collections

1. Rickey, *History of Custer Battlefield*, 70–71, 116–17.

2. Utley, "'Cap' Luce," 7; Luce to Nathalie C. Gookin, October 3, 1943, copy in LBAF (quote); SMR, September 30, 1943; SMR, October 31, 1943; SMR, November 30, 1943; Rickey, *History of Custer Battlefield*, 125–26; Greene, *Evidence and the Custer Enigma*, 26–27. See Dustin, *Custer Tragedy*, and Kuhlman, *Legend into History*. Luce's recommendation for an archeological study appears in Luce to Coordinating Superintendent, Yellowstone National Park, September 30, 1943, NPS Central Classified File, 1933–1949, National Monuments, Custer Battlefield 120, Box 129, Historical Records Custer Battlefield National Cemetery, File Folder 2, provided by Douglas D. Scott. Colonel Calvin Goddard of the Army Ordnance Department verified for Luce that the cases found were the type issued to the soldiers. SMR, September 30, 1943.

3. *Billings Gazette*, August 7, 1946; *Billings Gazette*, August 8, 1946; Luce to Acting Regional Director Howard W. Baker, August 27, 1946 (quote), copy in

LBAF. Luce wrote, "The physical evidences of battle artifacts found between the Reno–Benteen and Custer battlefields bear out very definite conclusions of a battle engagement lasting probably from a half to three-quarters of an hour. This battle phase has never been written up in the history of the Battle of the Little Bighorn River. We also believe that we have definitely located several points heretofore not definitely established, such as the Crows Nest, the morass, and the burning Indian tepee." SMR, July 31, 1946. Luce sponsored occasional directorate-authorized informal gatherings to pore over new thinking regarding the battle. Another was held on June 25, 1947, attended by Kuhlman; Dennis Moran of South Dakota, who as a Seventeenth Infantry soldier stationed at Fort Custer had visited the battlefield in 1877; D. L. Egnew of Hardin; George Osten of Billings; Casey E. Barthelmess of Custer County, Montana; Maurice Frink of Indiana; and historical aide Robert M. Utley. SMR, June 30, 1947; Luce to Nye, October 11, 1943, copy in LBAF; Frink, *Photographer on an Army Mule*, xiii; *Billings Gazette*, March 18, 1946; Bulletin No. 2, Custer Battlefield National Monument, September 23, 1946, "Enlarged Map of Custer Battlefield National Monument Area and Surrounding Country," copy in LBAF.

4. SMR, April 11, 1945; SMR, August 31, 1947; SMR, December 22, 1947; SMR, January 31, 1948; SMR, February 29, 1948; SMR, July 31, 1949; Luce to Miller, March 16, 1948 (first quote), copy in LBAF; letter from George H. Zacherle, *LBHA Newsletter* 11 (January 1977): 5 (second quote); Rickey, *History of Custer Battlefield*, 123; George G. Osten to B. William Henry, Jr., February 4, 1969, copy in LBAF; Acting Superintendent Neil C. Mangum to Associate Regional Director, Rocky Mountain Region, November 26, 1986, copy in LBAF. Rickey reported that the 1947 attempt to use the army mine detector "proved fruitless, as the device was not able to detect the presence of the copper cartridge cases and lead bullets, it being only sensitive to iron and steel." *History of Custer Battlefield*, 126.

5. Memorandum, Luce to Director, May 31, 1945, in SMR, May 31, 1945; SMR, June 30, 1945; SMR, December 31, 1945; SMR, July 1, 1946; SMR, October 31, 1947; SMR, December 10, 1948; SMR, January 31, 1951; SMR, April 30, 1951; SMR, October 6, 1958; SMR, April 2, 1964; Rickey, *History of Custer Battlefield*, 125; H. Raymond Gregg, Regional Chief of Interpretation, to Superintendent, Custer Battlefield National Monument, June 28, 1955, copy in LBAF; Luce to Regional Director, Region Two, June 27, 1956, copy in LBAF. On receipt of a body of National Archives copies late in 1950, Luce remarked, "All of these are valuable in our research, but one letter with accompanying drawing is particularly important. It is the report on the placing of the large memorial on Custer Hill and the re-interment of the bodies around this monument, the work being completed July 29, 1881. This report has been our object of search for many years." SMR, December 31, 1950. A brief amendment to Rickey's administrative history was prepared in draft in 1981. See Murray, "Ghost-Herders on the Little Big Horn." A copy of Rickey's draft document is in NPS TIC 381 D14, "Administrative History," September 29, 1958.

6. SMR, May 8, 1956; NPS TIC 381 D28, "Mission 66 for Custer Battle-field National Monument," 1956, 2, 4; Superintendent, Custer Battlefield National Monument, to Regional Director, Region Two, June 27, 1956 (quoted material); Gregg to Superintendent Aubuchon, July 3, 1956, copy in LBAF; Chief Historian Herbert Kahler to Regional Director, Region Two, July 19, 1956, copy in LBAF.

7. Roy E. Appleman, "Report of Visit to Custer Battlefield National Monument," September 25, 1956 (quote), copy in LBAF; Rickey to Major Frank Anders, July 16, 1956, copy in LBAF; SMR, July 5, 1956; SMR, August 31, 1956; SMR, October 3, 1956; SMR, November 1, 1956; SMR, September 3, 1957; SMR, July 6, 1965; Authorization note for project participation signed by Vaughn, counter-signed by Rickey, June 28, 1956, copy in LBAF; "Mission 66 for Custer Battlefield National Monument," *Yellowstone News*, September 13, 1956; Rickey, *History of Custer Battlefield*, 125–26; Greene, *Evidence and the Custer Enigma*, 22–35, citing research notes and metal detection reports, 1956–59, in the Research Files, CBNM. Regarding work in the area of Medicine Tail Coulee Ford, the superintendent reported, "Several items were recovered on the flat just east of the river, at the mouth of Medicine Tail Coulee, providing additional proof that some portion of the Custer battalion did actually approach close to the Indian camp site before taking up positions on Custer Battlefield." SMR, September 4, 1959. See also Vaughn to Loveless, July 3, 1965, copy in LBAF; and J. W. Vaughn, "Research Relating to Area," July 2, 1963, copy in LBAF. Respecting discoveries in Deep Coulee (North Medicine Tail Coulee) during October 1958, the superintendent wrote, "Mr. Vaughn completed researching a portion of the North Medicine Tail Coulee area, for a distance of about 200 yards East of the Battlefield road. All finds were staked, described in writing and separately stored. The area staff surveyed the find sites for permanent location." SMR, November 4, 1958. Rickey entertained the notion of using an underwater metal detector in the Little Bighorn River in the areas of Reno's retreat and Medicine Tail Coulee Ford. O. W. Judge to Rickey, undated, ca. 1959–60, copy in LBAF. The Indian positions discovered at Reno–Benteen in 1969 lay outside the park boundary. B. William Henry, Jr., to author, June 20, 1969.

8. SMR, July 3, 1958; "Restoration of Rifle Pits and Barricades in the Reno–Benteen Battle Area During June 1958," attached to ibid.; SMR, September 5, 1958; Rickey, *History of Custer Battlefield*, 53–54, 126; Robert T. Bray, "A Report of Archeological Investigations at the Reno–Benteen Site, Custer Battlefield National Monument, June 2–July 1, 1958," unpublished report in LBAF, 2 (quote).; "Map of Archeological Investigations and Historic Features, Reno–Benteen Battlefield," in ibid.; *Billings Gazette*, June 25, 1958; NPS TIC, Midwest Region, Master Plan Narrative, vols. 1–3, 1964; "CBNM Chronology," copy in LBAF. A summation of the 1958 restoration effort is as follows: "To the south and east of the Reno–Benteen Memorial are 3 restored entrenchments and 4 restored rifle pits. . . . The trench at [interpretive] trail post No. 4 . . . now [1975] appears to be 42½ feet long, 5 feet wise at the top and 2 feet deep and is slightly curved. The soldiers apparently faced west over a parapet. The trench at post No. 5, . . . faces east, is approximately 38 feet long,

6 feet wide at the top, 1½ to 2 feet deep, and is slightly cured at the north end. The trench at post No. 2 is L-shaped, apparently faces southeast, and is 15 feet by 17 feet, the long arm facing south. The rifle pit at post No. 13 . . . is C-shaped and approximately 4 feet by 2½ feet by 6 inches deep. The two rifle pits at post No. 14 . . . are roughly 3 feet across and one foot in depth. The pit at post No. 16 . . . is approximately 3 feet by 8 inches deep." Lance R. Williams and Lance J. Olivieri, "Classified Structure Field Inventory Report, Custer Battlefield Historic District," September 6, 1975, copy in LBAF. The preparers concluded in 1975 that "the entrenchments and rifle pits, which were restored in 1958, are reaching the point of being imperfectly discernable. The ground cover must be kept trimmed in order for the visitor to see them. Perhaps they should be restored again, relying on the report, map and other data of the 1958 excavation." See also the NPS brochure *Entrenchment Trail.*

9. George G. Osten to B. William Henry, Jr., February 4, 1969, copy in LBAF; "Correlation of Relic Finds in Custer Battlefield Vicinity," August 8, 1970, copy in author's files; Custer Battlefield Historical and Museum Association, *Quarterly Newsletter,* April 1979; W. Kent King to Rodd Wheaton, undated letter in *LBHA Newsletter* 15 (November 1981): 5. The 1970 compilation of artifacts was later integrated with known Indian accounts to produce a feasible scenario (for its time) of the defeat of Custer's battalion. Greene, *Evidence and the Custer Enigma,* 14–45.

10. *Montana Standard* (Butte), September 11, 1983; Richard A. Fox, Jr., "Preliminary Archaeological Survey at the Custer Battlefield National Monument," unpublished report dated October 31, 1983, in the folder "Artifacts, Archaeological Survey at Custer Battlefield National Monument," LBBNM. Particulars of the 1983 burn and its aftermath, together with initial park service reaction, appear in Parle, "History Revisited."

11. NPS, press release, May 15, 1984, copy in LBAF; *Sheridan Press,* May 8, 1984; *Time,* May 28, 1984:49. Robbins, "New Look"; Acting Superintendent Mangum to Director, NPS, November 7, 1985, copy in LBAF. For the 1984 season, see Scott and Fox, *Archaeological Insights.* A comprehensive presentation of the 1984–85 archeological surveys appears in Barnard, *Digging,* but see also the final assessment in Scott, Fox, Connor, and Harmon, *Archaeological Perspectives.* The 1985 dig was briefly interrupted by a failure of the battlefield staff to submit review documents in compliance with historic preservation law. See NPS, press release, May 15, 1985, copy in LBAF; *Billings Gazette,* May 15, 1985. See also coverage of the digs in the *Washington Post,* May 5, 1985.

12. D. Scott, "Cartridges," 28–30; *Wall Street Journal,* August 30, 1985; *LBHA Newsletter* 20 (November 1986): 6; D. Scott, "Archaeological Perspectives," 169, 173–77, 180–81; Jordan, "Ghosts on the Little Bighorn"; Mangum to Scott, November 7, 1985, copy in LBAF; Barnard, *Digging,* 64–65; Acting Superintendent Mangum to Director, NPS, November 7, 1985, copy in LBAF; Mangum to Michael Parks, October 8, 1985, copy in LBAF. In 1986 Historian Mangum urged that thirteen "spurious" markers be removed from the battlefield, based upon the archeological findings. He also called for replacing one unknown soldier marker

with a marker identifying the site to scout Minton ("Mitch") Bouyer, where a partial skull, forensically attributed to Bouyer with "evidence that would hold up in a court of law," had been located. Acting Superintendent Mangum to Associate Regional Director, Rocky Mountain Region, November 26, 1986, copy in LBAF; NPS TIC 381 D23, SAR, 1992; *Billings Gazette,* November 2, 1986; *LBHA Newsletter* 23 (July 1989): 7; *The Battlefield Dispatch* 9 (Winter 1990): 3; *The Battlefield* Dispatch 13 (Summer 1994): 6; *LBHA Newsletter* 24 (April 1995): 3; *The Battlefield Dispatch* 14 (Spring 1995): 3; NPS TIC 381 D23, SAR, 1995. Subordinate studies from which data tied to the archeology emerged included geomorphologist C. Vance Haynes's examination of Deep Ravine (1985) and forensic pathologist Clyde Collins Snow's analysis of human bones recovered during the survey. Regarding the public attention of the 1984–85 project, Neil Mangum wrote in 1987, "Unequivocally, the excavation produced unparalleled excitement and curiosity beyond wildest expectations. Record–breaking crowds converged on the site, many hoping to personally witness the unraveling of the battle's closely guarded secrets. Scores of journalists and TV crews literally besieged the archeologists and volunteers. . . . Daily events of the survey were broadcast around the nation and even circulated in England, Germany, and Austraila. Media coverage was prolific in terms of headline news. *Time, Newsweek, U.S.A. Today,* and the NBC *Today Show,* to name just a few." Magnum, "Popular Reaction to Custer," 61. For Utley's views, see Utley, "Digging Up Custer Battlefield," and Utley, *Custer and Me,* 191. Looting at Reno–Benteen is described in the *Denver Post,* April 1, 1985, and *USA Today,* April 2, 1985. Using the archeology findings together with historical data gleaned from an assortment of documentary materials, Archeologist Fox advanced a well-stated theory of the battle action in *Archaeology, History.*

13. For archeology subsequent to 1984–85, see D. Scott, "Cartridges," 24–30; D. Scott, *Little Bighorn Battlefield Archeology;* Scott and Bleed, *Good Walk;* Scott and Willey, "Human Remains Identification Project"; *LBHA Newsletter* 24 (July 1995): 3; *Missoulian* (Missoula, Mont.), May 28, 1989; *The Battlefield Dispatch* 8 (Fall 1989): 7; Barnard, "Reno–Benteen"; *The Battlefield Dispatch* 21 (Fall 2002): 8–14; *Billings Gazette,* May 8, 1996; *Billings Gazette,* May 18, 2003. Conclusions dealing with human remains recovered in 1983–84 appear in Scott, Willey, and Connor, *They Died with Custer.* The horse cemetery discovered in 1941 during repair work on the reservoir atop Custer Hill is discussed in SMR, April 30, 1941, and in Douglas D. Scott, "Archeological Investigations of the 'Horse Cemetery' Site, Little Bighorn Battlefield National Monument," unpublished report dated 2002, NPS Midwest Archaeological Center, Lincoln, Nebraska. Burial of the trooper's remains found protruding from the riverbank in 1989 took place in the cemetery on June 23, 1991. *Billings Gazette,* May 31, 1991. A complete bibliography of reports and studies resulting from the extensive archeological work on battlefield property, including that on private lands surrounding the park, is in "Archeology at the Battle of the Little Bighorn," http://www.cr.nps.gov/mvac/libi/bibliography.html, as well in the Cultural Sites Inventory of Little Bighorn Battlefield National Monument maintained at the NPS Midwest Archeological Center, Lincoln, Nebraska.

14. In February 1960 the superintendent reported that "we met with Jim Little Bird of Busby, and Albert Tall Bull and Marion King of Lamedeer [*sic*] to discuss items of interest to the Indians at the Monument." SMR, February 9, 1960. Stands In Timber told Rickey where Noisy Walking fell during the battle. He also showed the historian the petroglyth along the rimrock overlooking the north side of Reno Creek and locally termed Crazy's Horse signature. SMR, November 3, 1965. This latter resource on the sandstone was destroyed after 1968 either naturally or by an individual attempting to break it off. NPS TIC 381 D20, "Oral History of the Battle of the Little Bighorn," by Royal G. Jackson, 1985–86 (see also the commentary in Linenthal, *Sacred Ground*, 155–56); Mangum to Kenneth L. Diem, December 10, 1985, copy in LBAF; NPS TIC 381 D45, "Reptile and Amphibian Inventory at Grant Kohrs Ranch National Historic Site and Little Bighorn Battlefield"; NPS TIC 381 D44, "A Systematic Survey of Vegetation at Little Bighorn Battlefield National Monument." Some of Rickey's experiments are documented in Neil C. Mangum, "Commentary on Psychometry Experiments Conducted on Custer Battlefield," copy in LBAF. (Psychometry is the "divination of facts concerning an object or its owner through contact with or proximity to the object." *Webster's New Collegiate Dictionary*, 931.)

15. SMR, March 31, 1942; SMR, April 30, 1942; SMR, August 31, 1942; Rickey, *History of Custer Battlefield*, 105–106.

16. SMR, October 31, 1942; SMR, November 30, 1942; SMR, December 31, 1942; Rickey, *History of Custer Battlefield*, 106–107.

17. SMR, January 31, 1943; SMR, May 31, 1943; SMR, August 22, 1943; SMR, April 30, 1944; SMR, July 1, 1944; SMR, April 30, 1946; SMR, July 1, 1946; SMR, March 31, 1948; SMR, April 30, 1948; SMR, May 31, 1948; SMR, February 28, 1949; SMR, August 3, 1949; Rickey, *History of Custer Battlefield*, 107–108; Luce to Nathalie C. Gookin, October 3, 1943, copy in LBAF; Utley to author, March 5, 2005. The acceptance of the Elizabeth B. Custer Collection was mandated in a component of the 1939 Act of Congress authorizing "a public museum suitable for housing a collection of historical relics." NPS TIC 381 D42, "Scope of Collection Statement," July 26, 2000.

18. SMR, March 31, 1951; SMR, June 2, 1951; Rickey, *History of Custer Battlefield*, 108–109. Other noteworthy accessions include No. 18, O'Donnell Collection; No. 63, Bates Collection (includes Godfrey materials); No. 75, Snyder–Ronayne Collection (documents pertaining to Colonel Nelson Miles's campaigns); No. 77, Colter Collection (Indian art); No. 137, Scabery Collection (contains Indian photographs); and No. 153, McMurry Collection (material about fiftieth anniversary). Donation of the Snyder–Ronayne materials is discussed in SMR, February 29, 1956.

19. SMR, March 1, 1957; SMR, August 8, 1957; SMR, September 3, 1957; SMR, July 6, 1964; SMR, September 2, 1964; Rickey, *History of Custer Battlefield*, 109–10; "CBNM Chronolog," copy in LBAF.

20. SMR, June 8, 1959; "CBNM Chronology," copy in LBAF; Alberts to Associate Regional Director, November 2, 1964, copy in LBAF. The Hammer File was

basis for a publication, *Little Big Horn Biographies*, and, later, Hammer, *Biographies of the 7th Cavalry*.

21. SMR, February 5, 1964; SMR, December 3, 1964; SMR, January 8, 1965; SMR, April 5, 1965; SMR, May 6, 1965; Carson to Associate Regional Director, May 27, 1965 (quote), copy in LBAF; Interpretive Specialist to Associate Regional Director, June 17, 1965, copy in LBAF; SMR, April 3, 1967. Mrs. Nadezda Henry, wife of Park Historian B. William Henry, Jr., and a trained librarian/archivist, completed much of the book cataloging in 1969.

22. *Billings Gazette*, April 18, 1976; *LBHA Newsletter* 10 (July 1976): 13; Utley, *Custer and Me*, 151; NPS TIC 381 D7-A, "Statement for Management," 1975–76 (quote); Custer Battlefield Historical and Museum Association, *Quarterly Newsletter*, April 1979; Mangum, *Register*; NPS, press release, February 1, 1980, copy in LBAF; NPS TIC 381 D16c, "Final General Management and Development Concept Plans," August 1986, 7–11; *Billings Gazette*, June 24, 1979; Court to author, February 8, 2005. The purported price of the Miller paintings in 1989 was $2 million. Acting Superintendent McChristian to Associate Regional Director, Park Operations, Rocky Mountain Region, March 29, 1989, with supporting papers, copies in LBAF.

23. Mangum to William Sontag, Chief of Interpretation, Rocky Mountain Region, January 27, 1987, copy in LBAF; *The Battlefield Dispatch* 8 (Fall 1989): 4, 7. In 1998 the museum collections were "conservatively valued in excess of seven million dollars." NPS TIC 381 D43, "Superintendent's Annual Narrative Report, Fiscal Year 1998."

24. *The Battlefield Dispatch* 9 (Fall 1990): 5; *The Lakota Times*, May 8, 1991; *The Battlefield Dispatch* 10 (Spring 1991): 1, 9; NPS TIC 381 D23, SAR, 1991–92; *LBHA Newsletter* 26 (March 1992): 5; *The Battlefield Dispatch* 11 (Spring 1992): 3; *The Battlefield Dispatch* 12 (Summer 1993): 6; *The Battlefield Dispatch* 12 (Winter 1993): 4, 10. McChristian estimated the value of the McIntosh diary at $75,000. *Billings Gazette*, February 4, 1992.

25. Mitchell, "Archival Reorganization"; NPS TIC 381 D39, SAR, 1997; NPS TIC 381 D43, "Superintendent's Annual Narrative Report, Fiscal Year 1998"; *Billings Gazette*, September 2, 1998; "FY97 Curatorial Accomplishements," January 20, 1998, copy in LBAF; NPS TIC 381 D47, "Superintendent's Annual Narrative Report, Fiscal Year 2000"; NPS TIC 381 D48, "Superintendent's Annual Narrative Report, Fiscal Year 2001"; "National Park Service Little Bighorn Battlefield National Monument Museum Collection Access Policy," LBAF; "National Park Service Little Bighorn Battlefield National Monument White Swan Library Collection Access Policy," LBAF; *The Battlefield Dispatch* 22 (Spring 2003): 1, 16. A summary of the collections refurbishment appears in *The Guidon*, 3 (June 2000): 20. See also "Scope of Collection Statement," as revised 1999, LBBNM. Researchers are encouraged to schedule appointments with the park historian or the museum curator to use the library and museum collections. Researchers are required to complete the "Library Research Room Rules and Registration" prior to accessing materials.

26. NPS TIC 381 D42, "Scope of Collection Statement," July 26, 2000, 13–21; "Park Museum Collection Profile: Little Bighorn Battlefield National Monument," http://www.cr.nps.gov/museum/collections/libi.html.

9. Nonprofit Support Groups and Interest Groups

1. *National Park Service Reference Manual,* Director's Order 32 re: Cooperating Associations, Chapter 1, Section 1; "About Cooperating Associations," http://www.parksandhistory.org/about/coop.asp. Public Law 633 of August 7, 1946, authorized use of "nonprofit-sharing cooperating associations" and permitted their use of government building space. "The main purpose of and justification for these organizations is to assist in interpreting the Service areas to visitors. This purpose is achieved through the production and sale of interpretive literature, purchase of equipment used in interpretation, and in various other direct and indirect ways." U.S. Department of the Interior, National Park Service, *National Park Service Information Handbook,* 64. For period guidelines regarding "cooperating associations," see "NPS Administrative Manual, Organization Volume, 1960," National Park Service Cooperating Associations, Part 12, Chapter 1–5 (cancelled in 1969). The definition of "interest group" is interpreted from that appearing in *Webster's New Collegiate Dictionary.*

2. SMR, January 31, 1953; Rickey, *History of Custer Battlefield,* 110; *The Battlefield Dispatch* 9 (Spring 1990): 1; NPS TIC, Midwest Region, Master Plan Narrative, vols. 1–3, 1964 (quote). Beginning in 1943, ten years prior to the establishment of the CBHMA, the Yellowstone Library and Museum Association sold postcards and brochures at Custer Battlefield National Monument. Termination of the park's administrative relationship with Yellowstone National Park paved the way for creation of a separate "association for the furtherance of the interests in historical research and related subjects" at Custer Battlefield National Monument. Nichols, "CBHMA," 3. A copy of the then-current MOA is attached to Earle Kittleman, Rocky Mountain Regional Office, to S. Paul Okey, January 5, 1978, copy in the Vertical Files, Montana Room, Parmly Billings Library. Approved bylaws as of March 1978 are in ibid. For membership information, see the CBHMA web site at http://www.cbhma.org/about.htm.

3. SMR, July 31, 1955; SMR, January 6, 1960. Quoted material, without attribution, appears in Nichols, "CBHMA," 3–4; Neil C. Mangum, personal communication, August 20, 2004. In 1964 the bylaws were amended so that "the Park Historian automatically becomes the Executive-Secretary of the Association upon assignment to Custer Battlefield and that both the Superintendent and Historian automatically become ex-officio members of the Board of Directors upon their respective assignments to Custer Battlefield." SMR, July 6, 1964.

4. Ibid., 4; SMR, July 2, 1963; Ray H. Mattison to Associate Regional Director, August 21, 1964, copy in LBAF. As early as November 1953, the CBHMA explored ways to purchase land near the entrance to the park. Wrote Luce, "We hope

that within a few weeks the Association can purchase this land and then tender same to the National Park Service under the Historic Sites Act [of 1935] until such time as the monument boundaries are extended to include it." SMR, November 30, 1953. For the purchase and organization of the Dustin materials, see SMR, March 1, 1957; SMR, February 10, 1958. For the funding of the Reno–Benteen archeology and later interpretive brochures, see SMR, March 5, 1958; SMR, July 6, 1959; SMR, December 8, 1959; SMR, January 6, 1960.

5. Nichols, "CBHMA," 4–5; Koury, "A Bit of CBHMA History," 99 (quote); SMR, July 3, 1967; Mangum, "Popular Reaction to Custer," 56–57; Utley to author, March 5, 2005; "Custer Battle Centennial Commemorative Stamp Prospectus," undated, ca. 1975, in the Vertical Files, Montana Room, Parmly Billings Public Library; "Bulletin," CBHMA, undated, in ibid. The CBHMA scholarship went to Daniel O. Magnusson, who had been a seasonal ranger at the park. Magnusson, a World War II veteran, completed his dissertation at the University of Montana, Missoula. It was published as *Peter Thompson's Narrative of the Little Bighorn Campaign 1876: A Critical Analysis of an Eyewitness Account of the Custer Debacle.* The printing of Kenneth Hammer's earlier pamphlet, *Little Big Horn Biographies*, was underwritten by the CBHMA in 1964 and went on sale in the following year. SMR, December 5, 1963; SMR, January 7, 1964; SMR, October 5, 1965. Publication of Rickey's administrative history is in SMR, April 3, 1967, and SMR, June 1, 1967.

6. Nichols, "CBHMA," 5–6; "Ammendment [sic] to Article II. Members," and Rich Rambur, "For Amending Article II (members)," undated, ca. 1973, copy in the Vertical Files, Montana Room, Parmly Billings Public Library; Mangum, "Popular Reaction to Custer," 56. A copy of the bylaws of Custer Battlefield Historical and Museum Association, Inc., as of 1975–76, reposes in the Vertical Files, Montana Room, Parmly Billings Public Library. In that document, "Members" is addressed in Article III. The CBHMA perceived the NPS's circumvention of the group's constitution in disbanding the centennial committee and in altering the membership requirements as heavy handed. The decision came after an Internal Revenue Service audit suggested that some CBHMA members might have conflicts of interest with the book-selling apparatus at the park. Richard J. Rambur to Michael J. Koury, August 7, 1975, Koury Files. One critic termed the 1975 decision to open the membership "a blatant attempt to dilute the influence of the CBHMA." *The Battlefield Dispatch* 13 (Winter 1994): 4. Member Michael J. Koury believed that by opening membership to all interested parties, the park service "hoped to dilute the influence of the Association by the infusion of a large number of members, widely scattered about the country. This, they believed, would make the group easier to control." "A Bit of CBHMA History," 100–101. The 1975 Billings seminar included a panoply of longtime Custer and Indian wars luminaries, among them historian Brian W. Dippie ("Did You Hear the One about Custer's Last Words?"), artist Randy Steffan ("Arms, Accoutrements and Uniforms of the Indian War Period"), author Mark H. Brown ("The Genesis of the Sioux War of 1876"), and long-time battlefield devotee George Osten ("Personalities of the Old School of Custer Scholars I Have Known"). *Billings Gazette*, June 8, 1975.

7. Nichols, "CBHMA," 6–7; *Custer/Little Bighorn Battlefield Advocate*, 2 (Winter 1994): 11; Utley, *Custer and Me*, 150–51. Longtime CBHMA member Michael J. Koury believed that "the decision to abolish the Centennial Committee and tone down the scope of the 100th Anniversary was dictated by the very real fear of possible actions by American Indian activists." "A Bit of CBHMA History," 100–101. A member's critical view of the NPS's oversight of the centennial commemoration is in Koury, *Custer Centennial Observance*, 7–24. Custer's grand-nephew complained to President Gerald R. Ford about the centennial program at the park, specifically about Means's appearance, to which the NPS responded that to deny Means recognition at the event "would have risked confrontation and possibly even violence." Copies of George A. Custer III's letter to the president and the park service response repose in LBAF, as cited in Linenthal, *Sacred Ground*, 166.

8. Nichols, "CBHMA," 7–8. In 1982 the association helped sponsor a summer workshop titled War on the Northern Plains, 1862–1890, at Montana State University, with instructors including Michael Malone, Richard Roeder, Thomas Wessell, Robert M. Utley, Don Rickey, Jr., and Robert A. Murray. NPS, press release, March 31, 1982.

9. "Review of Financial Activities of the Custer Battlefield Historical and Museum Association, Incorporated, and the Custer Battlefield Preservation Committee, Incorporated, National Park Service," Office of Inspector General Audit Report, October 1984, Koury Files; Nichols, "CBHMA," 8–9; *Billings Gazette*, February 16, 1985; Memorandum, Acting Regional Director, Rocky Mountain Regional Office, to Chief, Administrative Service Division, NPS, November 27, 1985, regarding "OIG Audit Report," copy in LBAF; "Report of Custer Battlefield Publications and Interpretation Review Team," October 8, 1984 (quotes), copy in LBAF; Memorandum, Court to Regional Director, Rocky Mountain Region, October 22, 1985, copy in LBAF; Memorandum, Ditmanson to Regional Director, Rocky Mountain Region, February 5, 1987, copy in LBAF; Rouse, "Custer Battlefield Up-Date," 88; *The Battlefield Dispatch* 8 (Fall 1989): 2. Cost of the independent "Blue Ribbon" review team exceeded $5,000. Regional Director L. Lorraine Mintzmyer to Koury, October 15, 1984, copy in Koury Files. In the summer of 1990, CBHMA funded seven of ten interpreters at the park while subsidizing the printing of a new guidebook for the national cemetery. In 1991 the group funded a specially designed computer database program to implement registration of graves in the cemetery. *The Battlefield Dispatch* 9 (Fall 1990): 6; *The Battlefield Dispatch* 10 (Spring 1991): 2; *LBHA Newsletter* 26 (March 1992): 5.

10. Nichols, "CBHMA," 8–9; Koury, "A Bit of CBHMA History," 102–103; *LBHA Newsletter* 25 (April 1991): 4; *The Missoulian*, August 12, 1990; *The Battlefield Dispatch* 10 (Spring 1991): 2; *The Battlefield Dispatch* 13 (Winter 1994): 4; *Custer/Little Bighorn Battlefield Advocate*, 2 (Winter 1994): 11; *Billings Gazette*, July 15, 1992; *Lakota Times*, August 12, 1992; *Rocky Mountain News* (Denver): September 18, 1992; Nichols to Superintendent Booher, January 3, 1993, copy in LBAF; Candace Dempsey, "Historical Battle. Superintendent on the Firing Line

at Custer Monument," *Horizon Air Magazine* (March 1991): 32. In 1992 the association published its first major book on the battle, Nichols, *Reno Court of Inquiry. The Battlefield Dispatch* 11 (Spring 1992): 1. Another dispute had revolved around the Lawrence A. Frost book, *Custer Legends*, which had been likewise rejected by the book committee. Mangum, "Confessions," 5. Despite this, Frost's book was later sold at the park. Linenthal, *Sacred Ground*, 167. As one former NPS employee related, "The board members assumed the attitude that since they were paying for salaries, interpretive equipment, etc., they should have a strong voice in controlling those assets. This is where they lost touch with the proper role of a cooperating association." Douglas C. McChristian, e-mail message to the author, January 31, 2005.

11. Baker to Kennedy, August 10, 1993, enclosing briefing statement,copy in Koury Files; Nichols, "CBHMA," 9 (quote); NPS TIC 381 D23, SAR, 1991–92; Koury, "A Bit of CBHMA History," 103–104; *The Battlefield Dispatch* 13 (Winter 1994): 4; *Custer/Little Bighorn Battlefield Advocate*, 2 (Winter 1994): 11; Baker to Jo K. Johnson, August 27, 1993, copy in LBAF; NPS, press releases August 27 and September 30, 1993; *The Battlefield Dispatch* 13 (Summer 1994): 2; *The Battlefield Dispatch* 13 (Fall 1994): 1; *Denver Post*, August 31, 1993. Douglas McChristian, acting superintendent at the battlefield, reported that "while the Park Service recognizes the valuable contributions made to the battlefield over the years, the relationship had changed for the worse and a decision was made to seek a cooperating association that would be truly cooperative." Beyond the conflicts cited, "the association . . . has challenged decisions made on resource management and operational matters, even though those are clearly [within] the purview of the Park Service." *Billings Gazette*, August 28, 1993. See also *Custer/Little Bighorn Battlefield Advocate*, 1 (Fall 1993): 1–3.

12. Ditmanson to Regional Director Robert M. Baker, October 8, 1993, copy in LBAF. Mangum reflected on the early turbulence: "The chemistry of the board changed to the detriment of the park and I think to CBHMA. Board members began to meddle into park operations to the point that the cooperating association became very much uncooperative. Discontent mushroomed. . . . The seeds of discord rippled, with CBHMA assuming more the role of an adversarial group bent on dictating management policies instead of focusing on their mission as a cooperating association." "Confessions of a Park Ranger," 5.

13. Nichols, "CBHMA," 10–11; Bob Reece to author, August 10, 2004. See Roger G. Kennedy to Jo K. Johnson, November 17, 1993; Ron Nichols to Kennedy, December 10, 1993; and Robert M. Baker to Nichols, January 5, 1994, in *The Battlefield Dispatch* 13 (Winter 1994): 2; *The Battlefield Dispatch* 14 (Spring 1995): 2; *The Battlefield Dispatch* 14 (Winter 1995): 3; *Friends of the Little Bighorn Battlefield*, 4 (March 2004): 4; NPS TIC 381 D48, "Superintendent's Annual Narrative Report, Fiscal Year 2001," 3.

14. *LBHA Newsletter* 10 (January 1976) (quoted credo), 2;1; Frost, foreword to *Garry Owen, 1976*; Dale Kosman to author, July 21, 2004. See also Lawrence A.

Frost, "The Beginning of the LBHA," in *LBHA Newsletter* 11 (January 1987): 3–4. A later credo was "To seek the truth about the Battle of the Little Big Horn and all of Custeriana." "A Special Report to the LBHA Membership," *LBHA Newsletter* 19 (April 1985): 27. However, the group's 1983 constitution stated that the body was formed "for the study of the life and times of George Armstrong Custer." "Constitution (Code of Regulations) of Little Big Horn Associates (Association)," Koury Files. Historian Brian W. Dippie has described "the love/hate relationship between the Custer buffs [including members of the various groups], and the Custer Battlefield. An intense, unreasonable partisanship has led some buffs to make vitriolic personal attacks on battlefield staff over matters of interpretation and perceived bias. But an intense devotion to the subject also leads buffs to volunteer for archaeological digs and seasonal posts. Buffs spearhead the drives for funds to acquire additional land that will preserve the integrity of the battlefield site for future generations, serve on committees, attend conferences, present papers, lobby congressmen, and care. They can be peevish, mulish, and tiresomely obsessive. They can also be generous, receptive, and wonderfully informed, models of that enthusiasm and knowledge that define the buff everywhere." "Of Bullets, Blunders, and Custer Buffs," 80. Elsewhere, Dippie described "Custer buffs (that is, amateur historical enthusiasts)" as having the following concerns: "What happened at the Little Bighorn, and why? Who did what to whom? Who was responsible for defeat?" They are "not nearly as interested in right and wrong as they are in the fine points of orders and tactics and the character and performance of individual soldiers. . . . In the main, what the buffs resent—and resist—are not reinterpretations of the battle, but of the battle's meaning. They wage a rearguard action against Political Correctness [as in the name change], . . . just as they never accepted the double–whammy of the appointment of a Native American woman as battlefield superintendent in 1989." Dippie, *Custer's Last Stand* (Dippie's commentary appears in the preface to the 1994 reprint edition). While much solid research and writing has emanated from the LBHA members through the years, to many, especially during the group's formative years, "veneration and guardianship of the Custer myth and the sacred site were more important than dispassionate historical investigation." Linenthal, *Sacred Ground*, 144.

15. Linenthal, *Sacred Ground*, 130–31, 144–45, 146, 147, 149–50. About the centennial, Custer's grandnephew, Colonel George A. Custer III, remarked, "Twenty–five years ago [at the seventy-fifth anniversary] my father and mother were invited to stay with the monument superintendent. Now, I'm not even allowed to participate." Ibid., 145. *LBHA Newsletter* 14 (May 1980): 4; UNPS, press release, November 15, 1982; *Billings Gazette*, June 25, 1983. Among other things, Carroll had launched a lengthy letter-writing campaign to government officials seeking the ouster of Court and Mangum, while speaking out against, among other things, any proposed name change as well as the quotation from Black Elk ("Know the Power that is Peace") on the front exterior wall of the visitor

center. (Carroll had earlier mounted a similar vendetta against former park historian and CBHMA executive secretary Richard J. Rambur.) Carroll's defusing at the Billings meeting was partly, and artfully, facilitated by Robert Utley. Utley, *Custer and Me*, 188–89. Regarding the Black Elk quote, Chief Historian Edwin C. Bearss told Carroll that the quote "represents the highest aspirations of people everywhere" and contributed to "a discussion of the historical attitudes of those who fought" in the battle. Bearss to Robert Aldrich, February 25, 1986, Koury Files. Carroll also called for the appointment of a book review committee "completely unattached" to the park, and of a watch-dog committee "to oversee the activities of this park and their [*sic*] decisions." Carroll's views were endorsed by some members of the CBHMA leadership. The Inspector General's Office of the Department of the Interior reviewed the complaints and determined that the charges did not warrant further investigation. "History of Mr. John M. Carroll's Concerns and Conflicts with the Managers of Custer Battlefield Memorial [*sic*], 1976–1982," copy in the author's files. See also Acting Regional Director Jack W. Neckels to Assistant Director, Personnel and Administrative Services, February 1, 1985, copy in LBAF. Carroll likened the Black Elk quote to one by Tojo at Pearl Harbor's cemetery. Linenthal, *Sacred Ground*, 149. The LBHA board of directors later considered a resolution to the secretary of the interior calling for the removal of the "statement of a self-admitted brutal and savage killer of wounded United States Army soldiers emblazoned on the wall of the Visitors' Center." copy in Koury Files. The resolution did not pass. "Minutes of Board of Directors Meeting, Washington, D.C., Convention, July 1984, Manassas, Virginia," 4, copy in Koury Files. Discussion of the Black Elk quote imbroglio appears in *LBHA Newsletter* 11 (November 1977): 3–4; Mangum, "Popular Reaction to Custer," 57–58; *LBHA Newsletter* 17 (February 1983): 6–7; and *LBHA Newsletter* 17 (May 1983): 6–7.

    16. For examples of early tumult within LBHA, see Michael J. Koury to the Board of Directors, LBHA, August 24, 1984; Koury to Assistant Secretary of the Interior William Hartwig, August 24, 1984; W. Donald Horn to Hartwig, September 5, 1984; and Koury to the Board of Directors, LBHA, October 3, 1984 copies in LBAF; "A Special Report to the LBHA Membership," (also containing copies of much of the above correspondence); "Message from the Board of Directors of the Little Big Horn Associates" to its members, September 30, 1984, Koury Files; *LBHA Newsletter* 18 (November 1984): 5–6; Horn to Rocky Mountain Regional Director Lorraine Mintzmyer, June 25, 1985, copy in LBAF; Horn to William Wells, July 23, 1985, copy in LBAF; Court to Thomas Zoesch, August 12, 1985, copy in LBAF; *Rocky Mountain News*, July 15, 1985; *Custer/Little Bighorn Battlefield Advocate* 1 (Winter 1994): 15; *Denver Post*, June 25, 1996. See also Linenthal, *Sacred Ground*, 149–50, 160. Information on the "Blue Ribbon" review panel is also in Mangum, "Confessions," 4. One member of the LBHA succinctly decried what he saw as "an increasing close-mindedness" in the group now seemingly dedicated "to defend[ing] Custer's reputation, come what may. . . . In the end, it must inevitably thwart the Associates' stated goal of seeking the truth about Custer and the battle of the Little

Big Horn. The dispute over books at the Battlefield seems to me merely a symptom of the real malaise—a growing intolerance for opinions contrary to those of our pro-Custer members. . . . Do they, in short, *really* want to *end* the 'Great Custer Controversy'?" Brian W. Dippie to Koury, September 27, 1984, copy in Koury Files.

17. *Rocky Mountain News*, July 15, 1985; *The Battlefield Dispatch* 8 (Fall 1989): 3; *Billings Gazette*, November 24, 1993; *Newsletter, Little Bighorn Associates*, 28 (February 1994): 7; *The Battlefield Dispatch* 13 (Summer 1994): 1; *The Battlefield Dispatch* 13 (Fall 1994): 4; Linenthal, *Sacred Ground*, 157–58 (including quote); *Custer/Little Bighorn Battlefield Advocate* 11 (Spring 2004): 3; Superintendent to Harold Stanton, October 20, 1993, Koury Files. The land holdings of the CBPC are delineated on a map titled "Little Bighorn Battlefield National Monument and Custer Battlefield Preservation Committee Land Status as of January 15, 2002" (Hardin, Mont.: Custer Battlefield Preservation Commission, 2002). (As of 2005, Superintendent Darrell Cook continued to explore possible boundary expansion through partnering and land exchange with the Crow Tribe.)

18. NPS TIC 381 D43, "Superintendent's Annual Narrative Report, Fiscal Year 1998"; Friends of the Little Bighorn Battlefield Web site, http://www.friends littlebighorn.com; Doerner, "So That the Place Might Be Remembered," 11; *The Battlefield Dispatch* 19 (Spring 2000): 5; NPS TIC 381 D48, "Superintendent's Annual Narrative Report, Fiscal Year 2001"; *LBHA Newsletter* 35 (April 2001): 6; *The Battlefield Dispatch* 21 (Winter 2002): 5; *Friends of the Little Bighorn Battlefield* 4 (March 2004): 4; Bob Reece, e-mail message to author, August 21, 2004.

10. Indian Memorial

1. McCleary, "Stone Cairn Markers"; Doerner, "So That the Place Might Be Remembered," 6–10. The letter from Mrs. Beaverheart is quoted in Rickey, *History of Custer Battlefield*, 141. It is reproduced in *Peace through Unity*, a brochure privately published by the National Park Foundation in 2000 on behalf of the Indian Memorial Fund national campaign.

2. Linenthal, *Sacred Ground*, 134. The issue of remembrance and Indian history and the creation of a memorial landscape at the park up to and including the development of the Indian Memorial there is discussed in Horton, "Indian Lands, American Landscapes," chapter 4, "Remembering Little Bighorn."

3. Data regarding the 1970s proposals for an Indian memorial, as well as those suggesting a park name change, including quotes, are in Linenthal, *Sacred Ground*, 158–59. See also memorandum from Harris, December 12, 1971, qtd. in ibid., 146; memorandum from Historian David L. Clary, February 9, 1972, and Robert M. Utley, Acting Director, Office of Archeology and Historic Preservation, February 10, 1972, cited in ibid., 166.

4. *Billings Gazette*, October 14, 1972; *Hardin Tribune-Herald*, October 19, 1972; *Los Angeles Times*, July 4, 1988. A detailed account of the events of June 25, 1988, appears in Ditmanson's memorandum to the Regional Director, Rocky

Mountain Region, July 8, 1988, but see also Memorandum, Regional Director, Rocky Mountain Region, to Director, NPS, July 29, 1988. NPS director William Penn Mott commended the superintendent and his staff for defusing the situation "by their balanced non-judgmental responses to both Indian and non-Indian concerns." Memorandum, Mott to Regional Director, Rocky Mountain Region, August 25, 1988. Copies of correspondence provided by Dennis L. Ditmanson. See also Means, *Where White Men Fear to Tread*, 491.

5. Superintendent Ditmanson wrote that the AIM plaque was placed in the visitor center museum to be viewed as a "temporary symbol of our intent to develop a memorial that will represent the shared perspectives of the tribes involved in the battle. It also [serves] to represent certain contemporary native American attitudes about the National Monument." Qtd. in Linenthal, *Sacred Ground*, 161. Chauncey Whitright, a Sioux from the Fort Peck Reservation in Montana, acknowledged that "the whole purpose behind the plaque was to make sure we'd get a monument there." *Rocky Mountain News*, September 8, 1988. For documents outlining the course toward an Indian Memorial in the aftermath of the 1988 plaque installation, see Memorandum, Director to Regional Director, Rocky Mountain Region, August 26, 1988, "Indian Memorial, Custer Battlefield National Monument"; Memorandum, Ditmanson to Regional Director, Rocky Mountain Region, September 27, 1988, "Indian Memorial for Custer Battlefield"; Memorandum, Regional Director, Rocky Mountain Region, to Director, October 3, 1988, "Custer Plaque"; and Memorandum, Associate Regional Director, Planning and Resource Preservation, Rocky Mountain Region, to Superintendent, Custer Battlefield National Monument, "Task Directive to address a Native American Memorial," copies provided by Dennis L. Ditmanson.

6. Linenthal, *Sacred Ground*, 159–61; NPS TIC 381 D7-D, "Statement for Management, Custer Battlefield National Monument," December 1, 1990, 21; *The Battlefield Dispatch* 9 (Fall 1990): 2; texts of House Resolutions 847 and 848, February 6, 1991, in LBAF; *Billings Gazette*, June 19, 1991; *Denver Post*, July 14, 1991; *Rocky Mountain News*, July 26, 1991; *Billings Gazette*, July 26, 1991; *Denver Post*, July 26, 1991; *Lakota Times*, September 4, 1991; *Big Horn County News*, October 30, 1991; *Billings Gazette*, November 24, 1991; *Denver Post*, November 28, 1991; *Billings Gazette*, December 11, 1991; *LBHA Newsletter* 26 (February 1992): 3–4. Other considered locations were on the ridge near the army monument, a ridge at the south end of the national cemetery, and on Greasy Grass Ridge, west of the park road and overlooking the battlefield as well as the site of the Indian village. *Information Brochure for a Native American Memorial at Custer Battlefield National Monument* (1988), copy in LBAF; *LBHA Newsletter* 28 (December 1994): 6. Possible siting of the memorial on the battle ridge near the cavalry monument drew concern from battle students. See, e.g., *LBHA Newsletter* 24 (February 1995): 4. For hearings, see U.S. Congress, Senate, Select Committee on Indian Affairs United States Senate, *Hearing on Wounded Knee Memorial*, 12–14; U.S. Congress,

Senate, Subcommittee on Public Lands, National Parks and Forests of the Committee on Energy and National Resources, *To Authorize the Establishment of a Memorial*. For the act, see Public Law 102-201, in *United States Statutes at Large*, 105, Part 2, 1631–33. Other pertinent 1991 House bills were House Resolution 847 and House Resolution 770, 102nd Congress. The original Poor Bear–Two Moons 1989 statement read, "If this memorial is to serve its total purpose, it must not only be a tribute to the dead; it must contain a message for the living. We strongly suggest to you that 'Power through Unity' would serve us well." Available online at http://www.usd.edu/iais/bighorn/purpmem.html. Indian Memorial Advisory Committee member Paul A. Hutton later wrote that Poor Bear and Two Moons "spoke of the need for Indian people to stop fighting among themselves and finally unite to accomplish something important—but we changed it [to 'Peace through Unity'] at the urging of Lakota artist and philosopher [and fellow committee member] Arthur Amiotte so it would also appeal to white Americans." "An Indian Memorial for Little Bighorn," *Roundup Magazine* (February 2003): 4. Earlier bills in 1990 (HR Res. 4660 and S Res. 2869) affected only the Indian Memorial. Attitudes for changing the park name were mixed and continued as such. George A. Custer IV believed that his great-uncle had "become the nation's scapegoat for the guilt we feel about our country's failed Indian policies. . . . Have we come to putting the blame on one man?" "Letters," *Montana: The Magazine of Western History* 41 (Autumn 1991): 93. Yet Robert M. Utley recognized the need for change: "The time is now here to sacrifice that bit of history [the park's original name] as a concession to Indian sentiment." *Billings Gazette*, October 26, 1991. (See also "Robert Utley Reflections," http://www.friendslittlebighorn.com/utleyreflections.htm. "These people fought to save what they believed was theirs," remarked Senator Conrad Burns (Rep.-Mont.). "They did what any of us would have done to save and protect our own families and homeland." *Billings Gazette*, December 11, 1991. See also Utley's statement supporting House Resolution 4660, in U.S. Congress, House, Committee on Interior and Insular Affairs, *Hearing before the Subcommittee on National Parks and Public Lands*, 55–56; and Utley's testimony of April 23, 1991, before the Subcommittee on National Parks and Public Lands, House Committee on Interior and Insular Affairs, on House Resolution 847, House Resolution 848, and House Resolution 770, pertaining to the proposed Indian Memorial, copy in LBAF.

7. Public Law 102-201, in *United States Statutes at Large*, 105, Part 2, 1631–33.

8. U.S. Department of the Interior, National Park Service, *Management Policies, 1988*, 5:6, 5:11, 9:17. Current National Park Service management policies elaborate considerably on those prevailing in 1991. See U.S. Department of the Interior, National Park Service, *Management Policies, 2001*. The ground at the favored site had been previously disturbed by the establishment there of borrow pits during the period of War Department administration. A black-and-white aerial

photograph taken in 1959 shows the preexisting disturbed condition of the selected terrain. See photo number 30003-179-182L, Aerial Photo Drawer 12, White Swan Memorial Library.

9. *Billings Gazette*, November 10, 1992; *LBHA Newsletter* 28 (October 1994): 4; "Charter, Little Bighorn Battlefield National Monument Advisory Committee," December 18, 1992, copy in LBAF. Members of the Little Bighorn Battlefield National Monument Advisory Committee were Leonard Bruguier (chairperson), Nakota, director of the Institute of American Indian Studies, University of South Dakota, Vermillion; Arthur Amiotte, Lakota artist and adjunct professor of Native studies and art, Brandon University, Manitoba; Paul Andrew Hutton, executive director of the Western History Association and associate professor of history, University of New Mexico, Albuquerque; A. Gay Kingman, National Indian Gaming Commission, Washington, D.C.; Donald Malnourie, North Dakota, descendent of White Shield, an Arikara scout in 1876; Linda L. Pease, the Heard Museum, Phoenix, Arizona, vocational education director and art instructor, and descendant of White Man Runs Him, a Crow scout in 1876; Richard K. Pohl, associate professor of landscape architecture, Montana State University, Bozeman; Kevin Red Star, Crow Indian artist and rancher, Lodge Grass, Montana; Carol Redcherries, chief justice of the Northern Cheyenne Appellate Court, Lame Deer, Montana; Dennis Sun Rhodes, Northern Arapaho architect, St. Paul, Minnesota; and Chauncey Whitright, Lakota historian and Indian rights advocate, Wolf Point, Montana. Robert Burley, architect, of Waitsfield, Vermont, was selected as jury advisor to the committee. http://www.usd.edu/iais/bighorn/advisory.html; *The Battlefield Dispatch* 13 (Summer 1994): 5. Quotation is from Pease-Bell, "Indian Memorial," http://www.billingsnews .com/story?storyid=5271&issue=153.

10. *Call for Entries* brochure of the Little Bighorn National Monument Advisory Committee, ca. May 1996; *National Design Competition for an Indian Memorial*, program dated July 17, 1996, copy in the author's files; Bruguier to competitors, October 23, 1996, with accompanying "Contestant Questions and Responses," copy in the author's files; NPS TIC 381 D39, "Superintendent's Annual Report for 1997," undated. Some Oglala Lakotas objected that locating the monument on land lower than the army monument "makes it appear that the soldiers are still more important than our fallen warriors." Despite charter-mandated advertised advisory committee meetings, others claimed, "we were never notified or asked for our opinion and input . . . until eight months after the design was approved." *Indian Country Today*, July 27–August 3, 1998. Other Indians criticized the design competition as not being appropriately advertised to attract more Indian artists. *LBHA Newsletter* 27 (April 1998): 3. In response, committee member Chauncey Whitright wrote, "When the committee announced the design competition, we had to extend the deadline solely to ensure all of Indian country was aware of that process, too. . . . We had placed our meeting dates and places in the *Federal Register*, but as usual, no representatives would show up at these meetings even after giving these tribes three months notice." *Indian Country Today*, August 31–September 7, 1998. See also

Intermountain Region Indian Liaison Officer Barbara Sutteer (Booher), e-mail message to Project Manager Rudolph B. Lobato, February 24, 2003, 10:56 a.m., Rudolph B. Lobato Files, NPS Intermountain Regional Office, Lakewood, Colorado (hereafter cited as Lobato Files).

11. Public Law 102-201, in *United States Statutes at Large*, 105, Part 2, 1633; NPS TIC 381 D43, "Superintendent's Annual Narrative Report, Fiscal Year 1998"; NPS TIC 381 D47, "Superintendent's Annual Narrative Report, Fiscal Year 2000"; *LBHA Newsletter* 34 (March 2000): (including quote): 6. See also "Cost Summary of Preliminary Design Alternatives, 1998," copy in Office of Facility Management, Design, and Engineering, Intermountain Region, Denver Support Office, NPS.

12. NPS TIC 381 D47, "Superintendent's Annual Narrative Report, Fiscal Year 2000"; *The Battlefield Dispatch* 19 (Spring 2000): 5; *The Battlefield Dispatch* 19 (Fall 2000): 1; *The Battlefield Dispatch* 20 (Spring 2001): 12; Briefing Paper for Senators Max Baucus and Conrad Burns prepared by Superintendent Neil Mangum, February 2001 (first quote), copy in LBAF; *Sioux Falls Argus Leader*, June 26, 2001 (second quote); NPS TIC 381 D48, "Superintendent's Annual Narrative Report—Fiscal Year 2001"; Representative Denny Rehberg (Rep.-Mont.), press release, http://www.house.gov/rehberg/press/101201.htm; *Indian Country*, October 22, 2001; Mangum, "Confessions," 10; Hutton, "An Indian Memorial," 5.

13. *The Battlefield Dispatch* 21 (Winter 2002): 5; *The Battlefield Dispatch* 19 (Fall 2000): 1; NPS, press releases, October 3, 2002, and January 29, 2003; Kitty Deernose, e-mail message to Neil Mangum et al., April 12, 2002; Edward Tafoya, e-mail message to Violet Hugs, et al., May 8, 2002; Tafoya, e-mail message to Mangum, et al., May 8, 2002, enclosing revised statement of work for Spirit Warriors sculpture; Lobato, e-mail message to Tafoya, May 8, 2002; "Who's Sister Wolf?" http://www.sisterwolf.com/resume/sisterwolf.html; Lobato, e-mail message to Tafoya, et al., July 23, 2002; Tafoya, e-mail message to Lobato, et al., August 14, 2002, all in Lobato Files. During construction of a traffic island directly south of the army monument to accommodate Indian Memorial visitors, workers uncovered human bone fragments, wood, and nails from the 1888 reburials from the cemetery at Fort Phil Kearny, Wyoming, later removed to the national cemetery in the early 1930s. The remains were later reburied in the national cemetery. *LBHA Newsletter* 36 (September 2002): 2.

14. John R. Collins, e-mail message to Lobato, September 16, 2002; Memorandum, James Holloway, Roybal Corporation, to Craig Feldman, Roybal Corporation, June 24, 2002; Collins, e-mail message to Lobato, October 2, 2002; Tafoya to CCM, Inc., October 28, 2002; Collins, e-mail message to Lobato, November 21, 2002; Tafoya to CCM, Inc., December 10, 2002; Lobato, e-mail message to Tafoya, January 14, 2003; Darrell Cook, e-mail message to Lobato, February 24, 2003; Lobato, e-mail message to Holloway et al., February 26, 2003; Collins to Dwain Salveson, CCM, Inc., March 3, 2003; Holloway, e-mail message to Feldman, March 21, 2003; Lobato, e-mail message to Michael Snyder, April 14, 2003; Lobato, e-mail

message to George Horse Capture, April 16, 2003; Lobato, e-mail message to Bradley Acre et al., April 21, 2003; Lobato, e-mail message to Tafoya, April 25, 2003; Collins to Lobato, May 21, 2003; Cook, e-mail message to Lobato, July 17, 2003, all in Lobato Files. Early in 2004 Superintendent Cook projected the remaining work for the memorial—a sidewalk accessing the north side of the memorial for improved photographic opportunities, the development of permanent interpretive panels for the interior walls, development of wayside exhibits, and an interpretive guidebook and video. *Friends of the Little Bighorn Battlefield* 4 (March 2004): 3. For detailed progress comments variously throughout construction, see "Little Bighorn Battlefield National Monument Indian Memorial Title II 50% Contract Document Review"; Lobato to Thomas Watson, Roybal Corporation, April 9, 1999, relaying "Review Comments for 95% Construction Document Submittal"; Lobato to Watson, July 9, 1999, relaying "Final Review Comments for June 18th 95/100% Contract Document Submittal"; and "Scope of Work," December 2001, Intermountain Region, Denver Support Office, copies in Office of Facility Management, Design, and Engineering, Intermountain Region, Denver Support Office, National Park Service; commentary on prededication planning provided by Superintendent Darrell Cook, e-mail message to the author, March 2, 2005. On the evening of June 24, 2005, the battlefield hosted a recognition ceremony for approximately two hundred people who had contributed through the years to the success of the Indian Memorial. Ibid.

15. *Friends of the Little Bighorn Battlefield* 3 (September 2003): 1–2; *Billings Gazette*, June 26, 1976; *The Battlefield Dispatch* 22 (Summer 2003): 1, 15; *LBHA Newsletter* 37 (August 2003): 4; Resolution No. DOI-195 (2003): "Resolution of the Northern Cheyenne Tribal Council in Support of the Activities and Events for the Commemoration of the Indian Memorial," June 3, 2003, copy in author's files. Campbell's quote is from "Campbell Hails Dedication of Indian Memorial at Bighorn Battlefield," http://indian.senate.gov/108press/062503.htm. A commemorative booklet outlining the events culminating in the authorization and creation of the Indian Memorial is *Indian Memorial Dedication, "Peace through Unity," June 25, 2003*. Among other things, the booklet contains the names of those individuals from the various tribes who were known to have died during the battle, June 25–26, 1876. The erection of markers for individual warriors carried on a tradition rooted in the placement of Lame White Man's marker in 1956 and renewed by Doerner in the 1990s. Details of the return of the AIM plaque were provided in Cook, e-mail message to the author, March 2, 2005.

16. *Casper Star-Tribune*, June 23, 2003; *Billings Gazette*, June 26, 2003; *Philadelphia Inquirer*, June 25, 2003; http://www.newsday.com/news/nationworld/nation/ny-usind263346052jun26,0,3879362.

17. *Casper Star-Tribune*, June 23, 2003; *Billings Gazette*, June 23, 2003; *Philadelphia Inquirer*, June 25, 2003; *Custer/Little Bighorn Battlefield Advocate*, 10 (Summer 2003): 1.

18. Wayne Michael Sarf, "A Sense of Relief?" in ibid., 9.

19. "An Indian Memorial for Little Bighorn," 4; Linenthal, "Transformation," 42.

Afterword

1. Linenthal, "OAH Site Visitation, May 24–25, 1997," submitted June 16, 1997, copy provided by William P. Wells.

Appendix 1: Legislation

1. Custer Battlefield National Cemetery was added to this list by Executive Order 8428, effective July 1, 1940.

Bibliography

Manuscript Collections

Denver Public Library, Denver, Colorado.
  Western History Department, Robert Ellison Collection.
Greene, Jerome A., Files. Arvada, Colorado.
Koury, Michael J., Files. Johnstown, Colorado.
National Park Service, Denver Service Center, Lakewood, Colorado.
National Park Service, Intermountain Regional Office, Lakewood, Colorado.
  Intermountain Regional Office Library
  Rudolph B. Lobato Files.
National Park Service, Midwest Archeological Center, Lincoln, Nebraska.
Library of Congress, Washington, D.C.
  Edward S. Godfrey Papers.
Little Bighorn Battlefield National Monument, Crow Agency, Montana.
  Administrative Files.
  Administrative Research Collection. Accession 738.
  Walter M. Camp Collection.
  Elizabeth B. Custer Collection. Microfilm Reels 1–8.
  White Swan Memorial Library.
    Historical Research Files.
Montana Historical Society, Helena, Montana.
Nez Perce National Historical Park, Spalding, Idaho.
Parmly Billings Library, Billings, Montana.
University of Colorado at Boulder Libraries, Boulder, Colorado.
  Western History Collections.
  William Carey Brown Papers.

U.S. Military Academy Library, West Point, New York.
    Manuscripts Collection. Diary of John G. Bourke.

Government Documents

Davenport, Beverly P., comp. *Laws Relating to the National Park Service,
    Supplement VII, 102d and 103d Congresses, January 1991 to December
    1994.* Washington, D.C.: Government Printing Office, 2001.
Sturtevant, William C. *Handbook of North American Indians.* Vol. 13, *Plains,*
    ed. Raymond J. DeMallie. 2 parts. Washington, D.C.: Smithsonian
    Institution, 2001.
Sullivan, Thomas Alan, comp. *Laws Relating to the National Park Service,
    Supplement I, July 1933 through April, 1944.* Washington, D.C.: Gov-
    ernment Printing Office, 1944.
Tolson, Hillary A., comp. *Laws Relating to the National Park Service, Sup-
    plement II, May 1944 to January 1963.* Washington, D.C. Govern-
    ment Printing Office, 1963.
United States Statutes at Large. Washington, D.C.: Government Printing
    Office, 1927, 1929, 1931, 1939, 1992.
U.S. Congress. House. *Custer Battlefield Historical Museum.* 76th Cong.,
    1st sess., July 17, 1939. H. Doc. 1204.
————. *To Redesignate Custer Battlefield National Monument as the Little
    Bighorn National Battlefield Park.* 102d Cong., 1st sess., February 6,
    1991. H. Doc. 847.
U.S. Congress. House. Committee on Interior and Insular Affairs. *Autho-
    rizing the Establishment of a Memorial at Custer Battlefield National
    Monument to Honor the Indians Who Fought in the Battle of the Little
    Bighorn, and for Other Purposes.* 101st Cong., 2 sess., September 17,
    1990. H. Doc. 101-708.
————. *Hearing before the Subcommittee on National Parks and Public Lands.*
    101st Cong., 1st sess., September 4, 1990.
U.S. Congress. Senate. *An Act to Provide for the Erection of a Public Historical
    Museum in the Custer Battlefield National Cemetery, Montana.* Senate
    Bill 28. 76th Cong., 1st sess., 1939.
————. *A Bill to Provide for Building and Furnishing a Building at Custer
    Battle Field National Cemetery for Use as an Office for the Custodian
    and for the Convenience and Comfort of the Public.* S. Rep. 323. 68th
    Cong., 1st sess., 1924.
U.S. Congress. Senate. Select Committee on Indian Affairs. *Hearing on
    Wounded Knee Memorial and Historic Site Little Big Horn National
    Monument Battlefield.* 101st Cong., 2 sess., September 25, 1990.
U.S. Congress. Senate. Committee on Energy and National Resources, Sub-
    committee on Public Lands, National Parks and Forests. *To Authorize*

the Establishment of a Memorial at Custer Battlefield National Monument to Honor the Indians Who Fought in the Battle of the Little Big Horn, and to Redesignate the Site as the Little Bighorn Battlefield National Monument. HR Res. 848. 1991. 102nd Cong., 1 sess.

U.S. Department of the Interior. *Report of the Secretary of the Interior, 1933.* Washington, D.C.: Government Printing Office, 1933.

U.S. Department of the Interior. *Report of the Secretary of the Interior, 1940.* Washington, D.C.: Government Printing Office, 1940.

U.S. Department of the Interior. Bureau of Indian Affairs. *Executive Orders Relating to Indian Reserves Issued Prior to April 1, 1890.* Washington, D.C.: Government Printing Office, ca. 1890.

U.S. Department of the Interior. National Park Service. *Environmental Assessment, Deep Ravine and Keogh/Crazy Horse Trails, Little Bighorn Battlefield National Monument.* N.p.: National Park Service, 1999.

———. *Field Report, Little Bighorn Battlefield National Monument.* (Alternative Transportation System). N.p.: National Park Service, 2001.

———. *Interim Interpretive Plan, Custer Battlefield National Monument.* Denver, Colo.: National Park Service, 1976.

———. *Interpretive Prospectus, Little Bighorn Battlefield National Monument, Montana,* by Paul Lee. Harpers Ferry Center, W. Va.: National Park Service, 1997.

———. *Little Bighorn Battlefield National Monument 1999 Annual Performance Report, October 1, 1998–September 30, 1999.* N.p.: National Park Service, 2000.

———. "Little Bighorn Battlefield NM 1998 Visitor Survey Card Data Report." N.p.: National Park Service, 1999.

———. *Management Policies, U.S. Department of the Interior, National Park Service.* 1988, 2001. Washington, D.C.:, National Park Service, 1988, 2001.

———. *The Master Plan, Custer Battlefield National Cemetery.* N.p.: National Park Service, 1942.

———. *National Park Service Administrative Manual, Organization Volume.* Washington, D.C.: National Park Service, 1960.

———. *National Park Service Information Handbook.* Washington, D.C.: Government Printing Office, 1957.

———. *Planning Process NPS-2, General Management Plan.* Release No. 3, September 1982. Washington, D.C.: National Park Service, 1982.

U.S. War Department. *Annual Reports of the War Department for the Fiscal Year Ended June 30, 1903.* Washington, D.C.: Government Printing Office, 1903.

———. *Index of General Orders and Circulars, Adjutant General's Office, 1879.* Washington, D.C.: Government Printing Office, 1880.

———. *Index of General Orders and Circulars, Adjutant General's Office, 1886.* Washington, D.C.: Government Printing Office, 1887.

———. *Military Reservations, National Military Parks, and National Cemeteries. Title and Jurisdiction.* Washington, D.C.: Government Printing Office, 1910. Revised ed. 1916.

———. *National Cemetery Regulations.* Washington, D.C.: Government Printing Office, 1931.

———. *Report of the Secretary of War, 1879.* Washington, D.C.: Government Printing Office, 1879.

———. *Report of the Secretary of War, 1884.* Washington, D.C.: Government Printing Office, 1884.

———. *Report of the Secretary of War, 1885.* Washington, D.C.: Government Printing Office, 1885.

———. *Report of the Secretary of War, 1887.* Washington, D.C.: Government Printing Office, 1887.

———. *Report of the Secretary of War, 1889.* Washington, D.C.: Government Printing Office, 1889.

———. *Report of the Secretary of War, 1890.* Washington, D.C.: Government Printing Office, 1890.

———. *Report of the Secretary of War, 1891.* Washington, D.C.: Government Printing Office, 1891.

———. *Report of the Secretary of War, 1892.* Washington, D.C.: Government Printing Office, 1892.

———. *Report of the Secretary of War, 1894.* Washington, D.C.: Government Printing Office, 1894.

———. *Report of the Secretary of War, 1895.* Washington, D.C.: Government Printing Office, 1895.

———. *Report of the Secretary of War, 1897.* Washington, D.C.: Government Printing Office, 1897.

———. *Report of the Secretary of War, 1900.* Washington, D.C.: Government Printing Office, 1900.

———. *Reports of Inspection Made in the Summer of 1877 by Generals P. H. Sheridan and W. T. Sherman of Country North of the Union Pacific Railroad.* Washington, D.C.: Government Printing Office, 1878. Reprinted in *Travel Accounts of General William T. Sherman to Spokan Falls, Washington Territory, in the Summers of 1877 and 1883.* Fairfield, Wash.: Ye Galleon Press, 1984.

Published Sources

Abbott, Newton Carl. *Montana in the Making.* Billings, Mont.: Gazette Printing, 1964.

Anderson, Gary Clayton. "Early Dakota Migration and Intertribal Warfare." *Western Historical Quarterly* 11 (January 1980): 18–36.

———. *Kinsmen of Another Kind: Dakota–White Relations in the Upper Mississippi Valley, 1650–1862.* Lincoln: University of Nebraska Press, 1984.

The Army Almanac: A Book of Facts Concerning the United States Army. Harrisburg, Penn.: Stackpole, 1959.

Athearn, Robert. *William Tecumseh Sherman and the Settlement of the West.* Norman: University of Oklahoma Press, 1956.

Barnard, Sandy. "1989 Reno–Benteen Archeological Project." *The Battlefield Dispatch* 8 (Summer 1989): 5.

———. *Digging into Custer's Last Stand.* Terre Haute, Ind.: AST Press, 1986.

Barbour, Barton. *Fort Union and the Upper Missouri Fur Trade.* Norman: University of Oklahoma Press, 2002.

Beck, Warren, and Ynez D. Haase. *Historical Atlas of the American West.* Norman: University of Oklahoma Press, 1989.

Biographical Directory of the American Congress, 1774–1971. Washington, D.C.: Government Printing Office, 1971.

Bock, Jane H., and Carl E. Bock. "Ecology and Evolution in the Great Plains." In *The Evolutionary Ecology of Plants*, ed. Jane H. Bock and Y. B. Linnart, 551–77. Boulder, Colo.: Westview Press, 1989.

Bourke, John G. *Mackenzie's Last Fight with the Cheyennes: A Winter Campaign in Wyoming and Montana.* Governor's Island, N.Y.: Military Service Institution of the United States, 1890.

———. *On the Border with Crook.* New York: Charles Scribner's Sons, 1890.

Boyes, Bill, ed. "Visit to Custer Battlefield." *Little Big Horn Associates Newsletter* 23 (February 1989): 8.

Brown, Dee. *Bury My Heart at Wounded Knee: An Indian History of the American West.* New York: Holt, Rinehart, and Winston, 1970.

———. *Fort Phil Kearny: An American Saga.* New York: G. P. Putnam's Sons, 1962.

Brust, James S. "Fouch Photo May Be the First." *Greasy Grass* 7 (May 1991): 2–10.

———. "Little Big Horn: After-Action Photographs Offer Glimpses into Mysteries." *Greasy Grass* 9 (May 1993): 11–18.

———. "Stanley Morrow's 1879 Photographs of the Little Bighorn Battlefield." *9th Annual Symposium Custer Battlefield Historical and Museum Association, Inc., Held at Hardin, Montana, on June 23, 1995*, 47–78. N.p.: Custer Battlefield Historical and Museum Association, 1996.

Brust, James S., Brian C. Pohanka, and Sandy Barnard. *Where Custer Fell: Photographs of the Little Bighorn Battlefield Then and Now.* Norman: University of Oklahoma Press, 2005.

Burleigh, Mrs. E. R. "Little Big Horn, 1876–1951." *Montana Treasure* 2 (March 1952): 3.

Calloway, Colin G. "Sword Bearer and the 'Crow Outbreak' of 1887." *Montana: The Magazine of Western History* 36 (Autumn 1986): 38–51.

Clifford, Walter. *Captain Walter Clifford: A 7th Infantry Officer's Career in the Indian Wars*, comp. Norman Poitevin. Santa Cruz, Calif., 2002.

Coffman, Edward M. *The Old Army: A Portrait of the American Army in Peacetime, 1784–1898.* New York: Oxford University Press, 1986.

Court, James V. "Battlefield Preservation Complete." *Little Big Horn Associates Newsletter* 36 (February 2002): 6.

Custer National Cemetery. Tucson, Ariz.: Western National Parks Association, 2002.

Day, Arthur E. "Marcus A. Reno Reburied with Honor." *Little Big Horn Associates Newsletter* 2 (January 1968): 3–6.

Day, Carl F. *Tom Custer: Ride to Glory.* Spokane, Wash.: Arthur H. Clark, 2002.

Deep Ravine Trail. Tucson, Ariz.: Western National Parks Association, 2002.

DeLoria, Vine, Jr. *Custer Died for Your Sins: An Indian Manifesto.* New York: Collier-Macmillan, 1969.

Dippie, Brian W. *Custer's Last Stand: The Anatomy of an American Myth.* Lincoln: University of Nebraska Press, 1976.

———. "Of Bullets, Blunders, and Custer Buffs." *Montana: The Magazine of Western History* 41 (Winter 1991): 77–80.

Dixon, David. *Hero of Beecher Island: The Life and Military Career of George A. Forsyth.* Lincoln: University of Nebraska Press, 1994.

Dixon, Joseph Kossuth. *The Vanishing Race: The Last Great Indian Council.* Philadelphia: National American Indian Memorial Association Press, 1913. Revised ed., 1925.

Doerner, John A. "'So That the Place Might Be Remembered': Cheyenne Markers at Little Bighorn Battlefield." *Research Review: The Journal of the Little Big Horn Associates* 14 (Summer 2000): 2–11.

Dollar, Charles M. "Putting the Army on Wheels: The Story of the Twenty-fifth Infantry Bicycle Corps." *Prologue* 17 (Spring 1985): 6–23.

Doyle, Susan Badger. "Indian Perspectives of the Bozeman Trail." *Montana: The Magazine of Western History* 40 (Winter 1990): 56–67.

Dustin, Fred. *The Custer Tragedy: Events Leading Up To and Following the Little Big Horn Campaign of 1876.* Ann Arbor, Mich.: Privately printed, 1939.

———. "Dustin Describes the Re-Burials." In Graham, *Custer Myth*, 368–72.

———. "Some Aftermath of the Little Big Horn Fight in 1876: The Burial of the Dead." In Graham, *Custer Myth*, 362–67.

Entrenchment Trail. Billings, Mont.: Custer Battlefield Historical and Museum Association, 1959.

Ewers, John C. "Intertribal Warfare as the Precursor of Indian-White Warfare on the Northern Great Plains." *Western Historical Quarterly* 6 (October 1975): 397–410.

Fenneman, Neil M. *Physiography of Western United States.* New York: McGraw-Hill, 1931.

Finerty, John F. *War-Path and Bivouac; or The Conquest of the Sioux.* Norman: University of Oklahoma Press, 1961.

Foner, Jack D. *The United States Soldier between Two Wars: Army Life and Reforms, 1865–1898.* New York: Humanities Press, 1970.

Fowler, Loretta. *Arapaho Politics, 1851–1978.* Lincoln: University of Nebraska Press, 1982.

Fox, Richard A., Jr. *Archaeology, History, and Custer's Last Battle: The Little Bighorn Reexamined.* Norman: University of Oklahoma Press, 1993.

Frey, Rodney. *The World of the Crow Indians: As Driftwood Lodges.* Norman: University of Oklahoma Press, 1987.

Frink, Maurice. *Photographer on an Army Mule.* Norman: University of Oklahoma Press, 1965.

Fritz, Henry E. *The Movement for Indian Assimilation, 1860–1890.* Philadelphia: University of Pennsylvania Press, 1963.

Frost, Lawrence A. "Custer Battlefield Monuments." *1st Annual Symposium Custer Battlefield Historical and Museum Association, Inc., Held at Hardin, Montana, on June 26, 1987,* 98–103. N.p.: Custer Battlefield Historical and Museum Association, 1987.

———. *Custer Legends.* Bowling Green, Ohio: Bowling Green University Popular Press, 1981.

———. Foreword to *Garry Owen 1976: Annual of the Little Big Horn Associates,* 6–8. Seattle, Wash.: Little Big Horn Associates, 1977.

Graham, William A., comp. and ed. *The Custer Myth: A Source Book of Custeriana.* Harrisburg, Penn.: Stackpole, 1953.

Gray, John S. *Centennial Campaign: The Sioux War of 1876.* Fort Collins, Colo.: The Old Army Press, 1976.

———. *Custer's Last Campaign: Mitch Bouyer and the Little Bighorn Reconstructed.* Lincoln: University of Nebraska Press, 1991.

Greene, Jerome A. "A Battle among Skirmishes: Little Bighorn in the Great Sioux War." In Rankin, *Legacy,* 83–92.

———, ed. *Battles and Skirmishes of the Great Sioux War, 1876–1877: The Military View.* Norman: University of Oklahoma Press, 1993.

———. *Evidence and the Custer Enigma: A Reconstruction of Indian-Military History.* Kansas City: The Lowell Press, 1973.

———. "The Hayfield Fight: A Reappraisal of a Neglected Action." *Montana: The Magazine of Western History* 22 (October 1972): 30–43.

———, ed. *Lakota and Cheyenne: Indian Views of the Great Sioux War, 1876–1877.* Norman: University of Oklahoma Press, 1994.

———. *Morning Star Dawn: The Powder River Expedition and the Northern Cheyennes, 1876.* Norman: University of Oklahoma Press, 2003.

———. *Nez Perce Summer, 1877: The U.S. Army and the Nee-Mee-Poo Crisis.* Helena: Montana Historical Society Press, 2000.

———. *Slim Buttes, 1876: An Episode of the Great Sioux War.* Norman: University of Oklahoma Press, 1982.

————. *Yellowstone Command: Colonel Nelson A. Miles and the Great Sioux War, 1876-1877*. Norman: University of Oklahoma Press, 2006.

Hafen, LeRoy R., and Ann W. Hafen. *Powder River Campaigns and Sawyers Expedition of 1865*. Glendale, Calif.: Arthur H. Clark, 1961.

Hammer, Kenneth. *Biographies of the 7th Cavalry, June 25th 1876*. Fort Collins, Colo.: Old Army Press, 1972.

————. *Little Big Horn Biographies*. N.p.: Custer Battlefield Historical and Museum Association, 1964.

Hanson, James A. *Little Chief's Gatherings: The Smithsonian Institution's G. K. Warren 1855–1856 Plains Indian Collections and The New York State Library's 1855–1857 Warren Expeditions Journals*. Crawford, Neb.: The Fur Press, 1996.

Hanson, Joseph Mills. *The Conquest of the Missouri: Being the Life and Exploits of Captain Grant Marsh*. New York: Murray Hill, 1946.

Hardorff, Richard G., comp. and ed. *Cheyenne Memories of the Custer Fight: A Sourcebook*. Spokane, Wash.: Arthur H. Clark, 1995.

————. *The Custer Battle Casualties: Burials, Exhumations, and Reinterments*. El Segundo, Calif.: Upton and Sons, 1989.

————. *The Custer Battle Casualties, II: The Dead, the Missing, and a Few Survivors*. El Segundo, Calif.: Upton and Sons, 1999.

————, comp. and ed. *Lakota Recollections of the Custer Fight: New Sources of Indian-Military History*. Spokane, Wash.: Arthur H. Clark, 1991.

Hart, Robert L. "Changing Exhibitry and Sensitivity: The Custer Battlefield Museum." *1st Annual Symposium Custer Battlefield Historical and Museum Association, Inc., Held at Hardin, Montana, on June 26, 1987*, 34–53. N.p.: Custer Battlefield Historical and Museum Association, 1987.

Hassrick, Royal G. *The Sioux: Life and Customs of a Warrior Society*. Norman: University of Oklahoma Press, 1964.

Hatch, Thom. *The Custer Companion: A Comprehensive Guide to the Life of George Armstrong Custer and the Plains Indian Wars*. Mechanicsburg, Penn.: Stackpole, 2000.

Hathaway, Nancy. *Native American Portraits: Photographs from the Collection of Kurt Koegler*. San Francisco: Chronicle Books, 1990.

Hebard, Grace Raymond, and E. A. Brininstool. *The Bozeman Trail*. 2 vols. Cleveland: Arthur H. Clark, 1922.

Hedren, Paul L. *First Scalp for Custer: The Skirmish at Warbonnet Creek, Nebraska, July 17, 1876, with a Short History of the Warbonnet Battlefield*. Glendale, Calif.: Arthur H. Clark, 1980.

————. *Fort Laramie in 1876: Chronicle of a Frontier Post at War*. Lincoln: University of Nebraska Press, 1988.

————. "'Holy Ground': The United States Army Embraces Custer's Battlefield." In Rankin, *Legacy*, 188–206.

————. *Traveler's Guide to the Great Sioux War: The Battlefields, Forts, and Related Sites of America's Greatest Indian War*. Helena: Montana Historical Society Press, 1996.

————. *We Trailed the Sioux: Enlisted Men Speak of Custer Crook, and the Great Sioux War*. Mechanicsburg, Penn.: Stackpole, 2003.

Horton, Tonia Woods. "Indian Lands, American Landscapes: Toward a Genealogy of Place in National Parks." PhD diss., Arizona State University, Tempe, 2003.

Hoxie, Frederick E. *Parading through History: The Making of the Crow Nation in America, 1805–1935*. Cambridge, England: Cambridge University Press, 1995.

Hoyt, Colgate. "'Roughing It Up the Yellowstone to Wonderland': An Account of a Trip through the Yellowstone Valley in 1878." *Montana: The Magazine of Western History* 36 (Spring 1986): 22–35.

Hunt, Charles B. *Natural Regions of the United States and Canada*. San Francisco: W. H. Freeman, 1974.

Hunt, Fred A. "A Purposeful Picnic." *Pacific Monthly* 19 (March 1908): 233–45.

Hutton, Paul Andrew. "An Indian Memorial for Little Bighorn." *Roundup Magazine* 10 (February 2003): 4–5.

————. *Phil Sheridan and His Army*. Lincoln: University of Nebraska Press, 1985.

Hyde, George E. *A Life of George Bent Written from His Letters*. Ed. Savoie Lottinville. Norman: University of Oklahoma Press, 1968.

Ingersoll, L. D. *A History of the War Department of the United States*. Washington, D.C.: Francis B. Mohun, 1879.

"It Was Only 75 Years Ago: Custer Anniversary Is Observed." *Life Magazine* 31 (July 9, 1951): 41–44.

Jordan, Robert Paul. "Ghosts on the Little Bighorn." *National Geographic* 170 (December 1986): 787–813.

Josephy, Alvin, Jr. "The Custer Myth." *Life Magazine* 71 (July 2, 1971): 48–59.

Kappler, Charles J., comp., ed. *Indian Affairs: Laws and Treaties*. 2 vols. Washington, D.C.: Government Printing Office, 1904.

King, Charles. *Campaigning with Crook*. Norman: University of Oklahoma Press, 1964.

King, W. Kent. "Tombstones for Bluecoats: Misplaced Markers on Custer's Battlefield." *Research Review* 13 (September 1979): 3–16, 17–18.

Kinsley, Nora B. "Custer Memorial Highway." *American Review of Reviews* 64 (August 1921): 183–86.

Koury, Michael J. "A Bit of Custer Battlefield Historical and Museum Association History." *8th Annual Symposium Custer Battlefield Historical and Museum Association, Inc., Held at Hardin, Montana, on June*

24, 1994, 97–106. N.p.: Custer Battlefield Historical and Museum Association, 1994.

———, ed. *Custer Centennial Observance, 1976.* Fort Collins, Colo.: Old Army Press, 1978.

———. *To Consecrate This Ground: The Custer Battlefield, 1876–1976.* Old Army Press, 1978.

Kuhlman, Charles. *Legend into History: The Custer Mystery.* Harrisburg, Penn.: Stackpole, 1951.

Larson, Robert W. *Red Cloud: Warrior-Statesman of the Lakota Sioux.* Norman: University of Oklahoma Press, 1997.

Leckie, Shirley A. *Elizabeth Bacon Custer and the Making of a Myth.* Norman: University of Oklahoma Press, 1993.

Linenthal, Edward T. "From Shrine to Historic Site." In Rankin, *Legacy*, 306–19.

———. *Sacred Ground: Americans and Their Battlefields.* Urbana: University of Illinois Press, 1991.

———. "Transformation of Little Bighorn Battlefield National Monument." *Greasy Grass* 18 (May 2002): 38–42.

Little Bighorn Battlefield National Monument, Summer 2000. Tucson, Ariz.: Southwest Parks and Monuments Association, 2000.

Lowie, Robert. *The Crow Indians.* New York: Holt, Rinehart, and Winston, 1956.

Luce, Edward S. "Custer Battlefield Museum Dedicated." *The Westerners Brand Book, Chicago* 9 (August 1952): 41–42.

Mangum, Neil C. *Battle of the Rosebud: Prelude to the Little Bighorn.* El Segundo, Calif.: Upton and Sons, 1987.

———. "Confessions of a Park Ranger." *Friends of the Little Bighorn Battlefield* 4 (August 2004): 1, 4–5, 9–10.

———. "Popular Reaction to Custer: The Public's Perception." *1st Annual Symposium Custer Battlefield Historical and Museum Association, Inc., Held at Hardin, Montana, on June 26, 1987*, 54–61. N.p.: Custer Battlefield Historical and Museum Association, 1987.

———, comp. *Register of the Custer Battlefield National Monument Photograph Collection.* N.p.: Custer Battlefield Historical and Museum Association, 1984.

Magnusson, Daniel O. *Peter Thompson's Narrative of the Little Bighorn Campaign of 1876: A Critical Analysis of an Eyewitness Account of the Custer Debacle.* Glendale, Calif.: Arthur H. Clark, 1974.

Marquis, Thomas B. *Memoirs of a White Crow Indian (Thomas H. LeForge).* New York: Century, 1928.

———. *Two Days after the Custer Battle: A Clashing of Blue and Red as Viewed by a Gibbon Soldier.* Hardin, Mont.: Privately published, 1935.

———. *A Warrior Who Fought Custer.* Minneapolis: Midwest, 1931.

————. *Which Indian Killed Custer? Custer Soldiers Not Buried.* Hardin, Mont.: Privately published, 1933.

McChristian, Douglas C. "Burying the Hatchet." *Montana: The Magazine of Western History* 46 (Summer 1996): 50–65. Reprinted in *Greasy Grass* 18 (May 2002): 2–18.

McCleary, Timothy P. "Stone Cairn Markers on the Little Bighorn Battlefield." *Research Review: The Journal of the Little Big Horn Associates* 12 (Summer 1998): 2–7.

McDermott, John D. "Remarks on the 110th Anniversary of the Custer Fight." Advisory Council on Historic Preservation, June 25, 1986.

McGinnis, Anthony. *Counting Coup and Cutting Horses: Intertribal Warfare on the Northern Plains, 1738–1889.* Evergreen, Colo.: Cordillera Press, 1990.

Means, Russell. *Where White Men Fear to Tread: The Autobiography of Russell Means.* New York: St. Martin's Press, 1995.

Michno, Greg. *Lakota Noon: The Indian Narrative of Custer's Defeat.* Missoula, Mont.: Mountain Press, 1997.

Miles, Nelson A. *Personal Recollections and Observations of General Nelson A. Miles.* Chicago: Werner, 1896.

Miller, David Humphreys. *Custer's Fall: The Indian Side of the Story.* New York: Duell, Sloan, and Pearce, 1957.

Mills, Charles K. *Harvest of Barren Regrets: The Army Career of Frederick William Benteen, 1834–1898.* Glendale, Calif.: Arthur H. Clark, 1985.

Milner, Joe E., and Earle R. Forrest. *California Joe, Noted Scout and Indian Fighter with an Authentic Account of Custer's Last Fight.* Caldwell, Idaho: Caxton Printers, 1935.

Mitchell, Lynn Marie. "Archival Reorganization at Little Bighorn Battlefield." *CRM Online* 22, no. 2 (1999): 29–33.

Moore, John H. *The Cheyenne Nation: A Social and Demographic History.* Lincoln: University of Nebraska Press, 1987.

Moss, James A. "Military Cycling in the Rocky Mountains." *Spalding's Athletic Library* 6 (February 1898): 7–39.

Murtagh, William J. *Keeping Time: The History and Theory of Preservation in America.* New York: John Wiley, 1997.

Nichols, Ronald H. "Capt. Owen J. Sweet Reports on Marble Markers at Battlefield." *Greasy Grass* 19 (May 2003): 31–35.

————. "Custer Battlefield Historical and Museum Association Marks Its 50th Year." *Greasy Grass* 19 (May 2003): 2–11.

————. *In Custer's Shadow: Major Marcus Reno.* Fort Collins, Colo.: Old Army Press, 1999.

————, ed. *Reno Court of Inquiry: Proceedings of a Court of Inquiry in the Case of Major Marcus A. Reno Concerning His Conduct at the Battle of the Little Big Horn on June 25–26, 1876.* Crow Agency, Mont.: Custer Battlefield Historical and Museum Association, 1992.

O'Keane, Josephine. "The Band Played Garryowen." *Villager* (November 1951): 21–22, 43–44.

Page, Frank E. "Where Custer Fell." *Outdoor Life* 8 (December 1901): 6–9.

Parle, John J. "History Revisited: The 1984–85 Custer Battlefield 'Digs.'" *Little Big Horn Associates Newsletter* 22 (February 1988): 5–7.

Paul, R. Eli. *Autobiography of Red Cloud, War Leader of the Oglalas*. Helena: Montana Historical Society Press, 1967.

Peace through Unity: A Campaign for the Indian Memorial at Little Bighorn Battlefield National Monument. N.p.: National Park Foundation, 2000.

Pease-Bell, Linda. "Indian Memorial Can Bring Cultures Together." *The Billings Outpost*, September 24, 2003.

Plummer, William. "General Custer Loses at Little Big Horn Again as an Indian Activist Becomes Keeper of His Legend." *People* 33 (February 12, 1990): 93–94.

Powell, Peter J. *People of the Sacred Mountain: A History of the Northern Cheyenne Chiefs and Warrior Societies, 1830–1979, with an Epilogue, 1969–1974*. 2 vols. San Francisco: Harper and Row, 1981.

Rankin, Charles E., ed. *Legacy: New Perspectives on the Battle of the Little Bighorn*. Helena: Montana Historical Society Press, 1996.

Reece, Megan. "The Little Bighorn Battlefield National Monument and an Indian Memorial after 1988." Honors thesis, University of Colorado, Boulder, 2005.

Reno–Benteen Entrenchment Trail. Tucson, Ariz.: Western National Parks Association, 2002.

Rickey, Don, Jr. *Forty Miles a Day on Beans and Hay: The Enlisted Soldier Fighting the Indian Wars*. Norman: University of Oklahoma Press, 1963.

———. *History of Custer Battlefield*. Billings, Mont.: Custer Battlefield Historical and Museum Association, 1967.

———. "Myth to Monument: The Establishment of Custer Battlefield National Monument." *Journal of the West* 9 (April 1968): 203–16.

Robbins, Jim. "A New Look at Custer's Last Stand." *American West* 22 (July/August 1985): 51–57.

Robinson, Charles B., III. *A Good Year to Die: The Story of the Great Sioux War*. New York: Random House, 1995.

Robinson, Harry B. *Guide to the Custer Battlefield Museum*. Helena, Mont.: Naegele Printing, n.d. Reprinted in *Montana: Magazine of History* 2 (July 1952): 11–29.

Roe, Charles Francis. *Custer's Last Battle on the Little Big Horn, Montana Territory, June 25, 1876*. New York: Robert Bruce, 1927.

Rouse, Homer. "Custer Battlefield Up-date." *3rd Annual Symposium Custer Battlefield Historical and Museum Association, Inc., Held at Hardin, Montana, on June 23, 1989*, 87–90. N.p.: Custer Battlefield Historical and Museum Association, 1989.

Schmitzer, Jeanne Cannella. "The Wheels of War." *American History* 34 (April 1999): 26–30, 66–67.

Scott, Douglas D. "Archaeological Perspectives on the Battle of the Little Bighorn: A Retrospective." In Rankin, *Legacy*, 167–88.

———. "Cartridges, Bones and Bullets." *Greasy Grass* 18 (May 2002): 24–30.

———, ed. *Papers on Little Bighorn Battlefield Archeology: The Equipment Dump, Marker 7, and the Reno Crossing.* Reprints in *Anthropology*, vol. 42. Lincoln, Nebr.: J and L Reprint, 1991.

Scott, Douglas D., and Peter Bleed. *A Good Walk around the Boundary: Archeological Inventory of the Dyck and Other Properties Adjacent to Little Bighorn Battlefield National Monument.* Lincoln: Nebraska Association of Professional Archeologists and Nebraska State Historical Society, 1997.

Scott, Douglas D., and Richard A. Fox, Jr. *Archaeological Insights into the Custer Battle: An Assessment of the 1984 Field Season.* Norman: University of Oklahoma Press, 1987.

Scott, Douglas D., Richard A. Fox, Jr., Melissa A. Connor, and Dick Harmon. *Archaeological Perspectives on the Battle of the Little Bighorn.* Norman: University of Oklahoma Press, 1989.

Scott, Douglas D., and P. Willey. "The Custer Battlefield National Cemetery Human Remains Identification Project." *8th Annual Symposium Custer Battlefield Historical and Museum Association, Inc., Held at Hardin, Montana, on June 24, 1994*, 12–29. N.p.: Custer Battlefield Historical and Museum Association, 1994.

Scott, Douglas D., P. Willey, and Melissa A. Connor. *They Died with Custer: Soldiers' Bones from the Battle of the Little Bighorn.* Norman: University of Oklahoma Press, 1998.

Scott, Hugh L. *Some Memories of a Soldier.* New York: Century, 1928.

Sklenar, Larry. *To Hell with Honor: Custer and the Little Bighorn.* Norman: University of Oklahoma Press, 2000.

Smith, Burton M. "Politics and the Crow Indian Land Cessions, 1851–1904." *Montana: The Magazine of Western History* 36 (Autumn 1986): 24–37.

Smith, Sherry L. *Sagebrush Soldier: Private William Earl Smith's View of the Sioux War of 1876.* Norman: University of Oklahoma Press, 1989.

Stewart, Edgar I. "The Custer Battle and Widow's Weeds." *Montana: The Magazine of Western History* 22 (January 1972): 53–59.

———. *Custer's Luck.* Norman: University of Oklahoma Press, 1955.

———, ed. *The March of the Montana Column: A Prelude to the Custer Disaster.* Norman: University of Oklahoma Press, 1961.

Swisher, Ely M. "Controlling Mormon Crickets in Montana, 1936–1941." *Montana: The Magazine of Western History* 35 (Winter 1985): 60–64.

Taunton, Francis B. *Custer's Field: "A Scene of Sickening Ghastly Horror."* London: The Johnson-Taunton Military Press, 1986.

Terrell, John Upton, and George Walton. *Faint the Trumpet Sounds: The Life and Trial of Major Reno.* New York: David McKay, 1966.

Thom, W. T., Jr., G. M. Hall, C. H. Wegemannn, and G. F. Moulton. *Geology of Big Horn County and the Crow Indian Reservation, Montana, with Special Reference to the Water, Coal, Oil, and Gas Resources.* Washington, D.C.: Government Printing Office, 1935.

Thornbury, William D. *Regional Geomorphology of the United States.* New York: John Wiley and Sons, 1965.

Trenholm, Virginia Cole. *The Arapahos, Our People.* Norman: University of Oklahoma Press, 1970.

Unrau, Harlan D., and Willis, G. Frank. *Administrative History: Expansion of the National Park Service in the 1930s.* Denver, Colo.: National Park Service, 1982.

Upton, Richard, comp. and ed. *The Battle of the Little Big Horn and Custer's Last Fight Remembered by Participants at the Tenth Anniversary June 25, 1886, and the Fiftieth Anniversary June 25, 1926.* El Segundo, Calif.: Upton and Sons, 2006.

———. *Fort Custer on the Big Horn, 1877–1898.* Glendale, Calif.: Arthur H. Clark Company, 1973.

Utley, Robert M. "'Cap' Luce—A Superintendent Remembered." *Little Big Horn Associates Newsletter* 25 (February 1996): 6–7.

———. *Custer and Me: A Historian's Memoir.* Norman: University of Oklahoma Press, 2004.

———. *Custer and the Great Controversy: The Origin and Development of a Legend.* Los Angeles: Westernlore Press, 1962.

———. "The Frontier Army: John Ford or Arthur Penn?" In *Indian–White Relations: A Persistent Paradox,* ed. Jane F. Smith and Robert M. Kvasnicka, 133–45. Washington, D.C.: Howard University Press, 1976.

———. *Frontier Regulars: The United States Army and the Indian, 1866–1890.* New York: Macmillan, 1967.

———. *Frontiersmen in Blue: The United States Army and the Indian, 1848–1865.* New York: Macmillan, 1967.

———. *The Indian Frontier of the American West, 1846–1890.* Albuquerque: University of New Mexico Press, 1984.

———. *The Lance and the Shield: The Life and Times of Sitting Bull.* New York: Henry Holt and Company, 1993.

———. "On Digging Up Custer Battlefield." *Montana: The Magazine of Western History* 36 (Spring 1986): 80–82.

Vaughn, J. W. *With Crook at the Rosebud.* Harrisburg: Stackpole, 1956.

Vestal, Stanley, comp. *New Sources of Indian History.* Norman: University of Oklahoma Press, 1934.

————. *Warpath: The True Story of the Fighting Sioux in a Biography of Chief White Bull.* Boston: Houghton Mifflin, 1934.

Wagner, Glendolin Damon. *Old Neutriment.* Boston: Ruth Hill, 1934.

Webster's New Collegiate Dictionary. Springfield, Mass.: G. and C. Merriam, 1973.

Wheeler, Homer W. *The Frontier Trail, or, From Cowboy to Colonel.* Los Angeles: Times-Mirror Press, 1923.

White, Richard. "The Winning of the West: The Expansion of the Western Sioux in the Eighteenth and Nineteenth Centuries." *Journal of American History* 45 (September 1978): 319–43.

White, William H. *Custer, Cavalry, and Crows: The Story of William White as told to Thomas Marquis.* Fort Collins, Colo.: Old Army Press, 1975.

Whiteley, Lee, and Jane Whiteley. *The Playground Trail: The National Park-to-Park Highway: To and Through the National Parks of the West in 1920.* Boulder, Colo.: Privately published, 2003.

Wishart, David J. *The Fur Trade of the American West, 1807–1840: A Geographical Synthesis.* London: Croom Helm, 1979.

Wooster, Robert. *The Military and United States Indian Policy, 1865–1903.* New Haven: Yale University Press, 1988.

Index

Page numbers in italics refer to illustrations.

Aerial exhibitions: at Indian Memorial dedication, 236; at Little Bighorn Battle commemoration, 63, 64, 65
After the Battle (Ralston), 178, 209
AIM. *See* American Indian Movement
Alberts, Edwin C., 207
Alcatraz Island, 151
Allotment issue, 38
American Fur Company, 9
American Indian Movement (AIM), 148, 151, 157, 158, 159, 167, 172, 223, 227, 228, 236, 290n6, 314n5
American Indians: activism, 147–48, 151–52, 157, 159, 182, 208, 219, 228; historical artifacts, in museum exhibits, 206; and interpretation of Little Bighorn, 171–75, 177–80, 183–85, 188, 190, 191, 222, 225, 226, 227; intertribal rivalries and conflict, 7, 9; ledger art, 211; Little Bighorn anniversary celebrations, 34, 55, 62–65, 81, 83, 152–53, 162–63, 182, 189, 191, 223, 224, 228, 309n7; in park living history programs, 178; raising of social consciousness about, 96–97; seasonal rangers, 187; U.S. military conflict with, 9, 10, 11; U.S.

relations with, 9–10; weapons of, 202, 206. *See also* Indian Memorial; *and specific tribes and groups*
American Legion, and correction of Reno's record, 94
American Legion Post No. 8, Hardin, Montana, 54, 60, 65, 81, 84
American Revolution Bicentennial Administration, 152
Amiotte, Arthur, 315n6, 316n9
Amiotte, George, 237
Appleman, Roy E., 90, 91, 176, 198
Apsaalooke Bus Tours, 187
Arapahos, 6, 7, 9, 10, 161, 189; and Indian Memorial dedication ceremonies, 235, 236. *See also* Northern Arapahos; Southern Arapahos
Archeological investigations, 15, 88, *144, 146,* 163, 168, 184, 185, 187, 195, 197–203, 215, 217, 236
Arikaras, 163, 189; and Indian Memorial dedication ceremonies, 235, 236
Army, U.S.: class system of, 21; Indian conflict, 9, 10, 11, 17, 18, 38; officers of, 20–21; Santee Sioux uprising, 10. *See also* Little Bighorn, Battle of the

Army and Navy Journal, 30–31
Arnett, G. Ray, 223
Art, 178, 184, 209; Indian ledger art, 211
"Artists, Authors, and Historians" (seminar), 216
Assiniboins, 6, 191
Aubuchon, John A., 86, 176, 197, 259, *260*
Automated National Catalog Record System, 212

Babbitt, Bruce, 231
Babcock, Tim, 94
Baker, Gerard, 161, 162, 163, 187, 189, 191, 219, 220, 223, 229, 235, *261*, 262
Baker, Robert M., 220
Barry, David F., 34, 62, *108, 110, 120,* 206, 208, 211
Barthelmess, Casey E., *143*
Baskin, Leonard, 179, 215
Battlefield archeology, discipline of, 202. *See also* Archeological investigations
Battlefield Dispatch, The, 216
Bear's Paw battle monument, 150
Bear's Paw Mountain, Battle of the, 52
Bearss, Edwin C., 163, 312n15
Beaver Heart, 63
Beaverheart, Mrs. Thomas, 170, 226, 295n1
Beck, James Burnie, 40
Beckwith, James, 8
Benteen, Frederick W., 13–16, 34, 66, 67, 68, *102,* 206
Berger, Thomas, 96
BIA (Bureau of Indian Affairs), 7, 49, 68, 87, 151, 168
Bighorn Canyon, 7
Bighorn Canyon National Recreation Area, 216, 233
Big Horn Cooperative, 93
Big Horn County, Montana, 4, 68–69, 168
Big Horn County Library, Hardin, Montana, 205

Big Horn County Montana Centennial Committee, 95
Big Horn County Special Events, Inc., 95
Big Horn Mountains, 4, 5
Bighorn River, 5, 8, 263n2
Billings, Montana, Commercial Club, 61, 71
Billings Gazette, 89
Birds, 5, 83–84
"Bivouac of the Dead" (O'Hara), 52
Black Elk, quotation from, on visitor center, 152, 183, 223, 290n6, 312n15
Blackfeet Indians, 8
Black Hills, South Dakota, 7, 11
Black Whetstone, 63
Blummer, Joseph A., 195, 196
Bolsius, Victor A., 58, 259
Bonner, John W., 81
Booher, Barbara (Barbara Sutteer), 157, 158, 159, 161, 167, 187, 191, 219, 229, 232, 234, 235, 237, *261,* 262
Books, articles, movies, and TV programs on Little Bighorn Battle, 53, 78, 81, 96–97, 172, 179, 183, 185, 186, 219
Borgam Construction Company, 89
Bourke, John G., 25, 267n15
Bouyer (Boyer), Minton ("Mitch"), 163, 276n24, 304n12
Bowen, Gladys, 205
Bowen, William C., 205
Bowers, James, 92, 175, 262
Bowman, Dan, *143*
Boy Scouts, 89, 288n14
Bozeman, Montana, 8
Bozeman Avant Courier, 24
Bozeman Trail, 10
Brackett, Albert G., 27, 29
Bravo, Art, 83, *124*
Bray, Robert T., 199
Brennan, Walter, 88, *137*
Brigham Young University, 216
Brininstool, Earl A., 62, 72
Brown, Dee, 96, 219
Bruguier, Leonard, 231, 232, 316n9

Brushing Away Time (film), 187
Buell, George P., 28, 29
Buffalo, 5, 6
"Bugles in the Afternoon" (Haycox), 78
Bureau of Indian Affairs (BIA), 7, 49, 68, 87, 151, 168
Burkhardt, Samuel, Jr., 41, 276n24
Burley, Robert, 316n9
Burns, Ned J., 83, *133*, 174
Bury My Heart at Wounded Knee (Brown), 96, 219, 227
Bush, George H. W., 158, 229
Butler, James, 49, *143*, 194, 196–97, 276n24

Cabot, John B., 82
Caddle, Michael C., 23
Calhoun, James, 23, 24
Calhoun Hill, 15, 168, 200, 202
Call of the Bugle (Ralston), 178, 207, 209, 215
Camp, Walter Mason, 209, 211, 227
Campbell, Ben Nighthorse, 158, 162, 229, 233, 235–36
Campbell, James A., 35, 40, 44
Camp Crittenden, 34
Camp Poplar River, 43, 45
Camp Seventh Cavalry, 25
Canada, Indians' exile in, 18
Canyon Creek, Montana, 49
Carey, Minnie Grace Mechling, 163
Carroll, John M., 222–23, 311n15
Carson, Nan V., 207
Carter, A. G., 62
Cartwright, R. G., 195, 196
Case, J. Bronson, 61, 71
CBHMA. *See* Custer Battlefield Historical and Museum Association
CBPC. *See* Custer Battlefield Preservation Committee
CCM, Inc. (Cain Construction Management, Inc.), 233, 234
Charlie, Vincent, 276n24
Cheyenne River Sioux, 235
Cheyennes, 6, 7, 9, 10; Lakotas' alliance with, 11. *See also* Northern Cheyennes; Southern Cheyennes

Chicago, Burlington and Quincy Railroad, 53
Christopher S. Collins Studio, 233, 234
Civil Rights Movement, 172
Cleveland, Grover, 36, 243
Climate, in battlefield area, 5
Coal deposits, in battlefield vicinity, 5
Cody, William F. ("Buffalo Bill"), 53
Collins, John R., 231
Colorado, University of, plant succession study, 168
Colorado Territory, Sand Creek Massacre in, 9–10
Colter, John, 7
Colter, Mary Jane, 211
Comanche (horse), 176, 195, 216, 296n10
Commercialism, at commemoration of Battle of Little Bighorn, 64
Concordia College, Moorhead, Minnesota, 186
Congress, U.S., 17, 67, 70–73, 79, 158, 164, 229, 233
Connell, Evan, 186
Connelly, Kevin J., 238
Connor, Patrick E., 10
Cook, Darrell J., 193, 221, 233, 234, 235, *261*, 262
Cooke, William W., 20, 23, 24, 182
Cooney, Frank H., 58
Cop Construction Company, 86
Cordwood mound, on Custer Hill, 29, 30, *107*
Cotter, Mrs. R. E., 206
Counting coup, at battle anniversary, 224
Court, James V., 153, 154, 156, 200, 223, *261*, 262; and Custer Battlefield Historical and Museum Association, 217; and Custer Battlefield Preservation Committee, 224
Covered Wagon, The (movie), 70
Craig, Howard A., 81
Crazy Horse, 11, 12
Crittenden, John J., 23, 33, 34, 36, 39, 59, *107*

Crook, George, 11, 17, 25, 206; Battle of Rosebud Creek, 12

Cross, Floyd, *143*

Crow Agency, Montana, 4, 7, 37, 63

Crow Indian Reservation, 4, 36, 37, 38, 68, 69, 179

Crow Indians, 6–10, 34, 35, 42; and battle commemorations and anniversaries, 55, 63, 83, 152, 161, 163, 189, 191; and battle interpretation, 177; at Battle of Rosebud Creek, 12; in battle reenactments, 53, 61; casino, 169; compensation to, 245–46; and Custer Battlefield land acquisition, 155, 156, 162–63; and Custer Battlefield visitor center, 157; and Custer cemetery, 48–49, 50, 54, 59–60, 92; ethnological studies of, 54; and Indian Memorial dedication ceremonies, 235; at Legacy Symposium, 187; and North Shield Ventures proposal, 160; in park interpretive living history programs, 178, 184; at Reno's reburial, 94; in TV program, 88

Crow King, *103*

Crow Rebellion (1887), 38

Crow's Nest, 196

Crow Tribal Industrial Commission, 95

Curley (scout), 22, 51, 182

Curtis, Edward S., 54

Custer, Boston, 23, 40, 41, 47

Custer, Brice C. W., 81, 83, *133*

Custer, Elizabeth B., 21, 31, 55, 61, 62, 65, 67, 70, 71, *130, 131,* 182, 206, 270n25, 280n4; artifacts and manuscripts, collection of, 205, 207, 208, 211

Custer, George A., 11, 12, *102;* Baskin's drawing of, 179; at Battle of Little Bighorn, 13–18; burial and funeral of, 19, 21–24, 31, 266n10; exhibit of dress helmet of, 186; idolization of, 237; and interpretation of Little Bighorn, 171–74, 227

Custer, George A., III, 153, 311n15

Custer, George A., IV, 315n6

Custer, Thomas W., 19, 23, 24, 50

Custer and the Great Controversy (Utley), 96

Custer Association of Great Britain, 224

Custer Battlefield Highway, 55, 62

Custer Battlefield Historical and Museum Association (CBHMA), 154, 185, 186, 197, 201, 203, 214–22, 225; artifacts and collections donated by, 206; book review committee, 219, 220; and centennial of Little Bighorn Battle, 216, 217; college scholarship provided by, 216; constitution and bylaws of, 214, 215, 216; and Indian Memorial, 238; Little Big Horn Associates and, 222; membership of, 214, 215, 216, 219; and museum curator, 210; National Park Service and, 215, 217, 219, 220, 221; publications of, 216; revenues, sales, and funding of projects by, 215–19; symposiums, 218

Custer Battlefield (Luce), 173

Custer Battlefield National Cemetery (later Custer Battlefield National Monument), 4, 34, 35, 36, 74, 75, *111, 113, 114, 118,* 158; area of, 59, 78; authorization for (1879), 30; burials and reburials at, 38–39, 41, 42, 43, 45–52, 58, 59, 62, 163, 199, 202–203; condition of, care for, and improvements to, 33, 38–44, 48, 50, 51, 58, 76–77, 78, 165; costs and appropriations for, 39, 43, 44, 46, 51, 72–73, 249; Establishment Day, 30; fences and gates, 42, 44, 51, 52, 57, 58–59; flagstaff, 51; folders and leaflets, 173; Gettysburg Address, tablet with, 51; guidebooks, 185, 192; historical aides, 172–73; land issues affecting, 59–60; legislation, 241–50; living history programs, 177–78; master plan for, 171; Meigs's advocacy of, 31; Mormon cricket invasion, 59, 279n1; name change, 171, 250; as national cemetery of the fourth class, 30; parking area, 78; roads and sidewalks, 52, 53, 55, 59, 76, 78; rostrum, 58, *116*, 279n1; Sheridan's recommendation for, 26; social and commemorative outings at, 34, 54, 58, 60, 61, *116*; souvenirs and trophies removed from, 27; superintendent of, 42–43, 44; telephone and power lines, 51, 78; unknowns, remains of, 49, 64, 88; vandalism and defacing of, 42, 44, 49–50, 52, 57, *111*, 159. *See also* Custer Battlefield National Monument

Custer Battlefield National Monument (formerly Custer Battlefield National Cemetery; later Little Bighorn Battlefield National Monument): archeological project, 201–203; artifacts, relics, and manuscripts acquired by, 204–210; audiovisual programs, 182; boundary expansion, 154–56, 185, 196; brochure, 185; building program, 86–87; burials and reburials at, 80, 85, 92; bus tours, 155, 162, 183, 185–86; chief of interpretation and visitor services, 185; costs and appropriations for, 80, 82, 90; Custer statue, proposal for, 85; development and improvements to, 79–80, 82, 83, 86–87, 89, 90, 149–50; gates, 87; general management plans, 154–55, 184, 224; guided tours, 181, 182–83; hospital area, 199; houses and apartments, 86–87, *134;* library collection, 207–208; living history programs, 182, 184; master plans, 148–49, 171, 177, 180, 181; Memorial Day observances at, 84–85; name change from, 148, 158, 185, 219, 222, 228, 229, 252, 291n14, 315n6; name change to, 79,

171, 250; on National Register of Historic Places, 94; outreach programs, 186; parking areas, 87, 88, 90, 149; photographic collection, 208; Reno's reburial at, 94–95, *126;* Rickey's research agenda (1956), 197–99; roads and trails, 80, 87, 148–49, 176, 177; staff of, 92; "Statement for Management" (1975), 150, 228; study materials, collection of, 195; superintendents and managers, 147, 259–60; support and interest groups, 213–25; tape recordings, for visitors, 175–76; telephone and power lines, 93. *See also* Little Bighorn Battlefield National Monument

Custer Battlefield Preservation Committee (CBPC), 154, 156, 162, 217, 224, 291n12

Custer Battlefield Publications and Interpretation Review Team, 183

Custer buffs, 181, 221, 311n14

Custer Died for Your Sins: An Indian Manifesto (DeLoria), 97, 227

Custer Hill, 16, 24, 29, 32, 36, 39, 42, *106, 107, 114, 136,* 167, 168, 202, 228

Custer in '76: Walter M. Camp's Notes on the Custer Fight (Hammer), 216

Custer Monumental Association, 30, 65

Custer Monument (Custer Memorial; Seventh Cavalry Monument), 48, 76, 87, *109, 110, 112, 120,* 165, 166, 280n4

Custer Myth, The (Graham), 96, 209

Custer National Cemetery (part of Little Bighorn Battlefield National Monument), 229, 253

Custer's Fall: The Indian Side of the Story (Miller), 96

"Custer's Last Charge" (Whittaker), 270n25

Custer's Last Fight (Hoskins), 178, 209

Custer's Luck (Stewart), 96, 173, 185

Custer's River, 31. *See also* Little Bighorn River
Custer State Park, South Dakota, 71
Custer Tragedy, The (Dustin), 206
Cutschall, Colleen, 233

Dakota Territory, 10
Daly, B. H., 51
Dandy, George D., 39, 44
David F. Barry Collection, 206, 211, 215
Davis, Nelson H., 33
Davis range, 4
Deep Coulee, 15, 49, 199, 203
Deep Ravine, 16, 42, 200, 202, 203
Deep Ravine Trail, 167, 191–92
Deernose, Kitty Belle, 165, 191, 210
Deloria, Vine, Jr., 97
Department of Dakota, 38, 49
D'Ewart, Wesley A., 81
DeWolf, Dr. James M., 23, 24, 40, 41, 66, 68, 204
Dioramas, 178
Dippie, Brian W., 311n14
Ditmanson, Dennis L., 157, 220–21, 228, *261*, 262, 291n13
Dixon, Joseph K., 54
Dixon, Joseph M., 61, 71
Dixon-Wanamaker expedition, 53
D. M. Manning Construction Company, 69
Dodd, Verne A., 204
Doerner, John A., *129*, 165, 185, 187, 191, 236, 262
Dog Friend, 63
Dog's Backbone, *129*, 236
Dommitt, Daniel, 52, 54, 259
Dorman, Isaiah, 173
Drury, Newton B., 80, 174
Dudley, Nathan A. M., 34, 35, 36
Dustin, Fred, 195, 206

Eagle Bronze Foundry, 234
Eastern Montana College of Education, 151, 208, 217
Eastern Museum Laboratory, 178
Ecton, Zales N., 81

Edgerly, Winfield S., 62
Edmunds, R. David, 188
Education, 170; and park support groups, 213
Eisenhower, Dwight D., 86, 286n12
Elizabeth B. Custer Collection, 205, 207, 208, 211
Ellison, Robert S., 68
Elmer, May Custer, 62
Endicott, William C., 243
Entrenchment Trail, 199
Entrenchment Trail (booklet), 177

Fast Walker, 63
Fetterman Massacre (1866), 10, 39; markers for, 39, 41, 46, 277n24
Fifth Cavalry, 25
Fifth Infantry Monument, *117*
Fires, *145*, 168, 200, 204
First Cavalry, 42
Fisk J. Shaffer, firm of, 46
Fleming, Frank M., 27
Flinn, Edward, 47
Foch, Ferdinand, 56
Fool's Crow, Frank, 152
Foote, Stella, 183, 184
Ford, Sam C., 84, 85
Forest Service, U.S., 73
Forsyth, George A., 25
Fort Abercrombie, N.Dak., 43
Fort Abraham Lincoln, N.Dak., 12, 20, 21, 22, 24, 43, 45
Fort Assinniboine, Mont., 52
Fort Bennett, S.Dak., 43
Fort Benton, Mont., 9
Fort C. F. Smith, Mont., 35, 43, 45, *117*, 150, 166, 225
Fort Custer, Mont., 22, 26, 28, 29, 30, 32–35, 37, 41, 47, 48
Fort Ellis, Mont., 12, 41
Fort Harrison, Mont., 80
Fort Keogh, Mont., 34, 35, 51
Fort Laramie, Wyo., 9
Fort Laramie Treaty (1851), 6
Fort Laramie Treaty (1868), 6, 10, 35, 60
Fort Leavenworth, Kans., 22, 24, 193

Fort Logan, Colo., 59
Fort Mackenzie, Wyo., 51, 92
Fort Maginnis, Mont., 41, 43, 45
Fort Manuel, Mont., 7, 8
Fort McKinney, Wyo., 47, 52
Fort Meade, S.Dak., 65
Fort Pease, Mont., 22
Fort Pembina, N.Dak., 43, 45
Fort Phil Kearny, Wyo., 39, 41, 46, 59, *113*
Fort Reno, Wyo., 52
Fort Rice, N.Dak., 43, 45
Fort Shaw, Mont., 12, 43
Fort Sisseton, S.Dak., 41, 42, 45
Fort Totten, N.Dak., 43, 45
Fort Yellowstone, Wyo., 52
Fouch, John H., 24, *105*, 208
Fougera, Katherine, 205
Fourth Cavalry, 65
Fourth of July celebrations, at Little Bighorn Battlefield, 34
Fox, Richard A., Jr., *146*, 200–201
Frazier, Harold, 235
Fred Dustin Collection, 206, 215
French, John H., 39
Friends of the Little Bighorn Battlefield, 221, 225, 232
Frost, Lawrence A., 81
Fruitless Victory (Riley), 178
Fuller, Alvarado M., 32
Furey, John V., 44
Fur trade, 6, 7, 8

Gall, 12, 34, *103*
Garcia, Max R., 89
Garrett, W. H. H., 49, 50, 51, 259
Garry, Thomas A., 86, 91, *137*, 147, 259, *260*
Garryowen area, 62, 149, 155, 169, 185
"Garry Owen" (song), 55, 83
General Order No. 78, Headquarters of the Army, 30
General Order No. 90, Headquarters of the Army, 36
Germany, 163
"Ghost herders" (Crow name for cemetery superintendent), 49

Gibbon, John, 12, 17, 35, 72
Gibson, Francis, 205
Girl Scouts, 288n14
Godfrey, Edward S., 20, 34, 54–55, 61–65, 67, *123*
Goff, Orlando S., 208
Gold, discoveries of, 8, 10, 11
Goldin, Theodore W., 63
Good Day to Die, A (video), 185
Government Performance and Results Act (GPRA), 162
Graham, William A., 62, 96, 209
Grand Army of the Republic, visits to Custer cemetery, 54
Grant, Ulysses S., 10
Grasses, in battlefield vicinity, 5
Greasy Grass, 218
Greasy Grass Ridge, 201–202
Great Plains Physiographic Province, 4
Great Sioux Reservation, 10, 11, 17
Great Sioux War (1876–1877), 11, 17–18, 25, 188, 190; events leading to, 9. *See also* Little Bighorn, Battle of the
Grigsby, Fulton, 259
Grinnell, George Bird, 55, 61, 227
Groethe, Bill, 186, 210
Grover, Andrew N., 43, 44, 46–49, 58, 259, *260*
Guerilla warfare, study of, 193
Guide service, 171
Guy, William L., 179, 227

Hair, William C., 237
Half Yellow Face, 22
Hall, John, 34
Hammer, Kenneth, 207, 216
Hammer File, 207
Hardin, Montana: American Legion Post, 60, 65, 81, 84; Custer monument, 61; High School Memorial Day observance, 60; Lions Club, 65; Little Big Horn Days, 163; Middle School symposiums, 218; outreach programs at schools, 186
Hare, Luther, 62

Harries, George H., 206
Harrington, Grace, 65
Harrington, Henry M., 23, 51, 65,
   197, 276n24
Harris, William A., 81, 83, *133*, 147,
   178, 180, 200, 228, *260*, 262
Hart, Eugene D., 72
Hart, Richard T., *127*, 151, 152, 153,
   228, *261*, 262, 297n12
Hart, William S., 63
Hartung, Robert W., 178
Hartzog, George, 88
Harwood, Ben, 214
Hastings, Minnie, 205
Haycox, Ernest, 78
Hayfield Fight, 43
Haynes, Frank J., 208
Hazleton Tombstone Company, 51
Headstones. *See* Markers and
   headstones
Hebard, Grace Raymond, 61–62
Heier, Vincent A., 238
Heil, Anna, 205
Henry, B. William, Jr., 178, 179, 262,
   296n10
Herb Gruss Construction Company, 86
Here Custer Fell (von Schmidt), 184
Herendeen, George, 22
Hidatsas, 236
High Eagle, Joseph, 81
Highways, 61, 69, 240
Hilger, David, 71
Historians. *See* Park historians
Historic Preservation, Advisory Council
   on, 163
Historic preservation laws and policies,
   U.S., 77, 240
History of Custer Battlefield (Rickey),
   179, 185, 215
Hodel, Donald, 154
Hodgson, Benjamin, 23, 24, 41, 51,
   66, 68, 276n24
Hollow Wood, 63
Holt, Elmer, 65
Hopi Indians, 235
Horse cemetery, 196, 203, 236
Hoskins, Gayle, 178, 209

Hoxie, Frederick E., 188, 189
Hudson's Bay Company, 8
Huffman, Laton, 55
Hutton, Paul Andrew, 188, 189, 191,
   238, 315n6, 316n9

Indian Memorial, 157, 158, 161, 164,
   170, 172, 182, 185, 191, 193, 203,
   219, 221, 227–34, 253–55;
   dedication ceremonies, 234–38;
   significance of, 236–38
Indian Memorial Advisory
   Committee, 230–33, 253–54,
   316n9
*Indian Memorial Dedication, "Peace
   through Unity," June 25, 2003*
   (booklet), 318n15
Indians. *See* American Indians
Indians for Equality, 227
Indian war veterans, 34, 61, 62, 63, 64,
   65
Interior, Department of the, U.S., 60,
   67, 73, 194, 246–48; and Custer
   Battlefield Historical and Museum
   Association, 218; and Indian
   Memorial, 229, 230–31, 233
Interpretative markers, 175, 176,
   181–82
Iraqi War casualty, 235
Iron, Tom, 235

J. C. Boespflug Construction Company,
   81
James Louk Post, Veterans of Foreign
   Wars, 81
Jenkins, Edith M., 206
Jewell, Daniel, 63
Johnson, Lady Bird, 88
Johnson, Lynda Bird, 88
Josephy, Alvin M., Jr., 179

Karl May Museum, Germany, 163
Kellogg, Mark, 23, 41, 47
Kennedy, Roger G., 160, 220
Kent, J. Ford, 42
Keogh, Comanche, and Custer (Luce),
   72, 76, 194

Keogh, Myles, 23, 24, *107*, 176, 195, 197

Kicked in the Bellies, 6

Kills Night, 63

King, Charles, 62

Kingman, A. Gay, 316n9

Kipp, Fremont, 63

Koury, Michael J., 215, 309n7

Kuhlman, Charles, 195, 196, 215

LaFayette, Floyd, 174

Lakotas (Teton Sioux), 6–9, 158, 226; at battle commemorations and anniversaries, 34, 63, 64, 81, 152, 161, 163, 189, 191; and battle interpretations, 172, 175, 180; at Battle of the Little Bighorn, 13–18; Cheyennes' alliance with, 11; and Indian Memorial dedication ceremonies, 235; at Legacy Symposium, 187; portraits of, 209, 210; at Reno's reburial, 94; summer encampment of, 13; visit to Crows (1886), 38

Lalonde Construction Company, 87

Lame Deer, 276n24

Lame White Man, *140*, 167, 170, 191, 227, 295n1

Lame Woman, Tim, 236

Land Preservation Committee, 155

LaPointe, Ernie, 237

Larrabee, Lucille, 89

Last Stand area, 93–94, *112, 135, 136,* 155, 229

Last Stand at Little Bighorn (film), 190

LBHA. *See* Little Big Horn Associates

Leahy, William D., 81

Leavitt, Scott, 67

LeBorgne, Michael D., *261,* 262

Lee, Daniel E., 147, 259, *260*

Lee, Fitzhugh, 63, 64

Lee, Ronald F., 83

LeForge, Thomas H., 22, 35, 266n10

Legacy: New Perspectives on the Battle of the Little Bighorn (Rankin), 187

Lewis, Ralph H., 174

Lewis and Clark Expedition, 7

Life magazine, 179

Limpy, 63

Linenthal, Edward T., 182, 188, 240

Lions Club, Hardin, Montana, 65

Lisa, Manuel, 7

Little Bighorn, Battle of the, 11, 13–18; burial of dead of, 19–29, 33; casualties of, 17; commemorations and anniversaries of, 34–35, 54–55, 61–66, 81, *116, 121, 122, 123, 125, 127, 128, 133,* 151–53, 161–64, 182, 189, 191, 216, 223, 224, 228, 234–38, 280n4, 309n7, 311n15; commemorative medal, *124;* events leading to, 9; interpretation of, 170–93, 194–95, 204, 215, 219, 222, 223, 225, 226, 227, 237; movies, books, articles, and TV programs about, 96–97, 172, 179, 183, 185, 186, 187, 219; reenactments of, 53, 61, 65, 95, 163, 278n27; weapons, 202, 206

Little Big Horn Associates (LBHA), 221–22

Little Bighorn Battlefield National Monument (formerly Custer Battlefield National Monument), 213; area and boundaries, 90–91, 224; artifact and manuscript collections, 204–206, 210–12; audio tours of, 187; audiovisual programs, 190; bus tours, 187, 190; cultural collection, 212; degradation of surrounding property, 91; development, 169, 223, 224, 239; electronic battle map, 190; as endangered historic place, 169, 239–40; fee collection, 161, 164; fences and gates, 164, 165; funding and appropriations for, 38, 39, 43–44, 67, 69, 232, 233; general management plans, 187, 189–90; geomorphology, 4–5; guidebook, 192; handicapped access, 164; Indian Memorial, *128,* 150, 157, 158, 161, 164, 170, 172, 185, 193, 203, 219, 221, 227–34, 253–55;

Little Bighorn Battlefield National
Monument (*continued*)
Indian Memorial dedication
ceremonies, 234–38; Indian
Memorial recognition ceremony,
318n14; interpretive programs, 187,
239; land acquisition, 224; lecture
series, 190; living history programs,
189; location, 4; maintenance and
improvements, 27, 30, 66, 164–65,
239; Meigs's design for, 31; Mission
66, 90, 92, *134*, 176, 178; name
change to, *128*, 158, 187, 219, 229,
252, 291n14, 315n6; national
history collection, 212; and North
Shield Ventures, 159–61; operating
budgets, 161; paths and trails,
167–68, 188, 191–92; resource
management and protection, 166;
roads, 68–69, 70, 190; social and
commemorative outings at, 34–35,
163; staff, 162; support and interest
groups, 213–25. *See also* Custer
Battlefield National Cemetery;
Custer Battlefield National Monument; Custer National Cemetery
Little Big Horn College, 162, 186,
187, 191
Little Big Horn Days, Hardin,
Montana, 163
Little Bighorn Legacy Symposium, 187
Little Bighorn River, 4–5, 7, 8, 31, 34,
77
Little Big Man (Berger), 96
Little Big Man (movie), 172, 179
Little Bird, Geofredo, 237
Little Chetish (Wolf) Mountains, 4
Little Horn River. *See* Little Bighorn
river
Little Moon, 63
Little Wolf, Laban, 185
Living history theme park proposal,
159–61, 223
Livingston Marble and Granite Works,
67
Lobato, Rudolph B., 233
Locke, H. R., *111*

Lodge Grass Creek, 8
Lone Road, 167
Lone Wolf, 63
Long Road, 191
Long Robe, 163
Long Sioux, Clifford, 237
Lord, George E., 20, 23, 51, 197,
276n24
Louis Dog, 65
Loveless, Andrew M., 175, 178, 208,
262
Low Dog, *103*
Luce, Edward S., 75–80, 82, 83, 85,
86, 89, 92, *124, 133, 136, 143*, 147,
171, 172–75, 203, 227, 259, *260*,
284n2; artifacts, manuscripts, and
books collected by, 204–207;
bibliography compiled by, 197; and
Custer Battlefield Historical and
Museum Association, 214; and
Indian liquor consumption, 286n12;
and interpretation of Little Bighorn,
227; and scholarly studies of
battlefield, 194–97
Luce, Evelyn, 76, 173, 175, 196, 197,
205, 214
Luce Ridge, 196
Lujan, Manuel, 158, 231

Maguire, Edward, 23, 35
Malnourie, Donald, 316n9
Mandans, 236
Mangum, Neil C., 153, 154, 161, 162,
163, 169, 177, 184, 190–91, 193,
200, 208, 209, 211, 221, 223, 232,
233, 235, *261*, 262
Mansfield, Mike, 88
Many Bad Horses, Donlin, 237
Markers and headstones, 25, 35,
40–42, 44, 47–51, 57, 59, 68, 76,
108, 111, 113, 129, 140, 143, 150,
163, 166–67, 171–73, 176, 178,
190, 191, 194, 196–200, 225, 236,
276n24, 303n12. *See also*
Interpretative markers
Marquis, Thomas B., 72, 171, 182,
205, 211, 227

Martin, John (Giovanni Martini), 206,
209
Martinez, Daniel, 177
Martz, Judy, 235
Mattes, Merrill J., 81
May, Karl, 163
McChristian, Douglas C., 160, 161,
177, 187, 188, 209, *261*, 262, 310n11
McCleary, Timothy P., 189, 262
McDermott, John D., 163
McDonald, Alexander, 31
McDougall, Thomas M., 13, 34
McGowan, James, 52, 259
McIntire, John, 183
McIntosh, Donald, 23, 24, 40, 41, 68;
diary of, 159, 210
McMurry, George J., 64
Means, Russell, *127, 128,* 151–52,
157, 159, 182, 217, 219, 222, 228,
290n6, 291n13, 309n7; and Indian
Memorial dedication ceremonies,
236
Mechling, Henry W. B., 163, 210
Medicine Crow, Joseph, 95, 165
Medicine Tail Coulee, 15, 90, 199, 202;
commercial development in, 169
Medicine Tail Coulee Ford, 23, 69, 90
Medicine Tail Creek, 69
Meigs, Montgomery C., 31
Memorial Day celebrations, 34, 54,
58, 60, 84–85, *116, 121,* 163, 191
Memorials, miscellaneous, administered
by Interior Department, 248
Michaelis, Otho E., 20
Midwest Archeological Center, 201
Mickle, William O., 259
Miles, Nelson A., 17, 28, 51, 70, 269n21
Military Division of the Missouri, 25,
33
Miller, David Humphreys, 96, 209
Mills, Anson, 206
Minnesota, Santee Sioux uprising in
(1862), 9–10
Mintzmyer, Lorraine, 157, 217
Mission 66 program, 86, 87, 88, 90,
92, *134,* 176, 178, 192, 197
Missouri Fur Company, 8

Monroe County Museum, Michigan,
81
Montague, Harold, 75, 259
Montana, State of, 36, 66, 80
Montana Conservation Corps, 165
Montana Historical Society, 71, 187
Montana national guardsmen: in battle
reenactment, 53; Black Hawk
helicopter flyover, at Indian
Memorial dedication ceremonies,
236; at Reno's reburial, 94
Montana Territory, 9, 10, 11, 31;
centennial celebration, 95
Monuments, 30–33, 37, 38, 45, 48,
50, 52, 57, 67–68, 76, 87, *109, 110,
112, 117, 120,* 150, 165, 166, 280n4
Morgan, J. P., 54
Morris, William E., 63
Morrow, Joseph, 58, 259
Morrow, Stanley J., 30, *106,* 197, 208
Morton, Rogers C. B., 227
Moss, Lloyd C., *143*
Mott, William Penn, 219, 224
Mount Auburn Marble and Granite
Works, 31
Movies, 53, 70, 78, 96, 172, 179, 183,
187
Mural art, 178
Museums, 70–73, 80–83, 88, *131, 132,
133, 138,* 159, 174–76, 178, 185,
193, 205–206, 209–12, 249

National Archives microfilming
project, 207, 208
National Association for
Interpretation, 170
National cemeteries, 74, 248
National Custer Memorial Association,
61
National Custer Memorial Committee,
67
National Geographic, 185
National Historic Preservation Act of
1966, 93
National military cemetery, concept
of, 268n16
National military parks, 74, 247

National monuments, 74, 247–48
National Park Foundation, 232
National parks, 74, 247
National Park Service, 73–79, 83, 86,
    91, 186, 194, 246; archival holdings,
    assessment of, 210–11; centennial
    celebrations of Battle of Little
    Bighorn, 151–53, 309n7;
    conservation laboratory, 208, 209;
    and Custer Battlefield Historical
    and Museum Association, 215, 217,
    219, 220, 221; ethnographic policies
    of, 230; field conferences of,
    195–96; and Friends of the Little
    Bighorn Battlefield, 225; functions
    and activities of, 250–52; general
    management plans of, 154–56;
    handbooks of, 171, 173, 179, 184,
    215; and Indian activism, 151, 228;
    and Indian Memorial, 228–32; and
    interpretation of Little Bighorn,
    170–73, 179–80, 182, 188, 227; and
    Little Bighorn Battlefield support
    groups, 213, 224; Little Bighorn
    Legacy Symposium, 187;
    management policies of, 315n8;
    minimalist policy of, 178; and North
    Shield Ventures, 158–61; and park
    administrative histories, 197; park
    superintendents, 259–60; and
    protection and preservation of
    resources, 166
National Register of Historic Places,
    93–94
National Trust for Historic
    Preservation, 157, 169
Native American Graves Protection
    and Repatriation Act, 161, 189, 211
Naylor, Alex, 58, 259
Neihardt, John G., 62
Nelson, Clifford L., 221
Newsweek magazine, 185
Nez Perces, 6–7
Nez Perce War, 49, 51
Nichols, Ron, 219
Ninth Cavalry, 34
Noisy Walking, 157, 191, 305n14

Northern Arapahos, 7, 9, 163
Northern Cheyennes, 6, 7, 9–13, 158,
    226; at battle commemorations and
    anniversaries, 34, 55, 63, 64, 65,
    152, 161, 163, 189, 191; and battle
    interpretations, 172, 175, 177, 180;
    at Battle of the Little Bighorn,
    15–18; casualty sites, 191; and
    Indian Memorial, 232; and Indian
    Memorial dedication ceremonies,
    235; and Laban Little Wolf exhibit,
    185; at Legacy Symposium, 187; at
    Reno's reburial, 94; reservation, 37;
    Rickey's interviews of, 203–204;
    World Day of Peace, 163
Northern Cheyenne Tribal Council,
    235
Northern Pacific Railroad, 11
Northern Sioux, 10
North Shield Ventures, Inc., 158–61,
    186, 220, 221, 223
Norton, Gayle, 235
Nowland, Henry J., 20, 22, 23
Nye, Elwood L., 143, 195, 196
Nye-Cartwright Ridge, 195, 197

Oglala Sioux, 11, 236; Ranger Corps,
    177
O'Hara, Theodore, 52
Okey, S. Paul, 262
Old Bear, 11
Olson, Harvey A., 71, 259, 260
On the Little Big Horn; or Custer's Last
    Stand (film), 53
Order of the Indian Wars, 225
Oregon Trail, 9, 10
Organization of American Historians
    (OAH), 188, 189
Osage Indians, monument to, 244
Osten, George G., 68, 143, 153, 214
Owen, W. H., 44–47

Parker, Quanah, monument to, 244
Peace Policy, Grant's, 10
"Peace through Unity" (Indian
    Memorial theme), 229, 231, 234,
    235, 315n6

Pearl Harbor anniversary commemoration, 163, 186
Pease, Linda L., 231, 316n9
Penwell, George, 34
Peterson, Harold, 174
Petroleum, in battlefield vicinity, 5, 91
Petty, Warren J., 175, 262
Photography, 24, 30, 34, 54, 55, 186, 208, 210
Piestewa, Lori, 235
Pine (Cheyenne warrior), 63
"Place Where Custer Fell, The" (Fouch), 24, *105*
Plain Feather, Mardell, 184
Plain Shield land claim, 60
Plants, in battlefield vicinity, 5, 84; and fires, 168, 204
Plenty Wing land claim, 60
Plesiosaur, 4
Pohl, Richard K., 316n9
Poor Bear, Enos, 229, 315n6
Porter, Henry R., 34
Porter, James E., 20, 23, 40, 41, 51, 276n24
Powder River, 10, 11, 206
Pryor range, 4
Psychometry experiments, 204
Public Works Administration, 69
Pym, James, 206

Quartermaster Corps, 67, 69

Ralston, J. K., 178, 207, 209, 214, 215
Rambur, Richard, 151, 262, 312n15
Red Bear, Emmanuel, 237
Redcherries, Carol, 316n9
Red Cloud War, 10
Red Star, Kevin, 316n9
Red Sunday (film), 183
Red Tomahawk, 63
Reece, Bob, 225
Reed, Harry, 40, 41, 47
Remington, Frederic, 53
Reno, Charles, 94
Reno, Marcus A., 13–17, 34, 66, 67, 68, 94–95, *102, 126*

Reno-Benteen Defense Site (Reno battlefield), 48, 68–69, 77–79, 85, 88, 90, 91, *140, 141, 144,* 155, 167, 168, 172, 184, 185, 192, 196; entrenchments and rifle pits, 302n8; field research at, 198–99, 201, 203, 215
Reno-Benteen Entrenchment Trail (booklet), 177
Reno-Benteen Memorial, 67–69, 87, *115,* 243, 244
Reno-Benteen phase of Battle of Little Bighorn Battle, 34, 66–70; interpretation of, 174, 176, 179
Reno-Benteen trail, 176, 177
Reno Creek, 69
Reno Hill, 65, 67
Research Review, 222
Reyer, Eldon G., 178, 227, 228, *260,* 262
Reynolds, Alfred, 49
Reynolds, Charles ("Lonesome Charley"), 23, 68, 153
Reynolds, Joseph J., 11
Rhodes, Dennis Sun, 316n9
Rice, William W., 26, 30
Ricker, Eli S., 227
Rickey, Don, Jr., 90, 92, *144,* 175, 177, 179, 185, 197–99, 200, 207, 262; and Custer Battlefield Historical and Museum Association, 214, 215; Indians interviewed by, 203–204, 305n14; and psychometry experiments, 204
Ridenour, James, 159
Riley, Frances R., 81
Riley, Kenneth, 178
Rinehart, Mary Roberts, 63
Robbins, Daniel M., 81
Robertson, Francis R., 82
Robinson, Harry B., 81, 174
Rodeo, at Little Bighorn Battle commemoration, 63, 65
Roe, Charles F., 32–33
Rogers, Edmund B., 81, 83
Roosevelt, Franklin D., 73, 248, 250
Roosevelt, Theodore, 53
Rose, Edward, 7

Rosebud Creek, 8, 12, 206
Rosebud Sioux, 235
Rouse, Homer, 218
Roybal Corporation, 232
Running Bear, Oscar, 151
Russell, Scott, 165

Saga of Western Man (TV program), 88–89
Sand Creek Massacre (1864), 9–10
Sanders, William W., 33, 38
Sanderson, George K., 29, 30, *106, 107*, 269n23
Sandoz, Mari, *136*
Sanno, James M. J., 39
Santee Sioux uprising (1862), 9–10
Saturday Evening Post, The, 78
Scott, Douglas D., *146*, 201
Scott, Hugh L., 24
Scott, John W., 84
Scouts, 6, 17, 22, 23, 34, 35
Second Battalion, Seventh Cavalry, 235
Second Cavalry, 12, 32, 33, 72
SEPA (Special Emphasis Program Allocation System), 211
Seventh Cavalry, 11, 12, 13, 17, 22, 34, 49, 62, 75, 81, 83; in battlefield interpretations, 174; burials of casualties of Little Bighorn, 19–29, 33; at commemorations of Battle of Little Bighorn, 63, 64, 65, 189; exhibit at park visitor center, 182; and Indian Memorial dedication ceremonies, 235; records, relics, and manuscripts of, 204–207, 209, 211
Seventh Cavalry Memorial Association, 161–62
Seventh Cavalry Monument. *See* Custer Monument
Seventh Infantry, 12
Seventh U.S. Cavalry Association, 85
Sharp-tailed grouse, 84
Sheridan, Michael V., 21–24, 26, 266n10
Sheridan, Philip H., 17, 21, 22, 25, 26, *104*
Sherman, William T., 21, 25, 26, 27, 241

Shoemaker, James A., 61
Shoots Walking, 63
Shoshoni Indians, 12
Sioux, 8, 9, 10; and Indian Memorial dedication ceremonies, 235. *See also* Lakotas (Teton Sioux)
Sioux Indian Museum, Rapid City, South Dakota, 206
Sitting Bull, 12, 18, 38, 63, 64, *103*
Slaper, William C., 63
Slim Buttes, Dakota, 206
Slocum, Herbert J., 34
Small, Geri, 235
Smith, Algernon E., 23, 24
Smithsonian Institution, 186
Soldier Blue (movie), 172
Soldiers Falling Into Camp (Kammen, Marshall, Lefthand), 219
Son of the Morning Star (Connell), 186
Soubier, L. Clifford, 178, 180, 262, 296n10
Southern Arapahos, 7, 236
Southern Cheyennes, 7, 10, 12, 236
Southwest Parks and Monuments Association (Western National Parks Association), 187, 220, 221
Spanish-American War veterans, 58
Special Emphasis Program Allocation System (SEPA), 211
Spirit Warriors (sculpture), *128*, 232, 233, 234
Spotted Bird, Leland, 235
Standing Rock Sioux, 235
Stands in Timber, John, 203, 305n14
Stanolind Gas and Oil Company, 91
Stanton, Harold G., 154, 156, 224
Staples, Samuel E., 26, 30
Staples, Samuel F., 26
State, Department of, U.S., 246, 248
Steamboat navigation, 9
Stearns, Harold G. ("Hal"), *127*, 152
Stefanisin, Al, 89
Stewart, Edgar I., 96, 173, 185
Stocker, Albert R., 82
Stone lodge. *See* Superintendent's house
Stuart, James, 8

Sturgis, James G., 28, 51
Sturgis, Mrs. Samuel D., 269n21
Sturgis, Samuel G., 20, 23, *106*, 197, 276n24
Sun Bear, 63
Sun dance, 159
Superintendent's house (stone lodge), 42–43, 46–47, 51, 58, *115, 119, 137,* 150, 165, 182, 211, 215, 217, 220
Support and interest groups, 213–25. *See also* Custer Battlefield Historical and Museum Association; Custer Battlefield Preservation Committee; Little Big Horn Associates
Sutteer, Barbara. *See* Booher, Barbara
Sweet, Owen J., 40, 41, 42
Sword Bearer, 38

Tangney, William R., 172
Teapot Dome Scandal, 71
Television programs, 88–89
Terry, Alfred H., 12, 17, 19–22, 25, 28, 29
Teton Sioux. *See* Lakotas
Their Shots Quit Coming (film), 192
Theme park proposal, 159–61, 223
They Died with Their Boots On (movie), 78
Third Cavalry, 206
Thomas, G. W., 51, 52, 259
Thomas B. Marquis Collection, 205, 211
Thompson, Peter, 63
Time magazine, 185
Time-Warner Communications, 159
Tonka (movie), 96
Tourists. *See* Visitors and tourists
Towers, Allison J., 231
Trail of Broken Treaties, 228
Travel and settlement, 7–10, 53
Twenty-fifth Infantry, 39, 40, 48
Two Moon, 11, 12, 55, *103*
Two Moons, Austin, 229, 315n6

Udall, Stewart, 88
United Spanish War Veterans, 55
Universal Pictures, 63

Unknowns, remains of, 49, 64, 88, 236
Upper Missouri River, 9
U.S. News and World Report, 185
Utley, Robert M., 81, 96, *127,* 152, 160, 173–74, 179, 184, 202, 215, 227, 312n15, 315n6

Vance, Herman W., 39
Vandalism, 42, 159
Van Walkenburg, Carlton, 70
Varnum, Charles A., 62
Vaughn, Jesse W., 198–99, 215
Venne, Carl, 235
Vestal, Jay, 232
Veterans of Foreign Wars, 81
Vietnam War and postwar period, 147, 153, 172
Visitor center, 81, 89, *132, 134, 135, 138,* 149, 155, 157, 164–65, 177–79, 182, 184, 185, 188, 190, 192, 228, 314n5
Visitors and tourists, 49, 53–56, 60–61, 65, 76, 78, 80, 88, 89, 95, 148, 155, 162, 164, 169, 175, 177, 179, 187, 193, 240, 257–58
Volunteers, for field survey (1984–1985), 201
Volz, J. Leonard, 180
von Schmidt, Eric, 184

Wade, Karen, 232
Wainwright, Jonathan, 83, *124, 125*
Walsh, Thomas J., 67, 70, 71
Walter Mason Camp Collection, 209, 211, 216
Wanamaker, Rodman, 53, 54
War Department, U.S., 21, 22, 30, 35, 68, 69, 71–75; compensation for Crow Indian land claims, 60; control and authority over national cemeteries, 37, 48, 171, 194, 226, 246–48; park superintendents, 259
War of 1812, 8
Warren, Lawson S., 159
Washita River engagement, Seventh Cavalry, 12

Water supply, 49, 52, 58, 59, 77, 78, 86, 93, 149, 165, 166

Waud, A. R., *101*

Wayside exhibits, 192

Weapons, 202, 206

Wedemeyer, Albert, 81

Weir, Thomas W., 14

Weir Point, 15, 16, 69, 203

Wessinger, Eugene, 52–53, 54, 57, 58, 62, 170, 259, *260*

Western Archeological and Conservation Center (WACC), 210

Westerners National Service Award, 175

Western National Parks Association (Southwest Parks and Monuments Association), 187, 220, 221

West Point, New York, Custer's burial at, 21, 22, 24

Wheeler, Burton K., 71, 72

Wheeler, Homer W., 267n15

White, William H., 72, *137*, 283n16

White Bear, Russell, 63

White Bird Canyon, Battle of, 51

White Bull, 64, 65, *123*

White Goose land claim, 60

White Horse, 63

White Man Runs Him, 55, 64

White Swan, 34

White Swan Memorial Library, *119*, 165, 211, 212, 225

Whitright, Chauncey, 314n5, 316n9

Whittaker, Frederick, 270n25

Wildlife, in battlefield vicinity, 5, 6, 83–84, 204

Williams, Pat, 235

Williamson, Henry E., 38

Windolph, Charles A., 63, 65, 175, 197, 206

Wirth, Conrad, 88

Wister, Owen, 53

Wolf (Little Chetish) Mountains, 4; Crow's Nest in, 196

Woodring, Harry, 73

Woody, Kenneth, 185, 191

World Day of Peace, 163

World War I veterans, 58

World War II veterans, 80, *118*

Wounded Knee Massacre (1890), 38; occupation of site of, 151

Wraps-Up-His-Tail, 38

Wright, Oscar, 51, 53, 259, 276n24

Wyoming, white emigration in, 10

Wyoming/Montana Council for the Humanities, 187

Wyoming national guardsmen, in battle reenactment, 53

Yates, George W., 23, 24, 50

Yellowstone Library and Museum Association, 307n2

Yellowstone National Park, 7, 75, 80, 85, *172*

Yellowstone River, 5, 8, 10, 11, 12

Yellowstone Wagon Road and Prospecting Expedition, 8

Yellowtail, Robert, 69, 85

Young, J. D., 262

Young Hawk, 63

Zacherle, George H., *143*